ASIAN CROSSINGS

Praise for *Asian Crossings: Travel Writing on China, Japan and Southeast Asia*

'This timely and clearly focused collection of essays offers an illuminating introduction to accounts of travel to and from China, Japan and Southeast Asia. The travelogues challenge the reader to question many of the assumptions that characterise current studies in travel writing, revealing the richness of context-specific approaches that draw on a variety of journey accounts concerning common geographical zones. Highlighting issues of gender and ethnicity, of genre and history, *Asian Crossings* is essential reading for all serious scholars of travel literature.'

— Charles Forsdick, James Barrow Chair of French, University of Liverpool

'At last a travel book on Asia that is as revisionist as it is invigorating. Steve Clark and Paul Smethurst have produced a collection that will entice and intrigue both the scholar and the general reader. *Asian Crossings* challenges many of the stock scholarly assumptions about postcolonialism and Orientalism, and puts us in touch with a little-known history that is imperative for the West to understand. This book is as rich, complex and subtle as Asia itself. There is no better illustration of the range of narrative and analysis that can be attained within the genre of travel encounter when it is done with intelligence and flair.'

— Iain McCalman, Federation Fellow and Professor of History, University of Sydney

'Turning away from a generalised post-colonial theory approach, the essays in *Asian Crossings* offer focused and unusually fruitful analyses of the travel writings they discuss. The result is a superb collection, indispensable both for its historical and geographical accuracy and for the freshness and range of its insights.'

— Susan Morgan, Distinguished Professor of English, Miami University of Ohio

ASIAN CROSSINGS
Travel Writing on China, Japan and Southeast Asia

Edited by
Steve Clark and Paul Smethurst

Hong Kong University Press
The University of Hong Kong
Pok Fu Lam Road
Hong Kong
https://hkupress.hku.hk

© 2008 Hong Kong University Press

ISBN 978-962-209-914-2 (*Hardback*)
ISBN 978-962-209-915-9 (*Paperback*)

All rights reserved. No portion of this publication may be reproduced or transmitted in any form or by any means, electronic or mechanical, including photocopying, recording, or any information storage or retrieval system, without prior permission in writing from the publisher.

British Library Cataloguing-in-Publication Data
A catalogue record for this book is available from the British Library.

Digitally printed

Contents

Acknowledgements   vii

Contributors   ix

Introduction   1
Steve Clark

1. Between Topos and Topography: Japanese Early Modern Travel Literature   15
   Robert F. Wittkamp

2. 'The First Appearance of This Celebrated Capital'; or, What Mr. Barrow Saw in the Land of the Chinaman   31
   Joe Sample

3. A Reading of Readings: English Travel Books, Audiences, and Modern Chinese History, c. 1832 to the Present   47
   Ting Man Tsao

4. Travel and Business: The First Colombian in China   71
   Jacinto Fombona

5. Erasing Footsteps: On Some Differences between the First and Popular Editions of Isabella Bird's *Unbeaten Tracks in Japan*   87
   Shizen Ozawa

6. Discourses of Difference: The Malaya of Isabella Bird, Emily Innes and Florence Caddy   99
   Eddie Tay

7. China of the Tourists: Women and the Grand Tour of the Middle Kingdom, 1878–1923 113
   Julia Kuehn

8. Ruins in the Jungle: Nature and Narrative 131
   Douglas Kerr

9. Forbidden Journeys to China and Beyond with the Odd Couple: Ella Maillart and Peter Fleming 141
   Maureen Mulligan

10. Kawakami Otojiro's Trip to the West and Taiwan at the Turn of the Twentieth Century 149
    Yukari Yoshihara

11. Shaking the Buddhas: Lafcadio Hearn in Japan, 1890–1904 163
    David Taylor

12. *'Chambres d'Asie, chambres d'ailleurs':* Nicole-Lise Bernheim's 'Vertical Travels' in Asia 179
    Katy Hindson

13. *World Journey of My Heart* and *Homestay in the World:* Travel Programming and Contemporary Japanese Culture 193
    Mark Meli

14. After the Bubble: Post-Imperial Tokyo 209
    Steve Clark

Notes 229

References 265

Index 271

Acknowledegments

The editors would like to thank the School of English at the University of Hong Kong and Tim Youngs and the Centre of Travel Writing Studies, Nottingham Trent University, for organizing the 'Mobilis Mobile' conference (June 2006) at which earlier versions of these essays were originally delivered. We are also grateful to Julia Chan for assistance with formatting, proofs and index; to Colin Day, Clara Ho, Ian Lok and their colleagues at Hong Kong University Press for their courtesy and professionalism throughout; and to Tristanne Connolly, George Hughes, Ann Lane and John Phillips for comments on the manuscript. We would also like to thank John Stanmeyer for his evocative photograph of a girl crossing a bridge in the Chinese town of Ruili.

Contributors

Steve Clark is currently visiting professor at the Graduate School of Humanities and Sociology, University of Tokyo. Among his previous publications are *Travel Writing and Empire: Postcolonial Theory in Transit* (1999) and *The Reception of Blake in the Orient* (with Masashi Suzuki, 2006). Current projects include *Liberating Medicine 1720–1830* (with Tristanne Connolly), and a collection of essays on the late thought of Paul Ricoeur.

Jacinto Fombona received his *licenciatura* in Mathematics from the Universidad Simón Bolívar in Caracas, and his PhD in literature from Yale University. He is the author of *La Europa necesaria:textos de viaje de la época moderista* (2005) that explores the discursive construction of Europe from the Spanish American standpoint. His publications include articles on contemporary narrative and poetry. He is on the editorial board of *Brújula*.

Katy Hindson received her BA in French Studies from the University of Liverpool and her MA in Translation Studies from the University of Warwick. She is currently completing a PhD at the University of Liverpool. Her thesis engages with questions of travel and identity in late twentieth-century France and focuses more particularly on the dominant *Pour une littérature voyageuse* literary movement.

Douglas Kerr is Professor in the School of English at the University of Hong Kong. His publications include *Wilfred Owen's Voices* (1993), *George Orwell* (2003) and *A Century of Travels in China* (2007) co-edited with Julia Kuehn. More recent work has been concerned with the history of representations of Eastern people and places in English writing, from the time of Kipling to the postcolonial period. He is on the Editorial Board of *Critical Zone: A Forum of Chinese and Western Knowledge*.

Julia Kuehn is Assistant Professor of English at the University of Hong Kong. Her research interests lie in nineteenth and early twentieth-century literature and culture. She is the author of *Glorious Vulgarity: Marie Corelli's Feminine Sublime in a Popular Context* (2004). She is also co-editor of three collections of essays on travel writing: *A Century of Travels in China* (2007); *Empire, Form, and Travel Writing* (forthcoming); and *China Abroad* (in progress).

Mark Meli received his PhD in philosophy from SUNY at Buffalo, specialising in Japanese aesthetic theory. He went on to do graduate studies in classical Japanese literature at Osaka University. He now teaches comparative literature and culture at Kansai University in Osaka. His current research interests include Japanese travel writing, garden aesthetics, and the culture of food and drink.

Maureen Mulligan received her degree in English from Cambridge University and taught in Nottingham for several years, followed by teaching posts in the Seychelles, Sweden and Spain. For the last twelve years she has taught at the University of Las Palmas de GC. Her PhD thesis, defended in the ULPGC in 1999, was published in Spain as 'Prodigal Daughters and the Representation of Empire'.

Shizen Ozawa teaches in the Department of Literature at Chiba University. He received his PhD in literature in 2002 from the University of Essex. His primary research area is colonial and postcolonial literature, and his publications include articles on Rudyard Kipling and Amitav Ghosh. He also translated (with Masatsugu Ono) V. S. Naipaul's *Miguel Street* into Japanese (2005).

Joe Sample is Assistant Professor in the Department of English at Clemson University where he teaches a range of courses in professional communication as well as a course in American literary humour. His research looks at encounters between Eastern and Western thought as found primarily in eighteenth-century 'customs and manners' texts. He has an article on the Macartney embassy in *Genre: An International Journal of Literature and the Arts*, as well as essays forthcoming in several edited collections dealing with travel and its writings.

Paul Smethurst is Associate Professor at the University of Hong Kong, where he teaches travel writing, contemporary fiction and cross-cultural studies. His publications include *The Postmodern Chronotope* (2000) and *The Reinvention of Nature: Scientific, Picturesque and Romantic Travel Writing 1760–1840* (forthcoming). He has written the 'Introduction' to *The Travels of Marco Polo* (2005) and essays on travel writing in *Studies in Medievalism*, *Studies in Travel Writing*, and *Time Magazine*. He is currently working on a cultural history of the bicycle.

Eddie Tay is from Singapore and is Assistant Professor at the Chinese University of Hong Kong. His research and teaching interests are in the area of colonial and postcolonial Singaporean and Malaysian Anglophone literatures. He is the author of two poetry collections, *Remnants* and *A Lover's Soliloquy*.

David Taylor is Associate Professor of English at Tokyo Medical and Dental University. His publications include 'Bruce Chatwin: Connoisseur of Exile; Exile as Connoisseur' in Clark (ed.) (1999) *Travel Writing and Empire: Postcolonial Theory in Transit*, and monographs on contemporary poetry and the English literary ballad. He is currently working on a study of Samuel Beckett.

Ting Man Tsao is Associate Professor of English at LaGuardia Community College in New York. A graduate of Hong Kong Shue Yan College, he holds a PhD in English from Stony Brook University. He has published in journals such as *Victorians Institute Journal*, *The History Teacher*, *Teaching English in the Two-Year College*, *Peer English* and *Writing Macao*, as well as in the book *Illness in the Academy: A Collection of Pathographies by Academics* (Purdue University Press). Dr. Tsao dedicates his article in this collection to the memory of his father, Kung Shuen, who was devoted to educating young people in Canton, Hong Kong and New York.

Robert F. Wittkamp studied at the University of Cologne where he received his Master of Arts and PhD in Japanology, Chinese literature and cultural anthropology. He has lived in Japan since 1994, and now teaches at the Kansai University (Osaka). The focus of his research is landscape and travel literature as forms of cultural memory and ritual, especially as found in 'classical Japanese literature'.

Yukari Yoshihara is Associate Professor at the University of Tsukuba. She received her PhD in literature from the same university in 2004. Her publications include an essay on Japanese adaptation of the *Merchant of Venice* in *Performing Shakespeare in Japan* (2001) and 'Introduction' to *English Studies in Asia* (2007).

Introduction

Steve Clark

Within an Anglo-American context, the academic study of travel writing coincides fairly precisely with the emergence of postcolonial studies, for which the genre serves as a convenient paradigm of cross-cultural encounter, inevitably inscribed with the dynamics of power relations between centre and periphery.[1] The study of travelogue thus both enlarges the traditional literary canon and challenges any residual ideal of the classic text as aesthetically self-contained and autonomous. However, the applicability of such postcolonial models of reading may immediately be queried in an Eastern Asian context, whose primary geographical focus is China and Japan, expanding to include the somewhat amorphous zone of Southeast Asia.[2]

Edward Said's initial thesis of a monolithic Western will-to-power is almost entirely based on the Near East, with little consideration of the markedly different practices of British colonialism in India, let alone the complex and diverse European relations with Eastern Asia. The mercantile integration of the region may be traced back through the millennium-long evolution of the Silk Road trade route, and certainly predates significant European intervention by several centuries.[3] The late twentieth and early twenty-first centuries have undoubtedly seen a shift in the global balance of power back to Asia.[4] Whether or not one accepts the Oriental globalisation thesis in its strong form, it cannot be disputed that many technological innovations originated from China in particular (the calendar, compass, gunpowder, print and paper).[5] Recent revisionist histories of the industrial revolution indicate that, in the seventeenth century, methods of production and means of transport in China, India and

Japan for goods such as porcelain and textiles were much more advanced than in the West. In the course of the eighteenth century, Europe began to compete in an aggressive way, developing rival manufacturing systems and copying Asian goods in order to appeal to the consumerist appetite of a rapidly expanding new middle class.[6]

The case for China as a world centre to rival and surpass the West can be found not only in its famous 'firsts', but also in its massive one-way trade with America and Europe which at the end of the eighteenth century was worth close to $50 million a year, nearly all paid for in bullion due to restrictions on foreigners selling their wares into China. The introduction of opium would change all of this. But China's image of itself as the only true empire in a world of tribute-bearing barbarians (as any non-Confucian culture would be categorised) remained unshaken until the First Opium War (1839–42). Even up to the end of the eighteenth century (as demonstrated by the Macartney embassy [1793]), China felt no reason to treat the King of Great Britain's ambassador any differently from any other supplicant emissary. Even partial acceptance of such a viewpoint requires a move away from an Atlanticist emphasis in narratives of world history: Columbus after all accidentally encountered America while intending to voyage to Cathay; Marco Polo was travelling to, rather than from, what he knew to be the dominant imperial centre in China.[7]

Said's claim that Britain was in 'an imperial class by itself, bigger, grander and more imposing than any other' pales into insignificance against the *longue durée* of China's imperium.[8] Its inability to resist the superior firepower of the British gunboats in the First Opium War, and vulnerability to subsequent foreign incursions, though hugely damaging to Chinese prestige and still smarting in the Chinese psyche, may be regarded as a comparatively self-contained period, nicely bracketed by the colonial history of Hong Kong, ceded to the British in the Treaty of Nanking in 1842 and resuming Chinese sovereignty in 1997. This interlude is fairly brief compared to, for example, the collapse of the state for three centuries from AD 317 to 589 or the Mongol occupation from AD 1215 to 1368. *China: The Long-lived Empire* with its vast internal market, demographic strength and rapid industrialisation, is likely to assert its regional sovereignty ever more vigorously throughout the coming century.[9]

Japan has never been colonised, with the arguable exception of post-war US occupation, though any credence to claims of cultural exceptionalism (*nihonjinron*) must be qualified by its early dependence on Chinese and Korean culture.[10] From the Meiji era onwards, it has sought to establish itself as a latecomer empire modelled on European powers; the goal of control of raw materials, envisaged in the Greater East Asia Co-Prosperity Sphere, has been largely achieved after the Great Pacific War through economic neo-colonialism rather than military conquest.

With the Portuguese and Dutch holding parts of Indonesia, the French in Vietnam and Cambodia, and the British notably reluctant to acquire territory beyond what was necessary to secure trade routes, no colonial power possessed clear ascendancy in the region. It was possible to play regimes off against one another and retain sovereignty, as King Mongkur (1851–68) and Chulalongkorn (1868–1910) succeeded in doing in Siam. The tensions internal to the region should also not be underestimated, as well as the capacity for a variety of nations within the area to regard themselves self-consciously as empire-builders in their own right, from the Angkor regime in northern Cambodia through to the Indonesian occupation of East Timor.[11]

Furthermore, the recent economic resurgence of the region may be seen as founded to a considerable extent on the perpetuation of colonial infrastructures, education systems and administrative elites, in contrast to the majority of African and Caribbean states. The respective economic fortunes of Jamaica and Singapore, both granted independence in the early 1960s, make a striking and painful contrast. Japan was never formally colonised; recent debate on modernisation, however, has emphasised that the necessary infrastructures must have been already at least partially in place to account for the speed of subsequent transformation in the Meiji era.

Imperial-gaze models derived from Mary Louise Pratt are difficult to apply to travel writing about a region that has always contained many of the world's great urban centres. The original moment of contact involves a relationship of comparative parity and at times outright subordination: Magellan, for example, was enlisted into and eventually killed fighting local wars. There is no equivalent to the eighteenth-century South Sea voyages, or to Cook's power of naming supposed *terra incognita*.[12] Tokyo was the world's biggest city between 1600 and 1800; when the Macartney embassy arrived in 1793, Beijing was hugely more populous and imposing than contemporary European capitals; and since their foundation, Singapore, Hong Kong, Kuala Lumpur and Bangkok have all served as dynamic and highly cosmopolitan international entrepôts.[13]

Asians are travellers too, sometimes in forms inviting comparison with those of Europe, sometimes in distinctive regional traditions. The impact of the Chinese diaspora, travel without return, may be seen throughout the world; and within the country itself there have regularly been large-scale internal migrations due to the implosion of population vacuums or periodic bouts of political coercion (such as the exodus of intellectuals [*zhiqing*] to the countryside during the Cultural Revolution). In Japan, tribute missions to China are prominent from an early date (seventeen between AD 607 and 838–39, the final one recorded in the diary of the monk Ennin); even during the period of self-imposed seclusion (*sakoku*), with the practice of *sankin kotai*, the aristocracy were obliged to maintain a residence in the capital to pay tribute to the shogun and to visit their family members obliged to live in the Imperial Palace as hostages (*hitojichi*); and the process of late nineteenth-century technology transfer produced a host of memoirs of returnees (*ken'ou shisetu dan*) recounting their often traumatic encounters with Western modernity.[14]

The essays in this volume continually negotiate the vexed question of how far it is possible to transpose generic norms and developmental sequences based on European travelogue, whose multiple variants include pilgrimage, voyage literature, Grand Tour, natural history, picturesque sightseeing, and whose participants include colonial administrator, journalist-spy and postmodern pasticheur.

In both European and Asian traditions, the journey necessarily encodes ideology (what James Clifford in *Routes* terms its 'historical taintedness'), religious crusade, mercantile prospectus, mercenary campaign, imperial expedition and missionary indoctrination.[15] Similarly, there are the negative variants of diverse forms of captivity narrative such as exile, hostage, migrant and slave, and the distinctive female subcategories of not merely accompanying wife, but also of concubine and domestic worker. Yet even apparent similarity may be deceptive. In pilgrimage-narrative, for example, how far can the Buddhist concept of bodhisattva be mapped on to Christian models of expulsion from and continued desire for paradise, and a Biblical typology of interminable expiation (the motivating force of Mandeville)?[16] From the perspective of global homogenisation, pilgrimage may be seen as operating on the same schema as tourism. Asian populations become travellers when they reach a sufficient level of affluence, similarly besotted by sacred sites and souvenir relics.[17] (The Chinese have allegedly visited Japan primarily for Tokyo Disneyland, an attraction now likely to diminish subsequent to the opening of a version in Hong Kong.)

Prior to the emergence of postcolonial studies, narratives of the development of the genre of travelogue in a European context tended to concentrate on crossovers with the rise of the novel. In Japan, however, the genealogy of literary traditions is different. The *Tale of Genji*, a female-authored chronicle of considerable psychological complexity, predates other forms. There is no equivalent to the European evolution from romance to realist conventions, in particular the style of notation of particulars common to Dampier and Defoe; rather a reverse movement occurs from a highly self-conscious form of introspective lyricism to more directly referential description of the physical environment.

In Europe, the first classical tour-guide was Pausanias (c. AD 200), though Herodotus or even Caesar might also be nominated as proto-travelogues. However, as a distinctive combination of testimony, reflection, and narrativised anecdote, it would be uncontentious to regard the form as predominantly post-Renaissance (even granted medieval precedents such as Mandeville, Marco Polo and Columbus). However travel writing appears as a literary genre (*nikki bungaku*) much earlier in Japan (934–35) than in Europe, where it rapidly becomes a highly sophisticated and aestheticised form, as Robert F. Wittkamp argues in 'Between Topos and Topography: Japanese Early Modern Travel Literature'. The Japanese tradition is initially defined by concepts such as *jôshu* (mood, feeling, taste) and *hyohaku* (desire to wander), recognisable by its short narrative sequences, sentimental reflections and obligatory mention of place names. These seldom identify new locations, preferring instead to refer to what has always already been cited. There is a reverse sequence of the European development from cartographic survey to dramatisation of interior subjectivity. Instead the exquisite lyricism of Basho's *Narrow Road to the Interior* (1694) gives way to the information model represented by the copious writings of Sugae Masumi (d. 1829).

The question of equivalence is raised by Wittkamp's essay — the extent to which the Kinsei period in Japan (early seventeenth to late nineteenth century) can be mapped on to the European Middles Ages or early Modern Period. The aesthetics of the British picturesque are seemingly compatible with (and may well owe much to) Chinese-Japanese landscape art, but are bound up with the development of internal tourism during the Napoleonic wars, with its dependence on an expanded class-base and improved infrastructure of transportation. It also perhaps lacks the immediate political dimension of exclusion from the power-centre of the court which is a powerful and inescapable subtext not only in Basho but also in his Chinese precursors such as Li Po or Li Bai.

Trade Missions to China

The relative balance of power between Europe and Asia at the end of the eighteenth century is made brutally apparent in the reception of the Macartney embassy (1792–94). This is mediated through the multiple and competing narratives of Aeneas Anderson, *A Narrative of the British Embassy to China* (1795) and John Barrow, *Travels in China: a Narrative of the British Embassy to China* (1805) — with an additional text by George Staunton, *An Authentic Account of an Embassy from the King of Great Britain to the Emperor of*

China (1797), supplemented by the publication of Macartney's own original notes in 1962. Joe Sample's essay '"The First Appearance of This Celebrated Capital"; or, What Mr. Barrow Saw in the Land of the Chinaman' may be regarded as a test case for generic mutation through the stages of letter, archive and published narrative; and for travelogue as diplomacy, with specific political consequences, a high degree of cultural visibility, and an editing out of the highly collaborative nature of the endeavour (the legation was over 3000-strong). Barrow is better known for his South African travelogue, made famous by Mary Louise Pratt's exposition of the model of 'contact zone'.[18] At the moment of arrival at Beijing, however, the imposition of the imperial gaze does not prefigure subsequent conquest, but instead meets with an emphatic snub. The failure of the mission may be attributed to the lack of comprehension of the necessary rituals of self-prostration. Alternatively, China's refusal to deal with other nation states with anything like parity, and the insistence on tribute, kowtowing and draconian measures to protect trade (foreigners being afforded no rights whatsoever in the only port they were permitted, with all trade handled by Chinese middlemen) were the cause not only of this specific diplomatic fiasco but also ultimately of the Opium Wars. This is travelogue as humiliation, a cruel comedy of presumptuousness and mis-recognition. The mission arrives as vagabonds, paupers, almost ludicrously bedraggled, as Anderson wincingly acknowledges. Prior accounts of China had inevitably been mediated by the encomiums delivered by Jesuit missionaries and a mythical chinoiserie becoming ever more tangible in the form of export of consumer goods. These initial impulses of curiosity and wonder, evident in Anderson's emphasis on the carnivalesque, are punctured by the vengefully deflating observations of Barrow, instrumental in establishing a new rhetoric of China as inferior copy, stagnant, impotent and requiring prising open for both trade and missionary endeavour.

The impact of the Ship Amherst voyage and subsequent narrations is analysed by Ting Man Tsao, in 'A Reading of Readings: English Travel Books, Audiences, and Modern Chinese History, c.1832 to the Present'. The original journey involved a compact between Hugh Lindsay and Charles Gutzlaff, an alliance of British East India Company and missionary zeal. Both were motivated by the desire for the opening up of China to free trade and faith. The generic template for their self-presentation alludes back to the piratical heroes of Hakluyt, whose impetuous individualistic actions are to be celebrated over the pragmatic circumspection of state or apathetic complacency of monopoly. Even in the home culture, however, there was no unitary Orientalist reception. The cost of books and periodicals determines various strata of readership, each with different expectations and concerns. The incursion was frequently seen as reckless and incendiary, endangering rather than promoting both economic and religious interests. Female-oriented periodicals stressed the liberation of Chinese and Indian women (poor sisters) emphasising the potential role for female missionaries. Those directed to working-class constituencies were appealing to conservative values, sceptical of both trade and missionary proselytising, and intent on conveying an apparently apolitical knowledge. From a Chinese perspective, the incident has come to exemplify the humiliation of a weak and corrupt Qing regime in its failure to retaliate against foreign provocation. It, therefore, incorporates an imperial perspective into its own historiographic tradition. Yet there is no necessary linkage between the outcome of the later Opium Wars and the voyage itself, of which contemporary Chinese testimony was largely dismissive.

In 'Travel and Business: The First Colombian in China', Jacinto Fombona investigates Nicolás Tanco Armero as an exemplar of a Latin American cultural elite, simultaneously critical of and complicit in imperial exploitation. Armero's outspoken denunciation of British involvement in the opium trade (providing first-hand testimony of the Opium Wars and diagnosis of the weakness of cohesion that permitted such incursion) combines with an economic rationale of providing indentured labour to Cuba to replace slavery (it is a noteworthy feature of the Chinese diaspora that there was already a sizeable population present in Cuba). His scruples did not, however, prevent him from utilising opium clippers (as did Gutzlaff), or from eventually abandoning his supposedly invaluable native informant Achuy. His travelogue presents an overlay of Latin American and European perspectives, of new nation and old empire, whose audience is an imagined community exemplary of an early form of political modernity. The narrative itself is somewhat oddly prefaced by an introduction which denounces both the desire and performance of travel, resulting in a stylistic paradox of the journey being justified by often highly ornate disparagements of adornment of style. In Armero's text, China is crystallised (to use Herder's term) into a form notably more vivid and resonant in the Latin American cultural imaginary than actual Spanish colonies such as the Philippines. This is travel as loss and diminishment rather than as an enhancement of power, in which a utopian commitment to both secular progress and religious eschatology is counterbalanced by strategies of sombre remembrance.

The Travels of Isabella Bird in China, Japan and Southeast Asia

The next three essays offer versions of Isabella Bird (described by contemporaries, accurately enough, as 'Samson abroad'). Her oeuvre provides a usefully problematic exception to attempts to define an autonomous sphere or tradition of female travelogue. The first woman member of the Royal Geographical Society prefers robust taxonomy to empathetic phenomenology. If Bird deserves to be regarded as hero, it is for more traditional reasons than a dialogic openness to alterity.

Bird laments the Meiji project of modernisation that her own presence confirms: the more Japan resembles an advanced industrial culture, the more it is disparaged for vulgar imitation and loss of a putative authenticity. Shizen Ozawa, in 'Erasing Footsteps: On Some Differences between the First and Popular Editions of Isabella Bird's *Unbeaten Tracks in Japan*' analyses the political implications of the revisions made to this hugely influential text. The idealisation of the Ainu people, the culminating northern point of her journey, itself consigns them to historical defeat, victims of the racial struggle for existence. The composition of *Unbeaten Tracks in Japan* goes through several stages: familiar epistle to sister, expansive first edition, revised and contracted popular version. Each has a different implied readership, though who precisely controlled each stage remains tantalisingly elusive. There is a progressive heightening of authority, by downgrading the mediation of native informants (the continual business negotiation of the 'squeeze' or commission), not acknowledging dependence on other authorities (notably Sir Ernest Satow), and a whittling down of the comedy of cross-cultural encounter at her own expense. Particularly noteworthy is the changing role of missionaries, praised for their introduction of modern medicine and methods of schooling and so agents of progress, but also seen as ambivalent intruders: a Christian education making it more difficult, if not impossible, for girls to find husbands. There is an ultimate admission of the impossibility of converting Japan at the same time as acknowledging its impressively self-fulfilled task of modernisation to prevent colonisation by the West.

Isabella Bird's *The Golden Chersonese and the Way Thither* (1883) immediately invites comparison with two other near contemporary female travelogues, Emily Innes's *The Chersonese with the Gilding Off* (1885) and Florence Caddy's *To Siam and Malaya in the Duke of Sutherland's Yacht 'Sans Peur'* (1889). Eddie Tay, in 'Discourses of Difference: The Malaya of Isabella Bird, Emily Innes and Florence Caddy', examines both resemblances and divergences within these texts. Bird offers a form of mercantile taxonomy: in an unexpected reversal it is the British colonial officials such as Hugh Clifford who are feminised, as proponents of cross-cultural empathy. Her primary antagonism is towards the Portuguese and Dutch ('little better than buccaneers'). The history of colonisation prior to European intervention in the area is alluded to but passed over. Innes, as wife of a minor colonial official, shows rancorous envy towards Bird as an interloper, for whom travel serves as an aristocratic pursuit and leisure activity rather than as a form of incarceration. There are intermittent outbursts of paranoia, demonising both devious natives and the harsh environment; and the insights into the practical workings and inequalities of empire are articulated through self-pity for the suffering of the colonist (or in this case, more specifically, his wife). She can present herself as slave sympathising with other slaves, but in the course of criticising empire, favours a policy of outright annexation of Malaya rather than continuing its indeterminate protectorate status. Caddy embodies the onset of luxury tourism in the region, with colonial power structures reduplicated in the partitioning of space on the yacht in which she travels (the guest of the Duke of Sutherland, en route to bidding for a railway construction project). She does, however, show unexpected admiration for the industry of the Chinese in both Malaya and Singapore — wealth-generation centred on a non-European culture (though contrasted with the sloth of the Malays themselves). All three women are seen as not merely complicit but active in the promotion of colonisation. It is argued that rather than displaying greater nuance or openness, their narratives do not reject or subvert but rather reinforce both imperial and domestic ideology.

Julia Kuehn's essay, 'China of the Tourists: Women and the Grand Tour of the Middle Kingdom, 1878–1923', identifies a first generation of women's travel in China exemplified in Isabella Bird's *The Yangtze Valley and Beyond* (1899) and Constance Gordon Cumming's *Wanderings in China* (1888). Bird adopts a traditional masculine mode of travel as ordeal, Herculean physical endeavour, whereas Cumming perhaps may be categorised as a proto-modern consumerist sightseer. (The stylistic difference was mirrored in a personal relationship of mutual detestation.) The process of selection and evaluation of primary sites to visit establishes a reiterative structure of pre-recognition, seeing what has been seen before, with the final destination inevitably the urban centre of Peking. Tourist infrastructure had been established early after 1879: China was an already highly developed state, though with limited transport connections to the interior. The second generation of female travellers become more concerned with epiphanies of alterity, recognising parallels with Asian women who themselves are capable of reverse journeying to the West (as in the case of Mrs. Soong Ching Ling). The porous boundaries between travelogue and guidebook are demonstrated in Eliza Scidmore's *Westward to the Far East: A Guide to the Principal Cities of China and Japan* (1892); there is a growing overlap with popular novelistic representations (such as those of Pearl Buck) and also an unexpected degree of internationalisation. As Ellen Newbold LaMotte remarks in *Peking Dust* (1919), 'Fifth Avenue has nothing compared to Peking department stores'.

Confounding the Imperial Gaze in Southeast Asia

Douglas Kerr's essay, 'Ruins in the Jungle: Nature and Narrative', positions the reflective colonial traveller in the perplexing space of the jungle. Hugh Clifford reappears, this time in the guise of novelist and short story writer alongside Leonard Woolf as specimens of fin-de-siècle/late imperial travelogue. This is the colonial administrator as traveller, aware that the material benefits of modernity come at the cost of the inevitable erasure of native cultures and habitats, an encroachment personified by the very act of testimony and representation. The text displays not feminine empathy, but a masculine pathology of erotic engulfment, which may be seen as signifying a death-drive yearning for annihilation on both the individual and cultural level. The West has no jungle, the material and symbolic realm which entraps within a futile, endless and ultimately lethal circulation. Such Gothic and apocalyptic motifs have a distant ancestry in Caesar's representations of the Gallic barbarians and offer a prolepsis of an ultimate termination of empire (glimpsed in Kipling's 'Recessional'). Rather than being mastered by the imperial gaze, the landscape becomes an object for an elusive but all-powerful sublime experience of the jungle. Historical impasse is resolved by the mythologising of geographical specificity, with the final dissolution of the division between nature and culture in the recurrent image of the ruined and abandoned city (most vividly exemplified by Angkor Wat in Cambodia).

An Odd Couple in East Asia

Maureen Mulligan's essay focuses on two accounts of the same trans-Asian journey through China, India and Tibet: Peter Fleming's *News from Tartary* (1936) and Ella Maillart's *Forbidden Journey; from Peking to Kashmir* (1937). There is divergence of both gender and national viewpoint: Fleming, brisk, pragmatic, alert to the complexities of the Great Game, possibly already attached to the Intelligence Services (as were Freya Stark and Rebecca West); and Maillart, experienced journalist, stoic, resilient, durable, showing a Swiss neutrality and an attraction to Eastern spirituality. The journey for her is both literal and introspective: physical return cannot be reconciled with narrative closure. Their respective travelogues may be seen as exemplifying Fussell's thesis of the 1930s as the golden age of genuine travel thereafter supplanted by mere tourism;[19] equally, the couple may be seen as exemplifying generic features of the 1930s Hollywood screwball scripts as they 'act in a comedy' of banter, parity and vivacity. Both texts refuse the convention of romantic consummation, though what Fleming's fiancée in England made of their physical proximity remains an open question. The traditional motifs of forbidden journey and disguise as metamorphosis are combined with a redefinition of the traveller-hero, loyal companion, and also dwelling-in-travel, construction of an ideal residence while in motion.

Travels in and out of Japan

Post-1880 Japan as a latecomer empire may be regarded as simultaneously periphery with regard to Europe and America, and centre of its own emergent regional hegemony over such territories as Taiwan. Sympathy for countries under colonial rule (e.g. the Philippines annexed first by Spain, then by the United States) was by no means incompatible with Japan's own imperial ambitions. This paradoxical status at times resulted in a self-conscious process of mimicry, regarding cultural identity as a commodity that may be faked for international circulation, as Yukari Yoshihara demonstrates in her essay, 'Kawakami Otojiro's Trip to the West and Taiwan at the Turn of the Twentieth Century'. What is striking is not only the peripatetic globetrotting of the impresario's company, but the extent of the Japanese diaspora, with emigrant communities both eager for representations of their home culture and protesting at the self-caricature offered by Kawakami's shows. There are no actresses used in traditional Japanese drama; but as foreign audiences demanded a geisha, one was provided: Sado Yacco, the first Japanese actress was born in the United States.

Kawakami Otojiro is thus positioned as both a subversive outsider with regard to Japanese theatrical traditions and as a cynical agent of imperial expansion, utilising extravagant shows rather than highbrow art. *The Sino-Japanese War* becomes a pageant but one that must be played out in traditional costume rather than with contemporary weaponry, for American audiences whose fascination with the exotic combines with unease at the actualities of Meiji modernisation. The Japanese troupe displayed no scruples about pandering to American jingoism in the wake of the 1898 war with Spain ('Hooray Dewey'). Shakespearean texts are shown as capable of being deployed in the service of Asiatic imperialism, through the staging of *Othello* during a period of native Taiwanese uprisings against Japanese occupation. The structure of demonisation of and fascination with indigenous culture evident in Kawakami Otojiro's adaptation is equally apparent in the human zoos on display at international expositions during the period. Japan stages itself for Western consumption, but also insists on a strict racial hierarchy for other groups subject to its internal and external colonial dominance such as Taiwanese and Ainu.

David Taylor's essay, 'Shaking the Buddhas: Lafcadio Hearn in Japan (1890–1904)', explores this curious figure who may be seen as an early cultural hybrid and product of proto-globalisation: Greek-Irish origin, raised in Ireland and England, working as a journalist in the United States and the West Indies before settling in Japan (assuming both citizenship and the name of Yakumo Koizumi). Hearn's attempted acculturation is undercut by the limitations of his linguistic competence and consequent dependence on both his wife and native informants (underplayed if not altogether elided out of his travelogues). His nostalgia for an authentic Japan may be seen as a form of repression of the accelerated process of modernisation that the culture was undergoing. The fin-de-siècle exquisiteness of his prose, alternating a curious stasis with periodic vivid movement, may be read as simultaneous appropriation and attentiveness. As a parallel to Otojiro, his work offers the phenomenon of a version of japonaiserie originally addressed (and sold) to foreign audiences, mediated through the projection of such elements as Gothic and folktale, which is then re-imported to offer a seemingly authentic form of national identity by the Japanese themselves (among whom Hearn's reputation remains much higher than abroad).

Katy Hindson's essay, '"Chambres d'Asie, chambres d'ailleurs": Nicole-Lise Bernheim's Vertical Travels in Asia', compares two of the French writer's *récits de voyage*: *Chambres d'ailleurs* (1986), and *Saisons japonaises* (1999). In contrast to a French tradition of travelogues on Japan composed almost entirely by men, these are preoccupied with rooms, homes and shelters, as opposed to the non-places of postmodernity. These may be seen as corresponding to what Clifford terms 'dwelling-in-travelling',[20] and offering (as with Maillart) an alternative phenomenology of travel which involves a reconstitution rather than abandonment of home; a form of microscopic observation involving deceleration and inertia rather than continual movement. This mode of burrowing down ('nid douillet') attempts to negotiate and reclaim the archetypal, if not stereotypical, identification of the female with the domestic sphere. In Bernheim's first narrative, the relationship with her lover takes precedence over engagement with the native population, who are restricted to mere functional and instrumental roles; in the second, a greater length of duration and emphasis on the banal, anecdotal and everyday allows her to establish dialogic bonds with a surrogate family. The melancholy lyricism of self-performance generates an illusion of vulnerability, which may however be regarded as ultimately as manipulative and governed by ulterior motives as more traditional forms of representation. Certainly this would be indicated by the anger displayed by the host family at Bernheim taking photographs for commercial purposes. There remains the risk of yearning for reciprocity resulting in reification of a purely fantasy other and an idealisation of the state of ignorance (evident in the manifest lack of any linguistic competence). One might relate this to Bernheim's avoidance of specific sites of French colonial incursion, most obviously Vietnam, and also to a more general tendency to avoid questions of guilt and reparation in recent French *récits de voyages*.

Mark Meli's essay, '*World Journey of My Heart* and *Homestay in the World*: Travel Programming and Contemporary Japanese Culture', focuses on two specific shows: *Sekai wa ga kokoro no tabi/World Journey of My Heart* (running for 463 shows between 1993 and 2003); and *Sekai ururun taizaiki/Homestay in the World*. This raises the issue of generic mutation within televisual conventions: the persona fronting, the scripting and editing techniques, the inevitably collaborative status of the production, and the influence of advertising and revenue concerns. Such programming may seem to offer primarily a vicarious mode of satisfaction, but the centrality of travel in Japan was noted by Kaempher as early as 1691. More recently, distinctive groups such as parasite singles and affluent retirees have emerged as particularly itinerant; international travel also serves more generally as status commodity. *World Journey* offers a sophisticated exploration of the relation of individual and collective memory by allowing a temporal regression into early memories, family roots and formative encounters, introduced by an unusually wide range of (ethnically mixed) presenters. Historical links with Holland and Portugal are explored, as well as the frequently taboo memory of war in Asia. *Homestay in the World* stresses travel as residence but heavily mediated in this case through the influence of idol-making machinery, with glamorous young presenters selected as representative individuals (in contrast to the group tourism often associated with Japanese travellers). These are incongruously matched with supposedly authentic host families, acknowledging parity to Europe but flaunting their superiority over the developing world. (Designer clothes are worn in defiance of official government advice not to display excessive wealth abroad because of potential risk.) Each programme must conclude with *Ururun* (the sound of weeping) and appropriately hyperbolic displays of affection, which may be interpreted as simultaneously a placating of anxiety about Japan's international status and mode of appropriation. The Japanese term, *Sekai*, regards the world as defined by a binary opposition to Japan rather than within a part/whole relation, so the genre may be seen as both dissolving the boundaries between inside and outside as part of the process of global homogenisation and reinstating the *nihonjinron* claim to cultural uniqueness.

Meli's essay may seem to support the thesis of global homogenisation, as proposed in the bland and depthless travelogues of Pico Iyer. There are no Asiatic mysteries: any idealisation of a spurious essence is a form of repression; it is pointless to lament a postmodernity which is the precondition of international travel as consumerist lifestyle choice. Steve Clark's essay, 'After the Bubble: Post-Imperial Tokyo', seeks to restore a historicist dimension by emphasising the specific determinants of the urban phenomenology characteristic of recent representations of Tokyo, in particular the curious mixture of schadenfreude and supplication that characterises recent travelogues dealing with the mega-city.

The essays that follow are unified geographically and historically, but are not governed by a single overarching thesis. They do, however, share the emphasis of newer imperial history on cultural dispersal, multiple sources and resistance to teleological narratives of empire. After more than two decades of the near-undisputed ascendancy of postcolonial theorising, they represent above all a return to a more context-specific, empirically-grounded and formally-nuanced approach to the genre of travel writing.

1

Between Topos and Topography: Japanese Early Modern Travel Literature

Robert F. Wittkamp

Travel has always played an important part in the development of Japanese literature. In the *Man'yōshū*, for example, the first collection of poetry from the eighth century, about 2,000 of the 4,500 texts are connected to travel in the sense that an experience of a physical journey was the occasion for composing the poem. This, of course, can also refer to the grief and sorrow of a person from whom somebody has been taken away by travel (and who is reflecting on its consequences). There is still much work to do in order to get a grip on that 'strong desire to wander' (*hyōhaku*), which occupies a substantial part of the mentality of many, though not all, Japanese people. But if one is asked to name the most famous piece of travel literature, without any doubt the answer would be *Oku no hosomichi* (*Narrow Road to the Interior* 1694).[1] This travelogue by the famous Haiku-master Matsuo Bashō (1644–94) was the product of years of recasting and reworking of notes taken on a journey through the north-east of Japan in 1689.[2] Outside Japan, it is perhaps the best-known work of 'classical Japanese literature' and at the same time is usually taken as the most representative work of a body of literature which is summarised under the term *kikō bungaku* (travel literature).

This chapter will place the *Oku no hosomichi* in its cultural-historical context in order to show that it is indeed a work of the Kinsei period (*kinsei*, i.e. the early modern time from the beginning of the seventeenth to the second half of the nineteenth century) but not, as commonly assumed, the most representative one. To make this clear, I must reconstruct the 'paradigm shift' that occurs in this era, to use the term coined by Thomas S. Kuhn.[3] This will be achieved by examining the life and work of Sugae Masumi (1754–1829) who — at least in my view — is more suitable to represent the genre of early modern travel literature. I will approach this issue comparatively through a brief discussion of the central thesis in Karatani Kōjin's *The Origins of Modern Japanese Literature*. It will be shown that some of what Karatani takes as achievements of modern literature (*kindai*, i.e. from the second half of the nineteenth century to the Second World War) can already be found more than a hundred years earlier.

Two Mainstreams in Early Modern Travel Literature

What is described here as the paradigm or pattern of the Middle Ages not only concerns the travel poetry of that period (i.e. in our sense from about the tenth to the end of the seventeenth century) but also the way in which Japanese literary history since the end of the nineteenth century (*kokubungaku*) was — and sometimes still is — handling a corpus of texts subsumed under the name *kikō bungaku* (travel literature).[4] This fact already indicates that the paradigm shift is to be understood as both a diachronic *and* a synchronic matter, and may also be conceptualised in terms of social differentiation (as defined by the systems theory of Niklas Luhmann).[5] Gerhard Sauder notes a persistent oscillation within European travel literature since the eighteenth century between the poles of scientific-methodical travel (*die wissenschaftlich-methodische Reise*) and sentimental travel (*die empfindsame Reise*).[6] We can identify a similar set of coordinates in early modern Japanese travel literature. Even Kuhn does not claim the complete vanishing of a former paradigm with the appearance of a new one and, in many respects, it would be more appropriate to speak of them existing side by side rather than one after another. I will return to this point later.

I have to start with a brief reflection on the friction and tensions contained within the concept of *kikō bungaku* (travel literature). For the older Japanese history of literature (*kokubungaku*), this term denotes a small canon of belles-lettres writing, which reached its climax in Bashō's *Oku no hosomichi*. In opposition to this exclusively aesthetically-guided standpoint, proponents of more recent Japanese literary history after the Second World War define *kikō bungaku* in a broader sense to include travelogues, which were not written under the conditions of traditional travel literature.[7] Works dealing with travel without being diaries or even texts written to provide practical information may therefore also be included. The genre is no longer restricted to a narrow canon of *classical literature*, but expands to include all kinds of texts connected to travel. If I refer to the traditional paradigm of travel literature it will be — for the sake of convenience — to the earlier and limited classical canon.

Two major developments in travel literature clearly took shape in the seventeenth century. One direction (*Tosa nikki, Oku no hosomichi*) is connected to the Middle Ages and characterised by several criteria, such as poems following short narrative sequences and the obligatory mention of 'classical' place names (*utamakura, meisho*), or sentimental (self-)reflections. Kenji Watanabe proposed the name 'emotional' or 'introverted way' (*shujōteki*) for this paradigm. The other direction is extroverted, encyclopaedic and named by Watanabe as the 'intellectual way' (*shuchiteki*).[8] In opposition to the traditional model of travel literature as a form of belles-lettres governed by the ideal of *jōshu* (sentimental mood, feeling, atmosphere, aesthetic impression, refined taste), the new paradigm, as Yukihiko Nakamura emphasises, displayed particular interest in geographical description, and what Donald Keene terms, perhaps a little anachronistically, the 'scientific accumulation of information about all parts of Japan'.[9] For these reasons Yōko Itasaka calls this kind of text '*chishiteki kikō*' (topographical travel literature).[10] An early exponent of this paradigm is Kaibara Ekiken (1630–1714), and Tachibana Nankei (1753–1805) can be named as a later one. It should be clear, however, that emotional, introverted or self-reflective passages are part of their literary output as well as topographical elements and there is no abrupt break with the tradition found in the *Oku no hosomichi*.

Bashō and Ekiken were contemporaries and we can construct an axis, the ends of which are marked by their works, on which nearly the whole field of Japanese early modern travel literature can be located.

To Travel Means to Suffer: The Medieval Paradigm

The paradigm of 'traditional travel literature' is shown clearly in the opening lines of the *Oku no hosomichi*:[11]

> Days and months are travellers of eternity. So are the years that pass by. Those who steer a boat across the sea, or drive a horse over the earth till they succumb to the weight of years, spend every minute of their lives travelling. There are a great number of ancients, too, who died on the road. I myself have been tempted for a long time by the cloud-moving wind — filled with a strong desire to wander (*hyōhaku*).[12]

Self-reflection or self-examination (*jishō*, literally to light on or illuminate oneself) is an important element of this tradition. The roots of this kind of travel literature can be traced back to the chronicle *Kojiki* (720), or the poem-collection *Man'yōshū*, and distinct works in this style have appeared since the Heian period (794–1185). One peculiarity is the form already to be found in the *Tosa nikki*: relatively short prose passages climaxing in one or more poems in Chinese (*kanshi*), Japanese (*waka*) or what is called today Haiku (*haibun* style). Another characteristic is the restriction on the use of place names, because only those related to the canon of classical literature were accepted: *utamakura* (literally pillow worlds, poetic places taken from traditional *waka* collections) and other historical sites (*meisho*).

Another important issue can be epitomised by the Japanese phrase *tabi no urei* or *tabi no kurushisa*, the suffering, grief, sorrow, anguish and distress of a journey, or, as Keene puts it, the 'despair that marked the medieval travel diaries'.[13]

> I suffered severely from repeated attacks while I rode on horseback bound for the town of Kōri. It was indeed a terrible thing to be so ill on the road, when there still remained thousands of miles before me, but thinking that if I were to die on my way to the extreme north it would only be the fulfillment of providence . . .[14]

Comparing the long distance of this journey to the literary output (forty-six pages in a pocket edition) and considering how cautious Bashō was in selecting every single word,[15] we understand that there must be *deeper meaning* in his complaints. To emphasise, for example, the feeling of loneliness, the presence of travelling companions was often omitted:

> After many days of solitary wandering, I came at last to the barrier-gate of Shirakawa, which marks the entrance to the northern regions.[16] The voices of the fishermen dividing the catch of the day made me even more lonely, for I was immediately reminded of an old poem which pitied them for their precarious lives on the sea.[17]

The prototype of the suffering traveller can be traced back to a myth collected in the chronicle *Kojiki* (720), where Prince Yamato no Takeru no Mikoto was sent away by his father to conquer north-east Japan. Failing to accomplish his mission, he suffered and finally died on the road, leaving behind a couple of poems.[18] Other poets to whom Bashō is referring in the category of 'a great number of ancients, too, who died on the road' include Saigyō (1118–90), Sōgi (1421–1502), and the T'ang poets Li Po (699–762) and Tu Fu (712–70), to give only the most famous names. Another characteristic is the dense intertextuality within classical texts evident in highly self-conscious quotations such as 'travellers of eternity', taken from a poem by Li Po translated into Japanese, and many other similar allusions.[19]

Buddhist thought colours most of the works from the Japanese Middle Ages (in the sense of a *histoire de mentalité* employed by the Annales school of French historiography).[20] This is clearly apparent in the famous *waka* poet Nōin (born 988), an early representative of the *hyōhaku*-mentality ('strong desire to wander') expressed in *waka* poetry, who was strongly admired by successors such as the great wandering poet Saigyō, up to Bashō, who proves his adoration for both of them throughout the whole *Oku no hosomichi*. However, as mentioned above, Bashō himself was not only an exponent of the old paradigm. One can for example observe a different use of place names (*utamakura*),[21] and some passages from the *Oku no hosomichi* even show an occasional interest in topography:

> The islands are situated in a bay about three miles (*ri*) wide in every direction and open to the sea through a narrow mouth on the South-east side. . . . innumerable islands are scattered over (the bay) from one end to the other. Tall islands point to the sky and level ones prostrate themselves before the surges of water. Islands are piled above islands, and islands are joined to islands, so that they look exactly like parents caressing their children or walking with them arm in arm. The pines are of the freshest green, and their branches are curved in exquisite lines, bent to the wind constantly blowing through them.[22]

But in the end, Bashō's primary aim was not geographical description. As Haruo Shirane emphasises, he 'fundamentally refigures Matsushima one of the most famous *utamakura* in the north-east. through Chinese poetic structure and allusions'. The Matsushima section is 'a stunning haikai experiment in the Chinese *fu*'.[23] His writing is guided by the ambition of developing a new style, yet it remains as far away as the older literature from the ideal of describing the outside world.

Towards Modern Times: Sugae Masumi and the New Paradigm

The new paradigm starts to shift (or separate out) already in the fourteenth century but only achieves a distinctive form with the appearance of Kaibara Ekiken.[24] For Ekiken and his followers, travel did not any longer mean suffering and dying on the road. This new travel literature was reacting to the needs (i.e. practical knowledge) of a new time. Civil war was finally over, peace reigned over the country, and the reader was no longer interested in the mind of the suffering traveller but rather in his experiences on the road and what was actually going on in different parts of the country. Places connected to the canon of literature up to the end of the Middle Ages, which *classical* travel literature (*kikō bungaku*) felt obliged to mention, were losing their priority. Instead of these famous places (*utamakura*, *meisho*), the early modern reader was much more interested in information about unknown regions and daily life. There even appeared a kind of travelogue 'that contains not a single poem by the author'.[25]

For reasons described elsewhere,[26] the travel literature of Sugae Masumi is much more suitable to represent the new paradigm of the topographical travelogues (*chishiteki kikō*). Masumi was born in 1754 in the countryside close to present-day Nagoya. In 1783, he left his home for reasons which are still the object of speculation. From the beginning of his journey, which never brought him home, his destination presumably was Hokkaidō (Ezo). But it was five years before he finally succeeded in finding a passage to that largely uncharted island in the north, in 1788. During these years Masumi travelled all over the north of Japan and left many diaries filled with *waka* poems, paintings, and detailed descriptions of the land and people. He continued these works in Ezo, where he tried to learn the Ainu language and even worked on an Ainu-Japanese dictionary. After spending four years there, he went back to the north of Japan. Till his death in 1829, he spent almost all his time in that region which is called today the Prefecture of Akita (Akita-*ken*).

Many of his works, especially in his younger years, are similar to the classical paradigm of travel literature in that they are also interrupted by *waka* poems.[27] They are written in the style of *gikobun*, imitating the artifice of the old language of the Heian period, which was different from the spoken language. It was probably chosen to provide the diaries with the feel of serious literature (presumably to impress the local people in order to finance the journey).[28] Yet judged by their content, the diaries belong to the new paradigm since they describe land and people in a manner as detailed as possible without being restricted to *utamakura* and *meisho*.

In the last years of his life, Masumi worked on a complete topography of the whole area of Akita. The resulting *chishi* contain no poems but much data as well as colourful and detailed descriptions of the land, and the people and their customs. Today they are not only a treasure for research on local history but also have become objects of literary attention, and appear particularly well suited to the attention of cultural studies. Masumi died in 1829 on the road in the countryside of Akita trying to accomplish his huge project of mapping the topography of the region.

Travel, Landscape and Epistemology

'The Discovery of Landscape' — the first chapter in Karatani's *Origins of Modern Japanese Literature* — can be seen as central to his aim 'not to discuss the concept of "the history of Japanese literature"'. However, he does want to point out that such a narrative 'which seems so self-evident to us today, took shape in the midst of our discovery of landscape' which, he argues, occurred 'during the third decade of the Meiji period' (i.e. about 1900).[29] Of course, he has to admit that it already existed before that time but not *landscape as landscape*.[30] A similar argument might be made with regard to European conventions for scenic description subsequent to Petrarch's climbing of Mt. Ventoux in 1336: 'when talking about the landscape that predated "landscape" we face the contradiction [*hairi*; also: paralogism] that we are already looking at it through "landscape"'.[31] But when Karatani is still speaking vaguely of 'a kind of reversal' (*tentō*), we have to ask ourselves whether he is at all capable of distinguishing the epistemological constellation (*ninshikitekina fuchi*) of *landscape as landscape* from even a text by Bashō, which in his view has 'not a single line of description'.[32] It is argued that Bashō does not speak only about landscape by the use of different terms even as a kind of meta-language, but also is reacting consciously to a long tradition by 're-visioning' (Shirane) or by constructing 'anti-landscape'.[33] Even Bashō must have experienced an 'inversion' in order for this to become possible.

A closer look at early modern travel literature, which Karatani obviously was not willing to take, reveals a different perception and expression of landscape much earlier. This is already demonstrated in a short passage from the *Miso no ki* (1709; Records from Miso) by Kaibara Ekiken:

> The distance from Wada down to Suwa is about five *ri* and sixteen *chō*.... Between these places stands Mt. Wada with its long slopes. From the top to the bottom it is more than two and a half *ri*. The eastern slope is very gentle while the western slope is steep. But there are no unclimbable passages at all. Up to the end of the third month the peak is covered with snow, and even on the mountain path some snow sometimes remains.... The snow in this region is very deep.[34]

It has to be mentioned that Ekiken was a connoisseur of classical literature too, and he was also extremely self-conscious about his own literary style.[35]

A changed construction (i.e. perception and depiction) of landscape can be even better explained by Masumi's paintings, where he tries to provide reliable information for practical use (for example by offering topographical pictures from a bird's-eye view, where the place names were added in red ink), or in presenting a picturesque landscape, of a kind with absolutely no connection to earlier literary tradition.[36]

Figure 1.1 Sugae Masumi, 'Mount Shiribetsu ga Take'. From the travel diary, *Ezo no Teburi*. By permission of the Prefectual Museum of Akita (Akita-kenritsu hakubutsukan).

Between Topos and Topography 23

Figure 1.2 Sugae Masumi, 'Cape Inawozaki'. From the travel diary, *Emishi no Saeki*. By permission of the Prefectual Museum of Akita (Akita-kenritsu hakubutsukan).

Karatani is relying on a judgement by Yanagita Kunio (1875–1962), who was also the editor of a collection of 'travel essays'.[37] In this collection, Yanagita was full of praise for the travel literature of Kaibara Ekiken and the two topographical travelogues *Saiyū zakki* (*Jottings of Travel in the West*, 1783) and *Tōyū zakki* (*Jottings of Travel in the East*, 1788) by Furukawa Koshōken (1726–1807).[38] Yet we have to bear in mind that Yanagita was the founder of Japanese folk studies (*minzokugaku*). Though fully aware of the 'two distinct types' of travel literature,[39] his selection may be criticised for focusing only on material useful to folk studies.[40] Taking the works of Kaibara and Furukawa as a kind of new standard, it is indeed hard to discover 'a single line of description' in the *Oku no hosomichi*.

Now we can understand the reasons why in Karatani's book the 'discovery of landscape' is the kernel statement and why this denotes not only mountains and rivers in front of our noses and their description, but an altogether different way of seeing:

> When the ethnologist Yanagita Kunio began to use the term *jōmin* ('ordinary and abiding folk') in the early Showa period (1926–89), he was not at all referring to 'ordinary people', but to a kind of landscape which had become visible to him through the type of inversion of values I have just described.[41]

The inversion-based discovery of the 'ordinary and abiding folk' together with 'The Discovery of the Child' (Chapter 5 in Karatani's book) bring us to the question of the point of time when this may have occurred.[42]

If we search the *Oku no hosomichi* for concrete descriptions of people Bashō and his companion met on the road, the only and most 'colourful' description of a person is this:

> The gate-keeper was kind enough to find me a young man of tremendous physique, who walked in front of me with a curved sword strapped at his waist and a stick of oak gripped firmly in his hand.[43]

There are no more 'single lines of description' of all the thirty-odd people they met, hardly even an individual name. Furukawa, praised by Yanagita, is much more detailed in his descriptions of the local people but clearly keeping a distance and dividing himself from them. Bolitho, quoting from *Tōzai yuki*, writes:

> Of the shrine priest at Numakunai he Furukawa wrote, 'a very stupid person, who spoke nothing but absurdities to the inspectors.' He always seemed impatient with those local people assigned to the party as guides, referring

to one as 'the usual stupid sort of fellow', and saying of another 'if I were to tell people about him when I went home, nobody would believe me.'[44]

At least there were descriptions. Writing about the travel narratives by Kaibara Ekiken, Itasaka Yōko says that:

> ... it shows a new perception different from the traditional travel literature, i.e. a perception, which does not describe the rural life only as a part of a landscape or remote as in the *monogatari*-narratives. It is a kind of description, in which landscape, living people and their works are taking shape.[45]

Another travel writer who clearly broke the barriers between himself and the 'ordinary and abiding folk' was Masumi. On his journeys through the northeast he met many men, women, travellers, workers, farmers or children and left vivid descriptions of them. These are undoubtedly made by a man who was in close contact with the people, for example the children and their play, closely described in words or in paintings and sketches. Interestingly enough, this is also where Luhmann sees the 'semantic invention of the child' ('die semantische Erfindung des Kindes').[46]

Due to limitations of space, I will pick up just one more topic from Karatani's book, which again is related to the problem of landscape. The 'Afternote to chapter 1 (1991)' which was originally added to the English translation begins with the following remarks:

> What I have called the 'discovery of landscape' was not merely an 'internal' event: it was accompanied by the discovery of a landscape that was new in actuality and not enveloped in any way by ancient texts. This landscape was that of Hokkaido, the northern island which, until the Meiji period, had been inhabited by Japanese only in its southern tip. . . .
>
> Seen in this context, the 'discovery of landscape' in the Meiji period was a discovery — if we refer to Kant's distinction — not of the beautiful but of the sublime. For the vast wilderness of Hokkaido inspired awe in human beings, unlike the mainland which had been regulated for centuries and enveloped by literary texts. But in order to grasp this territory as sublime it was necessary . . . to take on the Christian attitude which regards nature as the handiwork of God. It was an attitude, at any rate, which was not continuous with Japanese thought as it had existed up to that point.[47]

The accuracy or otherwise of Karatani's account of the 'discovery of Hokkaido' cannot be discussed here; our object of reconsideration again should be its specific dating. Karatani is referring to the influential Meiji Christian thinker and critic Uchimura Kanzō (1861–1930) and the famous writer Kunikida Doppo (1871–1908) who, in his opinion, was the discoverer of landscape. As Itasaka Yōko shows in her résumé of early modern Hokkaidō travel literature, there existed already some texts on the region that were written about a hundred years before the time Karatani is referring to and in particular since the end of the eighteenth century when the Tokugawa shogunate sent pioneers to explore the territory.[48] When Masumi reached the shores of Hokkaidō in 1788, there had already been twelve books published dealing with the subject, such as the *Ezoshi* (1720) by Arai Hakuseki (1657–1725) or *Sankoku tsūran zusetu* (1785) and *Kaikoku heidan* (1786), both written by Hayashi Shihei (1738–93). A peculiarity of Hokkaidō travel literature is its distinctive 'synchronical intertextuality' and the fact that it contains many paintings and sketches made with the intention of providing exact information for practical use.[49] Of course, there was no classical literary tradition linked to Hokkaidō either, which is what makes it *a priori* different from classical travel literature. Taking into consideration the Hokkaidō travel literature (*Ezo kikō*), even Karatani would be obliged to admit that his 'epistemological constellation' developed much earlier than he acknowledges.

Bashō and Masumi: A Final Look

Since the works by Bashō and Masumi are very different, a complete comparison cannot be achieved here. Instead I will limit myself to only a few aspects, which supplement the points elaborated above. Some topographical and new elements in the *Oku no hosomichi* have already been mentioned and we can also trace the traditional paradigm of form and codes in Masumi's works. Let us take a look at *Waga kokoro*. This piece of *kikō bungaku* describes a climb on Mt. Obasute, a place famous in Japanese literature as a site to see the autumn full moon.[50] The travelogue begins very conventionally:

> I had been staying in Tsukama Country in the country of Shinano since the spring of Third Year of Tenmei (1783). I wanted to see the full moon over Mt. Obasute in Sarashina that fall, and spoke about this with some friends who also wanted to go. We made our preparations for the trip and set out from Motoseba village on the thirteenth night of the eighth month. We came to a field.
>
> Sarashina no　　　　　　　　Hearts set
> tsuki omou tote　　　　　　　on the Sarashina moon,
> shirube naki　　　　　　　　how dark was the path

> yami ni zo tadoru we followed in a field
> nobe no nakamichi with nothing to guide us!
>
> To someone who was wondering if the insect songs grew weaker at dawn, I said . . .⁵¹

We even find relics proving the old paradigm of *tabi no urei*, the suffering on a journey, as in the last line of the *waka* poem 'with nothing to guide us!' or in a passage like this:

> A notice on the gate of Tōkō Temple told how a thirty-year-old woman from somewhere had collapsed on the grass and died on the fourth of August, leaving behind a child of five or six. None of our party could read it without being moved to tears.⁵²

However, even in this passage (followed by two *waka* poems), one can observe a slight difference from the work of Bashō, since Masumi and his friends are not referring to a poet who died on the road with exquisite pathos or a place where a famous battle had been fought, but to the 'ordinary and abiding folk'. Japanese folk studies (*minzokugaku*) and even Yanagita Kunio, the name to which *minzokugaku* is linked, are now rightly recognising Sugae Masumi as the original founder of this field. This is particularly clear in his later works from the north-east of Japan and Hokkaidō, filled with detailed descriptions (in words and pictures) of the people, their lives, what they were eating and drinking, the tools they were using, the places in which they were living, their clothes and so on.

Compared to the traditional place names (*utamakura*, *meisho*), differences are evident in Masumi's use. The main intention of naming was to denote a place travelled through or visited during the journey but in his narratives this was not restricted to literature and history of the reading society in metropolitan cultural centres like Edo or Kyōto:

> Leaving our inn at a place called Kuwahara . . . We came to a place called Mine Village. . . . There are also people living on the mountainside in Sugi Village. . . . The mountains rose steeply from the banks of the Chikuma river to end in majestic peaks. We could see the summits of Mt. Ariaki and Mt. Kamuri in the east, and Mt. Hitoe to the west.⁵³

There are more place names in Masumi's climbing of Mt. Obasute, which took him just a week, than in Bashō's journey of about six months through the north-east. Masumi's interest in *place names as place names* providing topographical information is obvious, as is his particular concern not only with common people and unknown locations throughout Japan but also with any kind of information, including foreign countries too:

> On the way, Hinagawa Kiyotoshi, whom I had met the night before, spoke freely about many voyages that he had made from the island of Tsushima. He had crossed over to Korea during his childhood where, having learned the language, he worked as an interpreter. Because he had committed some slight crime, however, he was wandering about like this. When we stopped by the roadside, he wrote some Korean words in the dirt and explained what each one meant.[54]

It would be impossible to find a passage like this in the diaries by Bashō. Particularly in Masumi's works from Hokkaidō, the acute interest in foreign countries is apparent, for example in his attempt to gather information about Russia, which was in sharp competition with the Edo-*bakufu* to explore Hokkaidō.

Even in the *Waga kokoro* which — were it located on the hypothetical axis between the two paradigm-markers Bashō and Ekiken — would probably be the one closest to the 'Bashō-end', Masumi is obviously much too curious about land and people and their here-and-now life to be guided by ancient poets, *utamakura* and a vain wish to be an immortal poet (though judging by his biography there might have been a hidden wish to die on the road too). On the other hand, Bashō was distinctively very concerned with protecting the 'old paradigm'. In another short piece of travel literature he wrote:

> From time immemorial the art of keeping diaries while on the road was popular among the people, and such great writers as Lord Ki, Chōmei, and the nun Abutsu brought it to perfection. Later works are by and large little more than imitations of these great masters, and my pen, being weak in wisdom and unfavoured by divine gift, strives to equal them, but in vain. It is easy enough to say, for example, that such and such a day was rainy in the morning but fine in the afternoon, that there was a pine tree at such and such a place, or that the name of the river at a certain place was such and such, for these things are what everybody says in their diaries, although in fact they are not even worth mentioning unless there are fresh and arresting elements in them.[55]

Bashō by himself was setting the standards — rigid standards lasting up to our time — but the works of Ekiken or Masumi clearly show an independent paradigm. It would be hard to prove that their travel literature provides (or *allows*, in Luhmann's sense of social differentiation) more *information* than Bashō's, where one is forced to read the traditional canon too, but it is information of a different quality. At least the reader was (is) not so much interested in a suffering and lonely poet wandering towards his death on the road but in practical data about different people and regions — which of course would be even more welcomed if presented with a masterly use of language and profound education.

A translation of the complete travelogues by Sugae Masumi, in particular his records from Hokkaidō and north-east Japan, would make this transition much more comprehensible.[56]

2

'The First Appearance of This Celebrated Capital'; or, What Mr. Barrow Saw in the Land of the Chinaman

Joe Sample

> We entered the celebrated city of [Peking] early in the forenoon, but had no opportunity of seeing any thing, except immense crowds of people on each side of us, owing to the closeness of the carriages in which we were confined; all we could observe was, the walls, which were very high and strong, built of large bricks; and the houses were very low, and rather shabby, of the same materials. We had been induced to form so high an idea of its amazing grandeur, that I confess, we were somewhat disappointed; but no estimation could be formed from the little we saw.[1]

Readers familiar with Mary Louise Pratt's *Imperial Eyes: Travel Writing and Transculturation* should recognise the parallel in the title of this essay: 'Mr. Barrow' is John Barrow (1764–1848), author of *Travels into the Interior of Southern Africa,* one of the works that was instrumental in helping Pratt formulate her thesis that travel writing helped to create a domestic audience for European imperialism.[2] While Pratt acknowledges in an earlier essay that Barrow's Africa journal is not 'prominent on anybody's mental bookshelves' (Pratt 1986b, 140), she fails to mention in any of her writings that the journal Barrow produced following his participation in the much-heralded Macartney embassy (1792–94) occupies an important and permanent position on the 'mental' (and literal) bookshelves of scholars interested in Western representations of China.

The display quote from Samuel Holmes' journal contains several conundrums for travel writers that are addressed in this essay. The writer has arrived at an important location but the walls prevent him from seeing what he wants to see. Yet the conventions of travel writing virtually require that he write something. So Holmes, a soldier who kept part of his journal on loose rice paper purchased in China, writes a nicely balanced sentence about high walls and low houses and concludes his thoughts with a statement about his impressions of the city, even though he admits that he can make 'no estimation' of it based on the little that he was able to see. Holmes fulfils his travel writing obligation for his readers, whom he identifies as his family, while simultaneously helping to write a much more complicated narrative: his obstructed or denied view lends itself well to the Western trope of the inscrutable, or impenetrable, China. Indeed, early travellers to China did not only suffer from a 'traveling incarceration' because their own 'cultural baggage' (Dupee 2004, 315) prohibited them from 'seeing' (understanding, appreciating) the Chinese; instead, they were literally isolated, restricted, and forbidden from looking beyond the city walls or compound gates that surrounded them.

'. . . from the report of travellers'

In this essay, I read two journals written by members of the Macartney embassy to China by following a suggestion given by Barrow in the introduction to *Travels in China*. Specifically, he observes that because 'different people will generally see the same things in different points of view', he suggests that readers compare 'different descriptions and colouring . . . of the same object' so as 'to obtain the most correct notions of such matters as can be learned only from the report of travellers' (*Travels in China*, 2). As the title of this essay implies, the 'object' under consideration is the ancient and celebrated capital of China, Peking. Drawing on literary and anthropological approaches to the study of symbolic moments that commonly occur during cross-cultural encounters, this essay focuses in particular on the passages in the journals that tell the story of the embassy's entrance into the capital. One probably cannot overstate the significance of this moment for the British. After nearly a year of difficult travel, the last several weeks of which were spent in inland China, the embassy finally arrived at the capital 'said to be the greatest in the world' (*An Authentic Account*, 115). Their arrival not only afforded embassy members the opportunity to represent Britain to the Chinese, but they also experienced something that few other Westerners had had the opportunity to see, which gave them the chance to reflect and form their own opinions on Britain's supposed status as the world's most advanced and ordered society.

The Macartney embassy journals offer an exemplary opportunity to assess the value of travel writing beyond informational and entertainment purposes. Indeed, the journals offer the paradigm that Philip Edwards in *The Story of the Voyage* laments is so rare. More specifically, Edwards discusses his interest in the manner in which a journal travels from 'experience into the written word and the mutations of the written word as it moves into print', contending that 'the experience is inferred, not known; and the ideal paradigm of journal, manuscript draft and printed version, available from more than one individual engaged in the same venture, is seldom if ever found' (Edwards 1994, 6). Some of the original manuscripts from the Macartney embassy journals are extant and those who kept journals recorded the same events, each in their own words. The embassy participants freely borrowed from each other, so scholars are able to compare and contrast different treatments of the same events as originally narrated by a single writer. Multiple editions of most of the journals were published and 'A Delicate Inquiry into the Embassies to China and a Legitimate Conclusion from the Premises', which excerpted passages from the journals, was not published until twenty-five years after the embassy.[3]

The Macartney embassy marks Britain's first effort to make diplomatic contact with the Chinese court. The journals, however, have traditionally been regarded by scholars as personal accounts of real events as opposed to diplomatic reports of governmental affairs. Yet the journals have not been treated collectively as examples of travel writing, that 'particular species of entertainment' whose structure and function was 'easily distinguishable ... to eighteenth-century readers' (Batten 1978, 32).[4] If we approach the journals as written in a certain milieu, we can surmise that the writers were familiar with travel writing as a genre, a source of information, a form of entertainment, and even a forum for social and political commentary. And, to be sure, by the late eighteenth century the reading public was still fascinated by accounts from China: the journals then provided readers with an enormous amount of reliable, observation-based and entertaining information. Readers, in turn, could compare and contrast not only their own understandings of the country and the people with other accounts of life in the Middle Kingdom, but they could also compare the journals of the same embassy, and in particular the different versions of the same events that occurred during the embassy.

The latter opportunity is demonstrated in this essay by reference to the journals that were arguably most responsible for writing the story of the embassy, Aeneas Anderson's *A Narrative of the British Embassy to China* (London: J. Debrett, 1795), George Staunton's *An Authentic Account of an Embassy from the King of Great Britain to the Emperor of China* (London: G. Nicol, 1797), and Barrow's *Travels in China* (London: T. Cadell and

W. Davis, 1805). *A Narrative of the British Embassy to China* was the first to appear; and the publication of Barrow's account nearly ten years later marks a significant effort to rewrite the narrative of the embassy and change the image of China in Britain. In between these efforts was Staunton's *An Authentic Account*, the two-volume, eight-hundred-page official account of the embassy, which was, according to the title page, 'taken chiefly from the papers of His Excellency the Earl of Macartney; Sir ERASMUS GOWER, Commander of the Expedition, and of other Gentlemen in the several departments of the Embassy'. The works of Anderson and Barrow serve to frame the official history, and as such receive most attention here.

Writing China

The Macartney embassy is one of history's most anticipated and documented cross-cultural encounters, although 'collision' is the most common metaphor used to describe the events that took place when the British travelled to China in an effort to establish formal diplomatic relations. The embassy had six objectives: acquire one or two places near the tea-and silk-producing and woollen-consuming areas, where their traders might reside and British jurisdiction be exercised; negotiate a commercial treaty with a view to extending trade throughout China if possible; relieve existing abuses in the trade practices at Canton; create a desire in China for British products; arrange diplomatic representation at Peking; and open Japan, Chochin China and the Eastern Islands to British commerce (Hsu 1990, 156). Historically, the embassy has been regarded as a diplomatic failure because none of the stated objectives was accomplished. The only positive result of the embassy was the mass of information that was produced by the participants in their sketches and journals.

The British hoped that the Chinese, who were known to admire Western clockwork devices, toy automatons and certain kinds of scientific instrumentation brought to China primarily by early missionaries, would be eager to engage in trade. Unfortunately, the emperor was indifferent to the gifts brought by the embassy. The reception of these offerings and the infamous 'kowtow incident' have come to symbolise the contrasting British and Chinese worldviews. Macartney, a successful career diplomat who had previously served as ambassador to Russia and who would later become the colonial governor in Cape Colony, had been instructed by King George III not to perform the ceremonial obeisance, known as a 'kowtow', when he met with the emperor. (This gesture consisted of touching one's head to the ground three times thrice.) The rationale for this was simple: Macartney's conduct needed to reflect his understanding of the emperor as not being superior to his own king. The British viewed their efforts as a diplomatic endeavour based on 'principles of free trade and economic civility' (Schaffer 'Instruments', 218), but the Chinese insisted that the British were paying tribute to the emperor. Macartney, for his part, during his audience with the Chinese sovereign, kneeled before the emperor as he would his own king. Several days later, following a lavish banquet celebrating the Chinese ruler's birthday, the emperor, unfazed by Macartney's confidence and uninterested in more British curios, unceremoniously dismissed the embassy entourage from the capital and the country. The British stay in Peking lasted only forty-seven days, though they had been prepared to stay indefinitely.

The unique circumstances of the embassy require a careful consideration and contextualisation of the journals themselves, which can be broadly viewed as examples of the first-impressions subgenre of travel writing. That is, unlike those early travellers who ventured to 'unknown' lands or places about which a reading audience had very little prior knowledge, China by the late eighteenth century still enjoyed a symbolic and mythical status in the Western consciousness. With several spectacular exceptions, however, most accounts of China available in the West prior to the embassy were written by people who had never travelled to China or, as Barrow contends, never travelled 'five hundred yards beyond the limits of the European' settlements in Canton, the port city in southern China through which all trade was conducted (*Travels in China*, 19). Throw in popular texts by William Chambers and Oliver Goldsmith and most European readers had a rather hazy notion of things Chinese.

No one who purchased published editions of the Macartney journals or who read excerpted journal passages in popular magazines questioned whether they were written by people who had really been to and travelled throughout the country. In addition, China was not newly discovered in a manner similar to the South Sea islands visited by Captain Cook. Yet, at the same time, the country was obviously not as well known as places written about by those who completed the Grand Tour or who wrote about journeys to familiar, though nevertheless exotic, colonial outposts. These conditions, coupled with the embassy's lack of success, complicate our efforts to read the journals as representative of eighteenth-century travel and exploration narratives. However, therein lies the distinction that these artefacts offer to the travel writing researcher.

The diplomatic nature of the embassy allows us to identify and focus on a truly symbolic moment of cultural significance — the embassy's entrance into the capital of another great empire. Ideally, a visiting dignitary's arrival in a nation's capital would reflect the order and precision that one expects of royalty and command, but such a reception was rarely experienced by the British entourage, which was often slowed down by swarming crowds of curious onlookers. And then, when the travellers finally did enter the capital, the novelty of their arrival wore off quickly *for the Chinese*. Each writer noted that the Chinese pretty much went about their business after looking at the British visitors only briefly and, in general, laughing at the oddity that was the collection of foreign visitors. As Staunton noted, when the embassy entered the capital, he observed that the area was full of people 'who did not appear to be assembled for the expected sight' (115). The 'concourse of people', in fact, was only 'diverted for a while by the passing spectacle' (115).

To add to the psychological drama of the moment, the embassy participants were largely disappointed in their first viewing of Peking: not only did they not get to see enough of the capital but what they did see did not leave them with the impression that they were in an extraordinary city. Staunton readily admits that the city 'did not come up to the idea they previously had formed of China' (125). The mixture of British disappointment and Chinese lack of interest proved to be perplexing to the travellers and demonstrates how such encounters resist any simple categorisation.

Great Expectations

On 21 August 1793, approximately three weeks before Macartney met with the emperor, an entourage of upwards of 3,000 men arose at 2:00 am at a city outside the Chinese capital, and their day's journey did not end until they arrived at the Summer Palace at 5:00 pm. This leg of the trip covered only thirty miles but the ninety-six-degree temperature, coupled with the enormous crowds that not only hindered their progress but also kicked up clouds of dirt that filled the air, made for a gruelling fifteen-hour journey. The embassy travelled through the suburbs of Peking for about fifteen minutes before they reached the gates to the city, and then they only spent a few hours in the capital before heading to the Summer Palace where they had intended to stay.[5]

Of the writers considered in this essay, Anderson, more so than Staunton and Barrow, relies heavily on the conventions of travel writing, dutifully recording times, dates, locations and other common elements. Though simply written and lacking much insight with regard to diplomatic matters, Anderson's journal went through three editions in less than two years. His narrative begins and ends in England, and he only occasionally belies a chronological and on-the-spot reporting technique by including summative or evaluative statements of events that have yet to happen. As might be expected given his status as the ambassador's personal servant, Anderson does defend Macartney's ceremonial conduct; and further, given the enormous interest in the embassy, he reflects on the diplomatic disappointments. However, for the most part, his comments on the customs and manners of the Chinese are detached from the narrative and presented in a supplementary chapter, a construction commonly found in eighteenth-century travel texts.

Staunton's *An Authentic Account* also begins and ends in England and was written, according to a prefatory advertisement, to satisfy the demands of the public and despite the author's poor health. Though descriptive and informative throughout, both with regard to diplomatic matters and the customs of the Chinese, *An Authentic Account* is, according to one scholar, 'competent, worthy and dull . . . with a ponderous eighteenth-century rhythm which eventually dulls the reader's awareness'.[6] By the time Barrow writes *Travels in China*, we see a 'journal' that uses the conventions of travel writing in a very different way, revealing a deeper understanding of the historical story of failure that emerged regarding the embassy. More specifically, whereas Anderson's daily entries recount and describe, Barrow's, reflecting the benefit of hindsight, compare and critique — often through lengthy, scholarly digressions on the customs and manners of the Chinese — as his stated goal is to show the Chinese 'in their proper colours' (*Travels in China*, 4), not as they have been represented in the past by, presumably, less travelled, less knowledgeable or less objective writers. Furthermore, in the introduction, Barrow positions his work as a respectfully-written supplement to 'the able and interesting account' (1) already produced by Staunton.

All of the travellers shared a great expectation for the embassy, and in particular they were excited to see the Chinese capital. Anderson's journal, as the first embassy account to see publication, presents readers with the first impression of Peking. Barrow, ten years later, transforms the arrival, and Peking in particular, into a much broader cultural and historical narrative. Anderson represents the capital as it was experienced by him personally and he eventually reconciles his experience with his prior expectations. Barrow, by contrast, represents the experience as he believes it needs to be understood historically for the nation, and in the process lays the foundation for nineteenth-century representational practices.

First Impressions

Anderson's arrival scene might best be understood as a personal triumph. His entry for 21 August 1793 takes up an entire chapter of his journal, beginning with a report that the sound of drums awakened the travellers early in the morning and ended some fifteen hours later when all the suite retired 'to sleep off the fatigue of the day' (109). Early in his chapter he summarises the embassy's difficult journey to Peking with a paragraph that amounts to an apologia:

> I cannot but add to the obstacles which we received from the curiosity of the Chinese people, some small degree of mortification at the kind of impression our appearance seemed to make on them: for they no sooner obtained a sight of any of us, than they universally burst out into loud laughter: and I must acknowledge, that we did not, at this time, wear the appearance of people, who arrived in this country, in order to obtain, by every means of address and prepossession, those commercial privileges, and political distinctions, which no other nation has had the art or power to accomplish. (100)

From the beginning, Anderson focuses on the British. His observation that Britain, like other nations before it, had been unsuccessful in obtaining desired 'commercial privileges' (100) acknowledges and contextualises the diplomatic failures. A similar self-defence appears at the end of Macartney's journal when he cautions readers (who might happen upon his journal and be unacquainted with Macartney or China) that 'nothing could be more fallacious than to judge of China by any European standard'.[7]

The morning-until-dusk structure of the narrative helps readers gain a sense of the grit and determination that was required of the British as they made their way to Peking through the 'prodigious concourse of people who absolutely covered the road' (100). 'The pressure of the crowd was sometimes so great', in fact, that the British 'were obliged to halt, for at least a quarter of an hour, to prevent the accidents which might otherwise have happened from the passage of the carts amidst this continual and innumerable throng' (100). Readers are presented here with a non-imperial vision of an intercultural encounter. There are no empty spaces, no panoramas, and no erasure of inhabitants; how can there be — all they see are inhabitants: 'Of the country, which occupies the first miles from this place to [Peking], I have little to say, as the crowds of people that surrounded us either intercepted our view or distracted our attention' (101).

After the embassy passed through the city gates, Anderson presents the view as it might have appeared to the Chinese. In particular, he laments that by the time the embassy arrived at the city gates they were in no position whatsoever to make a 'very favourable impression of the manners and disposition of the English nation' (101).

> At two o'clock we arrived at the gates of the grand imperial city with very little semblance of diplomatic figure or importance: in short, for I cannot help repeating the sentiment, the appearance of the Ambassador's attendants, both with respect to the shabbiness of their dress, and the vehicles which conveyed them, bore a greater resemblance to the removal of paupers to their parishes in England, than the expected dignity of the representation of a great and powerful monarch. (102)

The Western representatives of royalty, reduced in appearance to paupers, are upended in this carnivalesque scene, and the privileged status of the English is thereby entirely removed. Yet unlike those arrival scenes where parodic reversals can serve to critique cultural self-centredness, Anderson's depiction does not appear to reveal a fissure in the imperial mindset, and the inward focus lends itself well to a triumphal arrival scene on the personal level.

The oxymoronic 'small degree of mortification' (102) that characterised Anderson's look in the mirror eventually disappears as he turns his attention to the city itself. The remainder of the chapter then paints a remarkably familiar picture of 'beautiful triumphal arches' (101), 'spacious streets' (102), city walls and gates, 'beautiful specimens . . . of . . . peculiarly attractive . . . Porcelain utensils and ornaments' (105), 'smiling countenances' (106), and, of course, several pages devoted to women dressed 'according to the fashion of the country' (106–8). Anderson loses himself in the wonders of the capital until some sort of confusion causes 'the whole procession . . . to halt' (109), which provides him with the opportunity to ease his cramped limbs and meet some of the people in the crowd.

> Perceiving a number of women in the crowd that surrounded us, I ventured to approach them; and, addressing them with the Chinese word *Chou-au* (or beautiful) they appeared to be extremely diverted, and gathering around me, but with an air of great modesty and politeness, they examined the make and form of my clothes, as well as the texture of the materials of which they were composed. When the carts began to move off, I took leave of these obliging females by a gentle shake of the hand, which they tendered to me with the most graceful affability; nor did the men, who were present, appear to be at all dissatisfied with my conduct, but, on the contrary, expressed, as far as I could judge, very great satisfaction at this public attention I paid to their ladies. It appears, therefore, that in this city, the women are not divested of a reasonable portion of their liberty, and consequently, that the jealousy attributed so universally to the Chinese men, is not a predominant quality, as least, in the capital of the empire. (108–9)

Anderson has arrived at more than the capital. In this encounter with the people of Peking, differences are acknowledged and 'subsurface similarities between peoples' are realised.[8] Reciprocity is achieved in the form of mutually-satisfied curiosity. Counter-knowledge is produced regarding the isolation of Chinese women and the inherent jealousy of Chinese men. Gender, cultural, and official boundaries that separate the Chinese and the British are crossed, and Anderson becomes a thoughtful traveller, one whose 'tolerant [observation] of human life' reflects Enlightenment desire to be a citizen of the world (121–2).

Staunton's *Authentic Account* includes a similar episode of unrehearsed contact on the day before the embassy arrived in the capital. As described in other places, he notes that the embassy's arrival interrupted the 'occupations of the people' but only 'for a while' (92) — an observation that reinforces his pose of innocence. He continues:

> Other Europeans, mostly missionaries, had traveled thro' the city; but in order to escape notice, they were clad in the long dresses of the country, and had suffered their beards to grow, in imitation of the Chinese. The short coats and smooth faces of the present strangers, form, therefore a new spectacle. The greatest surprise, however, was occasioned by a black servant, who attended one of the gentlemen of the party. He had been brought from Batavia, to supply the place of an European who returned home. The jet hue of his complexion, his woolly head, and features, peculiar to the negroes, nothing like which had been remembered to have been seen before, in this inland part of China, led some of the spectators almost to doubt, whether he belonged to the human species; and the boys exclaimed that it must be a black demon, fan-quee; but a good-humoured countenance soon reconciled them to his appearance, and they continued to stare without apprehension or dislike. (92–3)

Unlike Anderson, who personalises the contact narrative, Staunton positions himself outside the scene as a detached observer, one who is not only able to contextualise the encounter historically but who is also capable of speaking symbolically for the participants involved.

'It is the lot of a few to go to Pekin'

If Anderson's arrival scene is inwardly focused and sentimentally inspired, Barrow's scene begins as a timeless royal arrival scene but dissolves into a mockery of goodwill and understanding. To be sure Barrow's is different from other embassy journals because the work, in effect, is in response to the already published accounts and a contribution to the on-going discussion of diplomatic failure that actually predates departure — thanks to James Gillray's satirical print, *The Reception of the Diplomatique and His Suite, at the Court of Pekin* (1792) and Peter Pindar's *Ode to Kien Long, the Present Emperor of China* (1792) — and which was kept alive in works such as Thomas James Mathias' *Imperial Epistle from Kien Long, Emperor of China to George the Third, King of Great Britain* (1794) and Pindar's *A Lyric Epistle to Lord Macartney, Ambassador to the Court of China* (1797). But the gap in time between the embassy and the publication of *Travels in China*, coupled with the gap between what the work is and what it claims to be, allow us to read Barrow's journal with a sense of ironic deciphering.

As the title page tells us, the work is both a travel account and an explicit attempt to 'appreciate the rank that this extraordinary empire may be considered to hold in the scale of civilized nations'. Readers are invited to view *Travels in China* as more than a travel journal, and Barrow in turn needs the flexibility of the genre to ensure that people will read what he has written. He is trying to situate the embassy historically, so his extended title justifies why the journal should be read so long after the conclusion of the events it claims to describe. So whereas Anderson authored the first word on the embassy, Barrow is trying to write the last, and given the rather large rhetorical space in which he is operating — he is not confined by many travel genre conventions (such as observations or comments recorded on-the-spot) and importantly he has the benefit of hindsight — he is able to employ an expository strategy that relies on a sense of playfulness in his reader.

Throughout *Travels in China*, Barrow inflates China with compliments and then punctures it with negative comments here and there, a technique that David Porter in *Ideographia* has labelled 'deflationary parody' (Porter 2001, 214). The strategy is similar to the so-called 'Orientalist clause', which dismisses, though not outright, 'the significance of any particular Eastern achievement' so as to return to and maintain a 'Eurocentric vision' (Hobson 2004, 22–3). The vision that Barrow hopes to maintain, and in part constitute, is one that shows China as having slipped down from its once lofty position on the scale of civilisations. It had already passed its zenith, and the Chinese government, which at one time was regarded by European intellectuals as a model of efficiency and preferable to a monarchy, was now seen, especially after the embassy, as hopelessly despotic and ineffectual.

The travel portion of Barrow's journal is found mostly at the beginning and end of the book, specifically Chapters 2 and 3 and then 9 and 10. Chapter 1 offers 'Preliminary Matter' (9), which is largely a defence of the embassy's conduct, before Chapter 2 picks up with 'Occurrences and Observations in the Navigation of the Yellow Sea, and the Passage up the Pei-Ho, or White

River' (17). Chapter 3 then details the 'Journey through the Capital to the Country Villa of the Emperor — Return to Pekin — The Imperial Palace and Gardens of Yuen-Min-Yuen, and The Parks of Gehol' (59), the latter half of the chapter being copied from Macartney's notes. The next five chapters cover pretty much all aspects of things Chinese, including the 'Manners, Customs, Sentiments, and Moral Character of the People' (Chapter 3), the 'Manners and Amusements of the Court' (Chapter 4), language, arts, science, and medicine (Chapter 5), government (Chapter 6) and religion (Chapter 7), before Barrow narrates the embassy's departure from China.

In his Peking arrival scene, elements from all of these aspects of Chinese culture are present, and yet his narrative technique is consistent. For example, at the beginning of the chapter that describes the embassy's arrival in China, Barrow observes that the Chinese people are extraordinarily cheerful, adding that 'one could scarcely expect to meet' such a condition 'in so despotic a government' (62). This is typical of the sort of rhetorical game that he plays with his audience. He begins by noting the proficiency with which all the baggage and the gifts were recorded and loaded onto carts early on the morning of departure. 'The Chinese porters', Barrow writes, 'shewed [*sic*] such expedition, strength, and activity, as could not, I believe, be paralleled or procured in so short a time, in any other country' (59). Such factually ambiguous statements, however, are qualified as he muses that 'every thing here, in fact, seems to be at the instant command of the state', including 'the most laborious tasks' (59). Is this because the people are so civilised or because they live in fear of reprimand? 'A crowd,' after all in China, 'is not so tumultuous and unruly as it generally is elsewhere' (61). Is this a mark of a civilised nation or of a despotic government?

Barrow situates his work historically by comparing it with other noted books, claiming that *Travels in China* covers 'unbeaten ground by Britons' in explicating the English 'sentiments' regarding the 'manners, customs, and character of the Chinese nation' (2). He also stresses that he was one of 'those few favoured persons, who had the good fortune to be admitted into the suite of the British' (18), an idea expressed on the title page as well. His time in the capital not only allowed him to witness 'the government of such an extraordinary nation' but he was also able to experience 'all that was virtuous, and powerful, and grand, and magnificent, concentrated in one point — in the city of Peking!' (18).

Barrow devotes only a few paragraphs to describing the capital itself, which is odd given the billing that it receives on the title page and in the first chapter. The first eleven paragraphs describe, often with scientific precision, the various sites and sights outside the city gates. In writing about the difficult trip to the capital, Barrow notes thankfully that the journey would have been 'almost insupportable, but from the novelty of the scene, the smiles, the grins, the gestures of the multitude, and, above all, the momentary expectation of entering the greatest city on the surface of the earth' (61). There is an undeniable motif of expectation here, which Barrow is easily able to manipulate: when Peking first appeared after the long journey, he laments that 'the first appearance of this celebrated capital is not much calculated to raise high expectations; nor does it in the least improve upon a more intimate acquaintance' (62). The final clause is all that differs thematically from Staunton's account.

Once through the gates, Peking exhibits itself. Barrow concedes that 'although the approach to Pekin [sic] afforded little that was interesting' (64), when the embassy had passed through the gates 'a very singular and novel appearance was exhibited' (64). The travellers saw before them 'a line of buildings on each side of a wide street, consisting entirely of shops and warehouses, the particular goods of which were brought out and displayed, in groupes [sic], in front of the houses' (64). Here is another example of deflationary parody. After an immediate impression, informing us that a 'singular and novel appearance was exhibited', we read a long sentence that never clearly identifies what was singular or novel in the appearance that was exhibited. Indeed, despite all of the build-up, from the title page to the admiring crowds of curious onlookers, it seems as though only an inanimate 'line of buildings' (64) has captured Barrow's notice. Many details follow as he describes 'large wooden pillars', 'eaves of houses', 'inscriptions in gilt characters', and 'coloured flags, streamers' and 'ribbons' (64), all of which confirm Staunton's observations. Yet nothing matches the description (in terms of detail) that Barrow devotes to the walls that surround the capital.

At the end of the initial arrival scene paragraph, we finally come to the object that 'made the greatest show . . . coffins for the dead' (64). Whereas Staunton and others make specific observations about the Chinese funeral procession that they encountered while in the capital, Barrow only concludes that Chinese coffins are more impressive than those of the English. As he goes on to observe, 'the most splendid of our coffin furniture would make but a poor figure, if placed beside that intended for a wealthy Chinese' (64). This is Barrow's first reference to coffins; by the end of the book these become something of a running joke. In another arrival scene, for example, Barrow was able to observe more of the city and he lists 'butchers, and bakers' shops, fishmongers, dealers in rice and other grain, ivory-cutters, dealers in lacquered ware, tea-houses, cooks' shops, and coffin-makers', adding that coffin-making 'is a trade of no small note in China' (*Travels in China*, 357–8).

Following a paragraph about triumphal arches, Barrow adds to Staunton's observation that Peking is 'airy, gay, and lightsome' (*An Authentic Account*, 117) by providing a profusion of details: 'tinkers and barbers', 'cobblers' and 'blacksmiths', 'officers and soldiers', 'corpses', 'brides', 'husbands', 'peddlers', 'jugglers', 'fortune-tellers', 'mountebanks and quack-doctors', 'comedians and musicians'. The scene described in this long paragraph is buzzing with 'confused noises', and Barrow abandons his usual narrative style in describing the 'squalling', 'buying', 'selling', 'bartering', 'bawling', 'crying', 'wrangling', 'twanging', and 'jarring', all of which is punctuated by 'the mirth and the laughter that prevailed in every' group. The entire scene, he concludes, 'could scarcely be exceeded by the brokers in the bank rotunda, or by the Jews and old women in Rosemary Lane'. 'All was in motion' in the capital, leaving 'no space unoccupied' (*Travels in China*, 65).

The third paragraph marks the end of Barrow's effort at on-the-spot description. While some of the embassy proceeded onwards to the audience with the emperor, Barrow and several others stayed behind to manage the handling of the presents. He was able to visit Peking several times, yet he does not add much to Staunton's account. In fact, he only offers his impression 'that, on every day, throughout the whole year, there was the same noise, bustle, and crowd in the capital of China' (66). Barrow then appears to respond to a brief paragraph in Staunton's work. Staunton had concluded, well after he narrated his arrival in Peking, that 'the crowds of people at [Peking] do not prevent it from being healthy' (*An Authentic Account*, 156). 'The Chinese live', according to Staunton, 'in the open air . . . [but] the atmosphere is dry, and does not engender putrid disorders; and excesses productive of them seldom are committed' (156).

Barrow, however, offers his own take on Peking: the 'streets [are] covered with sand and dust' and the 'dreadfully nauseous' water supply in the capital is 'particularly disgusting . . . when mixed with tea' (*Travels in China*, 66–7). He then moves to a sustained discussion of human waste, acknowledging that Peking:

> cannot boast, like ancient Rome, or modern London . . . the conveniences of common sewers, to carry off the dirt and dregs that must necessarily accumulate in large cities, yet it enjoys one important advantage, which is rarely found in capitals out of England: no kind of filth or nastiness, creating offensive smells, is thrown out into the streets; a piece of cleanliness, that, perhaps may be attributed rather to the scarcity and value of the manure than to the exertions of the police officers. (67)

'The First Appearance of This Celebrated Capital'   45

Porter argues convincingly that circulation, the exchange of goods or ideas, was the controlling metaphor on which Barrow based his judgements of China (214–6). The only thing that is actually 'circulating' in the city is human waste. He claims to have encountered 'hundreds' of excrement-carrying carts between Peking and the Summer Palace (*Travels in China*, 67). Only three paragraphs removed from his descriptive treatment of the chaos that was Peking, Barrow writes in detail about the very efficient system that the Chinese have developed for processing waste — nothing else in the city circulates with comparable efficiency. Contrary to Staunton's claims, Barrow concludes that 'a constant, disgusting odour remains in and about all the houses the whole day long, from the fermentation of the heterogeneous mixtures' (66) that are not carried off by drains. Then, in what might be *Travels in China*'s most perplexing paragraph, Barrow relates an anecdote about the 'medical gentlemen of China' who do not quite compare to the doctors of Madrid in the middle of the previous century. In other words, he leads us far away from anything related to his arrival in China.[9]

Conclusion: Only in China?

What claims can we make about the different versions of the embassy's arrival in Peking? Anderson removes the privileged status of the British but presents a vision of China that in many ways meets his own and his readers' expectations. Barrow recolours the image of China in the Western mind, one that was largely left untarnished in Staunton's account. Barrow and Staunton both establish and maintain a space between themselves and the things they are reporting. Whereas Anderson found the Chinese reaction to the British to be humiliating, Staunton and Barrow largely do not. In fact, Barrow does not even acknowledge the Chinese reaction to the embassy's arrival until well after it has passed through the city gates. The only things that are exchanged, symbolically or otherwise, in Barrow's arrival scene are the glances and gestures between the travellers and travellees. As such, things do not happen to Barrow, such as chance encounters, in the same way that they happen to Anderson.

If Anderson really does manage to see the China he had hoped to see, Barrow's gaze shows a manifest lack of interest in what is witnessed. The Chinese capital offered 'little to engage the attention' because 'a single walk through one of the broad streets [of Peking] is quite sufficient to give a stranger a competent idea of the whole city' (*Travels in China* 68). Staunton, for his part, occasionally sees possible opportunities to establish trade with China.

Hence we also have competing narratives of discovery and failure to discover. The entire Macartney embassy was thus marked by intriguing cultural and ideological confrontations, not rhetorically-constructed East/West oppositions, but inescapable differences: tribute versus trade, ceremony versus diplomacy, cultural complacency versus scientific innovation. Perhaps the most dynamic confrontation though was between the real and imagined China.

In reading travel journals, the rhetorical critic is faced with a challenge of interpretation: when is a self-critical comment an attempt to expose the destructive values of one's own culture and when is it, as it appears in this case, just the result of a traveller simply feeling de-centred in the Middle Kingdom? The journals of the Macartney embassy can serve to focus our discussions about what actually constitutes travel writing and whether there should be a separate category, with its own generic conventions, for diplomatic travel. How do we handle a text such as Staunton's? Regarded as the official account of the embassy's experience in China, the production of this text — not to mention the attention it received — makes it markedly different from the vast majority of other travel books. Or does it? The burden of interpretation always seems to fall precariously on the reader to determine writers' sense of disavowal, or their refusal to acknowledge what they already know.

3

A Reading of Readings: English Travel Books, Audiences, and Modern Chinese History, c. 1832 to the Present[1]

Ting Man Tsao

Before China was defeated by Britain in the First Opium War and forced to open five ports to British subjects for 'mercantile pursuits' in 1842, the Qing government strictly confined the activities of foreign traders within a small designated area called the Factories by the Canton River, forbidding any foreigner from setting foot on Chinese soil beyond it. However, the first British incursion occurred a decade before the conclusion to the war. In 1832, Charles Marjoribanks, president of the Canton factory of the British East India Company (hereafter EIC), sent Hugh Hamilton Lindsay, the EIC's supercargo and Charles Gutzlaff, a Prussian missionary, on a secret mission 'to ascertain how far the northern ports of the Chinese empire may be gradually opened to British commerce.'[2] The voyagers loaded a private ship, *Lord Amherst*, with British products, disguised themselves, landed in several forbidden ports, distributed Chinese tracts about 'the English character' and religion and collided with the Qing authorities trying to drive them away. Upon their return, Lindsay and Gutzlaff lost no time in publicising the success of the voyage in 'befriending' the 'hospitable' Chinese people and frustrating the local governments' attempts to block their entrance. They wrote of themselves as if they were piratical heroes, defiantly barging into the defenceless coast of China and audaciously exploring a potentially boundless emporium and missionary field into which few Europeans had ever ventured. Self-representations of this heroic expedition filled Lindsay's official report and Gutzlaff's shorter counterpart, published as a parliamentary paper titled *Ship Amherst* (1833) and commercially reprinted under the title, *Report of Proceedings on a Voyage to the Northern Ports of China in the Ship Lord Amherst* (1833).³ In addition, Gutzlaff's own extended account about this voyage and two other excursions was published under the title, *Journal of Three Voyages along the Coast of China* (1834).⁴

The travel books stirred up a China craze in England, where public sentiment for expanding free trade to the East reached a new height with parliamentary discussions on the abolition of the EIC's China-trade monopoly. Even the most vociferous defender of the EIC's charter, John Barrow — despite his harsh criticisms of their rashness in angering the Qing government — had to praise Lindsay's and Gutzlaff's travel reports for exhibiting:

> in a style beyond all our previous conceptions, the imbecility and utter helplessness of the [Chinese] authorities then existing on the coast; their timidity on the appearance of a mere handful of [European] strangers, in a small private vessel; their humiliating conduct to get rid of them; and the totally unprotected state of some of the largest towns, seaports, and navigable rivers of the Chinese.⁵

Other commentators were equally enthusiastic about the voyagers' accounts which reinforced a familiar Orientalist tradition in seafaring literature. But how did Chinese historians writing after the establishment of the People's Republic of China (PRC) in 1949 receive these apparently imperialistic narratives of the incursion? Were they more critical about the travel reports when they, guided by a sense of anti-Western patriotism, believed that British, American and other European invaders had distorted their 'crimes' in Qing China? In 1952 Nan Mu wrote a short historical account of the voyage based mainly on the travel narratives of Lindsay and Gutzlaff. Compare the Chinese historian's comment with Barrow's:

> [Lindsay's and Gutzlaff's planned reconnaissance] was completely, completely successful. On the seas and lands of China, [the voyagers] were unbridled, jostling and elbowing their way everywhere without receiving any of the punishments that they deserved. During the voyage, they not only finished surveying the waterways of Xiamen, Fouzhou, Ningbo and Shanghai but also gained a better understanding of the Qing's political corruption, the lax and backward state of armaments and the economic conditions of different places.⁶

Despite a gap of more than a century, despite the received wisdom of the China-West opposition and despite their different political agendas, Nan's and Barrow's narratives coincide, rather tellingly, in their uncritical embrace of the travellers' reports with the images of daring white men, a penetrable country and above all a monolithic point of view that narrates 'facts' from 'above' and puts the European colonisers at the centre of history writing. Times had changed, culture had changed and politics too had changed, but the Eurocentric perspective of the voyagers' travel books remained (and, as I will show, still remains) remarkably tenacious, shaping modern Chinese people's collective memories of the 1832 incursion.

My purpose here is to problematise the traditional use of Lindsay's and Gutzlaff's travel writings as 'primary sources' for historical reconstructions of the voyage. I want to intervene in the Eurocentric historiography of the *Ship Amherst* voyage by writing a 'new imperial history' that reflects a greater diversity of perspectives.[7] Unlike its predecessors, this new history concentrates not on the course of the voyage per se (what the travellers did and how the Qing officials and Chinese people reacted). Instead, I radically shift the historiographic focus to the very publications of Lindsay's and Gutzlaff's travel accounts as *printed books*, tracing and contextualising the uneven dispersions of these travelogues among hierarchically different readerships in Britain and China from the 1830s to the present. Instead of re-reading, once again, the canon of the voyagers' narratives, I offer a new approach to the multifarious readings of these printed books for a wide range of audiences in histories and across cultures, an approach that will render visible *differences* — social, gender, cultural and historical — in accessing and reading English-language travel books. As the following pages will show, this very act was and still is a *privilege* not universally shared by all historical and contemporary readerships. Regardless of their political, critical and disciplinary stances, historians and literary scholars should no longer take for granted their own privilege of being able to access these books as 'primary sources' for historical reconstructions or cultural texts for postcolonial critiques.[8] For this privilege, responsible at least partly for making the old historiography of the 1832 incursion, is a *historical* and *material* problem in and of itself that demands examination.

Publication of Lindsay's and Gutzlaff's Travel Books

Although the results of the mission were clearly of interest to the mercantile communities along the eastern trade routes dominated by the British Empire — such as Canton, Singapore, Malacca, Calcutta and Bombay — and although English presses had been established in some of these trade ports, Lindsay and Gutzlaff, like most British explorers of the time, sent their travel book manuscripts to London, the imperial hub, for publication, targeting metropolitan readers. Once published, these accounts, which became instant bestsellers and ran to several editions, stirred up a craze for 'opening' China both to British commerce and the Christian mission or, in Barrow's words, a *'free-trade mania'*.[9] 'The intense enthusiasm aroused in England and America among political, commercial and religious people, by the reports of Gutzlaff's three voyages can now hardly be appreciated', observed Marshall Broomhall.[10]

This China-trade craze should be understood in the context of the decline of the EIC's monopoly and the rise of laissez-faire as a school of thought. However, it still prompts the questions: To whom was this free-trade discourse addressed? How widely was it dispersed? Who most enjoyed the chance of accessing and debating Lindsay's and Gutzlaff's ground-breaking reports? Which groups were left out? These questions can perhaps be best addressed by mapping the main medium through which the 'free-trade mania' was disseminated to Britain and other colonial and trade ports, namely the culture of print.

In the nineteenth century, the spread of Lindsay's and Gutzlaff's travel books, like that of other printed volumes, was determined first and foremost by economics. The first editions of *Ship Amherst* and Gutzlaff's *Journal* were high-priced, costing eight and twelve shillings respectively.[11] That even the thinner, and therefore lower-priced, *Ship Amherst* was considered costly can be seen in a contemporary reviewer's remark: 'The Report of the Amherst's Voyage if printed by the dealers in *cheap* publications, would be almost as entertaining as *Robinson Crusoe*'.[12] Yet as Richard Altick argues, even 'cheap' books (usually priced at half the cost of *Ship Amherst*) were beyond the buying power of the vast majority of the growing literate middle- and working-class populations.[13] Therefore, *Ship Amherst* and Gutzlaff's *Journal*, well bound and forbiddingly expensive, obviously targeted the upper end of the ever-expanding market for print, made up of the aristocratic and the well-to-do middle-class readers in Britain as well as the wealthy mercantile communities in colonies and overseas trade ports.

The book was the original but *not* the sole medium through which Lindsay's and Gutzlaff's travel narratives were dispersed. Nor was it the most popular medium. As J. Don Vann and Rosemary T. Van Arsdel observe, nineteenth-century periodicals and newspapers, cheaply produced and widely and quickly marketed, 'served a more varied constituency in all walks of life' and were thus 'more influential . . . than printed books'.[14] In fact, the burgeoning periodical press disseminated Lindsay's and Gutzlaff's ground-breaking representations of China to a broader spectrum of readerships, reaching not only potential book buyers, namely the well-off middle class, but also the middling and working classes and women. However, this wider dispersion of the China craze sparked by the voyagers' tales was not a unified movement, but was rendered uneven through different types of periodicals targeting different readerships. A comparative reading of how three types of periodicals — middle-class, female, and working-class — 'read' differently Lindsay's and Gutzlaff's new conceptions of China can uncover from this unevenness discernible patterns of mediation based on their projected readerships' class and gender.

Readings of the *Ship Amherst* Narratives in Middle-Class Periodicals

To categorise certain periodicals that reviewed Lindsay's and Gutzlaff's works as 'middle-class' can be misleading, because they represented a wide range of print enterprises. These periodicals include critical quarterlies and general magazines, representing different and sometimes opposite political stands, from the Tory *Quarterly Review* to the Benthamite radical *Westminster Review*. They may also include religious periodicals that were organs of different denominations and missionary societies such as the *Evangelical Magazine* of the London Missionary Society and the *Missionary Register* of the Church Missionary Society. The list of 'middle-class periodicals' is incomplete without including newspapers and magazines published in Canton, such as the *Chinese Repository*, a Sinological-cum-missionary monthly, and the *Canton Register*, a mercantile biweekly.

Despite differences in their editorial policies and audiences, these middle-class periodicals nevertheless shared some features that distinguished them from their working-class and women's counterparts in reviewing or responding to Lindsay's and Gutzlaff's printed works. First, they tended to provide fuller summaries of the voyagers' reports, give snapshots of their various encounters with the Chinese people and Qing officials, and quote long but interesting excerpts from the books. Some periodicals such as the *Quarterly Review* even put this mission in the historical perspective of Britain's two previous embassies to Beijing.[15] Of the three types of periodicals which reviewed or responded to the travellers' accounts, these middle-class periodicals offered readers the most comprehensive coverage of the voyagers' experiences and observations that were closest to a direct reading of the original books.

However, if economics helped determine the class of potential buyers of Lindsay's and Gutzlaff's books, it also played a role in restricting the spread of contexts in which they might be fully reviewed, for the middle-class periodicals, like the travellers' reports, were expensive and became more so in the 1830s, costing between two shillings and six shillings. These costs, as Altick succinctly observes, 'placed them out of the reach of most buyers; they were publications distinctly . . . intended for the subscription reading-rooms whose very existence was evidence that many readers on the cultural level to which these periodicals appealed could not afford to buy them outright'.[16] In this sense, these periodicals were economically 'middle-class' by confining the knowledge, albeit abbreviated and second-hand, of the *Ship Amherst* reports to a readership who could afford high-priced printed matter, by not helping filter down this second-hand knowledge to the poorer audiences.

If there is any truth in the motto 'Knowledge is Power', popularised by the defiantly unstamped weekly, *Poor Man's Guardian*, in the 1830s, then one may very well ask this question: For periodical readers who could somehow afford that second-hand 'knowledge' of the *Ship Amherst* narratives, what kind of 'power' came with it? This brings us to the second feature of the middle-class periodicals that reviewed the voyagers' books, namely the 'power' of accessing nation-wide debates about the mission. Representing different standpoints, these periodicals debated the insights gained from the voyage as a national issue that was of interest to the British public. For instance, in his review of *Ship Amherst* and four other pamphlets about the changing roles of the EIC in China and the free-trade question, Barrow 'distinctly . . . disclaim[ed] all party-feeling in any strictures we may be compelled to make'.[17] Yet, at a time when the fate of the EIC's China-trade monopoly was hotly debated, it did not take a politically astute reader to sense his pro-EIC 'party-feeling' when the conservative reviewer — despite his previously quoted praise of the *Ship Amherst*'s ground-breaking 'style' — criticised Lindsay for calculatedly encouraging attempts to force free trade on the China coast, for 'holding out examples of successful resistance to lawful authority' and, above all, for 'inculcating the doctrine of stirring up the *people* against their rulers'.[18]

While Barrow's anti-free-trade sentiment was echoed by other conservative periodicals such as the *Gentleman's Magazine*, liberal readers would not be disappointed with the free-trade interests' performance in the nation-wide debate. In the *Westminster Review*, John Crawfurd, employed by the Calcutta merchants to publicise the cause of laissez-faire, answered Barrow's criticism of Lindsay's dangerous rashness point by point by highlighting three positive results of the mission: 'the acquisition of useful information, the ascertaining that the natives of China were desirous of an extended intercourse with foreigners, and that such intercourse might be carried on in defiance of the local administrations who have not the power to prevent it'.[19] Although Crawfurd agreed with Lindsay's critics that the voyage was a commercial failure, he attributed this failure not to Lindsay's excessive independence but, albeit not totally convincingly, to his very connection with the EIC. 'Mr. Lindsay and his companions', the free-trade lobbyist explained, 'were in a false position; they dared not assume so unpopular a name among the Chinese, as that of the East India Company, and were obliged to feign themselves to be private traders'.[20] This anti-EIC sentiment, with its optimism about the prospect of 'opening' China to free trade, reverberated through many other London-based general magazines such as the *Eclectic Review* and the immensely popular *Monthly Review* as well as trade-port papers such as the *Canton Register*.

The privilege of accessing the heated debate about the 'Free Trade to China' question was not confined to wealthy readers of middle-class general periodicals and mercantile papers. It was shared, albeit differently, by readers of religious or theological periodicals that were relatively lower-priced (one to three shillings) but were still unaffordable to most middle- and working-class literate people. The majority of religious reviewers joined their colleagues of Whig and liberal general periodicals in celebrating the observations of the *Ship Amherst* narratives about the immense possibilities in the 'opening' of China not only to commerce but also to the propagation of God's words. This combination of commercial and missionary discourse may have appeared controversial for politically-informed Christian readers who had probably read about the illicit opium trade to China in published parliamentary debates and in the London and trade-port press. In fact, Barrow commented that Gutzlaff 'appears to have been less scrupulous than some of his religious brethren in the means he employed to accomplish his ends', alluding to his controversial use of an opium clipper on a mission following the *Ship Amherst* voyage.[21]

However, compared with Barrow, religious reviewers were conspicuously quiet about Gutzlaff's close ties with the EIC (the key player in the production of opium in India and the export of the drug) and private opium traders. Instead, these Christian writers subtly steered their pious readers toward supporting a Christianised version of the 'free-trade mania', a mild anti-monopoly (if not anti-EIC) cause. The *Evangelical Magazine*, the *Missionary Register*, the *Chinese Repository*, the *New York Observer*, the *Missionary Herald* and other Christian periodicals were replete with the two new insights concluded from Gutzlaff's published narratives: the Chinese people, in defiance of the Qing government's prohibitions, were not only 'friendly' to Europeans but also receptive of the religious and moralistic tracts written in Chinese. Based on these observations, the majority of religious periodicals reversed the pessimistic view of China as a prohibitive missionary field and began to circulate the ideas that 'NO COUNTRY IN ASIA, ruled by Native Princes, is SO EASY OF ACCESS', and that '*China* [is] *rapidly opening for the Propagation of the Gospel*'.[22]

Embracing Gutzlaff's vision of combining missionary work with commerce to 'open' China, the *Quarterly Christian Spectator* urged its audience to become more than bystanders in the China question debate. The periodical asked merchants to load their ships with Bibles and help in their distribution. Encouraged by Gutzlaff's success as a 'free' missionary, it also asked parents to have their sons 'properly educated' and send them on the mission of evangelising the world. After all, the *Spectator* believed that there had never been a more opportune time to carry out all the philanthropic missions than the 1830s: '[W]hen did ever an object stand before the Christian public more calculated to urge to such a state of [benevolent] feeling, than is now presented by the vast empire of China?'[23] Although the impact of this kind of appeal on the general public is now hard to gauge, it may nonetheless be interesting to note that Baron Schilling, an enthusiastic collector of Chinese works, once told his friends that he 'wishes likewise to have Gutzlaff and Lindsay's *Voyages*'.[24]

Not only did the well-off readerships of middle-class periodicals enjoy a more comprehensive coverage of Lindsay's and Gutzlaff's travel narratives and the privilege of following the 'Free Trade to China' debate, they also had a better chance of appreciating the new heroism embodied by the adventurers. This is the third feature that middle-class periodicals reviewing the *Ship Amherst* reports shared. Although, as just discussed, conservative and liberal general periodicals and religious magazines drew different, sometimes opposite, political inferences from the *Ship Amherst* reports, they all agreed that Lindsay and Gutzlaff were brave and heroic. They also found that the Qing officials, by contrast, were both impotent and inconsistent. The fearless image of European men penetrating the forbidden China coast, which the local governments were too weak to protect, was presented not only in Barrow's previously quoted excerpt but also in many other reviews in general and religious periodicals. For example, the pro-EIC *Gentleman's Magazine* condemned what Lindsay did in the voyage as 'a buccaneering or piratical enterprise'.[25] However, this criticism only served to liken the supercargo to the unconventional but admirable adventurers in popular seafaring novels of the time such as those by Captain Marryat.[26] Though with some reservations about his 'European prejudices' and 'deficiency in the political economy', the *Westminster Review* described Gutzlaff as an 'active, enterprising, and intelligent adventurer', who was 'inspired with a laudable desire of converting the heathens of Asia'.[27] According to the *Scottish Pilot*, 'Mr. Gutzlaff's voyages are replete with surpassing interest. He is a wonderful man, a heroic Christian, and a zealous philanthropist'.[28] Belonging to different political backgrounds, reviewers nonetheless repeated in chorus 'adventurer', 'enterprising', 'piratical', 'heroic' and above all 'man'.[29]

But why did periodical reviewers repeatedly single out Lindsay and Gutzlaff as the main heroes of this 'honourable' mission when it was widely known that the voyage was sponsored by the EIC and involved a large crew of seventy? This was perhaps due to the shifting political and cultural climates of the post-Reform Bill era, when, as one historian observes, '[m]onopoly in politics, in religion, in almost everything, was the object of widespread public suspicion'.[30] Time had indeed come for the white man, the individual hero, the free trader or the independent missionary to emerge as the new icon and replace, once and for all, the increasingly anachronistic mercantile monopoly in the rising empire of free trade. The reverberation of such terms as 'adventurer', 'hero', 'pirate' and so on through a wide array of middle-class periodicals that both praised and criticised the *Ship Amherst* voyage showed that masculinity was being massively redefined in terms of independent enterprise even when deemed 'rash', 'dangerous' and outright 'illegal'.

The gender and class biases of the middle-class general and religious periodicals' reviews of Lindsay's and Gutzlaff's travel reports become all the more apparent when compared with their women's and working-class counterparts. The latter adjusted and (at times) limited their coverage of or response to the books, providing scant detail about the voyagers' heroism or the China trade politics. This meant that in the increasingly specialised periodical industry of the 1830s, these kinds of content, albeit suitable for the general middle-class reading public, were deemed out of bounds for more narrowly defined audiences based on conventional, but not uncontested, conceptions of gender and class. If there was a 'British public' in the expanding empire of free trade in the early nineteenth century, the diversified periodical enterprises served to stratify this 'people', creating different readership identities within the larger imperial fabric through editorial adjustments and mediations.

The Responses of Women's Periodicals

What proper roles could middle-class women take when their nation was expanding to the East, to the potentially largest emporium and Christian field on earth? What should they do when their 'wonderful' and 'heroic' men such as Lindsay and Gutzlaff were pioneering commercial and missionary work 'out there'? Charlotte Elizabeth's *Christian Lady's Magazine* — established in 1834 for the dual purpose of providing middle-class Christian females with amusement and 'useful reference on topics of permanent importance'[31] — provided specific answers. The periodical was conspicuously quiet on the empire-wide 'Free Trade to China' debate, to which many middle-class general and religious periodicals contributed. However, this did not mean that Christian ladies had no business in the politics of the China question. To be sure, although admittedly 'it is the fashion of the age for women to leave their assigned sphere, setting themselves up for political agitators, political economists, and what not', Elizabeth, as editor of the religious women's periodical, had a 'far different' object.[32] She did not want to limit herself to 'the affairs of the senate-house', but would instead 'take a bird's-eye view of the world' in order to write about important political issues 'for the consideration of her own sex'.[33] This 'bird's-eye view' appeared to help the inexperienced editor identify from the highly politicised China-trade question a distinct problem for her readership's information, namely 'the unspeakably wretched condition of our own sex',[34] in 'China, India, and the East', which was used to title three consecutive short articles published in the *Christian Lady's Magazine* from 1835 to 1837.

Elizabeth began the first article by echoing the image of China, India, and the East as 'a field so immense',[35] an image already popularised by other middle-class general and religious periodicals. Yet she did not cite Lindsay's and Gutzlaff's reports about their pioneering work in China; nor did she refer to other male explorers' or missionaries' adventurous stories in other parts of that 'vast territory'. Instead, she confined the scope of the article to the Englishwoman's specific concerns in the field, namely 'the deeply affecting state of our poor eastern sisters'.[36] Elizabeth argued that the state in which Eastern women found themselves was 'so dreadful, that the practice of female infanticide becomes meritorious even in the mother's eye, who would far rather behold her offspring writhing in the agonies of a violent death, than bring her up to inherit the same bitter portion of oppressive cruelty, insult, and wrong'.[37] To speak patronisingly about the oppressed Chinese or Indian people was certainly not novel in English rhetoric of Elizabeth's times; similar descriptions about the Qing government oppressing its masses of people abounded in Lindsay's, Gutzlaff's and many other travellers' books. However, the identification of Eastern oppressed women as 'poor sisters' was a uniquely female rhetoric, for the most intimate descriptions that Lindsay and Gutzlaff gave to individual Chinese they had met were 'friendly' and 'hospitable' people, not 'brethren'. To extend a universal 'sisterhood' to the East was, therefore, to acknowledge, albeit implicitly, that English women and their 'Eastern sisters' shared a certain level of common fate as the 'oppressed' sex, which was non-existent between Gutzlaff and the Chinese 'friends' he had encountered. However, Englishwomen, with their English sense of superiority, could not be wholly equated with their 'Eastern sisters'. For the writer, what had set women in England apart from those in the East was religion: 'wherever christianity prevails, there is no longer male and female, according to the wide and degrading distinctions of privilege that had prevailed between them'.[38] With the blessings of God, Elizabeth believed, 'woman becomes again that for which she was originally designed, the companion and fellow-helper of man'.[39]

In what capacities could English women help their male counterparts in the East? For Elizabeth, the Ladies' Society for the Promotion of Female Education in China, India, and the East, newly established by the Duchess of Beaufort and other women dignitaries,[40] offered 'our christian ladies' opportunities for being instructresses in that 'vast territory'. She highly recommended this work to her readers because it was a 'truly christian, truly feminine undertaking'.[41]

If a Christian lady could be an instructress in the East, could she then undertake evangelical work as 'the companion and fellow-helper of man' there? Could she, for example, accompany 'heroic' missionaries such as Gutzlaff on voyages like the *Ship Amherst* mission and assist in the propagation of the Gospel? This kind of question sparked off a controversy since differentiating between 'female' and 'male' careers in the East could be problematic. In the second article, a correspondent for the *Christian Lady's Magazine* explicitly asks Christian ladies to answer 'the present importunate cry from the shores of India and of China' as well as to 'embark yourselves in this good cause, and spend your bodily and mental energies in the great work of evangelising the heathen.'[42] Such work was, however, deemed by another correspondent, called 'G. H. G.,' as 'unfeminine' because travelling from place to place to spread biblical tidings was considered the exclusive job of 'the Christian Missionary'[43] (i.e. the male missionary, such as Gutzlaff).

There was great difficulty in distinguishing between male and female missionary work in the East according to the British conception of separate men's and women's spheres because the extension of the Christian mission 'out there' necessarily involved 'manly' activities that Gutzlaff's *Journal* and other contemporary missionary writings had shown, such as extensive travel, encountering strangers of both sexes, and fighting local authorities. However, it was not impossible to make a very fine distinction between the two. As a response to the criticism of asking Christian ladies to carry out male missionaries' duties, a correspondent named J. S. redefined 'the work of an evangelist' in the third article in the *Christian Lady's Magazine* by constructing a colonial version of the separate male and female spheres. The writer argued that doing evangelical work involved 'nothing unfeminine' as Christian women engaged by the said Society would only devote themselves to 'promoting female education' in schools or orphanages. They would, in other words, 'remain stationary in one spot' and would not travel from place to place and be engaged in their male colleagues' activities.⁴⁴ By remaining 'stationary', female evangelists were able to preserve their 'domestic' femininity like the idealised lady in England, while actually working 'out there' in an inhospitable land. Since the work of educating female 'heathens', as J. S. contended, could only be performed by 'female agency',⁴⁵ women instructresses played their different yet indispensable part in the civilising mission. It was thus through the construction of a separate but necessary sphere in the missionary field that Christian ladies could join the master narrative of 'opening' China, India and the East.

Working-Class Periodicals' Responses

Like its middle-class women's counterpart, the working-class periodical press also adjusted its coverage of or response to the 'Free Trade to China' craze sparked off by Lindsay's and Gutzlaff's reports based on its projected audience's role in society. The term 'working-class periodical press', however, needs some qualification. Although there were numerous working-class periodicals in circulation in the 1830s, the ones that responded, either directly or indirectly, to China were mainly the products of another craze of the time — for cheap but 'respectable' literature. The most popular publications of the movement included the *Penny Magazine*, the *Chambers' Edinburgh Journal* and the *Mirror of Literature, Amusement, and Instruction*. Although intentionally published 'in form so cheap as to be accessible to the lowest class of readers',⁴⁶ this 'respectable', cheap press failed to filter down to the masses of literate labouring people at the bottom of the socio-economic ladder, specifically workers 'earning less than 16s. a week'.⁴⁷ Instead, it was mainly consumed by shopkeepers and skilled artisans who made up, in the words of the *Chambers' Journal*, 'the *élite* of the labouring community; those who think, conduct themselves respectably, and are anxious to improve their circumstances by judicious means'.⁴⁸ Mass-produced in an era of widespread agitation for political and economic reforms among the working and middling classes, the 'respectable' penny press could be seen as a conservative voice countering the radicalism propagated by the working-class, defiantly unstamped papers such as the menacingly popular *Poor Man's Guardian*.

In what ways, then, did the notions of working-class 'respectability' — 'respectable' thinking and behaviour, and 'judicious means' of self-improvement — shape the conservative penny periodical press's response to the China craze sparked off by Lindsay's and Gutzlaff's travel accounts? An exemplary response can be found in the *Penny Magazine*, established by the Society of the Diffusion of Useful Knowledge, an empire-wide organisation whose local committee in Canton boasted Gutzlaff as secretary and a leading British trader as chair.[49] For this magazine, as for other 'respectable' penny periodicals, the working-class readership won their respectability by understanding and respecting the world as it was, not by challenging or changing it as the radicals were championing, nor by debating it as middle-class intellectuals were doing.

To make its conservative appeal, the *Penny Magazine* both depoliticised the controversial 'Free Trade to China' subject matter by rewriting it into 'useful' but apolitical 'knowledge' and articulated the glorious history of the EIC. To counter the 'free-trade mania' of the time, the magazine issued a, by then, ultra-reactionary article that praised the EIC for its commercial achievements and its magnificent building at Leadenhall in London.[50] Yet, unlike the conservative middle-class general periodicals, it carefully avoided causing any controversy by refraining from defending the EIC's monopoly or attacking the 'piratical and buccaneering' rashness of the free trade interests. This editorial policy made the magazine conservative but *not controversially* conservative. To further acquaint the reader with 'useful knowledge' about China, the magazine published articles on uncontroversial topics ranging from the Chinese junk to Chinese poetry. There were, however, two episodic articles on the abject conditions of the Chinese people and one on the 'facts' of opium (without mentioning the EIC's notorious involvement in the opium trade to China).[51] Yet, amidst the middle-class waves of 'opening' China to commerce and religion, these articles did not cause any controversy for there was no question about the poor conditions to which the Chinese were subject or about opiate use in the East.

The even cheaper two-penny *Mirror* took a different approach to the China question based on its usual editorial practice of excerpting from books and other periodicals. However, like its competitor the *Penny Magazine*, the *Mirror* attempted to depoliticise the subject matter as much as possible by turning it into uncontroversial 'useful knowledge'. For instance, in extracting from a pamphlet on Britain-China relations, the *Mirror* apologetically explained that the work might seem irrelevant because of its 'political purpose', which was like 'chaff' to the reader. Yet, the editor explained that the pamphlet was nonetheless appropriate for the magazine because it did consist of certain 'facts' about the tea trade, which were as 'useful' as 'grains of wheat' to the audience. For this reason, the editor said he had to depoliticise such 'facts' and make them 'stand alone,' without weaving them into any political argument.[52] In stark contrast to most middle-class periodical reviews, which, guided by their overt political agendas were either supportive or critical of the China policy advocated by the books and pamphlets under consideration, the *Mirror* was openly apolitical and refrained from even mentioning, let alone debating, any of the pamphlet's statements about Britain's commercial relations with China. It confined its review to excerpting 'interesting' facts out of any trace of controversial context such as China's policy of seclusion and the 'origin of the tea trade of the East India Company'.

In the middle of the China craze, besides 'useful knowledge' articles similar to the *Penny Magazine*'s, the *Mirror* did issue two short extracts from Gutzlaff's *Journal*. However, these extracts were not drawn from Gutzlaff's account of his adventurous voyages but from its introductory essay written by Reverend W. Ellis on the history of the Protestant mission in the East. The first extract includes the descriptions by Mrs. Gutzlaff and Mr. Tomlin (Gutzlaff's fellow-missionary in Bangkok) on the 'barbarities' of the Siamese;[53] and the second is Mrs. Gutzlaff's 'graphic' description of a big fire in Bangkok.[54] None of these extracts contained any descriptions of Gutzlaff's unscrupulous missions to China, which nonetheless filled the pages of middle-class general and religious periodicals. The notable absence of Gutzlaff's accounts of his brave missions along the China coast in the 'respectable' penny press and the Christian lady's magazines indicated that colonial and imperial masculinity and heroism fell into the middle-class man's sphere and was deemed out of bounds for other groups.

Both the *Penny Magazine* and the *Mirror* won approbation from the upper and middle classes. Their (a)politically tactful coverage of the 'Free Trade to China' controversy may very well explain how the two-penny magazines earned respect 'from above'. By turning the controversial topic into 'useful knowledge' or apolitical 'facts', the magazines satisfied their readerships' thirst for a better understanding of the exotic world to which the British Empire was expanding, without alienating any major interests — the pro-monopoly, the Church, and even the pro-free trade. Like their 'respectable' working-class readers, and unlike the radicals, the magazines climbed the social ladder of 'respectability' by demonstrating to the upper classes that they knew their 'place' in the nation and empire, that they showed an eager desire for self-improvement by learning from the middle-class book and periodical, and that, most importantly, they, unlike the *Poor Man's Guardian*, also knew the 'proper' boundaries of their quest for 'knowledge'.

Readings in Chinese Historiography

How, then, did Lindsay's and Gutzlaff's travel narratives, dispersed widely albeit unevenly to large nineteenth-century English readerships, come to influence modern Chinese historiography as seen in Nan Mu's excerpt in the introduction? How were their narratives disseminated to and read by descendants of the very people whom the European voyages had explored and (mis)represented?

To address these questions, some background to nineteenth-century Qing reception of the English book is necessary. It is worth noting at the outset that the ambivalence and cross-cultural dynamics associated with the English book as a colonial tool of governance in British India, discussed by Homi Bhabha and Gauri Viswanathan,[55] have little if any relevance to the Qing Empire, which suffered from forms of imperial oppression other than complete colonisation. In a penetrable but uncolonised China, missionaries had to translate European secular and biblical learning into classical Chinese, drastically adapting it to fit the country's cultural, rhetorical, and typographic tradition in order to appeal to the masses of readers there.[56] However, the Chinese intellectual tradition was not uninfluenced by English books, periodicals and newspapers, which were circulating commercially in the foreign communities of Macao, Canton, and, after the Opium War, other treaty ports along the coast.[57] In the face of mounting menace from Western powers, Chinese official-literati, notably Lin Zexu and Wei Yuan, began to collect 'barbarian intelligence' through translation of English publications and incorporate Western knowledge into their geographical works.[58] However, these writings continued to cling to the old tradition by 'Sinicising' Western knowledge culled from English publications.[59]

It is in the light of this linguistic and cultural insulation that one can appreciate why Lindsay's and Gutzlaff's travel books and the English periodicals that reviewed them, despite their availability along the China coast, made little impact on the Qing historiography of the *Ship Amherst* voyage. The main historical records about the incursion were the local gazetteers of some of the town and counties that *Ship Amherst* touched, published mainly in the second half of the nineteenth century through to the fall of the Qing Dynasty in 1911.[60] In documenting the incident, the writers of these gazetteers — who relied on local recollections, uninfluenced by the English book or press — kept their narrative short, stating in a few sentences that a barbarian ship had illegally sailed into the port in order to trade in the twelfth year of Daogong [emperor] (1832). This event was usually noted right before or after the usually longer record of the 'English barbarian invasion' (namely the Opium

War) that described the bombings and killings. Significantly, Qing local historians, unlike their modern successors, made no effort to interpret the voyage teleologically by establishing a causal relationship with the 'English barbarian invasion'. They did not attach to the incursion any historical significance other than the literal: a barbarian ship appeared in an attempt to trade and later left without success. In fact, Qing local gazetteers, unlike modern Chinese histories, did not pay extra attention even to the 'English barbarian invasion', chronicling it as one of the countless events in the long local history since the Yuan Dynasty (1227) or earlier. There was a marked contrast between the terseness of these published Qing readings of the incursion and the enthusiastic though varied responses to the travellers' publications in the English-language periodical and newspaper press of the early nineteenth century.

Tellingly, however, as Lindsay's and Gutzlaff's travel books, together with numerous English historical sources, became comprehensible to an increasing number of bilingual intellectuals who had either studied in England and the United States or been educated in Western-style institutions of education in the new China since 1911, Chinese readings of the voyage forsook the Qing tradition and took on certain features of the English middle-class general and religious periodical press's readings. These readings have, in turn, formed a nationalist orthodoxy of comprehending the incursion as an event in the country's 'imperial past', an orthodoxy that remains strong and unchallenged even in today's China.

The first re-reading of the *Ship Amherst* voyage happened two decades before the publication of Nan Mu's article. In the Republican China of 1932, Zhang Dechang published a ground-breaking interpretation of the significance of the voyage *in Modern Economic History of China*,[61] a Chinese academic journal published by the prestigious Institute of Social Research based in Beijing. Modelled on European scholarly journals, distributed mainly in large cities such as Beijing and Shanghai, and forbiddingly priced at one yuan, the journal targeted an urban national elite who had received an exclusive Western or modern education.[62] For the masses of literate or semi-literate readers, particularly those in the rural areas, who had received limited but cheaper Confucian education, this periodical, like other urban modern newspapers, was both incomprehensible and out of reach.[63] Although social, cultural and political contexts had changed from Victorian England to Republican China, economics continued to be a factor in affecting the dispersion of Lindsay's and Gutzlaff's travel narratives.

Zhang's article was born out of a movement among the intellectual elite to sever the nation from its 'imperial past', to construct a 'correct' national memory for a newly established modern China.⁶⁴ To achieve these goals, historians systematically collected new primary sources including Qing government archives and Western-language sources and applied the methodology of Western social sciences to writing a new modern Chinese history.⁶⁵ Zhang, for one, used two sources, previously untapped by Chinese scholars, to study anew the *Ship Amherst* voyage. The first source was English publications, including the review of Lindsay's and Gutzlaff's travel books in the Canton-based *Chinese Repository*,⁶⁶ as well as Gutzlaff's *A Sketch of Chinese History*, which briefly discussed the voyage.⁶⁷ The second source tapped by Zhang was the recently available Chinese archival documents related to the *Ship Amherst* voyage, including Qing memorials and edicts as well as the correspondence between the voyagers on the one hand and the Qing authorities and the locals on the other.⁶⁸ Although this second source contained rich details about the Qing government's response to foreigners and the interactions between the European strangers and different segments of Chinese society, it was, not insignificantly, the first that played a leading role in shaping Zhang's nationalist narrative.

How did nineteenth-century English books and periodicals inform Zhang's chapter on modern Chinese history? Through references to the *Chinese Repository* and Gutzlaff's book, Zhang willy-nilly adopted the master narrative of 'opening' China to British free trade that these early-nineteenth century publications had chanted feverishly. With the benefit of hindsight, however, the historian expanded this narrative teleologically by establishing a causal relationship between the incursion on the one hand and Britain's post-Opium War demands on the other. Echoing Lindsay and Gutzlaff, the Chinese historian stated that their voyage 'enabled the English authorities to reach a correct understanding of China's long-standing weakness. It was, at the same time, a thorough reconnaissance of the ports along the coast of China'. Albeit without further evidence, Zhang jumped to the conclusion that this increased knowledge of China on the part of the British informed both their decision to go to war and their subsequent treaty negotiations: 'Therefore, when Lin Zexu strictly imposed a ban on opium, it gave [the British] an excuse to invade, quickly resorting to arms. Immediately upon defeating China, they pressed the demand to open five ports for mercantile pursuits'. Overlooking the uneven sharing and the multifarious readings of Lindsay's and Gutzlaff's China 'intelligence' among different Victorian interests, Zhang read an overarching mastermind into Britain's various imperialist activities in Qing China: 'It has now dawned on me that the Sino-British conflicts and the post-war demands in that era were acts of calculation on the part of the British, events that were eventually unavoidable'.⁶⁹ Considering the brief chronicle of the voyage by Qing local gazetteers, Zhang's linking of this event and the Opium War marked the birth of a teleological 'modern Chinese history' that sees the war as the landmark, endowing it with a lot of explanatory power.

Tellingly, Zhang's deterministic narrative that Britain's 'opening' of China was 'eventually unavoidable' coincided with the *Chinese Repository* and Gutzlaff's books in two images — an ever-victorious European aggressor and a weak, defenceless China. However, the Chinese historian went beyond these one-sided English publications to include Qing sources, thus resulting in what seemed like a more convincing historical narrative grounded in two national archives.

The historian's incorporation of Chinese and English sources was not, however, as bicultural as it appeared. Although his reading of Qing archival sources was quite incisive, he lost his critical acumen when approaching Lindsay's and Gutzlaff's narrative. Zhang's summary of Lindsay's feelings about Fujian, based on the *Chinese Repository*, was a case in point:

> In Fujian Lindsay and others got the impression that the Chinese people were exceptionally nice, desirous of trading with foreigners, but they were afraid of the officials' oppression. In the meantime the threats of the Chinese officials were completely feigned, lacking in any strength. Therefore they decided to cultivate the goodwill between the two peoples. As for the Chinese officials, they pressed for nothing less than equal, polite treatment.[70]

Identifying with the European explorer's point of view, Zhang was content to retell, almost word for word, the same laissez-faire narrative born out of the Victorian empire of free trade, the same rhetoric that the voyagers told their middle-class English audiences either directly or through the periodical press. Albeit writing for an economic history journal targeting a national elite, Zhang was so satisfied with what the transient explorers had seen, heard and thought that he did not need to further examine why 'the Chinese people were exceptionally nice, desirous of trading with foreigners' in the contexts of the coastal culture and economy.

Adopting the European point of view, how then did Zhang evaluate the Qing officials? For the Chinese historian, the latter had to be measured up to Lindsay and Gutzlaff as narrators of historical 'facts'. By paraphrasing the *Chinese Repository*, Zhang, for instance, adopted unquestioningly Lindsay's and Gutzlaff's delineation of events related to the *Ship Amherst*'s incursion into Shanghai:

> The English ship stayed in Shanghai for eighteen days ... Besides negotiating with the authorities, [the voyagers] also made a reconnaissance inside and

years, it has outlasted the latter and made a much greater impact on China's collective memories of the incursion. In 1958, communist historians reprinted Nan's essay in a major collection of articles on the Opium War published after the establishment of the PRC,[82] making no reference to Zhang's article and, for that matter, Republican China's historiography on the subject.[83] Not surprisingly, Nan's article, for all its colonialist narrative framework, has since then become the standard national narrative of the *Ship Amherst* voyage. Recent history books on the Western missionary enterprises reproduce the same kind of narrative as Nan's by uncritically excerpting or paraphrasing Gutzlaff's narratives.[84] Collections of historical sources on the Opium War include translations of the voyagers' books, thus enabling more readers to access these otherwise unavailable English documents.[85] The proliferation of the Internet in an increasingly globalised China since its participation in the World Trade Organisation has not led to new interpretations of the *Ship Amherst* voyage, but to a wider dissemination of Nan's decades-old narrative through the CCP's official websites.[86]

Conclusions and Interventions

What does one learn by reading the multifarious readings of Lindsay's and Gutzlaff's books about the *Ship Amherst* voyage for different audiences in histories and across cultures? From readings for the (implicitly male) middle class, the middle-class woman, and the working class in early nineteenth-century Britain to readings for Chinese audiences between the Republican era and today's PRC, one finds that, contrary to what many postcolonial scholars may have led their readers to believe, the imperial travel book cannot simply be seen as a text, a text in pristine form, and the impact of the English book cannot be solely gauged by its textuality. The text — either in the original book form or in mediated, excerpted forms such as reviews and articles in newspapers, periodicals and collective works — was and is *unevenly* dispersed among hierarchically and historically different readerships. This uneven dispersion of the imperial text is due not only to the political and cultural agendas behind each form of publication but also to its projected readership's identity informed by class, gender, nationality, education and other historical factors such as economics.

This observation has profound implications for historians and literary critics reading, tapping, and interpreting the colonial book. As I have shown, the very act of reading is a historical problem in and of itself that needs historicisation, and the relationship between the imperial text and the reader is not one of immediacy or transparency, but one of material and historical mediations that govern the practice of reading. If the text represents some form of colonial power, it then does so through these mediations so that empire, and its other, are *not monolithically* projected to and shared by all audiences. Therefore, it is dangerous for postcolonial scholars to simply read the English book as cultural text or 'primary source' without considering the complicated processes in which it was published, disseminated, edited, framed, summarised and translated before reaching the reader. In overlooking the mediations between the text and the act of reading, historians and literary scholars risk substituting their own reading — often done within the comforts of the modern (i.e. Western-style) academy — for a whole history of multifarious readings of empire by different agents in different contexts, under different limitations and above all for different audiences.

In this light, then, postcolonial scholars may no longer take for granted their very ability to access and read imperial and colonial books, which, as has been shown, was and still is a *privilege* not universally and evenly shared by all historical and contemporary readerships. Realising the historicity of this privilege may perhaps be a crucial step towards avoiding the predicament faced by Zhang and Nan in writing history based on 'primary sources' left by nineteenth-century colonisers, towards unbinding modern Chinese history from the canon of English colonial books, and towards writing 'new imperial histories' that reflect traditionally overlooked or suppressed perspectives.

4

Travel and Business: The First Colombian in China

Jacinto Fombona

> Negrero, sí, fue don Nicolás Tanco
>
> — Reinaldo Arenas

A year after arriving in Amoy (Xiàmén [廈門], Fújiàn province) as an agent for a British-Cuban company, Nicolás Tanco Armero proposes an exercise in observation to his readers of *Viaje de Nueva Granada a China*:[1]

> Let us start by observing the Chinaman in himself. Isn't this the strangest being a European or an American can face? It is true that the Indian of our Pampas; the ferocious Bedouin, or the savage Malay and Bengalese from the other part of Asia, are creatures that cause surprise because they present to man his primitive state. But, could you compare this surprise with that of looking at a Chinaman? Look at his physical complexion in which one can recognize features from every race: those shaved heads, always shining, with the beautiful ponytail or tresses floating on their backs; those very long faces reflecting vices and also intelligence; that careless poise facile and graceful: everything, everything in his aspect points to a being *sui generis*, a truly peculiar type. (373)

Several issues that involve shifting worldviews and positionings to accommodate the author's own perspective arise from this paragraph. To begin with, in Spanish the 'strangest being' posed in the rhetorical question is further displaced and singularised with the use of the Latinate *ente* (from *ens*). The description of the Chinaman by Tanco Armero follows here, as often happens throughout his texts — the blueprint of a naturalist or geographer who records observations of an object under scrutiny. Everything that is notable must be and is considered, discussed and classified according to a set of empirical guidelines whose archaeology might be traced back to Francis Bacon's essay 'Of Travel', written as 'directions' to the young traveller on how and what to observe when travelling abroad.[2]

In broad and general terms, Tanco Armero's travel writing is an exercise in Enlightenment thinking, characterised by a process of analysis and a system of reference that seeks to standardise the resulting observations. In this vein, a book by one of the founders and secretary of the Royal Geographical Society of England, Colonel Julian R. Jackson, entitled *What to Observe or the Traveller's Remembrancer*, offers a convenient summation.[3] Given Tanco Armero's education in London and Paris, it is not far-fetched to venture that he knew of this title in particular, or else was familiar with similar books on the subject. Jackson's book itemises the set of directives that Tanco Armero seems to be following when writing about his travels, and the knowledge he maintains he sought to acquire and make public for his readers. As Jackson states in his introduction: 'The object of this Work, as its title indicates, is to point to the uninitiated Travellers what he should observe, and to remind the one who is well informed, of many objects which, but for a Remembrancer, might escape him' (2). Notably, Jackson talks of his book not as a guide for travel, but a 'remembrancer', pointing on the one hand to a hierarchy of formal knowledge that guides for tourists would lack, and, on the other, making a gesture towards the kind of useful knowledge travellers, already formed within a profession, must 'remember' to direct their eyes to and really profit from in their travels. Such a gesture of remembering points writes to the moment and poses a narrating 'I' that, as in an autobiography, takes the double role of acting and telling. The distance between the narrating self that observes him/herself as a traveller and the actor/observed-self can vary considerably. In the case of Tanco Armero, the scene of writing is framed by the vicissitudes and joys of travelling as a retelling of very recent events in the author's life.

There are striking similarities between the table of contents of Jackson's book and Tanco Armero's own chapters about his travels in China especially, as well as visits to Cuba, Egypt and Palestine, the United States, England and France. He is quite meticulous in describing, as the 'remembrancer' recommends, aspects of history, population, uses and traditions of everyday life, religion, fine arts (or lack thereof), science, literature and a long etcetera, all in order to 'take nations as they are', as Jackson urges his readers. In *Recuerdos de mis últimos viajes, Japón*, Tanco Armero quite unambiguously stresses, in defending his travelling and the knowledge derived from it, that his is a first-hand account of life in the nations through which he travelled, and that he has indeed taken 'the nations as they are' (6). It is the knowledge produced and proclaimed by this kind of meticulous exercise in observation, as recommended by Jackson, that allows Tanco Armero — even when he is not a European with an imperial agenda — to cast himself (in the introduction to *Recuerdos de mis últimos viajes, Japón*) as a true traveller, an agent of useful knowledge, stressing the fact that he is not a simple tourist (11–17).

In *Viaje de Nueva Granada a China*, the chapter that asks the reader to 'observe the Chinaman in himself' begins with a generalisation:

> He who travels in the oriental countries, and particularly in China, does not experience *impressions* alone, because of all that is presented to his view, but also great *surprises*, since everything in this curious country, on top of being different from what we have in the West, is the contrary, diametrically the opposite. One would say the civilisation of the Celestial Empire is entirely the antipode to ours. (373)

Oriental spaces are for the author a source of difference, to the extent that it is not *impresiones* alone, but *sorpresas* (imprints and surprises, italicised in the original) that travellers in the Far East experience among people who are 'entirely the antipode' (both geographically to the South American, and anthropologically as a Westerner). Travellers find themselves among people who do everything backwards: reading and writing are done from right to left and 'vertically', he quips; even in putting on their shoes, the Chinese start with the left foot, since the left-side takes precedence over the right (375). In this upside-down world, the author calls his readers to observe the Chinaman, this 'truly peculiar type', while performing an authorial gesture that seeks a community of readers.

The description starts with a command in the first person plural and switches to the familiar address in the plural, *mirad* in Spanish. This is like moving from the first person plural of 'Let us observe' towards 'Y' all look!', to give an equivalent expression from the southern United States. Such a move stresses emplacement of the author's gaze who marks his American origin through the possessive pronoun, as in 'Indian of *our* pampas' — even if it is, as in this case, the gaze of an observer that can assume the role of a Eurocentric scientist or Orientalist courting a non-European reading public. The use of the term *pampas* by Tanco Armero is significant because this particular term for plains is not used in northern South America where the preferred usage is *llanos*. The author performs here a semiotic of inclusion that seeks a Spanish-speaking context of reception, that is willed to extend beyond national borders, in fact to the entire region. The use of the possessive reflects a time of nation-building rather than imperial expansion (to the extent that the two can be differentiated); the author writes at a point when the inclusion into the new societies of the diverse peoples and former colonial-time castes that lived in the Spanish regions of America is key for the rise and consolidation of the bourgeois republics.

For his implied audience, Tanco Armero takes on a persona that affords him a voice and carves him a space from which to parse and reassemble European discourses for an audience in Spanish America. Nonetheless, there is a problem in taking the voice of an empirically-minded travel writer. As with any kind of narrative, the travelogue inevitably allows for an element of literariness and in this case it provides the opportunity for the author, who claims not to be writing a piece of literature, to reflect on his writing style and his strategy in recording his travels. Thirty years after publishing *Viaje de Nueva Granada a China*, he seems to read into his texts a hybrid narrative where the accounts of personal experience introduce an element of storytelling that escapes his control. Perhaps he is merely repeating an often used trope, but he admits to reluctance to act as a simple objective and informative observer. He claims in the introduction to his second travel book, *Recuerdos de mis últimos viajes, Japón*,[4] 'I have never aspired to present myself as a man of letters; all my ambition has been reduced to stamp my impressions in the simplest manner, allowing my fellow compatriots to know the curious and far away countries I have visited' (6).

Who is this traveller whose declaration of purpose is to cast aside adornment in style and any pretension to literature, and yet whose name appears in the verse of a Cuban sonnet as a *negrero*, a slave-trader?[5] The answer to these questions requires examination of the set of textual strategies that arise in his travel texts in relation to the ideals of progress and civilisation he declares to profess, which provides a context for the interplay of cultural exchanges played out in his writings. His first book, *Viaje de Nueva Granada a China*, is a collection of impressions of his first trip around the world. It includes descriptions of places travelled to, as well as encounters with friends, travel companions and what he deems 'notable people' throughout his itinerary. The success of its publication in Paris in 1861 was followed some thirty years later by a second, more mature and also more formulaic, book on his travels in Japan, *Recuerdos de mis últimos viajes, Japón*, published in Madrid in 1888.

In 1851, the year that Tanco Armero left his native Bogotá, New Granada was in turmoil. Following the Liberal Party's reforms that included the abolition of slavery, pro-slavery, conservative leaders in two provinces — Cauca and Antioquia — rose in arms against the government. Tanco Armero, a young member of a distinguished family who had just returned from studying abroad, was jailed for three months in Bogotá for his writings and public speeches decrying the country's political and social chaos. The son of a secretary of Simón Bolívar's last Colombian government and of subsequent republican governments, Tanco Armero voiced opposition to what he saw as the barbarous Liberal Party regime that was strangling his country, one of the three nations into which Colombia fractured in 1830. Educated in the United States and Paris, thanks to the support of his older brother, Mariano, he studied economics under the French Restoration liberal, and traveller, Jérôme-Adolphe Blanqui (1798–1854), and later returned to Colombia where he became a politician and polemicist in conservative newspapers of the time.

Tanco Armero's narratives could be characterised as empiricist and articulating that faith in progress which in Spanish America would later be associated with scientific positivism. His impressions in Cartagena, for example, lead him to compare the monumental Spanish colonial bastion in the Caribbean to what he saw as the new monuments to progress: 'Banks, saving banks, railroads, the telegraph, shelter houses, exhibitions, are the monuments we have' (13). A key aspect to understanding Tanco Armero as a writer is to see him as a member of what Ángel Rama called *la ciudad letrada*, 'the lettered city' (in a key moment of struggle and transition).[6] This, according to Rama, consists of a core cultural elite whose members, as literati or *letrados*, are a 'pleiad' of religious and bureaucratic clerks, educators and lawmakers. Their function was the production of (civilising) meaningful discourses. Marked by writing, this elite established and built the discourses of the ideal rational city from which conquest, colonisation and, later, nation-building efforts stemmed. As such, these groups are for Rama an organising centre, armed by, and trafficking in, social distinction in order to control the unruly spatial and discursive territory of the nation. The figure of the letter is crucial in Rama's definition, reflecting the importance of the rule of law, as well as the role and semi-sacred aura of writing in the developing of the city and the nation in Spanish America.

The case of Tanco Armero is a good example of the importance of writing in the life and dealings of a member of the oligarchy. In him, we have an example of the *letrado* (in his case a conservative politician, travel writer and, to some, proto-sociologist) who is also a businessman who amassed an immense fortune in his dealings with the British in China.[7] In his writings, and in second-hand references to his public life, it is possible to glimpse the transformations that modernity is imposing on the *letrados*, or members of the lettered city. The compartmentalisation and setting of boundaries of knowledge and occupations brought forth by modernisation transformed the lettered city, slowly reshaping the city oligarchies and their relations with writing. In the travel texts of Tanco Armero, while it is possible to see an understanding of writing as a secondary, almost genteel exercise for the entrepreneur to occupy and amuse himself with between business engagements, the exercise of writing is also presented as a duty towards family and country, an instrument for progress that was to be facilitated by the social practice of travelling. Perhaps not surprisingly, his work coincides with a growing trend among Spanish American local elites to send their children abroad for education after the hiatus for these classes during the (civil) wars for independence.[8]

The 'selling points' of Tanco Armero's travel books are his representations of the Far East and, in particular, the aura of the 'Orient' instilled in these. The titles explicitly stress the main destination points — China in the first book, Japan in the second — but these somewhat erase the rest of the itineraries included in the travel narratives. They also reflect a hierarchy in the mappings of Oriental lands in Spanish American discursive constructions of the world, amounting to a geography and worldview. Here, and throughout the nineteenth century, China and Japan occupy a central place in the Spanish-American imagination of Asia, relegating other neighbouring lands to mere waypoints. For Spanish Americans, China and Japan can be thought of as the destination of an interrupted or broken itinerary, reaching back to the time of Columbus. Places such as India, Vietnam or the Philippines (despite its being a Spanish colony) all have a different 'value' or specific weight in this imagined geography. Tanco Armero's travel texts place the author in the privileged spaces of China, and later Japan, and invest him with a particular 'social distinction', to use Pierre Bourdieu's term.[9]

According to the introduction to *Viaje de Nueva Granada a China* by Pedro María Moure, his publisher and as a fellow Neo-Grenadian his countryman, the traveller arrived in China as a businessman to hire workers as bonded labourers, mainly from the Canton (Guangdong, 廣東) area, for the Cuban plantation economy, which was severely affected by the ban and consequent reduction in the slave trade. He was involved in what came to be known as the infamous 'coolie trade' that sent thousands of these workers to Cuba, Mexico and Peru, as well as to the British possessions in the Caribbean. As an agent for a British-Spanish (and Cuban) company, Tanco Armero was in charge of overseeing the contracts and the shipment of workers to Cuba, then a Spanish possession, to replace slave labour. The ordeals of these immigrants in the Spanish colony caused an international incident, and eventually led to the intervention of the Chinese imperial government which set up a commission in 1874 (its report was published in 1876 and has, among its documents, a sample contract issued in Chinese and Spanish and signed by

Tanco Armero).[10] The hiring of labourers, however, turns out to be a non-issue in both of Tanco Armero's narratives, although his second book was published twelve years after the commission's report. In his first text, the traveller does not dwell on any aspect of his work in China, and gives very few details of what he calls his 'business' there. Strictly speaking, this travel text is neither a journal (even if dates appear in each chapter, they do not structure the narrative) nor is it an account of detailed business transactions. The chapters and sections of his *Viaje* often read like letters home edited for a broader public. The reader is only informed about his motives for travelling in the introduction to *Viaje de Nueva Granada a China*. As a preliminary to the texts that follow, Moure's introduction gives biographical details of Tanco Armero's life and education, as well as some information about the Tanco family and its struggle after the death of the father, Nicolás Tanco.[11] Surprisingly, as the framing of a travel book, Moure's introduction also stands out as a caustic critique of the fashion to travel that gripped the youth of the time. It offers an extended appeal to rein in the youthful impetus to travel, and, with moderation, to dwell in the enjoyment of family and property. In short, the introduction stands as an apology for reading as a central (social) practice that would keep the family together. While presenting Tanco Armero as a driven young man who has written a useful and informative book, Moure develops a long-winded diatribe against the current obsession with travelling. These 'objections' to travel become the starting point for Tanco Armero to put forward a refutation in which, conversely, travel is presented as a useful social practice. This appears in the introduction to his second book, *Recuerdos de mis últimos viajes, Japón*, and is written by the traveller himself.

Among the complaints that Moure registers, there is an observation on what he calls 'immigration in reverse', a process that, according to him, created in Europe, mostly in Paris, numerous 'colonies' of South American families who seemed 'pushed [to travel] in spite of the difficulties and long distances', and who, in this process, were de-populating the new republics (vi–vii). Moure, it has to be noted, ventures this opinion when writing in Paris, where he is one of these emigrants 'in reverse', living and working in Europe. His diatribe against travel includes a counsel from himself, someone who recognises that he once had a passion for travelling, but who nowadays would offer the following advice:

> If we were asked, we would answer, without hesitation. Do not travel! At most ride your horse to the border of your valley, and at sunset, while you can still see the towers of the city or the belfry in the village, turn back so you can hear the last calls to prayer. (vii)

Travel, according to this introduction to a travel book, will only be the source of sorrow for those one loves, and the traveller's only satisfaction is returning home. Moure recommends an alternative to travelling:

> Read this book. Without expenses, without moving, without passport or customs houses, with no need to search for board, nor to pack or unpack trunks . . . without paying long, itemized accounts . . . this companion will take you to the four most important parts of the world. (xii–xiii)

The introduction to *Recuerdos de mis últimos viaje, Japón* affords Tanco Armero the occasion to answer in kind the 'eccentricity' of his friend's attack on the usefulness of travelling. As a well-read *letrado*, he displays his own set of readings and authors to answer his friend. His epigraph, a quote in French by Eugène Pelletan, poses the moral dilemma of disagreeing with one's highly respected friend when he is far from the truth. Tanco Armero's arguments flatly reject the idea, put forth by Moure, that 'a humble inhabitant will learn more from a tranquil reading than from a trip around the world' (12). In his opinion, such a dependence on second-hand accounts is manifestly deficient, as they are written by tourists, not by true travellers. This sort of travel writing is, according to the author, common among South Americans and Europeans alike, and 'is published as *«impresiones»*, plagued with inexactitudes, or referring to simple data found in *Guides*" (11–12, italics in original). Alexander Dumas writing on Spain, and the works of a *charlatán* like the Viscount of Gabriac on Bogotá,[12] are for the author poorly written texts that would only provide their reader, this *humble inhabitant*, with 'false and absurd notions' about the places travelled (15). In Tanco Armero's opinion, society will benefit from the education provided by the observation of other peoples and cultures. The *humble inhabitant* that both Moure and Tanco Armero talk about quickly transforms himself into the child of the rich and powerful who takes up travel as 'philosophy on foot', quoting Lamartine (10). Tanco Armero's introduction sets forth the idea of the traveller's life as an example to follow; but to a certain extent it misses the point of his publisher and friend whose attack on travelling might also be understood as a gimmick to sell the book he is publishing.

China is the key instance brandished by Tanco Armero in his arguments in favour of travelling. The rebuke to Moure's 'eccentricity' anchors itself on the Chinese 'counter-example' — China is 'that colossal Celestial Empire that I have had the occasion to closely study while living among its peoples'. In this, he coincides with Herder's influential work on cultures and history, in the diagnosis of Chinese society as *crystallised* due to its self-imposed ostracism.¹³ Herder, even if he risks falling into the category of 'cabinet travellers' that Tanco Armero criticises, is a clear influence on his approach to 'observing' Chinese spaces and culture. The very inconsistency of Herder's thoughts on Chinese civilisation, perhaps due to the unsystematic nature of his philosophy, combined with the first-hand experience and eclectic approach of the South American, seem to have an effect on Tanco Armero's opinions about China, and on the objective appraisal of the Chinese civilisation the traveller professes to attempt. For Tanco Armero, China's ostracism has led to a civilisation that is *crystallised*, as he calls it following Herder; but it is also (often) redeemable: the Chinaman, that 'truly peculiar type' he has asked his readers to observe, is also a graceful and intelligent being whose culture is fully adapted to his environment. Redemption will come to Chinese civilisation in the form of progress, thanks precisely to an idea spread by travel itself, Christianity. There is, however, another issue here — Tanco Armero's reason for being in China. As already mentioned, he arrives in China on business to 'hire' workers and ship them to Cuba as (cheap) labour for the sugar-cane fields. On the question of the 'immigration', as the hiring of coolie labourers was called, Moure finds it 'objectionable' on racial grounds, since the project of introducing into an already heterogeneous Cuba yet another 'strange and ugly' racial element will add another layer of complexity to its population. But the traveller, says Moure, in an interesting rehash of Father las Casas' story,¹⁴ saw it as 'a humanitarian issue', convinced as he was that the influx of Chinese labourers would further undermine African slavery in the island colony and, in the long run, completely eliminate it (xxv). Nonetheless, as a motivation for Tanco Armero's travel, the fact that he mentions barely any details of his dealings remains a rather loud silence, a conspicuous omission.

Such is the case even though Tanco Armero does comment on and condemn another business practice: the opium trade, the trade in 'foreign mud' sponsored by the British and other Western nations to force China to open its ports to international commerce.¹⁵ On this issue he is very clear: the Opium War (1838–1842) was an 'unjust' war that set aside any sense of 'justice, law and humanity' to 'protect smuggling', and 'to secure a market for India's main commodity' (307).¹⁶ In Hong Kong, he is often in the company of businessmen, many of them from the trading houses of Jardine, Matheson and Dent and Co., British companies involved in the opium trade. He witnesses these 'speculators' looking at the port from rooftop terraces, seeing the 'monstrous steamships arriving with their favorite *drug*!', and pointing to his companions ... [showing] satisfaction in observing the arrival and unloading of the poison that is immediately sent to the clippers to be distributed throughout the coastal region!' (314). He sees the happiness in the smiles of those 'speculators' induced by the prospect of the clippers' return loaded with silver, 'the valuable *sycee* from China, in exchange for the poison' (314). The author calls the people involved in the drug trade standing next to him 'poison-givers' — inhuman agents of a commerce that breaks Chinese laws with the sole aim of making money while 'killing and dulling millions' (314–5). The author's condemnation of the opium trade is powerful; however, he also describes (as necessary and unavoidable) the trips he took along the coast in the opium clippers, and is amazed at the luxury and speed of these vessels. In spite of his calls for 'philanthropy' and the 'humanitarian conscience' of the West to stop this hideous practice, he himself professes a selective blindness since there is not an inkling in any of his travel texts that his own business was at best questionable, if not tantamount to slavery for thousands.

Tanco Armero's travel narrative dwells on details of Chinese culture, religion, laws, history and the country's present situation. The origins of European presence, as well as the interplay between different Western empires in Chinese lands, is a matter of particular interest to the author. Although the reason for his trip is never fully addressed, it is neither completely absent nor fully erased from the text. There are a few traces that lead to abrupt silences, ellipses or erasures of his 'enterprise'. He obliquely mentions in passing the reason he is in China two or three times. But aside from sparse references to the shipments he has to attend to, and admiring comments about the ships themselves while in Chinese ports, it is only in Paris, preparing to depart, that any musings on the business that takes him to China are to be found. In Marseilles, Tanco Armero portrays himself as eager and deeply moved by reading the labels on his trunk, as travel to China presents itself no longer as an abstraction, but is made visible, inscribed on his personal belongings. At this point, he ponders about 'the knowledge I might acquire and the earnings that will stem from the major speculations that were taking me to those lands' (195). Any further details of his dealings with '*the* immigration', as he puts it, are left to the reader's 'speculations'. The definite article (my italics) — in the absence of any further elucidation of *what* immigration he is referring to — marks the tension between the heavily signifying silence, and the meaningful objective that articulates and justifies his presence in a foreign land.

Tanco Armero lived in China during a critical period for the Qing or 'Manchu' dynasty. He witnessed events in the Taiping rebellion of 1851, suppressed in 1864 (by that time considered the bloodiest conflict of the era), and lived through episodes of the so-called Second Opium War in 1857 that ended with the imposition by France and Britain of the treaty of Tientsin (Tianjin, 天津) in 1858, a humiliating treaty that forced the opening of Chinese ports to Western trade.[17] An occasion on which Tanco Armero makes reference to his dealings occurs just before the outbreak of the Opium War, and functions as a narrative lead into his experience of the war. Already in China, he writes that he had to return to Amoy (Xiamen, 廈門) 'for matters concerning the immigration' that were resolved with the shipping of two 'boats loaded with Asian colonists headed to the island of Cuba' (425). While the term he chooses to describe the Chinese labourers, *colonos*, invites other conjectures on the silencing of his dealings, Tanco Armero adds nothing else. He continues the narration of his return to Hong Kong to witness the unfolding episodes that led to war.

The war in Tanco Armero's text allows for a portrayal of a traveller's hard times as he attests to the increase in attacks on foreigners, notes the frustration he feels at being taken for an enemy when he is neither French nor British (even though he worked for a European company), and the anguish and anxiety that spread among people in the so called 'concessions', the self-administered communities of Westerners that lived in the open ports of China.[18] The episodes concerning the Opium War have an adventure novel quality to them. They include descriptions of escapes from danger; his experiences regarding the departure, following a decree, of all Chinese nationals working for the Westerners; accounts of squeamishness and searches for refuge in which to weather the conflict and wait for the cease-fire or the arrival of reinforcement troops that would quell the uprising; and the killing of the Spanish consul general, his personal acquaintance, by army men disguised as passengers — all of this among a storm of rumours and news that constantly promised the arrival of help.

On the origins of the war, Tanco Armero puts the blame squarely on British perfidy in foreign affairs, and in particular their ill-judged exertions seeking to expand commerce between the two nations which had provoked an international conflict. The author sees the war as unbecoming and dishonourable for the British, who in causing this conflict have endangered 'the dealings and lives of Europeans and other foreigners' (426). He marvels that:

> . . . in the midst of the nineteenth century, a century of enlightenment and progress, the nation that distils so much philanthropy, and boasts about being at the vanguard of modern advances, should be the one whose cruel hand will set fire to the torch of discord that will consume thousands in fortunes, and millions of human lives. (427)

For Tanco Armero, progress and its corollary, Christian civilisation, should be the guarantors of peaceful coexistence among peoples and commerce. The author does not consider far-fetched the opinion that Rear Admiral, Sir Michael Seymour, had 'previous orders from the Court of Saint James' to hasten the events that led to war (427). He discusses the horrors of the razing of Canton (Guangzhou, 廣州) by English warships and its predictable consequences for the foreigners or *'red haired devils'* (430, his italics). He explains the seeming lack of justifiable reprisals by the Chinese, addressing the stark differences and rivalry between Chinese regions:

> Every region's interest is different, and there is nothing that would enlist them under a single banner. The Cantonese have no contractual dealings whatsoever with the inhabitants of Fukien [福建], nor do these with the ones from Tche-kiang [浙江]: they differ in language or dialect, in traditions, and even in their feelings. (430)

The absence of any sense of national unity in China, and the priority that the accumulation of riches and material goods takes over 'fatherland, family, life, everything' explains, for Tanco Armero, the apparent lack of reaction of a nation affronted. The peace after the defeat of the Taiping forces did not last and he details the events that made the British forces abandon control of the Pearl River Delta, and leave for Hong Kong, where all the foreigners from the region had sought refuge. Without fully taking the Chinese side, Tanco Armero finds a way to signal instances of European barbarism such as the war and the opium trade, as well as to depict Chinese usages and customs as practices well adapted to their land and environment. He admires and considers 'worth noticing' that every Chinese person is able to read the 'difficult' writing system 'no matter how distressed or ignorant he might be' (405). That the Chinese considered every foreigner a barbarian is a commonplace in writing about China. A British interpreter, Thomas Medows, wrote in 1852 that the Europeans are for the Chinese 'people in a rude, uncivilised state, morally and intellectually uncultivated', simply put 'barbarians'.[19] Such a view of a world split between barbarians and civilised people provides familiar ground for Tanco Armero as a South American Creole who, encountering the European, faces a hierarchy that pushes his origins, and with them his status, and his claims, as a member of a European civilisation, away from Europe.

One of the reprisals engineered by the Chinese leader, commissioner Yeh Ming-ch'en who ordered every Chinese national to leave Hong Kong, is of particular interest to get a glimpse of the manner in which the author lived and travelled in China. Tanco Armero has to see off his servant *Achuy* (italicised in the text), who was his 'companion in pilgrimages, and whose Chinese dialect [Tanco Armero] had gotten used to' (435). The author stresses how elegantly Achuy was able to dress due to the generous pay he got from the agent traveller, and he laments the certain misery that awaits him as an unemployed man in the fields where he is being forced to return. It is at this point that the issue of war as a consequence of incommensurability comes up, embodied in the person of Achuy as one of the many victims of 'wars of race, that is between nations of foreign civilizations' (435).

Tanco Armero's world-view is an interesting mixture of mercantile liberalism and Christian redemption through progress. Achuy's rich clothings are for the traveller a mark of improvement in lifestyle that 'trickles down' thanks to (legally sanctioned) commerce. Not surprisingly, the dressing-up of Achuy reverts back to the first-person perspective, and points to the self-in-business in his dealings with the Chinese as a benefactor who seeks to understand the land he visits. Poignantly perhaps, one of the surviving photographs of Tanco Armero is his full-length portrait dressed up in Chinese clothing.

Figure 4.1 Nicolás Tanco Armero in full Chinese garb photographed by Juan Camilo Segura in Bogotá c.1870. From the collection of Doña Elvira Cuervo, Secretary of Culture, Columbia. Published with her kind permission.

Tanco Armero's dressing in Chinese garb appears in the text as part of a ruse to go inland into territories forbidden to foreigners. His transformation has been foreshadowed by his comments upon arriving in China when he writes, reflecting on the itinerary he has followed and the cultures he has visited, that 'I have worn every style of dress, and my head has sported from the serious round hat to the Indian turban: all I have left to do is to shave my head Chinese style' (290). The opportunity to try a new garb would soon arise.

In Fu-tchéu (福州), after overseeing the departure of a frigate to Havana, the traveller manages to convince a Protestant missionary, 'M. Burns' to 'penetrate the interior', to accompany him inland, and to quell the 'thirst for singularity' that made him 'anxious to know China better than any modern traveller' (405–6). Mr. Burns only agrees half-heartedly to such a dangerous adventure, and on condition they go in disguise:

> I was forced to agree to this just demand; albeit under great distress, since I had to shave my beard and head. Quickly I found someone to provide me with the necessary garb, made up simply of blue wide-on-top pants, but tied to the heels like undergarments; of a *cabaya*, a long cape of sorts; a pair of boat-shaped, wooden shoes with two-inch-thick soles: a beautiful fake braid of hair that floated on my back and reached to my feet. I was dressed exactly like a missionary. All I had to do was to speak to finish up the portrayal, but I was careful not to do so. (406)

The travellers are careful to disguise even their eating habits (they take neither 'wine nor abundant food' on the trip), a gesture that recalls Bacon's instruction not to stand out; but the narrator's transformation is bound to be incomplete, restricted by a language he does not master, so their disguise can only be partial. Their aim is not to become Chinese, but rather to gain access to the 'singular' lands the narrator wishes to see and experience, for which they have to assume another façade, that of the religious missionary: a privileged status different from that of the businessman. Mr. Burns, as a missionary himself, seems to lend a sense of truth to protect the traveller and narrator from being exposed, but he is a bit of a coward and a Protestant, an element that functions as a narrative device in the ridiculous adventure that will follow. The disguise did not work. Tanco Armero faults himself, blaming his body language as a traveller, his 'continuous state of surprise at everything he saw' (408) and the crowd of curious people, mostly boys, that started to follow them. Mr. Burns sensed the danger and they sought refuge in a little house that turned out to be a school. This episode is framed by a passing observation on the shipping of indentured workers to Havana, comments on the Chinese views of foreigners as devils or *fanguai*, and the use of his Colt revolver to disperse a menacing crowd, an event which led Mr. Burns and himself to jail (luckily, Tanco Armero admits, this episode took place before the war, and had no major consequences other than a trip back to Fu-tchéu in shackles where they were handed to the British consul, who freed them). Within this frame, the narrator offers his description of a first-hand contact with an elementary school in China where, in hiding from people who saw him as a trespasser, the traveller learns some Chinese from his host and schoolmaster among 'little Chinese boys with shaved heads, and little braids that made them look like mice' (414). The school allows the author to witness first-hand, and admire, the elementary school system in China, perhaps only surpassed, he says, 'by that of the United States of North America' (414).

Tanco Armero admires the moral foundations of China's civilisation, but this admiration hinges on a pervasive element that structures his text: religion, an element that is for many a traveller the grounds for an utmost disorienting otherness, since it informs a vision of this world and posits a future one in which the other is (ethically) entangled. In the case of Tanco Armero, it is Christianity and the idea of progress that comes forth throughout his text (and in a particularly coherent manner in the introduction to his second book). His is a view of progress enmeshed in the social practice of travel that stresses the evangelical, the globalising drive of Christianity. Faith in progress is for the author a way to embrace modernity; it pivots on travel as an 'imperious and fecund need of progress itself that will lead the traveller (not the tourist) to know and examine the planet where he lives in order to tame and beautify it with the creations of his mind, and make of humanity a single family' (*Japón*, 9). Such a globalised family dreamt by Tanco Armero as the product of the social practice of an elite would be, according to the author, the triumph of true civilisation, that of Christianity itself as imagined by Saint Paul the traveller.

In the case of China, however, the picture that Tanco Armero offers is always more complex. China is anything but a clean slate. Religion is another complicated and complicating subject here since the author finds himself facing a millenary civilisation that, as he recognises, has seen all kinds of philosophical propositions, including 'socialism'. The given 'Truth' of Christianity loses its force among the Chinese who see it as yet another element of life, even a subject for humour. In a passage that reproduces the riddle that is the other's laughter, Tanco Armero conveys the story of Catholic missionary priests who tell them of the Chinese laughing out loud at their explanations of religious 'truths' and references to the soul. This story brings Tanco Armero to lament that only money matters to the Chinese, and that 'everything that has to do with the spirit, that which concerns the soul, the world to come, the other life after this one, does not fret nor interest him' (372). Yet, these are the two strains that function as guidelines to Tanco Armero's writing, the lines of (his) fugue that structure his narrations as the 'observations' of a Creole businessman who travels and lives in a complex society that provides a constant source of 'surprises'.

5

Erasing Footsteps: On Some Differences between the First and Popular Editions of Isabella Bird's *Unbeaten Tracks in Japan*[1]

Shizen Ozawa

The narrative of Isabella Bird's *Unbeaten Tracks in Japan* reaches its climax when she meets the Ainu,[2] an indigenous people of Hokkaido, the northernmost region of the nation. She rapturously recalls:

> I never saw such a strangely picturesque sight as that group of magnificent savages with the fitful firelight on their faces, and for adjuncts the flare of the torch, the strong lights, the blackness of the recesses of the room and of the roof, at one end of which the stars looked in, and the row of savage women in the background — eastern savagery and western civilisation met in this hut, savagery giving, and civilisation receiving, the yellow-skinned Ito [Bird's Japanese interpreter] the connecting-link between the two.[3]

This scene, taking place at the location farthest from the point of departure, constitutes the most dramatic moment of Bird's travel narrative. The demanding two-month journey that precedes it is retrospectively characterised as a series of difficulties to overcome for the realisation of the encounter with 'magnificent savages'. In fact, the traveller leaves Japan as soon as she returns from Hokkaido. It looks as if she has quickly lost interest in the country once she has accomplished the main purpose of her journey.

This is how most of the currently available editions of *Unbeaten Tracks in Japan* end. These are reprints of the abridged edition first published in one volume in 1885.[4] Nevertheless, the original edition of *Unbeaten Tracks in Japan*, which appeared in two volumes in 1880, presents a rather different picture. After returning from Hokkaido, Bird stays in Japan for a few more months and travels widely in its western districts. She devotes as much as one-third of the second volume to the description of this succeeding trip.[5]

A close comparative reading of the two texts reveals that there is no substantial rewriting or addition involved in the editing process. Deletion is the chief means by which the longer version turns into the shorter one. While some chapters remain untouched, others are shortened to various degrees. Several, including those on the later journey, are completely edited out.

Anna M. Stoddart, the first biographer of Bird as well as her longstanding friend, records that the travel writer was busy in 1884 in compressing *Unbeaten Tracks in Japan* into one volume.[6] It is very likely, therefore, that Bird herself is greatly, if not totally, responsible for editorial changes. Nevertheless, the exact degree to which she could control the texts has yet to be investigated in the cultural context of the nineteenth-century publishing industry, as well as in terms of her friendship with the publisher John Murray. The aim of this paper is more modest. Rather than speculating upon Bird's possible authorial intention behind the revision of the two texts, I seek to examine the *effects* of editing in detail.

Shigetoshi Kusuya's observation offers a good starting point. Discussing the expunged chapters, he points out that the popular edition highlights the 'uncivilised' Ainu.[7] His argument is certainly convincing, given that the description of the Ainu is reproduced verbatim in the later edition; it is only the narrative of Bird's journey on the main island of Japan that is heavily abridged. However, Kusuya's analysis is too general in that he only briefly and cursorily considers the content of the chapters which have disappeared in the compressing process. Wishing to extend substantially his observation, I will firstly explore how editorial changes alter the character of the traveller. I will then examine how representations of Japan are accordingly modified. Finally, I will consider the most conspicuous difference between the two editions — the erasing of most of the references to missionary activities in Japan.

A More Authoritative Traveller

Evelyn Bach points out that women writers have been constrained by 'the conventions of feminine writing which required delicacy of reference, a good deal of polite self-deprecation and avoidance of authoritative pronouncements'. In this respect, she continues, the narrator of Bird's travel writing, while carefully retaining her femininity, often seems to assume a masculine voice by 'detailing events as they occurred, including statistical material, presenting her own observations without reference to male authorities'.[8] A comparative reading between the first and the popular editions of *Unbeaten Tracks in Japan* indicates that the narrative tone in question is partly a product of editing. Let me begin by considering the popular edition's description of a Nikko shrine as a typical example:

> Within is a hall finely matted, 42 feet wide by 27 from front to back, with lofty apartments on each side, one for the Shôgun and the other 'for his Holiness the Abbot.' Both, of course, are empty. The roof of the hall is panelled and richly frescoed. The Shôgun's room contains some very fine *fusuma*, on which *kirin* (fabulous monsters) are depicted on a dead gold ground, and four oak panels, 8 feet by 6, finely carved, with the phoenix in low relief variously treated. In the Abbot's room there are similar panels adorned with hawks spiritedly executed. The only ecclesiastical ornament among the dim splendours of the chapel is the plain gold *gohei*. Steps at the back lead into a chapel paved with stone, with a finely panelled ceiling representing dragons on a dark blue ground. (popular edn, 57)

Adopting the third-person present, Bird commandingly gives the exact size of the hall and describes it in detail. Using Japanese words without much explanation also gives an impression that she has a broad knowledge of Japanese culture. While pinning down 'masculine' elements in the quote might be difficult, it is nonetheless certain that the traveller exudes great self-confidence. This passage appears with slightly different punctuation in the first edition as well (1st edn, 1: 112). Nevertheless, its narrator admits a few pages later: 'Thus far, with Mr. Satow's help, I have gone over the principal objects of interest, omitting very many . . . I have reduced my description to the baldness of a hand-book in absolute despair' (1st edn, 1: 116). As the narrator openly and somewhat jokingly admits the limitation of her ability of description, her acknowledgement of intellectual debt to Ernest Satow — a British diplomat who was also famous as a Japanologist — characterises her as a self-deprecating figure. The excision of this passage makes the traveller of the popular edition much more confident and independent.

In fact, a similar point can be made about the very beginning of the narrative. The importance of arrival scenes in travel writing should be taken into account here. As Mary Louise Pratt points out, arrival scenes settle the terms of representation, thereby determining how the cultural contact will be narrated hereafter.[9] This being the case, it is remarkable that the first edition records the sense of disorientation Bird felt immediately after her arrival:

> But already the loneliness of a solitary arrival and the feeling of being a complete stranger have vanished, and I am suffering mainly from complete mental confusion, owing to the rapidity with which new sights and ideas are crowding upon me. My reading of books on Japan, and the persistent pumping of my Japanese fellow-voyagers for the last three weeks, might nearly as well have been omitted, for the country presents itself to me as a complete blur, or a page covered with hieroglyphs to which I have no key. Well, I have months to spend here, and I must begin at the alphabet, see everything, hear everything, read everything, and delay forming opinions as long as possible. (1st edn, 1: 23)

This passage frankly registers both her initial sense of 'loneliness' and the following 'mental confusion'. The relatively relaxed tone, as indicated by the interjection 'well', could be read as a residue of the intimacy that must have been openly expressed in Bird's original letter to her sister Henrietta.[10] It is as if the narrator were trying to cheer herself up in the face of difficulties lying ahead. In the popular edition, however, the quoted passage is completely excised. Without showing her bewilderment, the narrator starts depicting 'heavy, two-wheeled man-carts drawn and pushed by four men' (popular edn, 8), which the first edition describes only after the quote (1st edn, 1: 23). Compared with the earlier version, the popular edition's narrative sounds more assertive.

The subtle dramatisation of self-confidence also affects the ways in which Bird's relationship with European residents in Japan is described. As Olive Checkland points out, Bird's success in her difficult trip partly depended upon the help she was able to get from her new acquaintances: using her social status at home, she obtained no less than forty letters of introduction to her compatriots in Japan.[11] In fact, the first edition indicates that she was treated as a semi-official visitor during her stay in Tokyo. Before starting her journey, along with some staff members of the British Legion, she was formally invited to the opening ceremony of a new theatre (1st edn, 1: 53). After coming back from the Hokkaido trip, she participated in 'an afternoon entertainment given to the diplomatic body in the Shiba Pavilion, one of the Mikado's smaller palaces' (1st edn, 2: 202). Although she quickly dismisses the event as 'a mere imitation of an English reception' (1st edn, 2: 204), it is undeniable that she takes advantage of the various privileges that her good rapport with the British Legion confers. Such a close relationship with British officials is greatly obscured, if not totally suppressed, in the popular edition. Revealingly, the following passage is omitted: 'I can only allude to the kindness shown to me by others here, and to the way in which several people are taking a great deal of trouble to facilitate my arrangements for seeing Japan' (1st edn, 1: 23).

Deleting this passage, the popular edition implicitly highlights the traveller's self-reliance.

The popular edition also emphasises the traveller's independent-mindedness in a different manner. One of its letters on her Nikko experience ends with a description of the 'squeeze', the commission Japanese servants are alleged to charge secretly. She sighs: 'Your servant gets a "squeeze" on everything you buy, and on your hotel expenses, and, as it is managed very adroitly, and you cannot prevent it, it is best not to worry about it so long as it keeps within reasonable limits' (popular edn, 65). While this ending impresses readers with her ability to cope with even unpleasant foreign customs, the original version tells quite a different story. After mentioning the 'squeeze' in question, Bird moves on to describe several waterfalls she visited. During the excursion, she gets caught in the rain, and as a result:

> I arrived with clothing and baggage soaked, to find a foreign gentleman and lady drying their clothes on the front of my balcony, and my lovely rooms occupied. I was so rejoiced, however, to see people of my own race and speech, that I gladly took the back room, and as soon as we were all equipped in dry clothes, I made their acquaintance, and found that they were Mr. and Mrs. Chauncey Goodrich from Peking on their honeymoon journey. (1st edn, 1: 127)

Given the cultural and psychological strain of travelling alone in a foreign land, it is understandable that the traveller feels happy 'to see people of [her] own race and speech'. Still, such a seemingly candid expression of her emotion is perhaps at odds with the strength of mind that the popular edition seeks to highlight. Suppressing the friendship she establishes with her compatriots as well as the psychological comfort it must have offered, the popular edition implicitly dramatises her resilience. Ending the narrative with the episode of a 'squeeze', it highlights the difficulty of the journey and a fortitude which enables and entitles her to realise the eventual encounter with the 'savage' Ainu.

Representing an Old Japan

The editorial changes not only subtly modify the character of the traveller but also give her description of Japan a slightly different emphasis. The effects of editorial changes are apparent even at the very beginning of the travelogue. Both versions describe Bird's first impression of Yokohama as follows:

> The air and water were alike motionless, the mist was still and pale, grey clouds lay restfully on a bluish sky, the reflections of the white sails of the fishing boats scarcely quivered; it was all so pale, wan, and ghastly, that the turbulence of crumpled foam which we left behind us, and our noisy, throbbing progress, seemed a boisterous intrusion upon sleeping Asia.
>
> The gulf narrowed, the forest-crested hills, the terraced ravines, the picturesque grey villages, the quiet beach life, and the pale blue masses of the mountains of the interior, became more visible. (1st edn, 1: 14; popular edn, 7)

Phrases such as 'motionless', 'still' and 'scarcely quivered' all emphasise the fundamental absence of movement. The adjective 'picturesque' aestheticises the scenery, underlining further the static quality of what is perceived. In short, Japan is the epitome of 'sleeping Asia'. At the same time, identifying herself with the 'noisy, throbbing progress', Bird emphasises her vigorousness. The traveller's spiritedness stands out in contrast with the alleged motionlessness of Japan.

Nevertheless, immediately after this, the first edition records another aspect of Yokohama:

> Yokohama is not imposing in any way — these hybrid cities never are; its Bluff represents the suburbs of Boston; its Bund, the suburbs of Birkenhead, with a semi-tropical hallucination . . . Then there are the British Consulate, imposingly ugly, the Union Church, partly built with money contributed in the Hawaiian Islands, unimposingly so, a few other buildings scarcely less offensive, the Japanese Post Office, Custom House, and Saibanchô or Court House, new, and built substantially in foreign style by foreign architects, and a huddle of mean erections which look like warehouses. (1st edn, 1: 15)

Yokohama was one of the so-called 'Treaty Ports' where trade and the residence of Europeans and Americans had been officially allowed since 1859. By the time of Bird's visit, the influence of Western culture on the port town had become far more visible than elsewhere. The first edition records what it regards as cultural confusion. Ironically, the most conspicuous symbol of cultural hybridity is nothing other than the building of 'the British Consulate', the epitome of imperial power (here described as 'imposingly ugly'). In the editing process, however, such references to cultural contact are here and there deleted,[12] as a result the distinctiveness of Japan is emphasised more strongly.

When the popular edition does mention the effects of Westernisation, they are almost always described in a negative manner. For instance, Bird laments in Yamagata: 'At the Court House I saw twenty officials doing nothing, and as many policemen, all in European dress, to which they had added an imitation of European manners, the total result being unmitigated vulgarity' (popular edn, 138). The adoption of Western-style uniforms can be seen as an example of transculturation in the sense that less powerful groups 'select and invent from materials transmitted to them'[13] by a metropolitan culture. In Bird's eyes, however, it is nothing but vulgar 'imitation'. This comment also appears in the first edition (1: 269), but the traveller also pays close attention to instances of successful modernisation. Following the passage quoted above, she continues:

> I visited a filature where the managers and engine-tenders all wore European clothes, but they were singularly courteous and communicative. It is a light, lofty, well-ventilated building, running 50 spindles (shortly to be increased to 100), worked by as many clean, well-dressed girls . . . The machinery is run by a steam-engine of twenty horse-power, made and worked by Japanese. (1st edn, 1: 269–70)

As the added phrase 'made and worked by Japanese' indicates, Bird amusedly observes that some Japanese businessmen are competent enough to use modern technology for their own purposes.[14] Nevertheless, this observation is not included in the popular edition. As Kusuya also points out,[15] the Japan which this seeks to depict and emphasise is 'real Japan' (1st edn, 1: 20; popular edn, 7), a Japan that has hardly been influenced by contact with the West. While highlighting difference is a common strategy for exoticising the other, the othering in question is achieved by erasing less dramatic, but perhaps more nuanced, observations.

It is possible to read such differences as attempts to change generic emphasis. The prefaces of both editions assert: 'This is not a "Book on Japan", but a narrative of travels in Japan, and an attempt to contribute something to the sum of knowledge of the present condition of the country' (1st edn, 1: vii; popular edn, ix). Despite the disclaimer, some parts of the first edition of *Unbeaten Tracks in Japan* are much closer to a 'Book on Japan' than the writer might have wished them to be. This is particularly true of several 'Notes' that are occasionally inserted between the Letters. Written in the third-person present, these 'Notes' provide general information on given topics. 'Notes on Food and Cookery', for instance, describes Japanese food, explains how to cook it, introduces representative dishes, and ends with comments on the tastelessness of the cuisine (1st edn, 1: 232–40). Such a general and encyclopaedic description seems to point to the narrative's serious intention to 'contribute something' to the Western 'knowledge' of the country. These

'Notes' and several passages of similar nature[16] — which draw heavily on secondary sources — are not included in the popular edition. As a result, the characteristics of 'a narrative of travels' are more strongly felt.

To some extent, these modifications are made in order to render the travel narrative more enjoyable, and ultimately more marketable. The popular edition's emphasis on the narrator's movement defines the purpose of her trip more clearly; her chief goal is Hokkaido where the 'savage' Ainu live, and the main island of Japan is characterised as a space to be traversed to reach her 'final' destination. Nevertheless, as the example of the filature shows, the traveller's movement is foregrounded at the cost of the description of the cultural complexities that she witnesses during her journey: the Japan depicted in the popular edition is somewhat simplified.

To put it another way, the highlighting of mobility creates a certain sense of cultural aloofness on the traveller's part in that she moves on before establishing a certain relationship with the place she visits. One episode in Aomori is a case in point. Bird describes a children's game that she witnesses in an inn. In the popular edition, we do not know what this game is: it is described merely as 'a game which Ito says "is played in the winter in every house in Japan"' (popular edn, 195). In contrast, the original edition identifies it as 'I-ro-ha garuta', a traditional card game, and explains how to play it. Such an explanation, to a certain extent, conveys some sense of cultural complexity. This is particularly the case with the episode in question, because the first edition gives a rather lengthy explanation of the Japanese proverbs written on each card. There is something interesting about Bird's cultural position in the description of this scene:

> [After the game,] tea was handed round, and I gave sweetmeats to all the children. Then Ito made a rough translation of many of the proverbs, some of which, partly from the odd language into which he put them, and partly from their resemblance to our own, made me laugh uncontrollably, and my mirth, or my unsuccessful efforts to restrain it, proving contagious, it ended in twenty people laughing themselves into a state of exhaustion! I feel much better for it, and thoroughly enjoyed the evening.
>
> Ito has since written what he says is a good translation of the best sayings, or what he thinks the best, which I send. Is it not strange to find the same ideas gathered up into recognisably similar forms in Japan as in England . . . ? (1st edn, 1: 366–7)

The traveller here indirectly participates in the game by delightedly giving 'sweetmeats to all the children'. The 'contagious' laughter then symbolically diminishes, if it does not nullify, the cultural and psychological distance between traveller and travellees. This blurring of boundaries is precisely what makes Bird's observation of cultural similarity convincing. The scene captures a fleeting, but still significant, moment in which contact forces the traveller to rethink her own cultural footing. It is her capacity for such self-reflection that differentiates Bird from many of her contemporary travel writers. Erasing this small cross-cultural dialogue, however, the popular edition sets up a clearer distinction between the observer and the observed. Suppressing potentially complicated cultural interactions, its narrative highlights the traveller's mobility in the land of the Other.

Ambivalence towards Missionary Activities

While the examples discussed so far are relatively minor editorial changes, the most conspicuous difference between the first and the popular editions is probably that the latter deletes most of the references to Christianity and the activities of missionaries in Japan. It is true that the popular edition does contain some comments on the real or imaginary influences of Christianity among the Japanese. For instance, its Letter Thirty briefly records that three 'Christian students' visit the traveller (popular edn, 202). Nevertheless, the corresponding description in the first edition is much longer and even mentions the visitors' names (1: 376–8). In fact, although it is hard to imagine from any reading of the popular edition, Bird's wish to observe mission activities seems to determine her itinerary to a considerable extent. In 'Notes on Missions in Niigata', which appears only in the first edition, Bird clearly states that the main purpose of her journey to the place is to learn something about the Medical Mission work there (1st edn, 1: 200). Similarly, the purpose of her trip to Kobe and its environs, the description of which is totally deleted in the popular edition, is 'to see the process of missionary work' (1st edn, 2: 214).

In the first edition, the traveller's keen interest in missionary activities is inseparable from her sincere desire that Christianity should spread speedily in Japan. For instance, faced with the sheer poverty of a rural village, she asks herself:

> The villages of that district must, I think, have reached the lowest abyss of filthiness in Hozawa and Saikaiyama. Fowls, dogs, horses, and people herded together in sheds black with wood smoke, and manure heaps drained into the wells . . . Is their [the villagers'] spiritual condition, I often wonder, much higher than their physical one? They are courteous, kindly, industrious, and

free from gross crimes; but, from the conversations that I have had with Japanese, and from much that I see, I judge that their standard of foundational morality is very low, and that life is neither truthful nor pure. (1st edn, 1: 187)

She clearly links poor living conditions with degenerate morals.[17] This passage also appears in the popular edition (107), but its narrator immediately changes topics and starts describing the inn in which she is staying. In contrast, the narrator of the first edition continues her reflections:

All that remains to them of religion is a few superstitions, and futurity, whether as regards hope or fear, is a blank about which they hardly trouble themselves. Truly they are in sore need of ameliorating influences, and of being lifted up to that type of highest manliness and womanliness which constitutes the Christian ideal. (1st edn, 1: 187)

Here the 'ameliorating influences' of Christianity appear as a panacea. In Bird's eyes, it is only 'the Christian ideal' that could take the Japanese to a higher level of morality, which would somehow improve their material conditions. The extent to which the issue matters for her can be guessed at the ending of the first edition. The traveller finishes her narrative by recording her hope that 'in the reception of Christianity, with its true principles of manliness and national greatness, she [Japan] may become, in the highest sense, "The Land of the Rising Sun" and the Light of Eastern Asia' (1st edn, 2: 347). The disappearance of such remarks is striking, considering that Bird, the elder daughter of a clergyman, was increasingly drawn to the Christian cause as she got older.[18]

Undoubtedly, behind these editorial modifications is the popular edition's desire to emphasise Japan's cultural distinctiveness. Influences of Christianity are regarded as incompatible with an exotic Japan that the popular edition seeks to dramatise. Nevertheless, something more complex can be detected in reflections upon the potential influences of the missionary work, which are suppressed in the popular edition.

In Kobe, Bird witnesses several concrete results of the permeation of Christianity among the Japanese. Faced with what she imagined as desirable before, however, she cannot but have second thoughts. Instead of moral elevation, she finds that mission education results in what she calls 'the denationalisation of nations' (1st edn, 2: 221). As an example, she discusses critically the ways in which Christian schools for girls are run. In her opinion, these foreign schools are too keen on religious education and therefore do not pay sufficient critically attention to the 'housewifely education' which she takes as most highly valued in Japanese society. As a result, she claims, 'young men would not, indeed could not, seek for wives among the girls educated by the missionaries'. The mission work is clearly seen as weakening traditional ways of life. It might be possible to detect behind this comment a genuine cross-cultural sensitivity to local customs. As Checkland points out, Bird the quasi-anthropologist is often seriously worried that the intrusion of the Christian missionary will inevitably destroy the mores of indigenous society.[19] Still, there is another aspect to the traveller's anxiety:

> Of course, the first object is to give a Christian training, and raise the standard of morality, which must be low enough if it is represented truthfully by a superior sort of girl, who told the teacher that to form connections with foreigners is the great ambition of girls in her position . . . To foreigners, a girl in some degree accustomed to our usages, and speaking a little English, is, in many cases, more attractive than one solely Japanese in her language and habits, and with misguided female ambition on the one side, and the habits which prevail in the East on the other, there is much reason to fear that results may occur which would be to none so painful as to the missionaries themselves. (1st edn, 2: 219–20)

The traveller is afraid that education conducted in mission schools might Westernise Japanese women to some extent, making them more attractive to Western men. The introduction of religious education and concomitant cultural changes could unwittingly blur cultural and racial boundaries. Cross-cultural interactions throw into question the notion of stable cultural identity. In this case, the very notion of a 'Christian ideal' is itself subtly problematised because it might unexpectedly enhance cross-racial relationships, thereby 'relativising' its own values. What has been regarded as the epitome of morality now fosters immorality. As if to face away from the unbearable complications of cross-cultural interactions, the popular edition cuts out almost all references to Christianity. While Bird's ability as a traveller to embrace alterity is certainly distinctive, the erasure in question seems to indicate that she is much less capable of conceptualising cultural changes in a positive manner.

Perhaps the act of writing about travel is itself an effort to redefine identity, which contact with the other destabilises to some extent. If this is the case, differences between the first and the popular editions of *Unbeaten Tracks in Japan* cast an interesting light upon the ways in which cultural boundaries are redrawn in the process of recounting travel.

6

Discourses of Difference: The Malaya of Isabella Bird, Emily Innes and Florence Caddy

Eddie Tay

Isabella Bird's *The Golden Chersonese and the Way Thither* (1883), Emily Innes' *The Chersonese with the Gilding Off* (1885) and Florence Caddy's *To Siam and Malaya in the Duke of Sutherland's Yacht 'Sans Peur'* (1889) are narratives written by three very different women who were in Malaya under varied circumstances. By the time Bird embarked on her five-week visit to Malaya in 1879, she was already the renowned author of *The Englishwoman in America* (1856) and *The Hawaiian Archipelago* (1875), while *Unbeaten Tracks in Japan* was to be published the following year. In contrast, the name 'Emily Innes' would most likely have faded into obscurity if she had not written her book. She was the wife of James Innes, a junior colonial official who lived in remote parts of Malaya from 1876 to 1882. Florence Caddy set out in 1888 for Siam and Malaya as a guest on the Duke of Sutherland's yacht. While the ostensible purpose of the Duke's journey was to recuperate from an illness, he had also been invited by Prince Devavongse of Siam to submit a bid for a railway construction project.[1]

The visits by Bird and Caddy to Malaya were part of an extended trip. Bird's journey included visits to Japan, Hong Kong, Canton, Saigon and Singapore. She was hosted by prominent colonial administrators of the day, and it was during her stay in Singapore that an invitation was extended to her to venture northward into the Malay Peninsula. Caddy's journey lasted four months and included stops in India, Singapore and Siam, returning via Malaya, Ceylon and Egypt. She was hosted by the Duke of Sutherland who was in turn hosted by Thai and Malay aristocrats in Siam and Malaya. In contrast to

Bird and Caddy, Emily Innes lived in isolation (and misery, according to her narrative) in Malaya for close to six years. As Susan Morgan puts it, within the hierarchy of British colonial administration, 'the wife of a junior government servant is the lowest position in the imperial hierarchy, her husband occupying the second lowest'.[2] A significant portion of Innes' *The Chersonese with the Gilding Off* is devoted to the plight of her husband, who was forced to resign from the colonial service for having refused to issue warrants for the arrest of runaway slaves and for having accused his immediate superior, William Bloomfield Douglas, of withholding income from the Sultan of Selangor. James Innes was denied a significant portion of his compensation:

> Everything was refused — the compensation for six years' service, the compensation for privilege leave, and the passage-money . . . As, however, the passage-money had been paid, the Government . . . did not ask for it back again.[3]

Thus, much of the way Malaya is represented in Innes' text is filtered through her and her husband's bitter experiences with the colonial administration.

In *Discourses of Difference*, Sara Mills makes the point that since imperialism is constituted by an investment in 'constructing *masculine* British identity', women who wrote about their travels to colonised regions 'were unable to adopt the imperialist voice with the ease with which male writers did' [italics in original].[4] If the imperialist voice belongs to a masculine subject, then it is not a tone or style a woman might be able or willing to strike. Given this, 'how was [colonialism] negotiated in texts by women who were conventionally seen not to be part of the colonial expansion?'[5] This chapter engages with this question in relation to the writings of Bird, Innes and Caddy on Malaya, exploring the extent to which their works conform to the idea that women's travel writings might be considered as constituting 'discourses of difference'. It also makes the point that, apart from gender, there are other internal distinctions to be made within the 'discourses of difference'. These include differences in terms of class, marital status and the particular circumstances that brought these women to Malaya.

Isabella Bird: The 'Worlding' of Malaya

Even though it was in 1826 that Malacca, Singapore and Penang formed a single administrative unit called the 'Straits Settlements', it was the signing of the Pangkor Engagement in 1874 which marked the formal beginning of

British expansion in the Malay Peninsula. The years following the signing of the treaty were fraught with hostilities between the British residents and the Malay rulers due to differing interpretations of the treaty. J. W. W. Birch, the first resident of Perak, was killed because he sought to implement a system of revenue collection along with the abolition of debt slavery through the 'public humiliation' of Malay chiefs — the homes of the unrelenting chiefs were set on fire and their followers were made to surrender their weapons.[6]

It was barely four years after Birch's death that Bird arrived in Malaya, and the incident is described in her book:

> The Pangkor Treaty was signed in January 1874. On November 2d, 1875, Mr. Birch, the British resident, who had arrived the evening before at the village of Passir Salah to post up orders and proclamations announcing that the whole kingdom of Pêrak was henceforth to be governed by English officers, was murdered as he was preparing for the bath.[7]

In 'The Rani of Sirmur', Gayatri Spivak employs the term 'worlding' to describe a process of transforming a physical terrain into colonised space.[8] The worlding of Malaya, enacted by Birch, legitimised by the signing of a treaty and implemented through posters and proclamations, is depicted in the above passage. The process is consolidated in Bird's narrative in terms of causes and effects: (1) the treaty was signed; (2) Birch was the legitimate representative of the imperial order; and (3) he was murdered while engaged in the vulnerable act of preparing for a bath. Yet what the passage elides is the fact that Birch was notorious for his ill-treatment of the Malays and his insensitivity to their laws and customs. Frank Swettenham was to describe Birch in a diplomatic manner as follows: 'Unfortunately, he did not speak Malay, or understand the customs and prejudices of the people, and to this cause more than any other his death must be attributed'.[9] Consistent with the colonialist intent in consolidating this worlding of Malaya, the possibility that Birch's murder was an instance of anti-colonial resistance is not explicitly raised, denying any political agency on the part of the Malays.

Clearly, Bird was reproducing the colonised world of Malaya for her readers back home. The narrative employs the familiar strategy of depicting pre-colonised land as a *tabula rasa* that awaits colonial intervention. The second sentence of the book makes the point that 'the Golden Chersonese is still somewhat of a *terra incognita*; there is no point on its mainland at which European steamers call' (1). 'In fact', Bird tells us, 'it is as little known to most people as it was to [herself] before [she] visited it' (1). Yet, to say that a place is little known to herself and others is not the same as to say, as she does, that the place 'has no legitimate claim to an ancient history' (1). Furthermore, the Golden Chersonese is certainly not *terra incognita* to its inhabitants, whom Bird describes as 'a race of semi-civilised and treacherous Mohammedans' (1). The implication here is that the claim to history, ancient or otherwise, has to be legitimised via recognition from the metropolitan centre. Malaya is thus mapped onto a world predicated upon a Eurocentric framework.

In her descriptions, Bird depicts Malaya as a resource, emphasising its pragmatic and economic value. '[T]he Straits Settlements', we are told, is 'prized as among the most valuable of our possessions in the Far East', and she points out that the import-export figures amount to more than 32 million pounds (3). Of the land, we are told that 'Iron ores are found everywhere, and are so little regarded for their metallic contents that, though containing, according to Mr. Logan, a skilful geologist, sixty per cent of pure metal, they are used in Singapore for macadamising the roads' (5). Even the subject of food caters for the European palate: 'At European tables in the settlements the red mullet, a highly-prized fish, the pomfret, considered more delicious than the turbot, and the tungeree, with cray-fish, crabs, prawns, and shrimps, are usually seen' (12).

The chief trait of Bird's text regarding the people of Malaya lies in its shifts in tone. At first, she suggests that the Malays are, like the British, the colonisers of Malaya: 'The Malays are not the Aborigines of this singular spit of land, and they are its colonists rather than its conquerors' (12). However, one page later, she asserts that this is only a point of conjecture: 'The conquest or colonisation of the Malay Peninsula by the Malays is not, however, properly speaking, [a] matter of history, and the origin of the Malay race and its early history are only matters of more or less reasonable hypothesis' (13). Another change in emphasis occurs in the following passage:

> The Malays undoubtedly must be numbered among civilised peoples. They live in houses which are more or less tasteful and secluded . . . they have possessed for centuries systems of government and codes of land and maritime laws which, in theory at least, show a considerable degree of enlightenment. (18)

However, four pages later, we are told that these civilised Malays 'have no knowledge of geography, architecture, painting, sculpture, or even mechanics' (22). These acts of writing and re-writing, of vision and re-vision, of assertions and qualifications in her portrayal of the Malays are a function of ambivalence; they are perhaps a function of fluctuations between moments of complicity and resistance in relation to colonial rule.

Yet Bird's narrative is certainly concerned with depicting the benevolence of British imperialism. This can be seen in the way she contrasts British imperialism with that of the Portuguese and the Dutch. Malacca in the sixteenth century was deployed by Portugal as a collection point for spices. This was after 1511, when Albuquerque led a military expedition which ended in its seizure after more than a month of fighting.[10] In her chapter on Malacca, Bird has this to say: 'My sober judgement is that Albuquerque and most of his Portuguese successors were little better than buccaneers' (150). Dutch presence in the region can be traced to the amalgamation of small trading companies into the Dutch East India Company in 1602.[11] Of the Dutch, Bird notes: 'If the Portuguese were little better than buccaneers, the Dutch who drove them out were little better than hucksters, — mean, mercenary traders, without redeeming qualities, content to suck the blood of their provinces and give nothing in return' (151).

These sweeping statements are in contrast to Bird's glowing portraits of British colonial administrators she met during her trip. In Singapore, she met Cecil Clement Smith, then colonial secretary of Singapore; in Malacca, she was hosted by Captain E. W. Shaw, the lieutenant-governor; in Sungei Ujong, she was met by the resident, Patrick James Murray; and in Penang, she had lunch with Hugh Low, the resident of Perak, W. E. Maxwell, the assistant resident and William Robinson, the governor of the Straits Settlements. Her descriptions of these colonial administrators reinforce the idea of the benevolence of British colonial rule. Of W. E. Maxwell, then assistant resident of Perak, Bird says:

> He is a man on whose word one may implicitly rely. Brought up among Malays, and speaking their language idiomatically, he not only likes them, but takes the trouble to understand them and enter into their ideas and feelings. He studies their literature, superstitions, and customs carefully, and has made some valuable notes upon them. I should think that few people understand the Malays better than he does . . . I have the very pleasant feeling regarding him that he is the right man in the right place, and that his work is useful, conscientious, and admirable. As Assistant Resident he is virtually dictator of Larut, only subject to Mr. Low's interference. He is a judge, and can inflict the penalty of death, the regent's signature, however, being required for the death-warrant. (285–6)

In this passage, though we are told that Maxwell is virtually a 'dictator' because of his position, he is not so in person. Rather, he is a friend to the Malays — he understands them, likes them, speaks their language and enters into their ideas and feelings. Even though he is able to inflict the 'penalty of death', his power to do so is checked as secondary authorisation is required. Even as the passage testifies to the power of a colonial administrator over the people of Malaya, it assures the readers that this power is restrained, firstly because of the administrator's respect for Malay culture, and secondly because of administrative checks put in place.

In the passage, the justification for British presence in Malaya is supplemented with affective qualities. The author confides to the reader her personal feelings for the man — she has 'the very pleasant feeling regarding him that he is the right man in the right place'. Morgan identifies this narrative move as the 'rhetoric of emotion', which 'blends feminine domestic with colonial ideology'.[12] She observes that in Bird's text, 'colonial administrators are judged . . . according to a British domestic ideology which values sympathy and tenderness over a more aggressive representation of manliness'.[13] Bird's depiction of Maxwell is congruent with liberal values in Victorian England whereby personal qualities such as benevolence and kindness were endorsed; at the same time, it is in keeping with the civilising mission of imperialism, whereby other cultures are brought into the ambit of civilisation, transformed not by force but by compassion.

One feature of *The Golden Chersonese and the Way Thither* which requires mention is that the journey as narrated begins not with Malaya, but with Hong Kong, Canton and Saigon. 'Why begin a book on British Malaya with chapters on Canton?', asks Morgan.[14] The answer, she writes, is so that the 'narrative order . . . reiterate[s] the British trade route', beginning with China and ending with her leaving for the Bay of Bengal, thus framing the chapters 'within their primary imperial meaning'.[15] Travelling along this trade route, Bird was to compare the different governments of Hong Kong, Canton and Saigon so as to bring to the forefront her argument about the benevolent nature of British colonialism, a theme elaborated in her chapters on Malaya.

After describing in detail the horrifying conditions of the Chinese prison in Canton, where the innocent and guilty alike are incarcerated and subjected to torture, Bird quotes the prisoners' words, giving the impression, with some irony perhaps, that Hong Kong under the British is governed by compassion:

> 'Would I were in your prison in Hongkong', and this was chorused by many voices saying, 'In your prison at Hongkong they have fish and vegetables, and more rice than they can eat, and baths, and beds to sleep on; good, good is the prison of your Queen!' (71)

Of Saigon, Bird exclaims with some indignation that it 'has the wild ambition to propose to itself to be a second Singapore!' (94). After describing several scenes of extreme poverty and inspecting an army barracks which she calls a 'sickly station', where forty per cent of the soldiers are receiving hospital treatment for diseases, Bird concludes that 'The French don't appear to be successful colonists' (103). The comparisons between the prison systems in Canton and Hong Kong, and between poverty-stricken Saigon and prospering Singapore, are designed to legitimise the claims of British imperialism. Again, the implicit point here is that this is guided not by economic interests, but by compassion.

The repeated emphasis of *The Golden Chersonese and the Way Thither* on the compassionate nature of British colonial rule in Malaya has to be seen in the light of the Indian 'Mutiny' of 1857. As Morgan puts it, in Malaya 'the very notion of the glory of the British Empire [could be salvaged], tarnished as it had been by recent events in India'.[16] Much of Bird's writings were based on her letters to her sister, Henrietta. In a letter to her publisher John Murray, Bird describes Henrietta as her 'best public, [her] home and fireside'.[17] If Henrietta was to Bird the embodiment of her domestic reading public, then one of the key issues for Bird in her representation of Malaya was to write of it in such a way as to assure her readers that it would not turn out to be another India. It has to be said that a section regarding William Bloomfield Douglas, the resident of Selangor, was excised from the final version of the book. In a letter to Murray, Bird indicated that she planned to include the section; she wanted confirmation from Murray that Douglas had indeed resigned from the colonial service to avoid an inquiry on charges of corruption. As Bird puts it, this would validate her descriptions of him as presiding over 'a rule of fraud, hypocrisy, and violence'; at the same time, as Kay Chubbuck points out, it would also protect Bird from being accused of libel.[18] In the end, Bird decided to exclude the section, despite having received confirmation that Douglas had indeed resigned. The reason given was that she was abiding by the proverb 'Never kick a man when he's down'.[19] One may suggest another reason for excluding the section on Douglas — that it would undermine her portrayal of the compassionate nature of British colonial rule in Malaya.

Emily Innes: Colonialism and Its Discontents

In *The Chersonese with the Gilding Off*, Emily Innes has this to say of Bird:

> Miss Bird was a celebrated person, and wherever she went was well introduced to the highest officials in the land; Government vessels were placed at her disposal, and Government officers did their best to make themselves

agreeable, knowing that she wielded in her right hand a little instrument that might chastise or reward them as they deserved of her. (II: 242–3)

We could certainly forgive Innes her touch of jealousy. Unlike Bird, whose visit lasted five weeks, Innes was in Malaya for close to six years. She accompanied her husband, James Innes, who was sent to Kuala Langat to take up the post of collector of revenue and magistrate. In *The Chersonese with the Gilding Off*, she wrote of the difficulties of living in isolation. A dilapidated building served as office, courthouse and living quarters. The only steam launch belonging to the Selangor government was not at their disposal. When her husband took the rowing boat on inspection trips to tin-mines and fishing villages, Innes was left to herself for days without any means of contact with the outside world.

Like Bird's text, that of Innes displays a certain measure of ambivalence in its depictions of the natives of Malaya. At times, certain passages come close to paranoia and constitute instances of colonialist prejudice at its worst:

> The women who go out as ayahs [servants] in Malaya are the most degraded in the land. They are ready to steal, lie, drink, poison their master and mistress, or join in a plot for murdering them at any moment. (I: 24)

At other times, the text takes pains to vouch for the nobility of the Malay character:

> It seems to be the general impression in England that the Malay nature is 'treacherous, bloodthirsty, and cruel'; but I am so far from having found it so ... [the] country was far more peaceful than England, and life and property were more secure in it than in London ... and I know no 'civilized' country where it would be possible to leave your house perfectly open night and day for years as we did, without any serious loss of property. (I: 41–2)

As can be seen, the text moves between racist and empathetic portrayals of the local populace, between repulsion and acceptance, loathing and approval. On the one hand, native women servants are depicted as deceitful, dangerous and cunning; on the other, as in the passage above, the racist image of the Malays as being "'treacherous, bloodthirsty, and cruel'" is being challenged.

A large portion of Innes' text presents the author as a central character, laying bare her thoughts and reactions to her surroundings. While in a village shop, Innes is confronted with a crowd anxious to catch its first glimpse of a European lady. In response to this, she writes:

> It was no doubt flattering to find one's self looked on as the dove and olive-branch were on their return to the ark — a token that the troubled waters were abated; but I think if the original dove had been mobbed at the ark window by as motley and unpleasant a crowd of animals as the population of Klang, she would have flown away again very fast. (I: 8–9)

Here, her regard for the local populace is made clear. The affective quality that stands out is repulsion. There is an insistence on the differentiation of the self from the natives: the local population is to Innes what a 'motley and unpleasant . . . crowd of animals' is to a dove, a symbol of innocence and purity. This depiction of the crowd as a threat, as an undifferentiated mass of Chinese, Indians and Malays threatening to invade her innocent and vulnerable personal space, is metonymic of her encounters with the local populace.

The Chersonese with the Gilding Off is certainly a gendered text in the sense that it replicates the Victorian roles of the woman as inhabiting the space of domestic economy circumscribed within the harsh landscape of Malaya. We are told that Langat is no place for a woman:

> [Langat] is nothing but a mud-swamp . . . the house is an attap (palm-leaf) one, with no bath-room attached to it, the bathing-place being at some distance; there is no garden, not a tree, no flowers, scarcely even any grass . . . and no society. The mere landing is an acrobatic feat, and the isolation is such that it would be sheer imprisonment to any Englishwoman . . . remember, there is no European within a day's journey, man nor woman. (I: 3–4)

The landscape is presented as a colonial frontier, harsh and devoid of natural beauty. The relative isolation from a European community, the lack of an attached bathroom and the fact that the house is made of attap would offer no security to a woman.

In her book, Innes writes of her considerable efforts to maintain a Victorian home in such an environment. She writes of saving eighty pounds a year by obtaining groceries from England instead of from Singapore (II: 25). She laments the difficulties of obtaining fresh food and supplies. At one point, an order for condensed milk and biscuits resulted in a delivery of milk biscuits (II: 32). She writes of having to prepare a meal for ten persons: she 'arranged as fine a banquet as the combined resources of Singapore and Langat could be made to yield', only to be told at the last minute that the party was not coming (II: 35).

Given Innes' geographical isolation and the problems it entails, it is no surprise that she describes her plight with resentment. In a discussion with Hugh Low, then resident of Perak, regarding her husband's refusal to issue warrants for the arrest of runaway slaves in his capacity as magistrate, Low, in an unguarded moment, remarked that since all married women are slaves, Emily is a slave herself (II: 139). 'Just so', Innes retorted, 'That is precisely why I can sympathize with other slaves' (II: 139). It may seem that Innes, as a woman subjected to Victorian gender conventions, is at this point expressing sympathy for colonised subjects in Malaya. However, the fact that the book ends with a call for the annexation of the protected Malay States contradicts such a reading:

> I wish to point out that almost all the miseries from which we suffered in the Far East were a consequence, directly or indirectly, of the system of 'Protection.' Had the Malay Native States been annexed, how different would have been our position! . . . [T]he solitude and isolation which formed one of our greatest trials would have been modified, if not done away with altogether. (vol. II, pp. 245–6)

That annexation is called for to protect junior colonial officials (and their wives) from being oppressed by their superiors indicates that Innes' experience of Malaya and her views on its people is shaped by her resentment against the colonial administration, an administration which had relegated her to being the wife of a minor official sent to an obscure outpost of the empire. Thus, Innes' call for annexation is motivated not by empathy with the colonised subjects, but by her envy of the positions of senior officers. Innes' narrative does not question the basic tenets of colonialism. Rather, it draws attention to inequalities that exist among officers in the colonial administration.

What would happen to the Malays after annexation? 'Whether Annexation would be good for the Malays is another question', Innes concludes (II: 248). The final sentence of the book implies underlying doubt about the benevolence of British rule, as well as concern for the Malays' aptitude for independence and modernity. Referring to what is for her the archetypal Malay, Innes remarks that 'he cannot move with the times; and unless he moves out of the way . . . he will certainly be crushed beneath the wheels of the car of progress' (II: 250).

Florence Caddy: 'High Life in Asia'

If Innes was jealous of the attentions afforded to Bird by senior colonial administrators, she would have been bitter to have known of Florence Caddy's associations with the British aristocracy and the way she had been hosted by members of Thai and Malay aristocracies during her trip. Caddy embarked on her journey to Siam and Malaya in 1888 as a guest on the Duke of Sutherland's yacht. By that time, she was already the author of two novels, two books on how to manage a household and two biographies.[20] While writing her biographies, Caddy had covered the routes traversed by her subjects, Linnaeus and Joan of Arc, and thus she was already an accomplished traveller and writer.[21]

In *To Siam and Malaya in The Duke of Sutherland's Yacht 'Sans Peur'*, Caddy compares her work to that of Bird and Innes, making explicit reference to Bird's title in declaring that she has 'shown . . . in how much comfort it is possible sometimes to leave the beaten tracks of travel':

> We had read the 'Golden Chersonese' by Miss Bird, and heard of the 'Chersonese with the Gilding off,' by a resident in Singapore . . . but we found we must lay more gilding on, and deck our tale with jewels.[22]

Caddy wasted no opportunity in narrating the material ease and comfort of her travels. (One of the chapters in her book is entitled 'High Life in Asia'.) The yacht she sailed in is described as a luxurious vessel:

> The deck-house is lined with sofas; it has doors on each side and windows nearly all round, so that one can see the views while sitting at work or with a book. Above the wide, easy staircase that leads down to the saloon a folding table is spread, large enough to dine eight people, or a dozen at a pinch; the servants stand at the head of the staircase to wait, and the table does not impede their use of this short cut to the pantry, while the dishes are brought hot from the galley to the doors. (3)

'We have no privations on board the *Sans Peur*', writes Caddy (4). Indeed, the spaciousness of the yacht allows for the distinguishing of different spaces for pleasure and utility. From the pantry to the galley, from the head of the staircase to the staircase itself, these spaces are marked by differences of class, status and privilege.

'We always speak of the yacht as home', writes Caddy, and this English domestic space outside of England is to be defended against possible intruders (18). Just as the ordering of space within the yacht distinguishes nobility from their servants, that between inside and outside distinguishes the civilised from those construed as the barbaric other. While the yacht changes its location from place to place, these oppositions remain rigid and immobile. The array of weapons on board, including boarding-pikes, pistols, personal revolvers and a rifle serve to provide security for both passengers and crew. As the crew assures her, they are there 'in case the savages come . . . In case those heathens think there is anything worth taking in a vessel of this sort, we'll give them a warm reception' (6).

Such spatial ordering, distinguishing, on the one hand, between nobility and servants and, on the other, between English domestic space and the world beyond, is metonymic of the text's imbrication with the economic dimensions of colonialism. As Caddy points out, one of the reasons for the trip is that the Duke is interested to see 'if the application of English capital can benefit a colony or further British influence abroad . . . This is a thing that the workers cannot do for themselves. It requires leisure and capital' (77). The colonised subject is regarded as human labour just as colonies are regarded as sources of raw material. At one point in the narrative, Caddy remarks on the lush greenery and the easy availability of natural resources, lamenting, however, that because of the tropical climate, 'we [the British] . . . cannot dig, but only direct the digging' (p. 279).

The narrative makes a distinction between the ruling- and working-classes of the Malays as well. Referring to those of the working-class, Caddy laments that they refuse to work (279). In contrast, those of the ruling-class are mentioned in a positive light. They are regarded as enlightened for being willing middlemen for the British, amenable to the capitalist interests of the colonial regime:

> Sultan Abubeker is opening up the country energetically. He has attracted a multitude of Javanese, Chinese, and other settlers here; he has made Johore Baru a free port, with only small dues, and gives a free grant of land to settlers. He makes good roads, and villages spring up beside them as if by magic. By these and other enlightened measures the Sultan is yearly increasing his influence and his income. Instead of being crushed by the prosperity of Singapore, he is using the Lion City as a market, or rather a central depôt for the distribution of his native productions. (248)

If Caddy's admiration for the Sultan of Johore is undisguised, it is because he shares the same vision of Malaya as her, in that the Chinese, along with the Javanese and other settlers, are the workers of the land, transforming and excavating it for raw material. It is the Chinese that are singled out by Caddy as ideal workers:

> Sultan Abubeker encourages the industrious Chinese; he says he finds them valuable as original settlers, as they are indefatigable labourers, clearing the jungle, cultivating the ground, and turning everything to account: then, as he sees openings, — and he is always looking for them, — he can set up

companies for working mills, mines, &c., with Chinese labour under European direction. (265–6)

For Caddy, what is admirable about the working-class Chinese is that, in contrast to their Malay counterparts, they are willing workers for British capital. They may be regarded as diligent workers who will further the commercial interests of the British. In Singapore, Caddy is fascinated by the spectacle of Chinese industry:

> This China town swarms like an ant-hill with the yellow race, who appear industrious to the last degree. Chinamen here are always carrying loads in their pairs of baskets, or pails, slung on a bamboo across the shoulders. Exception: when not busily carrying about something, they are being shaved. There are plenty of jinrickshas, or 'rickshas' as they call them here . . . these are all drawn by Chinamen, some of them extremely fine men, often admirable models for a worker in bronze. (pp. 80–1)

In the above excerpt, the Chinese are first depicted as a mass of undifferentiated bodies at work, carrying loads, bearing bamboo poles and pulling rickshaws. Their bodies are scrutinised as if to distil from them the quality of physical strength, a quality objectified as 'bronze' metal. When her gaze rests on individual men, they are idealised as model workers.

As in the case of Bird's text, where comparisons are made between Canton, Hong Kong and Saigon to extol the benefits of British influence, Caddy's text makes comparisons between the peoples of Malaya and Siam. The private secretary to the Sultan of Johore finds favour in Caddy's eyes because he displays outward signs of British influence: '[He is] a highly intelligent young man in European dress, . . . speaking English fluently' (233). In contrast, she writes that 'It seems a grievous pity after the young Siamese have been educated in England to plunge them back into the semi-barbarism of the native habits' (126). At one point, Caddy goes so far as to remark that 'In Siam civilization is potential; in Johore it is at work' (254). As mentioned earlier, the reason for the Duke's trip to Siam was to bid for a railway construction project. As it turned out, the contract was in the end awarded to Sir Andrew Clarke, the governor of the Straits Settlements.[23] As Gullick suggests, it may be that the Duke's presence was meant to speed up the negotiations with Clarke.[24] So we may surmise that Caddy is displaying a measure of loyalty here to the Duke.

'A yacht', writes Caddy, 'is something like the magic carpet of the Arabian Nights, that can transport its owner where he wishes, or, better still, like Hans Andersen's "Flying Trunk," for you pack up and get into it, and it carries you where you wish' (1). Caddy's narrative projects and superimposes the multiple discourses of class, capitalism and colonialism onto Malaya. Her 'magic carpet' allows her to see precisely what she wishes to see — a land where British capitalists, aided by enterprising Malay middlemen and diligent Chinese workers, are involved in the work of harnessing raw material to be exported to Britain.

Taken together, the three accounts of British presence in Malaya demonstrate the variety of ways in which colonialism is articulated by women writers who were in Malaya between 1879 and 1888. What is striking about Caddy's portrayals of Malaya is that the economic basis of colonialism is laid bare. Whereas Bird writes of colonialism as a benevolent endeavour on the part of the British administrators, Innes draws attention to the inequalities that exist among administrators of different ranks. It has been said that travel allowed Victorian women to secure public positions as writers 'with experience enough to write about the wider world'.[25] However, their public positions as writers were secured because their narratives conform to a domestic ideology that sustained the imperial nation; at many points in their journeys, these women writers had never truly left home.

7

China of the Tourists: Women and the Grand Tour of the Middle Kingdom, 1878–1923

Julia Kuehn

> But whence are you, and whither do you make return?
> Over the mountain passes; through the Great Wall; to Kalgan — and beyond, whither? . . .
>
> Eunice Tietjens, *Profiles from China* (1919)[1]

This chapter looks at women travellers in China between the late 1870s and the early 1920s. Beginning with the two earliest, and probably most famous, journeys of Victorian women in the Middle Kingdom — those of Isabella Bird and Constance Cumming — the essay poses the question of whether their journeys served as more prescriptive itineraries for later women travellers and, in fact, established the frameworks of what we could call a Grand Tour of China.

The chapter focuses on female travellers of both British and American nationality. Given that the period under investigation is characterised by an increased assertion of women's rights in the West, the focus on women and their desire to express independence and learn more about otherness is especially pertinent. Even if these contacts with alterity happened in a highly mediated and often compromised form, it would still, in many cases, help these travellers to (re-)assess their own position and identity as Western women. Most important, however, the choice of texts by women results from the basic fact that it was mainly women, and not men, travellers who, in this forty-year period around the turn of the nineteenth century, wrote China travel and guide books. A look at Chadwyck-Healey's bibliography of 'Nineteenth-Century Books on China'[2] reveals that, of the 733 books on China published in the (long) nineteenth century, only about ten percent (categorised as 'Geography', as they map and describe the country) were travelogues, and these also include the works of Bird and Cumming. The large bulk of works on China is by (British) men and about 'Politics and government', 'Economics and commerce', 'Anthropology and sociology', 'History of China', 'Religion and philosophy', and 'Literature and the Arts'. All in all, there are fewer than twenty women writers mentioned in the bibliography, but it is particularly noteworthy that their (travel) writings emerge chiefly from around 1880 when their male counterparts focused visibly on socio-political and economic questions concerning China. Representative titles by male authors at the turn of the century include *The Chinese, Their Present and Future: Medical, Political, and Social* (1891), *China in Transformation* (1898), *China and the Present Crisis* (1900), *China and the Allies* (1901), *China in Convulsion* (1901), *The Awakening of China* (1907), *The Coming China* (1911) and *China Revolutionized* (1913).[3] As such, the travelogues by women from these years are important and exceptional, and arguably preserve an older tradition of a genre in which men specialised in writing political, historical or economic accounts of a country.

The shift from nineteenth-century British women to primarily American women travellers in the twentieth century requires a more detailed historical positioning. Women writers continued with the travel writing tradition, but Colin Mackerras suggests in *Western Images of China* that America replaced Britain as the central Western image-formulator for China in the early twentieth century.[4] If the imperialist British view of the Middle Kingdom was largely built on economic and political interests which necessitated an image of China as backward and in need of external governance, twentieth-century American views of China were, arguably, more positive, if no less ideological. The end of the Qing dynasty and the 1911 Revolution were consistent with America's belief that China was finally moving in a direction suitable to Western political, economic and social interests, and Americans wished to encourage this trend by furthering relations and knowledge between the two countries. From the late 1920s, the American journalists Edgar Snow, Anna Louise Strong and Agnes Smedley would — in support of the Communist creed — report on the country's political changes to a Western audience. At the same time, Chinese intellectuals such as the writer Lin Yutang and opinion-maker Madame Chiang Kai-shek went to the United States and addressed the American people, also trying to further Sino-American relations. Even Pearl Buck's hugely popular novels, starting with *East Wind, West Wind* (1930) and *The Good Earth* (1931), helped create a more favourable image of China in modern Western societies, and travelling to the Middle Kingdom was certainly not discouraged as the proliferation of American travelogues by women in these early decades of the twentieth century suggests. Ellen LaMotte, in her travel memoir, summarises the twentieth-century shift in American people's attitude towards China, even if she criticises its frequently uninformed nature: 'Like most Americans', she addresses her imagined reader in the Preface to *Peking Dust* (1919), 'you have a lurking sentimental feeling about China, a latent sympathy and interest based on colossal ignorance'.[5]

The number of British and American travelogues by women in the four decades around the turn of the twentieth century indicates a desire to impart and import knowledge about China's otherness. A first generation of British women travellers, including most prominently Isabella Bird Bishop (1831–1904), Constance Frederika Gordon Cumming (1837–1924) and Mrs Archibald [i.e. Alicia] Little (1845–1926), took the travel opportunities available to them through the existence of a British stronghold in China to explore the country and venture into areas hitherto unfamiliar to Westerners. The travel books these pioneers wrote, particularly Bird's *The Yangtze Valley and Beyond* (1899) and Cumming's *Wanderings in China* (1888), became models for the next generation of women travellers and travel accounts of China,[6] and a comparison of these with the later texts can help answer the question of whether a Grand Tour of China was hereby established. The second generation of female travellers who might have been influenced by this prescribed 'tour' includes the Australian travel writer and novelist Mary Gaunt (1861–1942), the professional American traveller and photographer Eliza Ruhamah Scidmore (1856–1928), the Wellesley professor Elizabeth Kendall (1865–1952), the American travel writer and women's rights activist Grace Seton (1872–1959), the American hospital nurse Ellen LaMotte (1873–1961), the American librarian Elizabeth Enders, and the American poet and journalist Eunice Tietjens (1884–1944).

Arguably, the beginning of this second phase of travelling and the emergence of a Grand Tour of China, which maps out places to visit and activities to undertake, lies in Scidmore's popular tour guide *Westward to the Far East: A Guide to the Principal Cities of China and Japan* (1892), which went through at least five editions up to 1900.[7] This booklet marks a shift of emphasis from independent, self-directed travel to and in China —exemplified by the women pioneers — to a more systematised and prescriptive travel itinerary as part of a Chinese Grand Tour. Arguably, we might also want to see this tour guide, which stands in the tradition of a Murray or a Baedecker guidebook, as marking the advent of tourism in China. The essay first traces Bird's and Cumming's travel routes, then introduces Scidmore's travel guide and finally moves into a discussion of how the second generation of female travellers describes the most prominent travel destination on their Grand Tour of China — the capital Beijing[8] — between 1900 and 1924.

British Women Travellers in China

With a few exceptions, it is hard to determine the exact routes of nineteenth-century travellers. Although their travelogues often provide sketches of places they have been to and thumbnail descriptions of the people they meet, a precise route description in the form of a travel journal is frequently missing. In contrast, Bird's and Cumming's very detailed descriptions and inclusion of maps enable the reader to retrace their steps faithfully and recreate their travel itineraries. Between them, these two Victorian women covered a lot of Chinese ground. On her second China trip, Bird crossed the entire country from Shanghai to Tibet and travelled on foot through large parts of Sichuan, while Cumming journeyed along the entire coastline from Hong Kong to Tianjin (Tientsin), and then to Beijing, stopping at almost every large settlement.

A depressed invalid at home, and suffering from spinal prostration after the removal of a tumour, Bird left all physiological impediments behind when travelling, and turned into a 'Samson abroad', as the *Edinburgh Medical Journal* put it.[9] She first came to China on her way from Yokohama in December 1878, stopping briefly in Hong Kong and Canton (Guangzhou) before continuing her journey to Malaya, as related in her *Golden Chersonese and the Way Thither* (1883).[10] Returning to China more than a decade later — at the age of sixty-three and after various trips to North America, Hawaii, Japan, Korea, Malaya, Persia, Kurdistan and Tibet — Bird found herself caught in the opening salvos of the Sino-Japanese War of 1894–95. After a few restless months in Shanghai, Yantai (Cheefoo) and Tianjin, she recklessly decided to travel to Mukden in Manchuria (Shenyang) to see how far the Japanese had advanced.[11] Her most extensive journey through China, however, was up the Yangzi River from Shanghai to Sichuan. She first spent seventeen days on a steamer to Wanxian, then travelled nine hundred miles by chair into Sichuan province and northwest to within range of Tibet, eastward again via Chengdu, Shuifu (Sifu) and Chongqing, and then returned the two thousand miles downstream back to Shanghai.[12]

The hardships undertaken and the dangers overcome included, in Bird's case, almost freezing to death in the snow-peaks of Batang and being attacked by a mob just outside Lo-Kia Chan, two days from Kuan, when a large stone aimed at the back of her head left her unconscious.[13] She only recovered from this blow, Bird writes, after a month. Her descriptions of these dangers and discomforts — including staying in Chinese inns adjacent to, above or in a pigsty, or being carried through Sichuan for several weeks in an open wicker chair fixed in the most elementary way to two long poles — are matter-of-fact. Eliza Scidmore, the American travel writer, reviewed Bird's *The Yangtze Valley and Beyond* in *The National Geographic Magazine*, and remarked that, according to some people's taste, Bird's descriptions were in fact 'all *too* clear and realistic', leaving little room for the imagination of a Chinese romance.[14] On her journey, Bird never questioned her right to explore China and penetrate into the furthest corners of the Middle Kingdom. For example, arriving at the last government post in Sichuan, Chinese officials tried to stop her from going further west where, they warned her, warring barbarians might pose a danger.[15] Their advice seems well meant and the result of a genuine desire to protect the elderly British woman for whose 'safety and comfort' they feared, given the perilous paths ahead, the uncertain weather conditions and the scarcity of food.[16] Bird, however, considered this 'meddling' an unwelcome obstacle towards her goal and she resolutely walked through the city gates of Li-fan, Sichuan, even passing an equestrian guard sent to obstruct her passage.[17]

Miss Constance Cumming was Bird's rival in travelling in remote places, but had, in contrast, an aristocratic background and connections, which greatly facilitated travelling for her and set a different agenda: rather than Bird's pursuit of exploration and adventure, Cumming sought entertainment, comfort and, to a degree, relaxation when abroad. Arguably, she marks a transition from travel to tourism in China, as will be further elaborated. Born into a wealthy Scottish family, Cumming travelled from an early age. On Christmas Eve 1878, the same time that Bird first arrived in Hong Kong, Cumming landed in Shanghai. However, she fled the city immediately because of its cold drizzle and boarded the next ship to Hong Kong, where the two rivals would not acknowledge each other's presence. The sisterly spirit that many later female travellers displayed — recognising each other's work and travels — did not motivate these two pioneers. The escape from rainy Shanghai is typical of Cumming's way of moving about. A creature of comfort, with the necessary wealth, connections and need for entertainment, she was less inclined to undergo hardships on her travels than Bird — even if, overall, Cumming's journey would probably look very comfortless to our modern eyes. With Cumming, we encounter what we can call the first sightseer in China, who turns distant places into tourist sites, even if she is still travelling by herself and not in groups as would the guests on Cook's European tours. Always accompanied by well-placed Western hosts and guides from the colonial world of China — which she prefers by far to the 'native' life — Cumming journeys rather hassle-free by ship along the coast from Hong Kong via Shantou (Swatow), Xiamen,

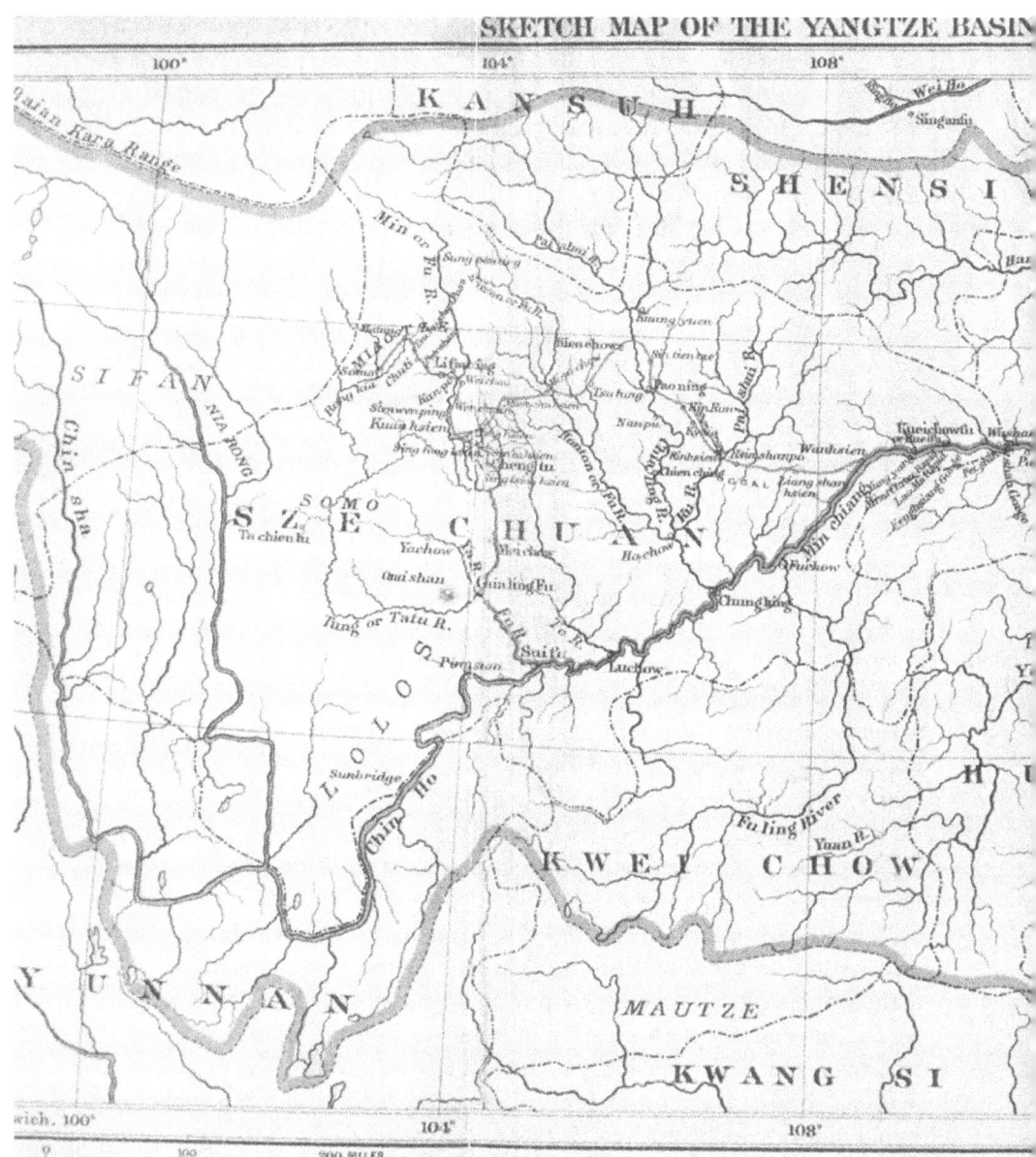

Figure 7.1 'Sketch Map of the Yangtze Basin Showing Mrs Bishop's Route'. In Isabella Bird, *Collected Travel Writings of Isabella Bird*. Vol. 11: The Yangtze Valley and Beyond: An Account of Journeys in China, Chiefly in the Province of Sze Chuan and among the Man-Tze of the Somo Territory. Bristol: Ganesha Publishing, 1997.

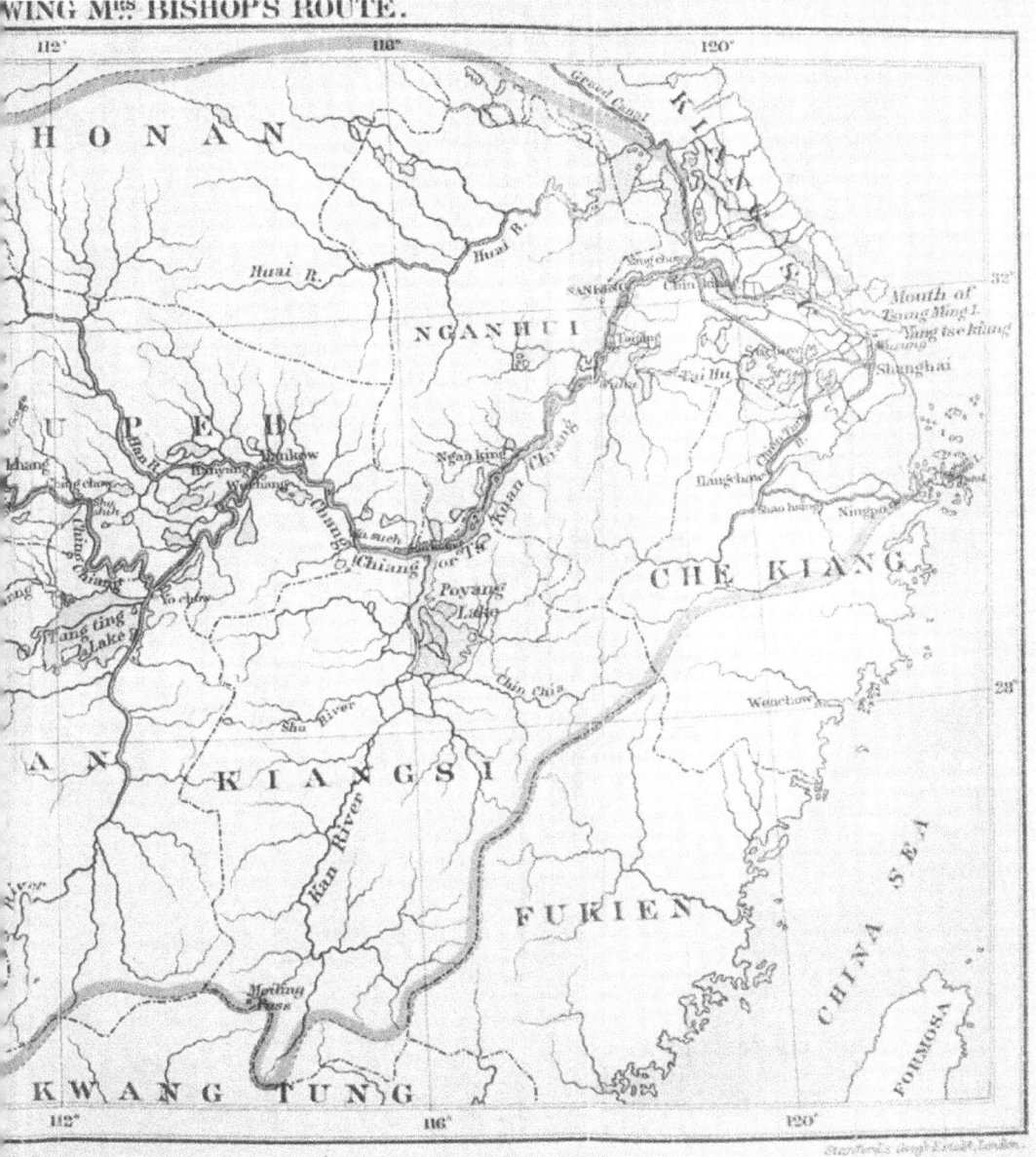

Fuzhou and Ningbo to Shanghai, Yantai, Tianjin and Tung Chou. It is only on the last leg of her journey, on the imperial highway from Tung Chou to Beijing, that Cumming travels uncomfortably like her rival Bird and endures the ride in a horse-drawn Peking cart, which represents the opposite of all the luxury usually appreciated. It is also only on these final moments of the journey that Cumming travels by herself, which may also be the reason for her initially unenthusiastic view of Beijing where she, all of a sudden, has to confront the Chinese locals she has successfully avoided until then, as other people previously dealt with the necessary Chinese servants, cooks and maids for her. Only when she is met by expatriate friends is Cumming in her element again.

A map of Bird's and Cumming's routes may give an idea of the sites and places these pioneers found worth visiting — the dotted lines signifying sea routes, the uninterrupted lines land routes.

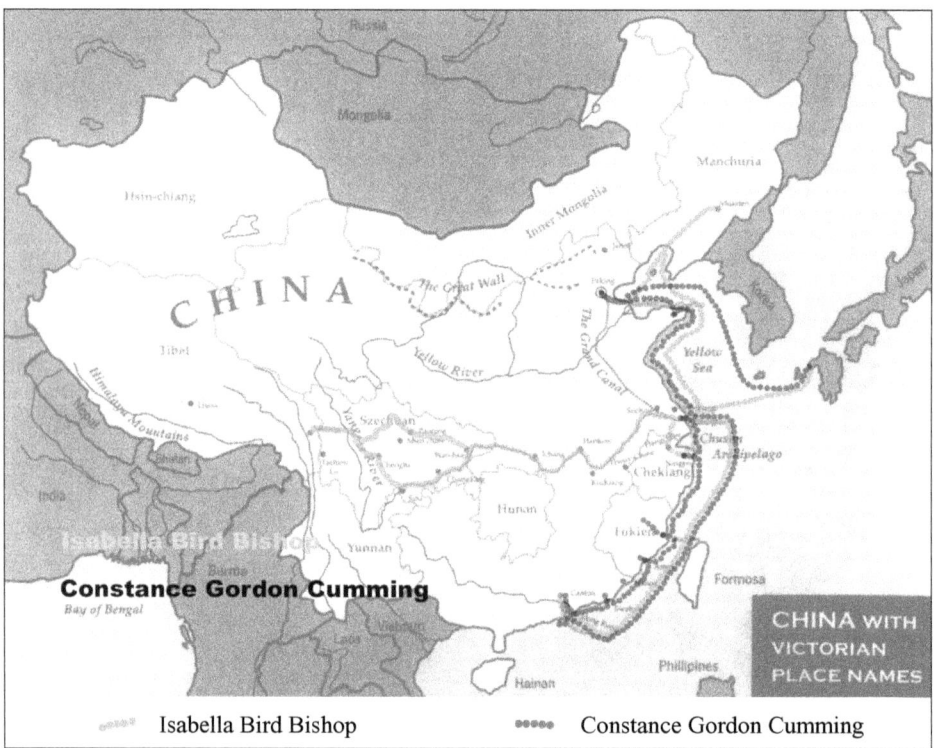

Figure 7.2 'Isabella Bird Bishop's and Constance Gordon Cumming's Travel Routes'. Map with Victorian Place names adapted from Susan Thurin, *Victorian Travelers and the Opening of China, 1842–1907*. Athens, OH: Ohio University Press, 1997. Reprinted with permission of the author.

We need to stay with Cumming a little bit longer, as her travel route — rather than Bird's — and her wants as a tourist are important for the emergence of the next batch of American visitors. Cumming's description of Ningbo in April 1879 is characteristic of her upper-class pursuit of comfort, amusement and tourist activities. Upon arrival, Cumming immediately directs her steps to the local English church mission run by Bishop Russell, her host. Her appreciation of the cleanliness of the mission school and the native children stands in stark contrast to her comments about the filth and dust of China outside the 'civilising' influences of the Western powers.[18] Despite her faith in the colonial mission and the superiority of the British, Cumming *does* appreciate Chinese life and culture in a very peculiar manner. For example, she praises the appealing nature of the local women's hairdos, is fascinated by the Buddhist temples and admires the wild azaleas, which display all the colours of the rainbow and are particularly pleasing to her eye.[19] However, most significantly, Ningbo is a shopping paradise for this aristocrat. In a gesture typical of the Grand Tour, where the traveller, after becoming familiar with the other culture and its art, seeks out select artefacts and collector's items to take back to Britain, Cumming, too, spends much of her time appreciating local handicraft and buying individual pieces. This acquisition of souvenirs epitomises the rather slight degree and the nature of contact this British woman has with Chinese culture and the Chinese people, which seems to be largely geared towards appropriation and commodification. It is as if, for Cumming, the buying of goods substitutes for a more intimate encounter with China itself. Visiting a neighbouring lake in the Ningbo area, Cumming and her female companion, a sister working in Bishop Russell's mission, are invited by local women to have tea. Cumming hastily refuses this invitation to receive an insight into native life. She seems almost glad that her friend is at the same time being accused by a gathering crowd of being a 'child-stealer'[20] — a common insult directed at missionaries who, according to the Chinese, took away their babies by converting them. When children start to throw stones at the two British women, they flee. The incident not only indicates Cumming's prevalent belief in the West's responsibility for civilising China, but also gives her an excuse not to mingle with the locals. Cumming's view of China is mediated mainly through the eyes of Western expatriates, and clearly she does not share Bird's aims to be an explorer and adventurer. In contrast, she is satisfied merely to touch the surface of the country and its culture by visiting select, mostly pleasing, sights and purchasing souvenirs.

Travel Itineraries, or Eliza Scidmore's 'China Guidebook'

Scidmore's seven visits to China between 1885 and 1900 resulted in a mere fifty-page guidebook *Westward to the Far East*, a number of articles in the *Century Magazine* and her major work, *China: The Long-Lived Empire* (1900).[21] It is the second part of Scidmore's *Westward to the Far East*, the travel guide to the main sites of China consisting of barely ten pages, which is the focal point of this section. After the description of her journeying in Japan, the American arrives in Shanghai. Written partly as an autobiographical travel memoir but primarily as a guidebook for future travellers, *Westward* not only recommends certain travel itineraries and comments on various places, but also communicates other useful knowledge. The information includes phrases for travel abroad (both in Chinese and Japanese), a list of the principal agencies for steamship travel in and between Japan and China, and a climate chart and table of distances for Japan. A list of further reading, the layouts of the three main steamers that operated between Japan and China (all owned by the Canadian Pacific Railway Company which also sponsored the printing of the book), and a log record — to be filled in at the traveller's leisure — complete the guidebook.

The traveller who arrives in Shanghai, explains Scidmore, is confronted by two possibilities. First, she can (after a short detour down the Yangzi river to Hangzhou and back to Shanghai) go south by ship to Hong Kong, stopping at will in Ningbo, Wenzhou, Fuzhou, Xiamen (Amoy) and Shantou (Swatow).[22] This southern coastal route follows Cumming's earlier coastal China trip to the letter — even if it takes the other direction and leaves out the detour trip up the Min River from Fuzhou — and suggests that the above-mentioned places on the coastline are 'must-see' places for the visitor, constituting prime sights on this Grand Tour of China.

The second route from Shanghai takes the traveller north. She can take another steamer upriver to Yantai (Che Foo), and from there further continue her journey to Tianjin and then by land route to Beijing. Again, this recommended tour up the coast is one that Cumming, and up to a point Bird, undertook in 1879 and 1894 respectively. Bird's journey to these coastal places was only a restless prelude to her main trip down the Yangzi river, and Beijing was an important omission (for unknown reasons), but nevertheless Cumming's and Scidmore's routes are identical, further supporting the case for the emergence of something like a Grand Tour itinerary. Scidmore's guidebook entry for Beijing should therefore be read alongside Cumming's description, complemented by Scidmore's 1900 description of the capital in her more detailed *China: The Long-Lived Empire*.

After her solitary trip to Beijing, Cumming's 1879 view of the capital is, again, through tourist eyes. Her acquaintances take her to see many local sights in addition to the British and American legations and the London Mission Hospital. These include the four walled cities, the Imperial City, the Temple of Heaven, the Temple of Agriculture, the Great Lama Temple, the Temple of Confucius, the Hall of Classics, the Examination Hall and the Summer Palace. Dragged along by her host, Dr. Edkins, who probably assumes more interest in the traveller than Cumming feels herself for Beijing, the scene in which the lady visits the Examination Hall may suffice to give an idea of her detailed, yet derisive, descriptions:

> Anything more dreary and dilapidated than this great theatre of national learning, could not be imagined. At its best it seems specially designed for discomfort, but as the examinations are only held here triennially, the place is allowed between whiles to fall into utter decay, and a fine crop of nettles, coarse weeds, and broken pottery gives the crowning touches of dreariness to the whole place.[23]

Cumming is aware of the importance of this Examination Hall in producing Tsin-tze, or 'advanced scholars', and future government officials; and she also knows that students must take three sets of tests for this particular examination (each lasting three days and three nights), together with thousands of other students, and live within the Hall complex during the examination. However, her language is utterly scathing. Like many of her contemporaries, she considers the old examination system outdated, when it is generally felt that China needs to modernise. Condemning the examination procedures — reciting 'fossilised' Chinese Confucian classics and the history of China, composing a poem and displaying a neat handwriting[24] — Cumming's portrayal of the site overall stresses its decay, inefficiency and inhumanity. Candidates stay in 'cells', are refused privacy or communication with other candidates and are held like 'prisoners' in abodes that resemble 'pigsties'.[25] If candidates die under the strenuous conditions, a hole is, according to Cumming, 'broken into the outer wall of the enclosure, and the corpse is thrust out, for a stringent regulation prohibits opening the gate while the men are in their cells, and traditional custom must be maintained in the presence of Death himself'.[26] Such dreary, morbid sightseeing under the conditions of heat, dust and noise is 'quite bewildering', writes Cumming, and the uncomfortable transport to and within Beijing is, to her, worsened by the deplorable lack of comfort in the form of decent accommodation.[27] In the capital, she writes, 'travellers are yet so scarce, that nothing of the nature of a hotel for foreigners exists'.[28] This would not actually have troubled Cumming as she always stayed with Western friends (here, most possibly the Edkins), but her criticism is yet another stanza in her overall dissatisfaction with Beijing, where comfort is her war-cry. When visiting the Examination Hall, she also deplored the lack thereof. There, 'not much attention [was] paid to the bodily comforts of the students', and they were 'without so much as one wadded quilt to save [their] bones'.[29] Cumming only changes the tenor of her narrative when she goes shopping.

> [W]hen Dr Edkins offered to escort me to a great fair which is being held in the grounds of a temple not very far off, I, of course, summoned sufficient energy to go there, and very amusing it proved. [. . .] I bought several fascinating curio stands in many compartments, made of pear-wood, stained black, and carved to resemble knotted bamboo; also lovely bright scarlet porcelain cups with patterns of bamboo foliage in white.[30]

More than a decade after Cumming's visit, Scidmore, in her China guidebook, now talks of the 'excellent Hotel de Peking' (today the Beijing Hotel),[31] which was erected by a French-funded bank precisely for the Western tourists who were streaming into the capital after 1879 when Cumming had lamented the lack of tourist facilities. Here, writes Scidmore, 'every comfort is secured, and every information and assistance given the visitor'.[32] Furthermore, she continues that, with the right currency in hand, the tourist can rather comfortably explore the city's main attractions and buy (like Cummings) local curios and gifts. The places of interest in Peking, however, laments Scidmore, 'are lessening in number each year because of the authorities closing them to foreigners'.[33] The sights she names include the ruins and gardens of the Temple of Heaven, the old observatory, the Mohammedan mosque and Catholic cathedral, and the foreign mission establishments and the Lamasery (i.e. Tibetan or Mongolian monastery of lamas) in the northeast of the capital. Although she still believes that 'Peking is sadly lacking in guide-book sights, in buildings, monuments, public works of art, or historic spots that can appeal to one to whom Chinese dynasties and rulers are but empty names, shibboleths, ciphers, and symbols of the ceramic craze only',[34] eight years later, in her 1900 travelogue, Scidmore adds the following sights: the Examination Hall, the Confucian Temple, the Lama Temple, the Clock and Drum-Towers, the Palace gates, the Temple of Agriculture, the Hall of Classics and the Imperial City. The similarities between Scidmore's description of the Examination Hall and Cumming's are striking: as scathing as Cummings in her evaluation, the later traveller even borrows the concept of 'cells' from Cummings, and the 'pigsties' turn into 'cattle-pens'.[35] However, Scidmore's dismissal of the examination system rests not so much on issues of comfort as on the problem of corruption. Even the honoured sphere of learning and knowledge, the American suggests, is invaded by fraud, bribery and collusion, which signals its looming decay. Despite Scidmore's rewritings of Cumming in *China: The Long-Lived Empire*, one cannot help but notice how her enumeration of Peking sights echoes the British woman's list, particularly when she also finds herself in the same shopping area in the Chinese City — or 'The Chinese Half of Peking', in Cumming's words[36] — as the aristocrat.[37] More caustic than Cumming about the shopping opportunities ('[i]f one would study and enjoy Chinese art, one should go where the great collections and the great art dealers in "Oriental" art are — to Paris, to London, to New York or Baltimore, to Dresden, Berlin, Weimar, or St. Petersburg, but not to Peking'),[38] the Chinese shopping district is, however, from now firmly put onto the sightseeing itinerary for subsequent tourists.

Most important, however, unlike Cumming who does not venture into Beijing's surroundings — maybe again for reasons of comfort — Scidmore strongly recommends seeing the Great Wall and the tombs of the Ming emperors, in both her 1892 travel guide and her 1900 travelogue. In her guidebook, she adds information about places to stay near the Wall, the cost of inns and modes of transportation, repeatedly warning the traveller about the basic nature of the lodgings and the often required cut-throat negotiation for the best price. Possibly as a response to Scidmore's recommending these stops on the Chinese Grand Tour, subsequent female travellers — including the Australian Mary Gaunt and the American women Ellen LaMotte and Grace Seton — all include the two sites in their travel itineraries in 1913, 1917 and 1923 respectively.[39] In fact, Gaunt's encounter with an American tour group who, rather than appreciating the sublimity of the Great Wall, are merely worried about the whereabouts of their disobedient teenage daughter Cora, shows how the Great Wall has turned into a tourist spot, much to the dislike of Gaunt. She, in whom the Great Wall inspires visions of the powers of mankind, civilisation and history, is rudely brought back to the reality of (American) tourism when 'a high-pitched voice' repeatedly screams 'Cora! Cora!! Cora!!!'[40]

Another point worth mentioning is that it was also Scidmore who, first in her *Westward* and more distinctly in her *Long-Lived Empire*, recommended — in the tradition of Isabella Bird — the river tour on the Yangzi as part of the 'real' China experience. Her trip on the Yellow River takes her a thousand miles into the heart of China, from the lower Yangzi into the Yangzi gorges and rapids, past Ichang.[41] The British novelist Alicia Little had, around the same time as Bird, but independent of her, also travelled on the Yangzi and into the remoter western provinces while her husband pioneered steamship travel on the Yellow River.[42] Mrs. Little is an interesting figure in the context of the exploration of China. She is what could be called a 'resident traveller' who, together with her husband, the merchant and trader Archibald Little, lived in China for over thirty years. In a period between her first arrival in the country in 1887 and her departure in the 1920s, she wrote several novels set in China and a number of travelogues and memories of her life in the foreign country.[43] However, it was only Scidmore's systematic mapping of the 'must-see' places on a Chinese Grand Tour, which would lead subsequent travellers — such as the Wellesley professor Elizabeth Kendall in 1919 and the American librarian Elizabeth Enders in 1923 —to follow in Scidmore's (and Bird's and Little's) footsteps and also undertake tours into the Chinese hinterland and on the Yangzi.[44] Theirs were individual and self-organised tours, but knowing that other women travellers had already undertaken them must have given reassurance that it would be worthwhile and possible.

Destination Peking: The Place and Its People

A large number of American women travelled to Beijing between 1900 and 1923 and visited the sights mapped out by Cumming and, more prescriptively, by Scidmore. The Grand Tour of China, which now meant the journey along the Chinese coast from Hong Kong to Shanghai, with a short detour on the Lower Yangzi, and up to Tianjin and Beijing with the Great Wall and the Ming Tombs close by, was now firmly established and hereafter the routes of travellers would coincide on this 'beaten' track. This essay concludes by referring to a phenomenon which is associated with the Grand Tour but which would become increasingly important in the twentieth century, particularly when a new form of Western interest in China emerged: contact with the local people. The contact with foreigners was originally part of the agenda of the young aristocrat's European Grand Tour. Cynical commentators, however, considered this originally desirable and potentially instructive contact between self and other — the main purpose of which was to educate in and further diplomatic relations with the country's elite — as a failure, with the young men's exposure to otherness more often turning to contact with so-called low life and manifesting itself in whoring and drinking. With a renewed and revised interest in otherness in later decades came more complex encounters. Our women travellers' interest in the local population, particularly Chinese women, is striking, and all of them describe at least one such encounter. If Bird and Cumming were hesitant about making contact, the next generation showed a great willingness to meet Chinese women, possibly as the contact with them would help them reassess their own (proto-)feminist agendas back at home. As the poet Eunice Tietjens writes in the poem 'Woman' in her 1919 collection *Profiles from China*:

> Strangely the sight of you moves me.
> I have no standards by which to appraise you; the outer shell of you is all I know.
> Yet irresistibly you draw me. [. . .]
> It is your eyes, I think, that move me.
> They are so bright, so black!
> They are alert and full of curiosity as the eyes of a squirrel, and like the eyes of a squirrel they have no depth behind them.
> They are windows opening on a world as small as your bound feet, a world of ignorances, and vacuities, and kitchen-gods.
> And yet your eyes are witchery. When you smile you are the woman-spirit, adorable.
> I cannot appraise you, yet strangely the sight of you moves me.
> I believe that I shall dream of you.[45]

Hence, contact with the locals, particularly if they strike a particular chord within the observer, becomes more important than visiting the prescribed places (*vide* Enders's remark of 1923 that Beijing's famous monuments, temples and bazaars still constituted the 'real China') and doing the prescribed shopping (*vide* LaMotte's comment that Fifth Avenue was nothing compared to what she called Peking's department stores).[46] Despite their interest in traditional sightseeing and tourist souvenir-hunting, both Enders and LaMotte are interested in their local servants and in Chinese upper-class women.[47] As Tietjens suggests, as different as Chinese women are, there is still a similar 'woman-spirit' in them, which the Americans also possess. In the early 1920s, Enders finds herself caught in the middle of one of the many occupations of Beijing, this time by Chang Tso-lin's Fengtien army who battle for the control of the post-revolution Beijing government. She offers shelter not only to her Chinese staff, but also to her friend Miss Ling and an old Manchu princess, claiming that she can protect them if they join her in the American legation.[48] In a similarly sisterly spirit, LaMotte confesses to a female Chinese acquaintance in 1918 that, looking at the ongoing Western exploitation of China, she now understands the Boxer Uprising and peoples' desire to get rid of the West.[49]

The most interesting and detailed description of an encounter between a Western and a Chinese woman, however, can again be found in Scidmore's landmark travelogue. In Beijing in 1899, Scidmore makes, like Enders, the acquaintance of an old Manchu noblewoman. Aided by a female Western friend who acts as translator when sign-language fails, their encounter has a dialogic and circular structure when, first, Scidmore visits the aristocrat in her home and is then visited by her in her own quarters. A Chinese tea ceremony with dumplings, sesame wafers, almond purée, honeyed fruits and nuts is answered with a Western tea-party with layered chocolate cake, fruit cake and maple-syrup, and in the course of two afternoons both Scidmore and the old tai-tai learn more about each other's culture. Most interesting, Scidmore learns that her predisposition to think of Chinese women and China in general as backward and conventional must be revised. She learns in astonishment from the tai-tai's doctor that the Chinese ladies have been discussing the latest discovery of X-rays and were very intrigued to hear that their friend Li Hung-chang had already undergone the procedure with a foreign doctor to locate a bullet the Japanese had fired at him.[50] China possesses as much modern medical knowledge as the West does, learns Scidmore, and if Western women discuss this progress, so do Chinese women. The focus on otherness and difference here gives way to feelings of sameness and solidarity, which might, however, be as much a class-bonding as gender-bonding. The tai-tai and the American woman part as 'friends forever', writes Scidmore, who speak the common language of the heart, but not of the tongue. Here, the meeting between self and other has become what the phenomenologist Hans-Georg Gadamer would call a dialogic 'hermeneutical conversation', which leaves neither partner unaffected, and in which self and other find a common, if non-verbal, language.[51] Tietjens is haunted by what she senses to be an unspoken sisterly bond between a Chinese and a Western woman; Enders and LaMotte take this solidarity for granted and act as protectors and confidantes; Scidmore more eloquently theorises the encounter as a 'merging of horizons', in Gadamer's words, between two different entities who both learn from the encounter and then build their newly found knowledge and experience into a revised view of the world. With the later female travellers in China, the Grand Tour agenda of learning about the other and possibly using this knowledge to reassess the self has been built into the travel experience.

The American suffragette Grace Seton then fully embraces this new agenda to gain knowledge about Chinese women. Her 1923 trip through China, on which she stops in Hong Kong, Guangzhou (Canton), Soochow, Shanghai, Hangzhou, Nanjing, Wuxi, and Beijing and its environs, if not in such a neat order, has the self-expressed aim to 'throw a little light on what is happening there, [and] especially upon the "dark places" of the "woman's quarters" of New China, where the white light of publicity has not yet beaten'.[52] Knowledge about Chinese women here merges with a political agenda that derives from Seton's role as president of the Connecticut Women's Suffrage League and her experience in organising and commanding women's action groups. Thus, Seton discusses the American women's vote with the Chinese president Li Yuan-hung, and her background provides interesting material for discussions with Mrs Soong Ching-ling, Sun Yat-sen's wife, also a progressive thinker on women's rights.[53] '[R]aising the status of women', says Soong Ching-ling to Seton during their first meeting in Shanghai in February 1923, and 'enlarging the opportunities for their education and participation in the general work of the country' is the challenge at hand, and she summarises, hitting a keynote with the suffragist Seton, 'a happier womanhood in China is bound up with a successful Republic in China'.[54] Seton's project is not one-sided or imperialist as her 'education' of Chinese leaders might suggest but is, in contrast, based on the exchange of knowledge. Her project also lies in meeting what she calls 'the New Women of China'. These include suffragettes (who would, however, have to wait until 1949 to see the women's vote implemented), writers, journalists, actresses, doctors, YWCA welfare officers, teachers and other educators, philanthropists and social ladies; and Seton interviews them and exchanges knowledge and ideals about women's rights and women's (future) role in society. At this stage, the Grand Tour of China has fully embraced the initial design not only to undergo an aesthetic education through the visiting of sights and the purchase of artefacts, but also to undergo a political, social and personal education through an intense contact with the other culture and its inhabitants.

Conclusion

It was women rather than men who, in the period between 1879 and 1923, claimed China for travelling and for tourism, and who continued writing travel books about the country. The accounts of pioneering British women led to the more systematic travel itineraries of succeeding American women. At the end of the essay, however, one central question remains: What initially motivated Bird, Cumming and Scidmore to visit certain places rather than others, so creating itineraries which would subsequently be followed by generations of travellers? One reason must, surely, have been the simple fact of infrastructure and available modes of transportation. These women went where they could go, primarily by ship, by Peking cart and, in rarer cases, by sedan chair. Only Bird was a walker, if an unwilling one who would consider this the last resort. Another reason, however, seems to have been an interest in culture and history, as in the case of the Great Wall. And a final motivation, visible in the river journey through the gorges, must have been aesthetic. Travelling educated not only the mind but also the senses and feelings, as the recurring encounters with Chinese women show.

8

Ruins in the Jungle: Nature and Narrative

Douglas Kerr

When W. Somerset Maugham, 'in a far island away down in the South East of the Malay Archipelago', encountered a great cockatoo which stared at him, his first instinct was to look about for the cage from which it must have escaped.[1] In the jungle, he says, he never quite got over his surprise at seeing at liberty birds and beasts whose natural habitation seemed to him a Zoological Garden. Maugham's little joke is a rather late instance of a trope that had been a nineteenth-century commonplace, a differentiation between Europe and the Orient that expressed itself in the opposition of civilisation and nature, the domesticated and the wild. As the cultural artefacts of Asia were being amassed by Western museums, its natural objects might be encountered in Kew Gardens or the London Zoo, and to the urban sophisticate Maugham was pretending to be, this was where they 'naturally' belonged.

The West has no jungle: that is to say, it is a word (itself of Hindi origin) that cannot apply to anywhere in Europe or North America. To Western observers of Asia, the jungle is the other habitat *par excellence*, the location and symbol of everything most foreign about the foreign parts penetrated by the European empires and later their vast shambling international rearguard of tourists. With its fascinations and dangers and its extreme difference from home, the jungle was as much a challenge to colonial and travel writers as it had been to the explorers clearing a trail through it. This essay considers some ways in which that challenge has been met. The issue here is representations of the jungle, and these constitute a discourse and a tradition which embrace fictional and non-fictional writing. I will be moving back and forth, in what follows, across the boundary between representations of actual and of imaginary experience, a boundary which is notoriously permeable in travel writing of all kinds, and at times as indistinct as any other artificial boundary in a jungle.

To read about the jungle is often to be struck by a recurrent figure of ingestion, an anxiety about being swallowed up by the scene of nature, never to reappear. In writing about the tropical East, the uncharted and unaccountable vastness and darkness of the jungle is often metonymic of the troubling enormity of the Orient itself, into which the unwary intruder may vanish and be lost. The jungle may be a refuge for the savage, the outlaw or the holidaymaker, but it can also engulf people who cross its threshold. When two adventurers enter the jungle in one of Hugh Clifford's stories, '[t]heir little expedition slipped into the forest, and the wilderness swallowed it' — they enter in the form of an abstract nominative ('expedition') which is an agential subject, but are immediately transformed, in the syntax of the sentence, into objects of the place's incorporation.[2] To those unfamiliar with it, the jungle has as few landmarks as the open sea, and an equally insatiable appetite. Those who broached the jungle might find themselves swallowed historically as well as geographically. Colonial administrators like Clifford — trained to observe, knowledgeable, highly literate, and usually sharing a common background with the literary elite at home — are a particularly valuable source of writing about outlandish places. When Leonard Woolf came as a young colonial officer to Hambantota district in Ceylon in August 1908, he too at first felt as engulfed as Clifford's adventurers had been, as if he had disappeared into some dark ahistorical otherworld, so that he could not establish where he was by triangulation with the familiar landmarks of his own past. 'I have no connection with yesterday', he writes to Lytton Strachey in October; 'I do not recognize it nor myself in it'.[3] He felt he had lost his place in the story.

The jungle was, to be sure, the place of nature, and a contrast between nature and modernity was one of the staples of a Western art and literature whose agenda was set by Romanticism. The contrast between the jungles of Africa, Asia and South America, and the cities of an industrial society which the travellers who visited them had left behind, became increasingly marked with the increasing transformation of both city and country in the West. But at issue here is not just the difference between the modern and an earlier phase of historical development. The point was that as the West changed, the jungle seemed changeless. Modern people in an evolutionary process had exchanged nature for history — or, in a slightly different teleology, they had fulfilled or transcended nature in becoming historical beings. A European parallel may be found in Julius Caesar's response to the German forest two millennia before, when he crossed with his army from the west to the east bank of the Rhine. The forest was not just the absence of civilisation it was the opposite of civilisation.[4]

The Rhine is the crucial east-west dividing line in the geography of *The Gallic War*. The Gaulish tribes to the west, however rebellious, were tractable material for the Roman imperium, and they had a way of life, customs and religions that could be mapped to a Roman idea of culture. But the east bank of the Rhine was the threshold of the incorrigibly savage, where, Caesar had been informed, wild and unwholesome people lived in the trackless darkness under the trees. In the German forests to the east, as Caesar describes them, distinctions blurred, distances were incalculable, there was no law, and the people were in every sense close to beasts. Caesar had more sense than to march his troops far into this forbidding region, whose inhabitants appeared to live in the place of nature as Thomas Hobbes was to imagine it — cruel and ignoble and unredeemed. They seemed prehistoric, for the jungle also has no history, and indeed in both its changelessness and its unfathomability, it is the enemy of history. 'The more you are in jungle, particularly if you are alone, the more one tends to feel it personified, something or someone hostile, dangerous', Leonard Woolf was to remember. 'I twice lost myself in jungle, a terrifying experience, and each time it was due to carelessness, to forgetting for an instant to be on one's guard against the treachery of the jungle'.[5]

The disorientation of the familiar lost-in-the-jungle anecdote brings a kind of relapse, for not only is the destination — the teleological direction of the journey — lost, but the traveller is condemned to a futile and endless circulation, a story that is a travesty of narrative because it has no shape, no beginning or end. Getting lost in the jungle is already the end of the story. In Maugham's 'Neil MacAdam', Angus Munro describes how he lost his way in thick jungle, realising (this is another familiar motif of the jungle narrative) that he has been walking in circles; after a few hours of frantic wandering, he says, he would have blown his brains out if only he had had a revolver. But he survives, of course, to tell the tale. Later in the story, Munro's wife Darya is abandoned in the jungle and never seen again, and we can only imagine what happened, how long she will survive and how she will die. She simply disappears off the map of the narrative; she has lapsed from history into nature, rejoining the life of the beasts.[6]

There is a similar moment at the end of Leonard Woolf's novel, *The Village in the Jungle* (1913). As colonial district officer in Hambantota, responsible for the inhabitants' welfare, Woolf had seen how thin was the line separating the region's Sinhala peasants from ruin and starvation. In his novel about their lives, various tragedies overtake the family of Silindu. Their village is eventually depopulated and forgotten and disappears into the jungle from which it had sprung, and the last survivor, Punchi Menika, who has been living on roots and leaves, lies dying of fever and starvation, alone in the tumbledown remains of her hut. 'When the end was close upon her a great black shadow glided into the doorway.'[7] Whether it is a wild boar, a hallucination, or a devil, she recognises that the jungle has come for her, and in this moment the narrative ends as the jungle folds over it: there can be no more story. What will happen next is unspeakable, and invisible, for there can be no human being to witness and recount it: there is only the darkness and silence of an engulfing alterity.

If the jungle was the state of nature in this Hobbesian sense, malignant and hostile and constantly at war with human efforts to subdue, cultivate, civilise and narrate it, then there can be no more potent image of this struggle than ruins in the jungle. In Kipling's *The Jungle Book*, the monkey people, the Bandar-log, kidnap Mowgli and try to recruit him to their travesty of human civilisation in the ruins of an abandoned city.[8] This is a complicated case, because Kipling's jungle is overdetermined, being at once an unforgiving natural environment, a model of a rule-governed society and the idyllic playground of a privileged child. In the story 'Kaa's Hunting', the important contrast is between the glamorous but anarchic society of the monkey city, and the sober but law-abiding polity of the jungle, guaranteed by Mowgli's tutors the panther and the bear. We are not told who built the city or why they abandoned it: perhaps it simply succumbed to the greater power of the forces of nature. In any case, it offers no temptation to any of the jungle creatures except the monkey tribe, and their encampment in its ruins is proof that, in Kipling's eyes, they are not worthy citizens of the jungle. Yet nor do they properly belong in a built environment. Clever but lazy, the monkeys have constructed a mimic and inauthentic civility, and the ruined state of their city testifies to their damning lack of creativity.

In 'The King's Ankus' in *The Second Jungle Book*, Mowgli returns to the ruins for an adventure involving an ancient cobra who still guards the king's treasure in a secret vault beneath the overgrown ruins. Mowgli steals a jewelled elephant goad (the pointed stick with which the mahout controls the elephant), with tragic results, and then returns it, having learned his lesson that the emblems of human history (and property) do not belong in the pastoral scene of his jungle life, because they are at odds with its idyllic changelessness: 'I will never again bring into the Jungle strange things', he resolves.[9] This little episode of 'imperial Gothic' reminds us of an important fact: ruins in the jungle are uncanny and usually haunted.[10] An odour of Gothic seems to cling to them, bringing with it an idiom which the most sober of writers may be unable to resist. When Hugh Clifford, on colonial business, travelled to the decayed city of Brunei, he reported, for example, 'Today we behold not Brunei, the land of ancient story, but its shrivelled mummy and the gray ashes of its empire'.[11] Meanwhile the curse of the elephant goad teaches Mowgli that the natural world embraces history at its peril and is better off without it, a lesson that will be more cruelly driven home when he himself is expelled from the jungle upon becoming an adult human. Actual jungles have generally had less success in protecting themselves from human encroachment.

Like their African equivalent in popular tales about cursed and mummy-infested Egyptian tombs — such as Bram Stoker's *The Jewel of Seven Stars* (1903), or the burial vault of kings in Rider Haggard's *King Solomon's Mines* (1886) or the palace of Ayesha in his *She* (1887) — ruins in the Oriental jungle are generally represented as uncanny, whether they are the relic of an indigenous civilisation or an earlier foreign invader. In Hugh Clifford's story 'The Skulls in the Forest', Martin Halliday thinks he has found a specifically ahistorical spot, a place of unfallen nature — 'The place where he was standing had never suffered profanation: it had no past, no history; it was straight from the hand of its Maker'[12] — only to discover under the brushwood the earthworks of an ancient fort of European design. His attempt to colonise the place with settlers ends in disaster and many deaths, for what seemed like a jungle idyll is in fact haunted by a terrible history. The unappeased spirits of the earlier settlement (apparently Portuguese of the fifteenth century) exact a wholesale vengeance on the new arrivals, and the place is left at the end of the tale, as it was at the beginning, uninhabited by a living soul. Purged of human activity, it reverts to empty hinterland, and to its natural function of simply being there.

Ruins, especially if they are overrun by an encroaching nature, encourage thoughts about the mortality of civilisations, as the Roman Forum inspired Gibbon's *Decline and Fall of the Roman Empire*, and the accounts of Egyptologists lie behind Shelley's 'Ozymandias'. Asia, like Latin America, has several sites where the jungle has laid waste the works of a great civilisation, and none more spectacular than the Khmer temples and palaces at Angkor. Hugh Clifford speculated about its mysterious history. André Malraux, notoriously, stole from it. Pierre Loti had plundered it only for literary copy, purporting to find in it 'un lugubre accueil', a dismal welcome.[13] The resourceful Loti managed to write a whole book about Angkor, though he had spent less than two days at the site, in November 1901 — his narrative adds a third full day to the visit, which in fact he spent travelling back towards Phnom Penh. Loti's ruins in the jungle become the occasion for flights of the egotistical sublime. 'Le voilà donc ce sanctuaire qui hantait jadis mon imagination d'enfant et où je ne suis monté qu'après tant de courses par le monde, quand c'est déjà le soir de ma vie errante!'[14] Somerset Maugham stayed longer at Angkor, and wanted never to leave it. He said he had never seen 'anything in the world more beautiful' than Angkor's temples; the desolation was a strong part of the beauty, and the overgrown city presented itself irresistibly as a *paysage moralisé*. 'For centuries nature has waged its battle with the handiwork of man; it has covered, disfigured and transformed it, and now all these buildings that a multitude of slaves built with so much labour lie a confused tangle among the trees.'[15]

For Hugh Clifford, descriptive travel writing about Angkor was not enough; he was moved to give the ruins a story. His *The Downfall of the Gods* (1911) is a scholarly historical novel — though the title is Wagnerian, the model may well be Flaubert's *Salammbô* — which imagines how the great medieval Hindu Empire at Angkor came to grief, through revolution, anarchy and invasion.[16] Clifford's fascination with the lost story of Angkor must have been similar to that of his fictional Halliday pondering the ruined fort in 'The Skulls in the Forest': 'It has got a queer grip upon me, this place: it seizes my imagination — I can't win free of it. How often I stand looking at those huge, silent trees, and long for them to have voices wherewith to speak, that they might tell me of the sights which they have seen the tragedy of that abandoned fort, of this deserted fairyland'.[17] The ruins seem to contain a story, but are unable themselves to tell it.

For Clifford as for Halliday, the ruins in the jungle become an obsession because they are the signs of a history that has been struck dumb. There is no written record of the collapse of Angkor, and it becomes the function of the traveller to give the place the gift of history, and supply it with the story that has evaporated from its ruins. Clifford had already speculated on the question in his non-fictional writing, in *Further India* (1905), where he suggested that earthquakes may have caused the inhabitants to abandon Angkor. His local knowledge was the warrant for this speculation, with its demystifying tone: 'As regards the encroachment of the forest, that, I think, need occasion no surprise. I have myself seen a ploughed field in tropical Asia covered in the space of fifteen months with dense undergrowth twelve feet in height, through which a man could pass only with the greatest difficulty, with the aid of a stout wood-knife'.[18]

Several years later he returned to the theme of Angkor's tragedy in *The Downfall of the Gods*, as if the wreck of Angkor demanded not only a geographical but also an imaginative interpretation. Clifford's novel is an aetiological myth, a work of not archaeological but narrative restoration of the ruins. (There is a kind of analogy with the speculative and controversial restoration by Arthur Evans of the Minoan palace at Knossos, over several decades beginning in 1900.)[19] At the end of *The Downfall of the Gods*, Thai invaders overrun and sack the city, the people of Angkor revert to being a 'race of jungle-dwellers,' and the principal surviving characters are reduced to living in a forest hut. 'Already the trees of the forest begin to invade the sanctuaries, and the wild fig vines thrust their tendrils between stone and stone.'[20] The jungle puts an end to history and story, reasserting the apparently changeless rhythms of nature. But as the jungle turned civilisation into ruins, Clifford the belated traveller can turn the ruins back into narrative, resurrecting a buried history from them, but resurrecting it only as a story of loss, and a *memento mori*. He meets the challenge of otherness by what might be called an appropriation, but in a narrative which proves to be only too appropriate to his own history.

With the return of the jungle, *The Downfall of the Gods* ends in the same way as *The Village in the Jungle*, or indeed as Kipling's 'The Judgement of Dungara', in which the jungle swallows up the mission house as soon as the missionaries depart in failure. Kipling, Clifford, Woolf and Maugham all seem to have taken a melancholy satisfaction in the spectacle of the defeat of human handiwork by the irresistible might of nature. The jungle in this aspect may be said to be an important manifestation of the Oriental sublime. Like other instantiations of the sublime, it creates an awareness of the potential annihilation of the self. It is one of those sublime natural phenomena which, according to Kant, challenge the subject's attempts to appropriate and contain them, and demand from us 'courage to be able to measure ourselves against the seeming omnipotence of nature'.[21] Kant had shown how the conscious mind is able to meet and rationalise the awesome challenge of the natural sublime; but the prospect of ruins in the jungle seems by contrast to stand as testimony to a crushing victory of non-human nature over the human. Sometimes, so omnipotent is nature that not even ruins are left to testify to a defeated human effort. Sailing upriver towards the decayed town of Brunei in Borneo — which would strike him, as we have seen, as exhibiting 'the shriveled mummy and the gray ashes of a former empire' — Hugh Clifford felt that the resumption of sovereignty by 'the spirits of the jungle' was even merciful in its completeness. 'Those hillsides, we knew, were filled with the memory of ancient tragedies, records of wrong and oppression, or murder and ruthless robbery; and Nature was even now slowly covering from sight the scenes of so much wickedness.'[22] Here the baleful trope of ruins in the jungle is itself turned, by the traditional pastoral trope of the restorative power of nature, and the returning jungle is seen as benign, healing, or at least covering up, wounds inflicted by human depravity.

We do not have to look far to see why Clifford was drawn to the ruins of Angkor, and what led him to conjure the story of the downfall of an empire from its stones. In his distinguished forty-five year career as a colonial administrator, he was a notably ambivalent imperialist.[23] This was not as uncommon as might be thought (Leonard Woolf in Ceylon was another such case, and went on to become a prominent campaigner against imperialism). Clifford was convinced of the material benefits of modernity which European incursions brought to Asia and Africa. However, he was also aware of the tragic costs of these changes in terms of the destruction of habitats and cultures he had come to know and love in his work as a colonial civil servant in Malaya (and Ceylon). In this he was voicing an ambivalence shared by other colonial personnel, as Philip Holden has argued in his study of the contradictions of modernisation and nostalgia in the rhetoric of British Malaya: 'The British construction of Malaya seems, in hindsight, driven by two narrative imperatives: first, to justify creeping colonization of the peninsula in terms of modernization; second, to inscribe Malaya nostalgically as a medieval society . . .'[24] Clifford could appreciate in Malaya a romance which had disappeared from the modern world, but his own arrival there, as an agent of modernity, was a guarantee that that romance would soon be destroyed. In the circumstances, a reminder that no encroachment of civilisation could stand forever against the forces of nature was a thought that had its consolations.

The story of the fall of Angkor is then, like Kipling's 'Recessional', a warning of what may befall a proud empire — the ruins in the jungle performing the function of the emblematic skull at the feast — but there is also a sombre gratification in contemplating the mutability of secular might. In an article that makes mention of his own observations of the temples at Angkor and the uninhabited forest in Pahang, Clifford was to congratulate Leonard Woolf on his discovery of a 'profound truth' in his Ceylon novel *The Village in the Jungle*. 'That truth is that, in all the long history of man in the tropics, the Jungle has always in the end triumphed over mankind.'[25] Ruins in the jungle were death's other kingdom, but in the long run all kingdoms are death's kingdom. Kipling himself, though he never admits in his prose that the British Empire in the East might come to an end, allows this tragic insight in his poetry, notably in 'Cities and Thrones and Powers', a poem in which he contrives to sound like Thomas Hardy as he grimly celebrates the blindness of humans to their necessary end.

> So Time that is o'er-kind
>   To all that be,
> Ordains us e'en as blind,
>   As bold as she:
> That in our very death,
>   And burial sure,
> Shadow to shadow, well persuaded, saith,
>   'See how our works endure!'[26]

This is very much the moral that adheres to the trope of ruins in the jungle, whether the ruins are actual or figurative, and it is consistent not only with the ancient religious and literary theme of mutability, but also with the strange dark vein of pessimism that accompanied the imperial triumphs of the late Victorian age, perhaps best exemplified in the 1894 Prolegomena to T. H. Huxley's Romanes lecture of 1893, 'Evolution and Ethics'.[27] There the great evolutionist had argued that civilisation was waging a losing struggle against the 'State of Nature' which would continue until 'the evolution of our globe shall have entered so far upon its downward course that the cosmic process resumes its sway; and once more, the State of Nature prevails over the surface of our planet'.[28] As for Hugh Clifford, of course it was the power of the British Empire that had enabled him in the first place to travel to and write about the ruins of imperial Angkor. But as he contemplated the temples and palaces overgrown by the jungle, it is hard to tell if he would have been surprised, or distressed, to learn that his own writing about them would outlast the empire he served.

9

Forbidden Journeys to China and Beyond with the Odd Couple: Ella Maillart and Peter Fleming

Maureen Mulligan

Forbidden Journey: From Peking to Kashmir by Ella Maillart (1937)[1] and *News from Tartary* by Peter Fleming (1936) demand to be read in parallel, as they offer a unique opportunity to consider the perspectives of a Swiss woman and an Englishman who undertook a journey together to a part of the world that was off-limits to Westerners. Ella 'Kini' Maillart travelled as an accredited journalist for a French newspaper, *Le Petit Parisien*, and Peter Fleming was at that time special travel correspondent for *The Times*. Their route, through China, India and Tibet, involved crossing the Gobi Desert, and their aim was to report on the current political situation, about which practically nothing was known in the West because of Sino-Japanese conflict and the rise of communism. They had other, more personal motives too, involving the desire to find alternatives to life in the West, and the need to prove their physical and mental capacities on a gruelling journey. They were partners in adventure, both young writers seeking fame, both experienced travellers, but not a couple (at least as far as we are told),[2] and their individual experiences of this remarkable trip reveal very different perspectives on what it meant to write in the 'golden age' of travel.

The journalistic and political involvement of certain writers of the decade was closely connected with the governing powers of the time: Paul Fussell speculates on the probability that Peter Fleming (brother of Ian Fleming) was involved in undercover work for MI5 during his travels even before his acknowledged work in this area during the Second World War (Fussell 1980, 175); similarly, travels by Freya Stark and Rebecca West in this period rendered maps and local information of direct usefulness to the British powers, apart from their interest to the general reader.[3] But in many ways the trip was not only a professional journalistic investigation, but one which, by its end, had become overwhelmingly a journey undertaken for the sake of travel itself. It was a chance to enjoy a golden age in which people with a European passport and money were still able to move relatively freely around the earth, looking back on their own society from a perspective of critical distance. They could still enjoy a sense of liberty and lack of national identity that was soon to be lost as Fascism took over Europe and resulted in another war.

Maillart, a Swiss-born sailor, skier and traveller, had travelled to the Soviet Union as a young woman in the 1920s to study film-making. Her travels were mainly motivated by her increased distaste for the militaristic and materialistic West, and her life-long search for spiritual peace and satisfaction in a simpler life in the East. In *Cruises and Caravans* (1942), she writes of the way she adopted the persona of a writer interested in film and sport:

> These two subjects of study were 'safe' — they would involve me in no political discussions; they were like a shield behind which I could hide my undefined personal quest for a true life (32).

In her 1934 book, *Turkestan Solo: One Woman's Expedition from the Tien Shan to the Kizil Kum*, she also explored this theme of travel as an escape from the West and a search for more primitive forms of existence:

> Cost what it may I am determined to go East. The nomad's life enthrals me. ... The Kirghiz are simple, hospitable, and above all, free ... It was that quality which made its deepest appeal to me. Wherever I go, it is always the secret of such simple, straightforward races that I seek, people whom a fair sky is sufficient to content. Only by returning to their way of living, can we ever hope to find a way out of the bogs in which we vainly stumble. (4)

Ella Maillart made her 'forbidden journey' in 1934–35. She and Fleming were not especially well-suited travel companions, both priding themselves on their ability to survive alone in inhospitable country: she had just written *Turkestan Solo* and he *One's Company*; he was in a hurry and she wanted to dawdle, and she felt the restrictions of being in a group, especially when they joined a caravan. Maillart's version of her initial unenthusiastic decision to share the journey is succinct: 'Fleming: "You can come with me if you like". Maillart: "I beg your pardon. It's my route and it's I who'll take you, if I can think of some way in which you might be useful to me". The controversy still rages' (1937, 8). The restrictions involved in the pragmatic decision to travel with a companion for the sake of safety, and the need to produce copy for a newspaper, are of far less importance to Maillart than the sense of freedom and escape from modernity she anticipates in the journey itself:

> I was devoured with curiosity as to what the immediate and uncertain future was going to be like. And very sensible of a feeling of relief at being free of man-made obstacles! Overjoyed to think that every day would be a new day, that no day would be the same as the one before! And determined on observing only one solitary rule — to go straight ahead! (73)

Their allocation of tasks on the very difficult journey followed a traditional gender division of labour: Fleming hunted while Maillart cooked and provided health care. Fleming sets out two lists of their responsibilities, introduced by the idea that 'Perhaps one of the main reasons for our getting on so well was that Kini always had a certain friendly contempt for me and I always had a sneaking respect for her; both sentiments arose from the fact that she was a professional and I was eternally the amateur' (Fleming [1936] 1995, 172). He goes on to say:

> I suppose I was the leader, because I made decisions more quickly, guessed more quickly, knew more quickly what I wanted than Kini did. But she did all the work that required skill or application ... we both knew that she was, so to speak, the better man, and this knowledge evened things out between us, robbed my automatically dominating position of its power to strain our relations. We had complete confidence in each other. (173)

The relationship held together for the duration, with a mixture of bantering humour and rivalry between the two travellers who had very different aims and philosophies; this is Maillart's version of where they parted company:

> Peter thought me too serious and I did not understand British humour ... I had the bad taste to lay down the law about the art of living. P. was bored by my craving to understand the thousands of diverse lives that make up humanity and bored, too, by my need to relate my own life to life in general. How could anybody be so crazy as to want to find out whether men's efforts brought about an improvement in human nature? Peter was troubled by none of these things. In his imperturbable wisdom he looked on human beings as characters in a comedy. (148)

There are moments of intimacy — Fleming describes how 'we made cocoa and I did my best to massage Kini, who had been in agony all day' (284); and his understated humour comes through: 'Her talk made so vivid and so valuable a decoration to the long slow hours that sometimes even I was shamed out of silence into some pawky anecdote about an alligator' (174). Maillart was well aware of the romantic possibilities of the journey, but claims she was not at all interested in fulfilling the role of romantic heroine; she explicitly suggests and then rejects the situation in terms of a standard novelistic plot that she refuses to write, instead asserting her own satisfaction in physical space and personal achievement, not in the arms of the hero:

> Walking along at an even pace I felt in great form, filled with such joy as I used to experience setting out on my skis on very dry winter mornings. There on the high table-lands of Asia I was singing, 'I'm sitting on top of the world'. I even laughed at the wide heavens. It was an odd situation Peter and I were in together at the centre of that continent. Indeed, it was like a situation in a novel, and if I were writing a best-seller, it should be that very day or never that the hero or heroine fell into each other's arms in mutual love and gratitude for rescues — on one side, rescue from the result of poisoned food, and on the other, rescue from a dangerous mist. Well, the novel-readers would have to go without. (147)

Evidently, we can only know what they choose to tell us about their domestic relationship, such as the sharing of tents and rooms, as there are no other witnesses. Fleming was engaged to a woman back home, and the conventions of the time mitigated against the revelation of such intimate personal details in travel writing. He also refers to the fictional stereotype of their relationship, and explodes it with similar irony:

> In the routine of life there was only one extraordinary feature, and that was how well Kini and I got on. We had been travelling together for three months already, and the journey lasted another four; all the time we were living together at the closest of quarters in conditions which were often uncomfortable and sometimes rigorous. By all the conventions of desert-island fiction we should have fallen madly in love with each other; by all the laws of human nature we should have driven each other crazy with irritation. As it was, we missed these almost equally embarrassing alternatives by a wide margin. (172)

Both record a revealing misunderstanding when Fleming, struggling with Chinese, responded to the question 'How old is she?' with the response 'No, only friends' (Maillart 1937, 71; Fleming 1995, 98). He mentions briefly that he has recently been married; Maillart when talking about memories refers to places and activities, but not people. Apart from that, neither traveller gives any detail about their private lives or previous relationships — a noticeable contrast with later travel writing, especially that by women. But their writing suggests an enormous respect for each other: this is Fleming, describing the end of a particularly long day's march:

> I got, during our seven months together, so used to regarding Kini as an equal in most things and a superior one in some that perhaps I have paid over-few tributes to (among other things) her powers of endurance. Praise, and especially praise in print, is an over-valued commodity, and I know that Kini has little use for it; nevertheless — because it is just as remarkable as any of the strange things that we saw — I should like to place it on record that, at the end of a fourteen hours' march in the middle of a hard journey (rising almost always before dawn, eating almost always a little less than enough), Kini went supperless to bed without, even by implication, turning a hair. The best that I can do in the way of eulogy is to say that I thought nothing of it at the time. (223)

In this generous tribute, Kini has been accepted as 'one of the boys' due to her lack of 'feminine' fuss and complaint. Another time Kini treats their camel for worms in a festering sore, and he praises her again in terms of her difference from most women: 'It was a real triumph for Kini. She was dog-tired and in some pain; and she thought she had almost no chance of doing good. But she forewent a needed siesta in the shade to do a job which would have made most women sick (282).

Another aspect that both books share is the break from the travel narrative to provide dense chapters of political information. Maillart justifies her chapter, which is detailed but inexplicit about sources, by explaining that 'as the obstacles liable to make a trans-Asiatic journey impossible are mainly political, it is only by discussing them that I can make it clear why our expedition was hazardous' (204). She deals with the subject in seventeen pages and a map, with the text divided into sections such as 'Forces Present in Sinkiang' or 'Events in Kashgar'. Her declared lack of interest in the political side of things is suggested by her preference for a rhetorical rather than analytical approach:

> What is going to happen? . . . Did the Soviets encourage Ma to take Kashgar three years ago, for fear England might get the upper hand in a Moslem republic in Turkestan? . . . Or did Ma, who set off as a powerful chief going to Moscow to discuss the terms of a possible alliance, fall into a trap in which he remains restive? . . . Heaven knows. (221)

In later books, such as *The Cruel Way* (1947), Maillart is clearly less interested in political analysis than in individual experiences; whether she lost interest as her journeys went on, or she was acting as a professional journalist merely for the cover and funding it provided her with in order to travel legitimately at the time, is not clear.

Fleming's book offers more political analysis (twenty-one pages, divided into four chapters e.g. 'Dirty Work' or 'Russian Racketeers'), equally unsourced, and introduced by an apologetic disclaimer acknowledging that few people are interested in politics, especially distant politics:

> Though we know that all men are brothers and that the peoples of the modern world are knit together in a great web of sympathy and understanding, we still find it impossible to be deeply stirred by things that happen to those fellow-beings whose skin is of a different colour to our own. (249)

For many readers, the political analysis may be the least interesting part of both books now, except for those interested in the historical details of the area in question in terms of the 'Great Game'; but the space devoted to it suggests both writers felt obliged to write something more than a personal travel book. The importance of the local political situation to outsiders, especially the British, is obvious, as well as the relevance it had to their journey, which was beset by problems over passports and visas demanded at all stages by policemen and army officials whose bureaucratic systems frequently held up the travellers or sent them off the main routes to avoid controls. Again, unlike more recent travel writing, this concern to go into detail over the local conditions shows the effort made by both writers to look beyond their own experience and document the situation they encountered.

The idea of the 'forbidden journey' to the East reminds us of a long tradition of travel writing which includes Sir Richard Burton's account of his entry into Mecca, disguised as a Pathan: the first Westerner to see the holy city and escape with his life. Alexandra David-Neel's *My Journey to Lhasa*, published in 1927, describes how the author disguised herself as a Tibetan peasant in order to defy the authorities who refused entry to foreigners. She claimed that her main motivation for the journey was political in the sense that it challenged:

> above all, the absurd prohibition which closes Thibet [sic] [. . .] I took an oath that in spite of all obstacles I would reach Lhasa and show what the will of a woman could achieve! I had sworn that a woman should pass, and I would. 'If heaven is the Lord's' the earth is the inheritance of man, and

that consequently any honest traveller has the right to walk as he chooses all over the globe which is his. (David-Neel [1927] 1988, xxv)

For Maillart, this journey marked the beginning of a lifetime avoiding what she felt was the evil of Western society, through a search for spiritual peace, continued later in travels to Iran, Afghanistan and India, which would later become the standard escape route for disillusioned Westerners. Maillart's own biography is reminiscent of Freya Stark's or Isabelle Eberhardt's in its lack of a sense of national identity and rejection of the normal mould for young women of the age, in favour of a life committed to exploring a foreign culture, and perhaps through this, discovering something of the self. Maillart questions the urge to travel that possesses her, and emphasises a sense of her own personal, existential value that needs space and freedom to be explored:

> What mattered was myself, I, who was living at the centre of the world — that 'I' who did not want to disappear without accomplishing something worthwhile, something that would carry me on, that would save me from nothingness, and satisfy — however humbly — the craving for eternity that existed in me. (268)

The physical struggle of the journey provides a metaphor for the psychological struggle involved in the decision to choose life and travel rather than give in to the pressures of death or immobility, as the series of metaphysical rhetorical questions slides into a realistic description of a tricky climb:

> What was the cause of the curiosity that spurred me on, of that need to see, to understand? Perhaps I created difficulties for the pleasure of surmounting them? What was the origin of those calls to me which I followed blindly and which made up my mind for me? There were still so many things to learn ... No, I didn't want to slip now. I must keep away from the dangerous scree. So I negotiated a ridge and, as my luck was in, I got safely back to the pasture grounds. (269)

The end of *Forbidden Journey* deals with the difficult trope of the return 'home'. They arrive at a hotel in Srinagar, amusing themselves by causing outrage to the prim couples dining there by their 'shabby clothes, untidy hair and buccaneer-black faces which no topee had ever shaded', though the amusement soon wore thin: 'It was depressing to be so near that world, all dressed up as though it was going to act in a comedy' (298). She knows her freedom has come to an end, as the threat of war forces them to return directly to Europe, in which 'although [it] was so small, misunderstanding was more rife than ever amongst its occupants. Yet they all have fresh water and grass growing on their lands . . .' (299). Fleming is aware that Maillart is less keen to end the journey and return to domesticity than he is, and comments on the differences in their natures:

> Getting back meant less to her than to me, who had, paradoxically, at once more ties and more detachment: a greater capacity to enjoy a life to which at frequent intervals I feel myself a stranger, and at the same time more friends and facilities with which to enjoy it. I wished it was not like this. On the road we had, I think, found much the same kind of happiness in much the same kind of things; and I would have liked the end of the road to have given us both an equal pleasure. But it is foolish to expect life to treat you and your friends fairly; and Kini was at least reasonably excited and proud and curious. (386)

Despite her sadness at leaving the 'careless life of the trail', Maillart ends her book by describing a sense of release or fulfilment, which reflects her need to escape a Western focus on 'civilisation' which placed Europe at the centre of the world:

> Night was falling when the vast swarm of lights that was Paris appeared in the north . . . Suddenly I understood something. I felt now, with all the strength of my senses and intelligence, that Paris, France, Europe, the White Race, were nothing . . . The something that counted in and against all particularisms was the magnificent scheme of all things that we call the world. (299)

Both accounts of the journeys combine familiar traditions: the remnants of nineteenth-century exploration in the adventure tale in forbidden lands; the attempt to explain the world in political terms and to question the nature of imperialism through journalism; and the post-romantic urge to explore the soul by seeking out exotic locations and rough terrain and turning these to a series of metaphors. In this final aspect, we see the greatest difference between the two writers, in that Maillart is clearly more interested in analysing her interior life and convinced of its innate importance than is Fleming, a tendency that is to become more generalised in travel writing by women as the century advanced.

10

Kawakami Otojiro's Trip to the West and Taiwan at the Turn of the Twentieth Century

Yukari Yoshihara

At the turn of the twentieth century, Japan was placed in the contradictory position of being both at the periphery of global Western hegemony and itself at the metropolitan centre of a colonial empire. This essay examines Otojiro Kawakami, one of the founders of Japanese modern theatre, and his travels to the West and to Taiwan under Japanese colonial rule; and it analyses them as cases testifying to the complexities surrounding Japan's geopolitical role during this period.

Models which set a European metropolitan centre against Asian colonial peripheries, in their simple forms, cannot be applied to Japanese travel writing. In his accounts of the United States, and Europe, we can perceive Otojiro's ambivalence towards such an opposition, for while admitting how hegemonic they might have become, he tries to challenge, question and subvert any stark dichotomy between the West and its others, by the very means of exaggerating the stereotypes of the Orientalist imagination at Western theatres. Another aspect of Otojiro is what Ayako Kano[1] calls the process of 'twisted double vision', by which Japanese people, themselves objects of the Western colonising gaze, were not only ready but eager to adopt a similarly appropriative perspective.[2] This may be seen in Otojiro's writing on his visit to the Penghu Islands (Taiwan) during the period of Japanese colonial rule and his adaptation of *Othello*, in which indigenous Taiwanese people sing and dance in praise of their Japanese masters. Otojiro is quite openly Orientalist, if I may use the term rather loosely, in his gaze on exotic Taiwan: only in this case metropolitan Tokyo is situated at the centre of the geopolitical map.

Otojiro Kawakami (1864–1911) started his career as an anti-governmental activist-performer in the late 1880s. His political activity was theatrical: he performed extravagant songs and dances in order to attract people's attention to the Movement for Civic Rights and Freedom (*jiyu minken undo*). However, his subversiveness was largely contained by the mid-1890s when he established himself as a central figure in the Westernisation of Japanese drama (called *engeki kairyo undo*, literally, theatre improvement movement), under the patronage of prominent politicians such as Hirofumi Ito (the first prime minister in 1885 and the first colonial governor of Korea in 1905) and Kencho Suematsu. Being a total outsider to the traditional Japanese drama, without any proper formal training in its conventions, Otojiro was notorious for his disregard for theatrical protocol, for his outrageous performing style, and for his overt admiration for the Western stage.

Otojiro travelled far and wide.[3] His first trip to Europe was in 1893, when he went alone and did not perform. The second was in 1899–1901, with his wife, Sadayakko, and his theatrical troupe to the USA and Europe. According to Otojiro's boast,[4] even Sir Henry Irving was impressed by their performance. In Europe, they performed as an attraction at the Paris International Exposition in 1900. After returning briefly to Japan in 1901, the Kawakami troupe set out on their second world tour to Europe where they performed in England, France, Germany, Austria and Russia.

Otojiro went to Asian countries also. In 1894, he visited the battle sites of the war between China and Japan, partly as a journalist, partly as a photographer, and he used his first-hand experience of the conflict to stage *The Sino-Japanese War* — a play which, because of its yellow-press

Figure 10.1 Otojiro's *The Sino-Japanese War* (Fukuoka City Museum)

sensationalism and its bloody spectacles, became a smash hit. Around this time, his themes became explicitly imperialistic, conforming to the Japanese ideology of expansion and colonisation recently adopted from the West.

After returning from Europe in 1902, Otojiro visited the Penghu Islands, located between mainland China and Taiwan, as a preparation for the planned staging of his adaptation of *Othello*. The region was an outstanding symbol of Japanese overseas expansion, for it was there that the Japanese military landed to initiate the colonisation of Taiwan in 1895. Otojiro wanted a first-hand experience of the Penghu Islands' reputedly tempestuous weather, barren soil and 'barbarous' pirates, to make his staging plausible.

It would be safe to say that Otojiro's performances in the United States and Europe were consumed as exotic shows, rather than as examples of the high-brow art of imperial Japan. Circuses, teahouse maids, *jujutsu* masters, *geishas* and stage performers went across the sea to the West just after, or even before, Japan opened its doors to the world in 1854. A circus, *Teikoku Nihon Geinin Itiza* (T. Maguire and Prof. Risley's Imperial Japanese Troupe), organised by Americans, visited San Francisco, New York, England, France, the Netherlands, Spain and Portugal in 1866–68. In 1885, when Gilbert and Sullivan's *The Mikado* was being performed, a Japanese village in Knightsbridge was simultaneously attracting huge crowds. By the time the Kawakami Otojiro troupe visited the United States and Europe at the turn of the century, Japanese exotic spectacles were a fairly established staple at major entertainment venues, especially in sideshows at international fairs.

Yumeto Kushibiki (?–1924), manager of the Kawakamis' US tour in 1899–1901, was one of the central figures in organising Japanese spectacles in America and Europe. He was famous, or notorious, for featuring lower-class jugglers and *geishas* at his tea gardens. His shows had great appeal to American audiences, but the Japanese tended to condemn them as an insult to national pride.

We can see one instance of Japanese antipathy to Kushibiki's enterprise in their reaction to his adaptation of *The Mikado* in New York in 1900. An article in a Japanese newspaper condemns this version as a disgrace to the country:

> I have often heard that in foreign lands stage performances claiming to display Japan represent our country ridiculously and they look simply outrageous to our Japanese eyes. A person coming back told me that currently in New York, USA, a play titled *The Mikado* is being shown, and the organizers are two Japanese, Arai and Kushibiki . . . It is especially unforgivable because it is Japanese who organise this outrageous show.[5]

Criticism directed against the japonaiserie of Kushibiki's 'outrageous show' could easily be applied to Kawakami's performance of savage *samurais* and love-crazed *geishas* while touring the United States and Europe. This is evident in the *San Francisco Chronicle* report of the arrival of the Kawamaki troupe to San Francisco on 20 May 1899. The headline reads: 'Madame Yacco, the leading geisha of Japan, coming here' with a large picture of Sadayakko.

The contemporary commercial craze for Japan in America was one factor that made Otojiro and his troupe's tour successful. Around this time, theatre classifieds abounded with advertisements for 'Oriental' plays such as *The Geisha* and *The Mandarin* (both at the Tivoli Opera-House). An article about 'Japanese day at the exhibition of industrial arts' features a drawing in which *geishas* are playing a *shamisen* guitar and dancing with a fan.[6]

In another register, we can relate the success of Otojiro's performance tours to the globalisation of the Asian labour force. Japanese immigrants to America, hungry for entertainments from 'home', formed a large part of the audience for the earlier phase of the tour. Japanese immigration to the mainland United States, in its government-sanctioned form, only began in 1884; but as early as 1880 there had been 148 Japanese residents and by 1900 Japanese immigrants numbered over twenty-four thousand. The Kawakami troupe started its American tour by performing for these communities in San Francisco, Tacoma, Seattle and Oakland, and then played for a general audience at the California Theater in San Francisco in June 1899.

This increase in the number of Asian workers caused American panic over the potential threat from this 'yellow peril'. Around the time the Kawakamis toured around the United States, vehement sentiments against Asian immigration were widespread. Because newcomers from China and Japan worked for cheaper wages and did not participate in the labour union movements, they were perceived to be threats to the white working population. Newspapers of the day were full of articles showing openly racist attitudes, such as demands for 'Restrictions on Jap Immigration'.[7] Under these circumstances, civic leaders in the Japanese immigrant community in San Francisco tried to persuade Otojiro's company to go back because their seedy performance was regarded as a great stain on the reputation of the Japanese in America.

One review article shows an ambivalent combination of fascination with exotic Japan and unease with the actual process of modernisation of Japan. What is particularly interesting about it, moreover, is that it situates the Kawakami troupe's performance in the context of American expansion in Asia.

It was a very quaint, curious and undoubtedly artistic performance . . . [T]he Geisha . . . made us realize a poetic value in all those quaint figures we see on vases which we have always considered fanciful . . . The first part of the second act showed to them that there was a modern spirit come into the Japanese acting in the last quarter of a century . . . The last piece had evidently been concocted to attract the American public. Mme. Yacco had a series of dances celebrating Dewey's victory . . . [O]ne of the Japanese girls entered in a blonde wig, with a gray suit, and swinging herself in imitation of the free American woman, greeted the vessel in English, although the only thing we heard distinctly was 'Hoora, Dewey!' The audience quite recognized the kindly intention of the strangers, but they are better in their truly Japanese plays.[8]

The writer highly appreciates the *geishas* and *samurais* in the shows as 'quaint, curious and artistic,' 'charming,' 'novel' and 'picturesque', but is uneasy about a 'modern spirit come into the Japanese acting', by a Japanese mimicking a modern American woman hooraying for Dewey. The quotation refers to Commodore George Dewey (1837–1917), who defeated the Spanish fleet at the Battle of Manila Bay (in the Philippines) in May 1898. At the time the Kawakami troupe was performing in the United States, Dewey fever was sweeping across the country. Anything and everything possible was created bearing his image, from soap to furniture to toys.[9] Otojiro was savvy enough to take advantage.

Japan also had its own colonial ambitions towards the Philippines. The political situation there had drawn much attention since the 1880s. For example, Suehiro Techo, a novelist, published his travelogue from Yokohama to Europe via the United States (*Oshi no ryokou*: 'Travel of a Deaf Mute' 1889), in which Jose Rizal (1861–96), a novelist and national hero of the Philippine independence movement, appeared in a fictionalised form as a 'gentleman from Manila'.[10] Some Japanese political activists are known to have been involved in the Philippines War of Independence.

It must be pointed out that, even by the late 1890s, Japanese sympathy towards Asia under Western colonisation had degenerated into an oblique justification of Japan's own colonial expansion to Asia, and Otojiro was no exception. Little is known about his show mentioned above. In all probability, it was simply a hurried improvisation designed to appeal to the American audience at the height of the Dewey craze. Otojiro was full of contradictions in his attitudes towards Asia. While he celebrates imperial American expansion over the Philippines in the 'Hoora, Dewey' show, he is, in other works, more critical of Western colonial rule in Asia. For example, in 1909, he performed an adaptation of Sir Hall Caine's *Bondman*, in which the scenes are set in

Mindanao Island in the Philippines. In the adaptation, a Japanese man appears as a benevolent settler who protects the innocent but lazy 'natives' of the Philippines from colonisers from Spain and the United States.

In Otojiro's tour of the United States, the Japanese actress in Western dress in the previous quotation, an apparent icon of Japan's sordid modernisation, may be regarded as a loose equivalent of the 'Japanese to-day in San Francisco in the hand-me-down suit of Western civilization' in the next review article.

> Nothing was ever more regretted by the foreigners who lived in Japan than the relegation to innocuous desuetude of their picturesque costumes, and their old-fashioned, beautiful rites and ceremonies. We don't need to ask why. We see the Japanese to-day in San Francisco in the hand-me-down suit of Western civilization; the women in the inappropriate fashions of our own race . . . [A]s I sat at the California Theater the other night . . . that battle scene would have done credit to Sir Henry Irving's stage management — the acting was modern . . . Still more noticeable was the remarkable performance of Kawakami . . . But that scene was more decidedly an example of the modern spirit in Japanese acting. Some of that development may be due to Kawakami's study of the European theaters.[11]

The writer, Peter Robertson, a prominent theatre critic who had lived in Japan in the 1870s, is nostalgic about the period before Westernisation. He contrasts 'picturesque' Japan with the shabbiness of actual Japanese workers in San Francisco and 'the women in the inappropriate fashions' (the phrasing is suggestive of Japanese sex-workers). His praise for Kawakami's performance as an 'example of modern spirit in Japanese acting' sounds half-hearted at best. He simply attributes any modernity in Kawakami's performance to his visit to Europe in 1893 — a telling sign of the writer's simplistic assumption that modernity can be equated to the West.

What did Otojiro have to say about such an Orientalising gaze of the West towards Japan? He responded with practical exploitation of these attitudes — making the most of Western expectations of the 'exotic' and 'quaint'. Initially, Otojiro intended to play his *The Sino-Japanese War* in modern military dress to show that Japan was a fully-fledged contemporary nation equipped with the up-to-date technology of mass-murder, but he was persuaded this would not appeal to American audiences. In a later interview, he explains the reason why his troupe instead chose to play traditional programmes.

> When I first went to the West to perform, I wanted to show that the Japanese were loyal and courageous subjects to the emperor. We would sacrifice

everything, we would commit ritual suicide *hara-kiri*, for the sake of loyalty and duty. To that purpose, we performed *The Sino-Japanese War* in which we killed the enemy soldiers in the bloodiest manner . . . They said, 'how barbarous and savage to play such bloody scenes. We have no interest in watching the Sino-Japanese war played on stage . . . We want to see Japanese actors in the guises of *samurais* in traditional *kimonos*, helmets and arms, we do not want to see you in western clothes'.[12]

American audiences had little interest in Japan as a modern, colonising nation-state. In order to please them, Otojiro produced extravagant shows full of bloody *samurais* and love-crazed *geishas*. He never hesitated to adapt and arguably travesty the basic plots of traditional Japanese dramas by adding unnecessary *hara-kiri* scenes and a *geisha*'s love-suicide. He was true to his spirit as an entertainment entrepreneur.

Otojiro and his troupe were expected to be 'authentic' native informants of 'genuine' Japanese culture. Yet, ironically, they were almost total outsiders to Japanese traditional drama. Strictly speaking, their performance did not even remotely resemble contemporary drama in Japan. Similarly, the introduction of Sadayakko as a Japanese actress on stage violated the conventions of traditional theatre which did not admit women on stage. Originally she had no intention of performing in America as an actress, but she was forced to become one because the Western audience wanted to see a genuine *geisha* in the flesh on stage. Ironically, the first Japanese actress was born in the United States.

Japanese reactions to the Kawakami troupe's exaggerated performance of exotic Japaneseness were, understandably, critical. One theatre critic condemned Otojiro as a betrayer of his native land. For him, Otojiro, like Kushibiki in his *Mikado* show, was a disgrace to the Japanese nation-state, for he performed a stereotypical 'Japaneseness', and thereby legitimised distorted images of Japan: he was, according to the critic, an Oriental who fawned upon the Orientalist discourse that defined Japan as different, 'exotic', and hence, inferior and savage. He complains that Otojiro 'should not have said to Western people that Japanese theatre in general was absurd, ridiculous, good only for erotic shows', and continues:

> You, Kawakami, it is nobody but you that performed absurd plays for the Western audience. You say Japanese theatre is degenerate, in need of improvement: if you know that, you must be also conscious that it is a great national shame to let the people in civilized countries watch what you call degenerate plays. Money is more important to you than national pride.[13]

Otojiro's overemphasis on the 'picturesque' and 'quaint' qualities of Japan surely helped to strengthen cultural stereotypes. However, it seems very probable that he performed such images of Japan as requested by audiences overseas in full knowledge that they existed only in the West's imagining, even though they appeared powerful enough to invent the 'reality' of Japaneseness.

A few years later, Nyozekan Hasegawa (1875–1969) wrote of his surprise at the British-Japan exposition in 1910: 'It looks so strange and absurd, to my Japanese eyes, that Japan thus shown never seems to represent today's Japan, nor Japan in the past century. In sum, such a Japan exists only in international expositions'.[14] In the case of Otojiro's exotic shows, this version was manufactured through a collaboration between the West that expected of Japan something 'quaint' and 'picturesque', and Otojiro's more-than-willing entrepreneurial spirit to satisfy such expectation.

At stake is who has the authority to represent Japaneseness and to whom? In the following quotation from a theatre review of Blanche Bates' performance in Belasco's *The Darling of the God*, it is the West, not Japan, that assumes the authority to represent 'genuine' cultural identity:

> But we can not quite believe that there was as much refinement of manners among the people of ancient Nippon as there is among the characters which Miss Bates and her players portray. We ought to be thankful that everything has been veiled to suit Western ideals . . . We don't want the Princess Yo San exactly as she might have been. We want her exactly like Blanche Bates.[15]

According to this review, it is the Western actress who can dictate the most ideal mode of Japanese femininity: Japonaiserie images are made in the West, for Westerners.

Otojiro's self-consciously extravagant performances of Japaneseness can be regarded as one instance of parody through exaggeration of the stereotypical. From Otojiro's memoir of his world tour, we learn that he intended to secretly ridicule the American audience who were fascinated by his exotic shows without knowing their real contents. For example, he staged an adaptation of *The Merchant of Venice* in Boston in nonsense Japanese. Otojiro's answer to Sadayakko, nervous because she did not know the lines to recite in her role as Portia, shows his rather wicked humour. He recalls that, just before the curtain opened, 'Sadayakko asked me "What shall I say?"', to which he replied 'Whatever. The audience would not know what you are saying. Say any old nonsense. Only be dramatic in body movements and in the ways you deliver the speech, they would think you are reciting the most heroic speech.'[16] In other words, Otojiro could be certain that an American audience would be fascinated with the Japanese version of *The Merchant of Venice* in so far as the performance suited their prior expectations of things Japanese.

Baron Kencho Suematsu (1855–1920), a politician, diplomat and patron of Otojiro and Sadayakko, criticised commercialised Japonisme in the West as a sign of the reluctance to admit the fact that Japan was a modern, Westernised country. In *The Risen Sun*, published in English in London (1905), he writes:

> We are often told that it is a pity that Japan should have lost her own antique customs . . . whereby she is in danger of ceasing to be one of the artistic objects of the world. It may be true to some extent, but we cannot afford to be deterred from promoting the growth of our own country, along the only path which will enable it to keep pace with the progress of the world, merely for the sake of pleasing the globe-trotters . . . The Westerners are well acquainted with many small objects of Japanese art such as *netsuke* or ivory carvings, and in admitting their artistic excellence, such critics are apt to call the Japanese 'grand in small things'. This is true to some extent, but it is not quite fair . . . If we stick to old modes we will remain for ever in the position of some inferior animal in the eyes of the Westerners.[17]

Japan simply cannot afford to remain one of 'the artistic objects of the world' in order to survive in the modernised world.

According to Suematsu, Westerners' fascination with Japan is similar to their attitude to exotic animals, positing a hierarchy of species in which the West is situated firmly at the top. An analogous structure may be discerned in Japan's own colonial version of the exotic, as exemplified in Otojiro's adaptation of *Othello* (1903). In a vivid scene with no equivalent in the original play, the indigenous Taiwanese people sing and dance in praise of Japanese colonial rule.

> *The natives worship the morning sun, shout strange and weird magic spells very loudly, hopping and jumping. They sing*: 'Ever since the Japanese came to rule Taiwan, peace prevails / We are grateful for Japan because we can now live without fear of burglars. / We can live happily and contentedly thanks to the good rule of the general [referring to the Othello figure]. / In these four or five years since Japan came to rule, we feel as if we were living under the bright sun every day.[18]

According to Otojiro, these words are based on a real song by the indigenous Taiwanese which he had collected: a claim which may well be greeted with incredulity.

A brief survey of the history of Japanese colonisation of Taiwan is appropriate here. Following its defeat in the First Sino-Japanese War (1894–95), Qing China ceded Taiwan and Penghu (the Pescadores) to Japan. Taiwanese resistance was largely crushed by 1902. Around 1903, when Otojiro's *Othello* was performed, the Japanese government was in the process of killing thousands of Taiwanese people who had rebelled against colonial rule. Local resistance persisted, however, with its last major manifestation, the Wushe Uprising led by Mona Rudao, occurring in the late 1930s: an incident in which over 150 Japanese officials were killed and beheaded during the opening ceremonies of a school sports meeting. The rebellion was subsequently put down with the help of the modern technology of mass destruction, poison gas.

Otojiro visited the Penghu Islands in 1902 — just after his tour to Europe in 1901–02, and, more importantly, approximately at the same time as the Taiwanese resistance was being crushed in the bloodiest of ways. His purpose was to gain first-hand experience of the exotic scenery and 'savage' culture and people in Japan's new colony, which could then be utilised in his adaptation of *Othello*.

He published a travelogue titled 'Kawakami Otojiro's adventure in the Pirates Islands' in the *Miyako Shimbun* (18–24 December 1902). From my perspective, it is clear that Otojiro projected his own preconceived stereotypes of the Penghu Islands upon the actual islands he visited, in spite of his claims that his observation is based on his genuine first-hand experience there.

In one episode, he talks about having difficulty in buying food from the local people.[19] He suspected that they were trying to extract money from him, thinking he was an ignorant coloniser-tourist — which he was. Finally, he succeeded in obtaining provisions. Local people offered him fuel to cook it with, but he did not know what it was. He thought it must be something other than coal, which people here could not be so 'civilized' as to know how to use. The fuel, it turned out, was dried cow dung. His tone is comic, but it must be said his travelogue is vulgarly colonialist. In addition, the episode has a cruel implication, for the Penghu Islands were suffering from severe starvation due to an exceptionally bad harvest at the time of Otojiro's 'adventure'.[20] There were good reasons for the local people's reluctance to sell food.

Apart from the doubtful authenticity of the song in Otojiro's adaptation of *Othello*, it is important to notice that the scene reflects some essential elements in the Japanese colonial imagination about the indigenous Taiwanese people as the quintessential embodiment of the exotic, primitive and picturesque. Contemporary travelogues about Taiwan abound with descriptions of their lifestyle and culture, which despite their marked fascination, are nonetheless colonialist: while the metropolitan Japanese highly appreciate their artefacts as signs of primitive purity and innocence uncontaminated by civilisation, they do not hesitate simultaneously to condemn the indigenous people as blood-thirsty head-hunters and cannibals. In Otojiro's adaptation, for example, a Japanese servant says of them that 'they are more fearful than malaria, for they eat men'.[21] The mainland Japanese do not seem to have felt any contradictions between their demonisation of indigenous Taiwanese people and their enchanted fascination with their picturesque folk-craft, dancing and music. Bloodthirsty at the same time as artistic: these two aspects were, from the standpoint represented by Otojiro, signs of the indigenous people's exotic otherness.

Otojiro's adaptation is remarkable in its somewhat confused discourse on ethnicity and class-formation in imperial Japan. The protagonist is named Washiro, a military officer rumoured to be of *eta* origin, a lower caste that was viciously discriminated against. He is sent out to Taiwan to become the first Japanese colonial governor. When he murders his wife, Tomone, in the most 'savage' manner, he compares himself to an 'ignorant' Taiwanese. At least partially, Washiro's rumoured origin from an ostracised caste is imaginatively compared to the supposed savageness of the indigenous Taiwanese.

It will be helpful to compare this with Otojiro's adaptation of *The Merchant of Venice*, which was performed in nonsense Japanese to an American audience in Boston. Little is known about the performance there, but according to Otojiro's memoir, he adapted the original play as a story of a money-lender in Hokkaido, the northern island in the Japanese Archipelago, colonised in the nineteenth century. Otojiro's memoir tells us much about his attitudes towards ethnic and class discrimination not only in Japan but also in the West.

> We loyal subjects of Japan gave much importance to charity and righteousness. There is no atrocious money-lender like Shylock in Japan . . . Some might say that Shylock in the West is an equivalent to *eta* in Japan, a mean and base tribe, that there is no wonder that a Western *eta* like Shylock commits cruel deeds. But even *etas* in Japan, who once were not treated as human, have never been cruel and savage like Shylock, even in novels and dramas . . . In the adaptation, I turned Shylock into a fisherman in Hokkaido, because the location would give some credibility to the savage and uncivilized deeds the Shylock figure commits, as Hokkaido is still largely uncultivated and a barbarous place full of ignorant and illiterate aboriginals.[22]

At the turn of the twentieth century, the *eta* or the *burakimin* people were often compared to racial minorities like the Ainu (the original inhabitants of Hokkaido), the Jewish people and the Native Americans — even though they are not a racial group, but a caste-like minority among the ethnic Japanese.[23] In 1871, the Meiji government abolished most derogatory names applying to the *burakumin*; but despite this, the new laws had a limited effect on the social discrimination faced by the formerly ostracised caste and their descendants, as is evident in Otojiro's words. Comparison between Shylock and the *burakumin* people was widespread in early twentieth-century Japan. Discrimination against this caste-like minority was often racialised.

Racial hierarchy in imperial Japan may be seen not only in Otojiro's adaptation of *Othello*, but also, in the same year as it was staged, 1903, in the anthropology exhibit scandal at the Fifth Domestic Exposition in Osaka, where four aboriginal Taiwanese, two Okinawan people, five Ainu people, two Koreans, three Chinese, three Indians and one aboriginal Javanese were put on display. Various people, especially elites from Okinawa, protested against the exhibit where ethnically different people were put on show as if they were animals. The issue raised vital questions concerning Japan's status as a multi-ethnic empire. An article in the *Ryukyu Shimpo*, a newspaper in Okinawa, succinctly summarises the scandal as follows.

> The anthropology house exhibits living human beings as a spectacle. Nowadays, even animals are protected against violation of their rights: needless to say, it would be against the spirit of civilization to put our fellow human beings on display even if they were inferior in terms of their knowledge and living standards . . . We must not insult the indigenous Taiwanese and the Ainu in Hokkaido by putting them on show, for they are subjects of the Japanese emperor engaged in the process of trying to become fully Japanese. What should we say about the Okinawan people on show, when they are not much different from the metropolitan Japanese both in their knowledge and life-style?[24]

The point at issue is: Who has a legitimate claim to be a proper Japanese subject? Another article calls the indigenous Taiwanese on show 'Taiwanese devils',[25] contrasting them with the Okinawan people who were deemed to be much more advanced in the process of Japanisation. This is symptomatic of subordinated peoples divided against each other, of one group demonizing another for the purpose of elevating its own position in the colonial hierarchy. One contemporary newspaper article says 'at the Taiwanese native section, the natives were not there to be seen. But I could imagine how they must be savage and barbarous, when I watched the shelves on which human skulls were displayed'.²⁶

As is well known, 'human showcases' similar to the show in which Okinawan and Taiwanese people were put on display provided a common form of entertainment at numerous international fairs at the turn of the century, including the Paris International Exposition in 1900 where Otojiro performed his *hara-kiri* shows.²⁷ Otojiro's performance must have been perceived by Western audiences as something quite close to these displays. These 'human zoos' were designed to serve as 'a system of signification in which objects and people were arranged in exhibits to suggest a world cultural hierarchy,'²⁸ denoting the exclusive right of the Western gaze to classify cultures and peoples other than their own as 'savage'. When Baron Suematsu wrote '[i]f we stick to old modes we remain for ever in the position of some inferior animal in the eyes of the Westerners', it is probable that he had 'human zoos' in mind.

So, 'human showcases' of the indigenous Taiwanese, Okinawa people and Ainu people at the Fifth Domestic Exhibition in Osaka in1903, and the 'savage' spectacle show of the aboriginal Taiwanese in Otojiro's *Othello* were, we may safely conclude, designed to satisfy Japan's desire to regard itself as the possessor of a similarly dominating gaze. The mainland Japanese and their culture were placed almost at the top of the hierarchy, almost on a par with a hegemonic West, in a manner designed to legitimitise Japan's colonial venture against the backdrop of the supposed primitive 'barbarity' of its colonial others.

I started this chapter by claiming that Japan had been placed in a contradictory position of being both at the periphery of a global Western hegemony and itself at the metropolitan centre of an empire. As I have tried to show, Otojiro was no less Orientalist in his attitudes towards the colonised peoples of imperial Japan. Obviously, it is not merely Otojiro's personal failing: rather, it is a product of a structure that situates Japan (especially Tokyo) both at the periphery and centre of imperial geopolitics.

By way of conclusion, let me refer to the British-Japan Exposition in 1910. It represented Japan both as a modern nation complete with an expansionist agenda, industrial and military power, and as an 'exotic' land — but this time, however, elements from Japan's colonised peoples were emphasised, rather than japonaiserie elements in *samurais* and *geishas*. Japan was represented in contradictory ways: on the one hand, as a contemporary state allied with the British Empire, and on the other, as the domain of 'curious' Taiwanese and the 'hairy Ainu'. *The Daily News* reports 'Ainu's Farewell: How London Impressed The Curious People,' making fun of the Ainu people's innocence.²⁹ One Japanese reporter, ashamed of the indigenous Taiwanese and Ainu displayed at the Exhibition, writes: 'One Englishman said, "I have heard lot about the Anglo-Japan Alliance, but we have never imagined that we have been allied to such people" '.[30] One of Japanese reporters, Hasegawa, whom I cited previously, wrote that such a 'human exhibition' violated the basic rights of the people involved, and 'the Japanese should never attempt to set up such a shameful show'.[31]

The organiser of this show was, significantly, a Japanese — Yumeto Kushibiki — who had introduced the Kawakamis to the Western stage.

11

Shaking the Buddhas: Lafcadio Hearn in Japan, 1890–1904

David Taylor

Out of the East, Lafcadio Hearn's 1895 collection, has the significant subtitle 'Reveries and Studies in New Japan', and yet despite the apparently upbeat emphasis on a contemporary scene, the work's principal urgency is an admiration of Japan's past. The volume contains 'The Red Bridal', a tale of a romantic double suicide based on fact with a developing agricultural village as its background, and giving a version of Oriental pastoral impinged on by Westernising modernity:

> Strange tall men with red hair and beards — foreigners from the West — came down into the valley with a great multitude of Japanese laborers, and constructed a railroad. It was carried along the base of the low hill range, beyond the rice-fields and mulberry groves in the rear of the village; and almost at the angle where it crossed the old road leading to the temple of Kwannon, a small station-house was built; and the name of the village was painted in Chinese characters upon a white signboard erected on a platform. Later, a line of telegraph-poles was planted, parallel with the railroad. And still later, trains came, and shrieked, and stopped, and passed - nearly shaking the Buddhas in the old cemetery off their lotus-flowers of stone (VII, 195).[1]

Seen through the eyes of the young lovers, Taro and O-Yoshi, at this point children, the arrival of the West may be construed as fearsome intrusion accompanied by architectural and religious desecration. The rural Japanese are subject to a seemingly foreign will for construction and change; and in this instance, the Chinese characters though intrinsic to the Japanese language, placed here in the list of innovations assume an air of unfamiliarity. Fixed location wavers momentarily, with the 'multitude of Japanese laborers' transplanted by an employment opportunity implicitly contextualised by the construction of the North American 'railroad', a usage resonating with the native Indian grievance of trespass upon its sacred sites. That human conflict foreshadows the imminent slaughter of the couple here, thwarted in love, and, with the will of 'samurai blood' (VII, 210), finally able to take advantage of the new technology, ending their lives with the train wheels, which 'passed through both — cutting evenly, like enormous shears' (VII, 213). Responsibility for their deaths stems from the profit motive of O-Yoshi's unscrupulous stepmother, O-Tama, who sets up a more lucrative match with a wealthy farmer and who, personifying the evolution of the peasant class, is 'a strong disbeliever in all the old ideas about character distinctions between samurai and heimin'[2] and is possessed of 'hard economy . . . concentrated into a perfect machinery within her unlettered brain' (VII, 207). The (advocated) ethos of the older period asserts itself in this allegory targeting the current mercantile drives encouraging the 'cunning speculators of the most vulgar class' (VII, 208).

'The Red Bridal' exemplifies Hearn's permanent distaste for modernisation's threat to what he regards as former Japanese sensibilities, beliefs and artefacts, and here, remarkably, he enters the consciousness of the Meiji period citizens, with an acute sense of their subordination to the now strongly centralised Tokyo government exerting increasing control. The narrative excels in its portrayal of the collision between past and present, with this historic moment of internal territorial reclamation — part of Japan's home nation-building vital to imperial domination in Asia — intimated as a rationale for the lovers' tragedy. Hearn's versions of traditional tales and especially notable human dramas drawn from newspapers, as in 'The Red Bridal', are in the habit of lauding the high morals of the former military aristocracy in stoic acts of commitment to duty; and this piece reiterates routine traits in Hearn's writing, such as a dubious, unquestioning nostalgia for the samurai, alongside a contempt for modernisation and its potential benefits.

However, intriguingly, Hearn's stories often eschew a single line of sympathy and propose a variety of contending perspectives. The satiric and garish theatricality of the 'red hair and beards', representing the specialist and invited foreign engineers, runs up against the scene's plausible historical accuracy and naturalistic detail, while the outrage conveyed in the symbolic assault on the Buddhist sculptures also borders on comedy. At school, the children are interested in learning about the mechanics of the trains, despite envisaging them as 'screaming and smoking, like storm-breathing dragons', and are engaged by 'the still more marvelous operation of the telegraph' (VII,

195). Hearn, the magazine writer provides copy from within the archipelago's far-flung regions, surely joining his characters in their enthusiasm for recent gadgetry. If the railroad is 'a long-expected and wonderful event' (VII, 194) of which both foreign traveller and local populace could not have ultimately disapproved, it is also the means by which the lovers end their lives in grim rejection of the militaristic imperial [ideology propounded by] their teacher: 'they should love their noble Emperor, and be happy even to give their lives for his sake' (VII, 190).

Hearn's skills in self-qualification — the journalist's manipulative and insightful awareness of the likely forums of reception — make it possible to read his works as complex narratives, subtle and surprising in both their enthusiasms and antagonisms, their polemics and counterarguments. His interest as a canonical observer of Japan increases when he is witnessed participating in the varied gambits of the commercially attuned performer, reliant both on the financial backing of the international readership and the career support of the host economy. This essay examines Hearn's success as resting on a professional dexterity which mediates a fiction of Japan's cultural authenticity while accommodating anxiety over a growing industrialised nation state. His decidedly partial representation of Japan as a self-conscious creation invites reassessment as travel writing, both as a negotiation with a journalistic marketplace and as an aesthetic construct in its own right.

The grafting of the American frontier onto provincial Japan has its origins in a proleptic letter of December 1883 to the musicologist, H. E. Krehbiel, a friend met in Cincinatti. Complaining of writer's block, Hearn also bemoaned diffidently 'another great affliction . . . [his] inability to travel'. But he then went on to announce a far from diffident ambition: 'I would give anything to be a literary Columbus — to discover a Romantic America in some West Indian or North African or Oriental Region — to describe the life that is only fully treated of in universal geographies or ethnological researches . . . If I could only become a Consul at Bagdad [sic], Algiers, Ispahan, Benares, Samarkand, Nippo, Bangkok, Ninh-Binh — or any part of the world where ordinary Christians do not like to go!' (XIII, 289). Hearn's aversion to Christianity, and in particular the late nineteenth-century missions, was to become manifest in his Japan writings, and his dismay over temporary stasis is equally understandable. Hearn's suitability for international journalism was rooted in the resilience necessary for the picaresque demands of his early and middle life prior to his departure for Japan. Born in Greece in 1850 to an Anglo-Irish army surgeon and Greek mother, a marriage that was short-lived, he was taken to Dublin in 1854. Here he was placed in the care of an Irish aunt, Sarah Brenane, a Catholic convert, who may have instilled in Hearn his distaste for formal Christianity.³ This antipathy developed at St Cuthbert's College, Ushaw near Durham, a strict Catholic institution where Hearn boarded for four years, and where he suffered a disfiguring accident that permanently blinded his left eye.

In 1869 the financial straits of his relatives sent him from London to Cincinatti, where he began his career as a journalist, gaining a reputation for sensational reports on the city's poverty, lowlife, and brutal dispatch of its criminals and their gory felonies, and where he entered an unsuccessful marriage with a creole woman, Alethea Foley. Journalism remained Hearn's source of income after moving to New Orleans in 1877, which, after ten years, he left for Martinique, where he lived and wrote for two years. Periods in Philadelphia and New York were followed by an expenses-paid journey by train through Canada arriving in Yokohama on the steamship *Abyssinia* on 4 April 1890.

Hearn made for Japan under contract for a variety of good reasons, including his fraught financial situation, and the emotional aftermath of a number of acrimonious personal and business relationships. The opportunity to leave New York on a paid voyage was the conclusion to a lengthy period of dissatisfaction with Western metropolitan life in which Hearn had contemplated Asia as a possible alternative. His strong interest in Japan was probably sparked by the Japanese exhibit at the New Orleans World Exposition in 1885, when, for the readers of *Harper's Magazine*, he immediately began to rehearse a stylistic approach to the Japanese exotic.⁴ Hearn arrived in Yokohama, sponsored to produce an article to accompany the artist C. D. Weldon's illustrations of Japan, an assignment which was completed successfully; but the arrangement with his publishers ended after some characteristically rancorous exchanges over payment with the *Harper's* editor, Henry Alden.

Initially without employment, Hearn began the last phase of his short but prolific life, never to leave Japan. He wrote extensively on the country, recording daily customs, local myth and history, alongside creating numerous episodes of travelogue. With the essential assistance of his wife, Setsuko Koizumi, he compiled and recreated a great number of national folk tales, and to support her and their four children, he went from being journalist to high school teacher to lecturer in English at the Imperial University of Tokyo. Hearn became a Japanese citizen in 1896, taking the name 'Koizumi Yakumo', at a point when his celebrity as a mediator of Japan for Western audiences — notably in America, England, France and Germany — was secure. He backed Japan in the wars against China (1894–95) and Russia (1904–05). Hearn's fascination, if not obsession, with the Buddhist doctrines of evolving, 'inherited' selves and accruing, remembered identities developed in Japan, but these ideas are strongly paralleled in the journeying palimpsests of his own writings,[5] with Eastern religion, Western evolutionary theory and the journalist's indefatigable resources cohering in this archetypal itinerant finally wanting to leave Japan, but due to illness, confined to run on the spot in the increasingly sought seclusion of his study. He died of heart failure in Tokyo in 1904.

Hearn remains one of the most engaging writers on Japan, paradigmatic generically in his proffered desire to live in the country 'not simply as an observer but as one taking part in the daily existence of the common people, and *thinking with their thoughts*',[6] before discovering with anxiety and ultimate resignation the impossibility of this wish. Yet the numerous expressions of retrospective regret have as their medium the prodigious professional output of the foreign correspondent, and, with his 'writing block' over, Hearn was to add richly to his already substantial body of journalism on the United States and the West Indies — the standard Koizumi edition comprising sixteen volumes, excluding a large body of literary criticism, aesthetics and philosophy. Hearn's reputation, despite often adverse criticism, survives; and the renewed interest throughout the 1990s to the present has been less concerned with maintaining his (now assured) literary status than with evaluating the multiple intercultural tensions within his writing. Sukehiro Hirakawa has commented that Hearn's antique vignettes have kept their attraction for the Japanese due to their 'ineradicable narcissism',[7] but that the writings' popularity did not emerge until much later than in the West. Their earlier success abroad can be attributed to the already well-established vogue for japonaiserie, the phenomenon which sent Hearn to Japan in the first place.[8]

The first collection, *Glimpses of Unfamiliar Japan* (1894), published four years after Hearn's arrival, and with the opportunity taken to revise and polish initial notes, opens with the important account of Yokohama, 'My First Day in the Orient', and initiates an overall technique of transcribing the perceived with shifting styles in close proximity. A stark objectivity is achieved in the 'wooden houses, mostly unpainted, with their first stories all open to the street, and thin strips of roofing sloping above each shop-front, like awnings, back to the miniature balconies of paper-screened second stories' (V, 5). Then a typically intense sighting heightens perception of 'an atmospheric limpidity extraordinary, with only a suggestion of blue in it, through which the most distant objects appear focused with amazing sharpness' (V, 4); or the traveller's delighted sense of discovery is relayed with a note of triumphant melodrama: 'all is unspeakably pleasurable and new . . . the real sensation of being in the Orient, in this Far East so much read of, so long dreamed of, yet, as the eyes bear witness, heretofore all unknown'(V, 4). Natural and cultural specificities are energetically collected and lyrically displayed: 'The path before me, is white with the soft, thick, odorous snow of fallen petals. Beyond this loveliness are flower pots surrounding tiny shrines; and marvelous grotto-work, full of monsters — dragons and mythologic beings chiseled in the rock' (V, 26). Indeed, Hearn claims a somewhat factitious tirelessness in his search for 'revelation', and within this lengthy piece's jostling, copious details — emblematic of his best writing as a whole — the tropes that will feature prominently in the Japan writings come to the fore: the rhetorically assured and opulent lyricism that marks him as a representative voice of the *fin de siècle*; a permanent aestheticised hunt for the rare and the exotic to the exclusion of mundane modernity; and a repetitive and highly stylised palette of vocabulary,[9] which Hearn revisits and recycles in the description of discrete experiences. Ordered to 'observe that the same rich dark blue which dominates in popular costume rules also in shop draperies' (V, 6) we note, as we might of the atmosphere, the roofs, the sea, sky and shaved head of a novice, that here, as in all subsequent publications, Hearn has a penchant for the word 'blue'. By 1897's 'The Dream of a Summer Day', the ubiquitous shade has become a mannerism, if an effective one:

> All was steeped in blue — a marvelous blue, like that which comes and goes in the heart of a great shell. Glowing blue sea met hollow blue sky in a brightness of electric fusion; and vast blue apparitions — the mountains of Higo — angled up through the blaze like masses of amethyst. What a blue transparency! (VII, 12)

Hearn's passionate, cadenced lyricism, with its Paterian aspirations[10] to a (sometimes ostentatious) musicality, charges his epiphanies of Japan artistically, or, despite the insertion of dynamic naturalistic detail, has a lesser, narcotic lulling effect. Nevertheless, his great success as a purveyor of Japan to Western audiences can be attributed to the various skilful transitions within his style, vivid, evocative 'impressions' juxtaposed with discordant, often melancholy undertones, all of which are difficult to reconcile with the declared motivation of ethnological research. Actually, Hearn's substantial output features relatively little analysis, consisting instead of set-piece sketches produced under the constraints of publishing scenarios and a foreign readership, and eliciting a voice attuned to the commercial opportunities of the Western taste for things Japanese.

More often than not, specific and original positions are less in evidence than the corroboration of a pre-existent set of expectations. The first essay introduces by way of contrast to the careful (though probably source-dependent) accuracy given to architecture, an admiring but, as Hearn concedes, provocative[11] displacing of the Japanese themselves, 'forty millions of the most lovable people in the universe' (V, 12), into 'fairy-land' where 'all movement is slow and soft, and voices are hushed — a world where land, life, and sky are unlike all that one has known elsewhere' (V, 10). This is casually contradicted two pages later: 'On a pavement, such as that of a railway station, the sound [of Japanese wooden clogs] obtains immense sonority' (V, 14). Hearn's naturalistic concern over his rickshaw driver, Cha, (his 'heart-beats and muscle-contractions' (V, 9), his 'coaxing' dishonesty (V, 8)) is undercut by the whimsical condescension which depicts the local people as 'lesser and seemingly kindlier beings, all smiling at you as if to wish you well ... Hokusai's own figures' (V, 10, 14). Regularly, Japan and the Japanese have their own aesthetic of the miniature directed back at them — 'Elfish everything seems; for everything as well as everybody is small, and queer, and mysterious' (V, 5) — this presaging the later countless uses of 'little', 'miniature', 'tiny' and 'dainty'. Hearn's belief in his 'consciousness . . . transfigured' gives context to his representations of the Japanese race, whose otherness, beyond their diminution, is favoured in a hyperbolic vocabulary of polarities ('never', 'always', 'unchanging', 'perfect') in which realism and fantasy commingle:

> Looking sunward, up the long Ohashigawa, beyond the many-pillared wooden bridge, one high-pooped junk, just hoisting sail, seems to me the most fantastically beautiful craft I ever saw — a dream of Orient seas, so idealized by the vapor is it; the ghost of a junk, but a ghost that catches the light as clouds do; a shape of gold mist, seemingly semi-diaphanous, and suspended in pale blue light. (V, 163)

Overt celebration of specific phenomena combines with a generalised configuration of the Orient, verging on the abstract and the fictional. The dissonant, anachronistic 'junk' crosses into the spirit world, at once standing for a private utopia and rendering it futile in the velocity of progress.[12] Yet, as the vision dissolves into evanescence, a despondent solipsism, reminiscent of late nineteenth-century spiritualism, is as pervasive as ecological regret, the entry into 'fairyland' reminiscent of W. B. Yeats's Celtic mythological ideals [as expounded in essays such as 'Irish Fairies' (1890).] If the beauty of Asia is under threat, is it best preserved in exaggeration of what is to be lost, or transformed, and savoured as a realm within the imagination?

Hearn has become a template for a central convention of travelogue on Japan, in which an idealisation of the traditional culture eroded by imported modernity gives way to enervated disillusion. Yet the Meiji acceleration towards an industrial economy had already largely occurred by 1880, a decade before Hearn's arrival, rendering the effects of his rhetorical stances the more complex and poignant. His writings are less factual renditions of Japan in a state of flux than belated elegies for an already complete metamorphosis. Hearn's epiphanic declarations occasionally resound with self-persuasion:

> When, for the first time, I stood before the shrine of the Great Deity of Kitzuki, as the first Occidental to whom that privilege had been accorded, not without a sense of awe there came to me the thought: 'This is the Shrine of the Father of a Race; this is the symbolic centre of a nation's reverence for its past.' And I, too, paid reverence to the memory of the progenitor of this people. (VI, 146)

Hearn's (clearly untrustworthy) self-projection was designed to appeal to the expectations of an international readership, whose appreciation of the novelty of Asian forms had probably been influenced by Matthew Arnold's definitions of racial and cultural essence.[13] The experienced and enlightened commentator had permission from a turn of the century public to evoke the distinctive traits of an older, disappearing world as much as analyse it, and Hearn manifestly understood his own talent for the former.

In a letter to Ellwood Hendrick, Hearn wrote that 'I am the only man who ever attempted to learn the people seriously; and I think I shall succeed' (7 October 1891).[14] However, the exaggerated claims of inaugural encounter ('the first Occidental') habitually elide any reference to the substantial foreign population of professional diplomats, teachers, merchants and other imported specialists already *in situ* aiding Japan's policies for Western-style imperialism, and vital to Hearn's own career progress around Japan. Instead, a calculated appeal to a Western audience is conducted in a sophisticated range of tones and personae, posited largely as entertainments. The original reader might well have been engaged by an ostensible East-West synthesis:

> . . . a shop of American sewing-machines next to the shop of a maker of Buddhist images; the establishment of a photographer beside the establishment of a manufacturer of straw sandals: all these present no striking incongruities, for each sample of Occidental innovation is set into an Oriental frame that seems adaptable to any picture. (V, 11)

Yet the harmony in this flexible absorption of the foreign is short-lived, and then denied, in the implicit self-contradiction that the Western objects do in fact stand out as 'striking incongruities'. 'My First Day in the Orient' introduces a trusted device, being a voice of sharp hostility towards the Western presence in Japan, accompanied by a willed involvement with the people and their customs — or, an inevitable observational distance is maintained, with the Lilliputian 'illusion' destroyed 'by the occasional passing of a tall foreigner, and by divers shop-signs bearing announcements in absurd attempts at English' (V, 5). The disgruntled visitor's sneer at linguistic incompetence swivels into animosity for the West and its influence, inviting the reader to 'imagine the effect of English lettering substituted for those magical characters; and the mere idea will give to whatever aesthetic sentiment you may possess a brutal shock' (V, 6). Hearn's agile displacements of sympathy install an ease of self-contradiction from one essay to the next, with the perpetual difficulties of inhabiting the role of *gaijin* (outsider) in conflict with the goal of nonchalant abandonment of the West. Both tendencies collaborate in 'Strangeness and Charm', from the final collection *Japan: an Attempt at Interpretation* (1904), where by way of thematic return to 'My First Day in the Orient', the hyperboles of pleasure and predicament intensify:

> The mere sensation of the milieu is a placid happiness: it is like the sensation of a dream in which people greet us exactly as we like to be greeted, and say to us all that we like to hear. (XII, 16)

The above enacts a characteristic shift in register subsequent to the daily alienation of life amongst 'emblems incomprehensible' (XII, 8):

> No adult Occidental can perfectly master the language . . . Could you learn all the words in a Japanese dictionary, your acquisition would not help you in the least to make yourself understood in speaking, unless you had learned also to think like a Japanese — that is to say, to think backwards, to think upside-down and inside-out . . . Experience in the acquisition of European languages can help you to learn Japanese about as much as it could help you to acquire the language spoken by the inhabitants of Mars. (XII, 11, 12)

Veneration for the 'magical' Japanese language in 1890 recurs in this highly reminiscent re-evaluation of 1904 in which the Chinese characters, commonplace elements for communication in the daily life of Japanese native speakers, retain their 'wizardry' in governing 'this fantastic world' where the outsider's knowledge may never 'diminish the sense of strangeness' (XII, 8). Ebullient overstatement of the mystique of this outwardly intractable language becomes a means to generate atmospheres of mystery and adventure. At the same time, the team of native informants and translators — the *sine qua non* for Hearn's writing — is screened out, a convention that makes virtual absences of his wife, relatives, colleagues and students, who enjoyed a degree of celebrity in biographies and interviews after his death. Among those who offered crucial assistance in overcoming the limitations in Hearn's Japanese,[15] and were largely unacknowledged as translators and interpreters, along with Setsuko Hearn and his colleague at Matsue Middle High School, Sentaro Nishida, are three male pupils from the Matsue school: Otani, Adzukizawa and Tanabe. In exchange for helping him with information on the language and customs, Hearn paid them to assist with their education in higher institutions, but 'was exceedingly detailed and ruthlessly specific in getting out of Otani and Adzukizawa what he wanted from them' (Stevenson, 246). Strikingly, Adzukizawa goes unmentioned by name in Hearn's account of his ascent of Mt. Fuji, despite being pivotal as translator in the expedition. Setsuko Hearn gives a parallel account to that of his students as to Hearn's methods of composition involving native speakers, in particular his firm instructions on wanting literal translation from idiomatic or spoken Japanese.[16] The traveller's blithe ignorance is inverted into a self-bestowing authority, liberating Hearn from the rigours of scholastic procedure, and enabling the omnivorous scope of the sketches as exercises in literary style. Attitudes disingenuously disowning the West are attended by a covert intimacy with the required Western reader, who, anticipating guidance, ghosts and Gothic, can also expect to be lambasted regularly and directly with charges of inferiority:

> For the Japanese do not brutally chop off flower-heads to work them up into meaningless masses of color, as we barbarians do: they love nature too well for that; they know how much the natural charm of the flower depends upon its setting and mounting, its relation to leaf and stem, and they select a single graceful branch or spray just as nature made it. At first you will not, as a Western stranger, comprehend such an exhibition at all: you are a savage in such matters compared with the commonest coolies about you . . . despite your Occidental idea of self-superiority, you will feel humbled. (V, 195)

This extract from the 'The Chief City of the Province of the Gods' — Hearn's long tribute to the city of Matsue, isolated and spectacularly resistant to modernisation — is collected with another of his extended pieces, 'In a Japanese Garden', where a love of nature is less in evidence than the 'cunning . . . art of the ancient gardener who contrived all this' (VI, 24), but who is warding off 'the withering influence of the utterly commonplace Western taste' (VI, 11).

Hearn often echoes the received Japanese epithets [for *gaijin*] to describe the 1853 arrival of Commodore Perry's fleet, 'the "Black Ships" as they were then called', and the 'foreign "barbarians"' they brought (VII, 398, 399). 'Of Women's Hair' is one of the many pieces which continues the conceit of the Westerner's inferiority:

> The hairdresser (*kamiyui*) first sends her maiden apprentice, who cleans the hair, washes it, perfumes it, and combs it with extraordinary combs of at least five different kinds. So thoroughly is the hair cleansed that it remains for three days, or even four, immaculate beyond our Occidental conception . . . Far beyond the skill of the Parisian *coiffeuse* is the art of the kamiyui. (VI, 88, 90)

Or:

> [t]here are no better surgeons in the world than the Japanese. (VII, 271)

Or:

> 'Ho-ke-kyo!'
> My uguisu is awake at last, and utters his morning-prayer. You do not know what an uguisu is? An uguisu is a holy little bird that professes Buddhism. (V, 166)

The multiple, impacted tones, in these instances ranging from the insider's lofty expertise to the genial, sentimental children's storyteller, seem to mark concerns over the creation of personae and with which culture to identify, as much as to inform the home auditor. A fluid back-and-forth motion between East and West is essential to Hearn's tactics ('What a great thing is the West! What new appreciations of it are born of isolation');[17] and by including himself ('we barbarians') in the midst of the exclusive, mocking 'you's', the impossibility of integration or any complete renunciation of the West is signalled through a nuanced irony. In 'Diplomacy', an intercultural ventriloquy conveys the self-confident voice of Imperial Britain through the samurai warrior who, Sherlock Holmes to Watson, is able to allay the illogical fears of a retainer as to a possible haunting:

> Oh, the reason is simple enough . . . Only the very last intention of that fellow could have been dangerous; and when I challenged him to give me the sign, I diverted his mind from the desire of revenge . . . you need not feel any further anxiety about the matter. (XI, 189, 90)

Then there is the comic-gullible persona caught in peevish dramatic dialogue with the unreliable natives:

> 'What utter humbug!' I exclaimed ... 'Now,' my friend protested, 'you are unjust to the woman! You came here because you wanted a sensation ... You did not suppose that ghost story was true, did you?'(IX, 288)

In this conclusion to 'A Passional Karma', one of Hearn's most successful versions of Japanese Gothic, with aristocratic lovers communing in life and death, skilled fictional technique is at odds with the insistent omniscience of the footnotes, as in the (unimaginative) assertion that the differences between the speech of samurai and lower classes 'could not be effectively rendered into English' (IX, 268).

Hearn, when holding the definitive mores of both Japan and the West at an authorial distance, still invokes the breadth of mind of the Western reader, who aside from sharing the blame for Japan's aesthetic decline, and being the willing recipient of Hearn's syndicated articles, is invited to accommodate the hybrid range of identities — cosmopolitan traveller, journalist, teacher, academic, late-Romantic prose stylist — amalgamated in the writer himself. The works have as their chief unstated irony the fact that they are sanctioned by the very forces of modernisation which repel their author; Hearn's presence in the country as part of the nation's educational reforms compromises his devoted search for authentic national rituals and beliefs, not least his conviction as a Tokyo University professor that 'it is a great mistake to teach English Literature in Japan'.[18]

Most of the 'weird', 'strange', 'exotic' and 'quaint' phenomena Hearn examined did not concern potentially extinct remnants of pre-Meiji Japan, with the paradox of his later reputation as a preserver of vanishing cultural forms involving the concomitant irony that much of the Japan he describes is still recognisable. Moreover, the kind of empirical efficiency and expertise of the catalogues of data provided by Isabella Bird (the first female member of the Royal Geographical Society) is noticeably absent in Hearn, passed over for soft-focus historical generalisations:

> The traveler who enters suddenly into a period of social change — especially change from a feudal past to a democratic present — is likely to regret the decay of things beautiful and the ugliness of things new. (V, 10)

The simplistic associations of the 'feudal past' with beauty, and democracy with 'decay', might be a gauge of the traveller-aesthete's superficial grasp of a developing political situation; alternately, he might be credited with near-prophetic apprehension of the outcome of nationalist hubris:

Will she stumble? It is very hard to predict. But a future misfortune could scarcely be the result of any weakening of the national spirit. It would be far more likely to occur as a result of political mistakes — of rash self-confidence. (VII, 176)

For Hearn, this polarised attitude, valorising samurai ethics while deriding Meiji, largely synonymous with Westernisation, results in the jarring eruptions of hostility in his correspondence and personal dealings, offering predictable discrepancies between his publications on Japan and his privately stated feelings. As early as 1893, Hearn confided to his academic sponsor and, then, close friend the Tokyo Professor of Philology, Basil Hall Chamberlain:

> The illusions are forever over . . . I know much more about the Japanese than I did a year ago; and still I am far from understanding them well. I love the people very much, more and more the more I know them. Conversely I detest with unspeakable detestation the frank selfishness, the apathetic vanity, the shallow vulgar scepticism of the New Japan, the New Japan that prates its contempt about Tempo times, and ridicules the dear old men of the pre-meiji [sic] era and that never smiles, having a heart as hollow and bitter as a dried lemon.[19]

Yet as Hearn's recommendations for the nobility of Japan's samurai past mount up, the reader is also provided with revelations of a violent hierarchical society of beheadings, live burials and severe social regulations,[20] which somewhat mitigates against his dismay at the West's head-chopping in flower arrangements, and prompts the possibility that Hearn's earlier journalistic preoccupation with macabre inhumanity propels his interest in ancient Japanese principles.[21] The education of the young samurai son in 'A Conservative' (1896) involves a 'Spartan discipline', including witnessing executions and being forced to go alone at midnight to retrieve a decapitated head 'in proof of courage' (VII, 394). One year later, disenchanted with pedagogy, Hearn's 'With Kyushu Students' regrets the passing of 'the mutual love of other days in the old Samurai Schools' (VII, 50). Similarly, the late retreat into the violent ghost stories of *Kwaidan* (1904) leads us through a sadistic world of cannibalistic monsters and vengeful spectres, reflective of the true-to-life greed and deceit of their human counterparts in Hearn's other tales, and in contradistinction to the sentimental stereotype of 'the dear old men of the pre-meiji [sic] era'.

Hearn is vulnerable to the charge of oversimplifying the allegiances of the period's protagonists and political structures. Historical analysis of the Meiji Restoration and dynasty (1868–1912) largely rejects a clear-cut division between the values of modernity and the samurai class,[22] with the financial implications of Western influence seen as welcomed by the former military caste:

> The young reformers, who started in 1868 to make Japan into a modern nation able to hold its own on terms of equality with the Western powers, saw their ambitions realised within their own lifetimes. With the aid of a strong army and navy, an efficient government, an obedient and technically competent citizenry, and vigorous industry and commerce they made Japan within a few short decades a world military power and won recognition of equality from the occidentals, who had in the past tended to look at upon all Asia as essentially "barbarian" and outside the family of civilized nations . . . Japanese leaders, with their samurai backgrounds, enthusiastically embraced the current imperialism of Europe and soon outstripped the Western imperialists in their determination to win colonies. (Reischauer, 134)

Reischauer, writing from the mid-twentieth century, interim perspective gives the accepted general outline of the period's energetic national transformation. His revised history of Japan's phases of modernisation continues with a recognition of the breadth of beneficiaries during the Meiji restructuring:

> To stabilize revenues and clarify land ownership, fixed monetary taxes were substituted in 1873 for the traditional percentage of agriculture yield, and the payers of the tax, who were the peasants themselves, were confirmed as the outright owners of the land. Modern Japan, unlike postfeudal Europe, has had no continuing problem of land ownership by the old feudal classes. (Reischauer, 83)

Fluid financial partnerships between the ancient classes were also a dynamic possibility:

> The Mitsui, which in late Tokugawa times had become a wealthy merchant family, created the largest of . . . economic empires. Next to the Mitsui came the Mitsubishi interests, developed by a *samurai* family, the Iwasaki, from a merchant firm of the Edo period. (Reischauer, 83)

Hearn's omission of the complexity of Meiji class interaction has its origins in his opposition to Western capitalism, which goes undiscussed in his support for Japan's colonial victories, despite, for example, many of the warships responsible for the Japanese naval triumphs having been built in England.[23] This curious silence continues in Hearn's support for the comparatively homogeneous and authoritarian nation state of Meiji Japan, which is repaid for its hospitality in unrelenting slights on the Occident: 'the wisdom of China was voluntarily sought, while that of the West was thrust upon her by violence' (VII, 380). In the context of their parallel colonial trajectories, there is scant logic in permanently situating the West as Japan's opposite in such a schematic way.

Hearn presents himself as swept up in the widespread popular rejoicing over Japan's undeniable military achievement:

> But in this radiant spring of the Japanese year 2555, the koi might be taken to symbolize something larger than parental hope — the great trust of a nation regenerated through war. The military revival of the Empire — the real birthday of New Japan — began with the conquest of China. The war is ended; the future, though clouded, seems big with promise; and however grim the obstacles to loftier and more enduring achievements, Japan has neither fears nor doubts. (VII, 332)

The Western observer, impressed by Japanese colonial expansion at this juncture, is forced to acknowledge that Japan's new-found status as a military power has its dominance grounded in expert use of Western-style weaponry,[24] with the martial codes of samurai Japan and the Meiji state in lethal alignment, a continuum without commentary in Hearn. In 'After the War', written in the wake of the Sino-Japanese conflict, and the intervention of Russia, France and Germany 'to bully' Japan into giving up Liaotung peninsula, statements weave between subjective belief and journalistic reportage of Japanese patriotism. Hearn's proclaiming of Japan's 'glorious purpose' and 'the national spirit' leads him to wonder 'whether Western civilisation has not cultivated the qualities of the individual even to the destruction of national feeling' (VII, 172). It is an unbalanced moment, as if the human loss incurred through Asian warfare is to be occluded in substantiating Hearn's philosophical rejection of Western individualism and his (palpably untrue) theory of declining patriotism.

Yet as Hearn enlists copious acts of extreme heroism and sacrifice from Japanese youth, such as the wounded bugler who resists rescue to blow a fatal signal of attack (VII, 334), his absolutist marshalling of arguments for Japan's military culture adjusts to encompass humanist sentiment:

> I could not help feeling it was cruel to send such youths to battle. The boyish faces were so frank, so cheerful, so seemingly innocent of the greater sorrows of life! 'Don't fear for them,' said an English fellow-traveler, a man who had passed his life in camps; 'they will give a splendid account of themselves.' 'I know it,' was my answer; but I am thinking of fever and frost and

Manchurian winter: these are more to be feared than Chinese rifles. (VII, 342)

A fellow outsider's voice galvanises doubt concerning Japan's warmongering, 'splendid' having been Hearn's favourite word several pages earlier for the Japanese naval command and its vessels. Meanwhile, the wisdom of hindsight — official at the point of writing that the majority of Japanese losses in China were due to illness — detracts from a Japanese sailor's excited rationalisation, 'If we had not had to fight against Western gunners, *our victory would have been too easy*' (VII, 341). Hearn does not baulk at portraying the soldiers' return from a notable campaign in terms of human defeat, with the West easily superimposed over Japan's uniqueness:

> The features showed neither joy nor pride; the quick-searching eyes hardly glanced at the welcoming flags . . . perhaps because those eyes had seen too often the things which make men serious. (Only one man smiled as he passed; and I thought of a smile seen on the face of a Zouave when I was a boy, watching the return of a regiment from Africa — a mocking smile, that stabbed.) (VII, 344–5)[25]

It is a judgement removed from the fervent tones devoted to integration and apologia, a sombre inflection that does not conform to the languid paeans to art and landscape, or to the splenetic confidences of the correspondence, but must also reach out to the West in paradoxical reliance to sustain the record of the East.

Any just appraisal of Hearn, particularly of his Japan writings, may commend a nuanced, finely constructed style, which elevates sharp anecdotal detail and cultural reportage into an accomplished, humane oeuvre, of its time, but enduring. Yet, this remarkable body of work has an important alternative interest in its divergent strains of authenticating Japan to the West while anxiously but astutely averting its gaze. To many, Hearn's Japan might be unfamiliar indeed.

12

'Chambres d'Asie, chambres d'ailleurs': Nicole-Lise Bernheim's 'Vertical Travels' in Asia

Katy Hindson

Traveller, writer, novelist and journalist, the late Nicole-Lise Bernheim (1942–2003) left a diverse body of work which reveals her passion for travel. This author's work ranges from journalistic *reportages* for newspapers such as *Le Monde, L'Express* and *Le Matin*, to production work for French radio station *France-Culture*. However it is two of Bernheim's *récits de voyage* which are of interest here, namely *Chambres d'ailleurs* (1986) and *Saisons japonaises* (1999). These texts, which evoke her experiences of travel and travel-in-dwelling in Japan, Hong Kong, Sri Lanka, Taiwan, Singapore and India, allow an exploration of the way in which the writing of one author can evolve through different modes of travel and different approaches to the exploration of place and provide a valuable case study for issues of gender and self-performance in travel and travel writing.

Chambres d'ailleurs is the account of the author's six-month journey around a number of countries in Asia, in the company of her partner. As the title suggests, Bernheim uses the rooms in which she stays as a central motif throughout the text, suggesting both the fragmentary nature of the travel undertaken and its account, and the importance of these temporary homes and shelters to the traveller as places of refuge.[1] Although these *chambres d'ailleurs* do not always fully reflect the sense of place in which they are located, they are not as anonymous or as easily relocated as the non-places described by Marc Augé.[2] Instead a sense of place is implied by the traces and spectres of other travellers, previous inhabitants and also by the details of each room. Perhaps this approach to travel and place should be seen, as James Clifford suggests, as 'dwelling-in-travel',[3] where the focus lies upon the preservation or invention of a sense of home in a series of transitory abodes. While travel seems at first to imply an abandonment of the home by the traveller, this text suggests the fluidity of the concept of home. The author seems to challenge the traditional binary opposition of the home and 'foreign' space, by recreating aspects of home with her in travel.[4] While many of the places visited during this journey are described and travelled through only fleetingly, there is a sense in which Bernheim's attention to detail and everyday experiences creates a type of microscopic travel, where the reduction of the traveller's field of vision and experiences, rather than being limiting as it might at first seem, actually highlights the complex interaction of home and abroad in travel and travel writing. Microscopic travel is taken here to indicate a mode which enables the traveller to stop and focus on the small details and textures of the places she travels to and through. Deceleration and attention to detail are characteristic of this approach to place, allowing a reactivation of the senses and a re-inscription of the travelling body into the experience of travel. Michael Cronin discusses this in terms of a 'fractal travel mode' which he offers as a counter to the discourse of exhaustion expounded by critics such as Paul Fussell. Such an approach, which can be traced back to Xavier de Maistre's *Voyage autour de ma chambre* [1794],[5] allows for infinite possibilities for travel within a finite space. The moments of deceleration and inertia between periods of motion which punctuate and direct *Chambres d'ailleurs* (conveyed stylistically by the division of the text into short sections) allow stasis to become as important to the travel experience as the displacement which usually is seen to characterise it.

The more recent *Saisons japonaises* is the account of the author's prolonged, lone, stay in Koyasan, a Japanese town, famous as a site of pilgrimage. This narrative, in certain ways, stands in contrast to the author's earlier text. Having travelled to Koyasan as part of the journey described in *Chambres d'ailleurs,* Bernheim returns, this time alone. Now the traveller burrows down in the place and carries out an extended version of the microscopic travel commenced in the earlier narrative.[6] The focus shifts, in this text, from the transience and brevity found in *Chambres d'ailleurs,* to what we might call travel-in-dwelling, or 'vertical travel': exploring a place, culture or community in depth while residing there. This affords the traveller the time and space to create what is narrated as a real bond with her surroundings and the town's inhabitants, although in this case, it is perhaps also a means of creating a bond of sympathy with her French readers.[7]

Having portrayed the sense of tension between her love of writing and her love for her companion in the earlier text, it becomes all the more apparent in *Saisons japonaises* that this encounter with Japan is intended to be understood as solitary, with the traveller made vulnerable and potentially more receptive to the world around her than when travelling with the security afforded by a companion. In one of the opening passages to this text the narrator describes herself as:

> Solitary, intrigued, receptive and happy to wander the little, temple-lined streets and in the necropolis. Unable to speak the language, I become deaf and illiterate here. It is as if I had just been born — I no longer know how to speak, how to read, nor how to write. I know only how to absorb, like a sponge.[8]

The emphasis on her status as solitary traveller is closely linked here to her supposed receptiveness to her surroundings, and sets up the premise of a passive, innocent interaction between traveller and the other culture. Two key issues spring from this pre-emptive declaration of vulnerability: that of self-performance and also the question of translation. While the narrator admits her inability to speak Japanese at this early stage in the narrative, and touches upon the presence of translation once or twice later in the narrative, she seems keen to downplay its importance in her travels, unless it can serve to highlight her initial feelings of vulnerability. In spite of the mention of a member of the host family acting as interpreter early on in the narrative, it remains unclear whether the traveller ever learns Japanese during her stay and, for the most part, any awkward linguistic problems are erased from the text. In *Across the Lines: Travel, Language, Translation*,[9] Michael Cronin discusses the similarities and tensions present between translation and travel writing and suggests the different manifestations of this uneasy relationship. In *Saisons japonaises* it would seem that Bernheim partially eclipses translation issues when they might impinge upon the narrative or, worse, remind the reader that the traveller is not as integrated into the Japanese culture as she would wish, and yet appears content to pepper the text with untranslated culture-specific words, such as *o-furo* (communal bath) and *yukata* (light summer kimono), as 'general markers of foreignness'.[10] This dual approach to translation and the translator's invisibility highlights the author's shrewd manipulation of her experience in the process of textualisation and reveals the extent to which travel writing can be seen in terms of self-performance. While part of the charm of these two narratives lies in the impression of innocence and authenticity, created in part by the apparently frank narrative style and the astute admissions of instability and vulnerability, it is evident that Bernheim's strategies of self-presentation are carefully managed in order to prove her initial naivety and later the extent of her 'knowledge' of the culture to which she travels.

Geographical, Historical and Textual Zones

In spite of the evident divergence in focus between these two travel narratives, it is clear that they both concentrate upon travel in the same geographical area: Asia.[11] Holland and Huggan suggest in *Tourists with Typewriters* that Asia has long been treated as an 'Oriental zone' which repeatedly draws the attention of Western travel writers whose texts can supposedly only perpetuate 'tropological myths' of a singular monolithic Asia.[12] Yet such an argument can only be seen as reductive of the potential of travel in the way in which it rules out any possibility for new ways of approaching place, and also in its assertion that a singular Asia exists. While both narratives studied here fit, geographically, neatly into Holland and Huggan's notion of travels to the 'Oriental zone', it is debatable whether or not Bernheim's texts manage to challenge certain aspects of this rather inflexible approach to travel. Certainly it can be suggested that the modes of travel employed by Bernheim go some way towards problematising these continental monoliths. In *Chambres d'ailleurs,* the fragmentary narration of the journey and its clear segmentation into chapters focusing on the different stages of her journey (Japan, India, Taiwan, Hong Kong, Singapore, Pakistan etc.) shatter the impression of continuity. In *Saisons japonaises,* the specificity of place demanded by vertical travel avoids continental stereotypes. The privileging of the personal and the domestic in both narratives gives the impression of a more intimate experience of the places visited, based upon an interpretation of the travel undertaken that privileges the traveller as much as the travel itself.[13]

And yet it can be argued that the specific cultural associations that Bernheim, as a French traveller, brings to her encounter with this zone are difficult to escape.[14] In spite of the scope of her travels in *Chambres d'ailleurs*, Bernheim only once sets foot in a country with a former French colonial history: India. That she visits Pondicherry and remarks briefly on its former links with France, and the traces left by the French colonial powers, indicates an awareness of the history with which she must journey as a privileged Western, and more importantly French, traveller in this part of India. Perhaps the limitation of her visit to this one place with former colonial significance, and her avoidance of countries such as Cambodia and Vietnam, speaks of a solipsistic unwillingness to engage with places problematised by French imperialism.[15] Japan, never having been colonised directly,[16] demands a very different approach from the Western traveller.[17] Akane Kawakami's text *Travellers' Visions* and Holland and Huggan's *Tourists with Typewriters*, while focusing on literary encounters with Japan, both speak only of male travellers, such as Pierre Loti, Pico Iyer,[18] Roland Barthes, Henri Michaux and Michel Butor. Holland and Huggan justify this by stating that '[i]n Western representations, Japan has most often figured as an alluring yet elusive feminine "other".'[19] This leads us then to question how a French female traveller negotiates her path into this space deemed feminine in the Western imagination. Is her approach any different, ultimately, to that of her male predecessors?

Gender in Travel

Whether travelling as part of a couple or as a single woman, Bernheim's accounts enable an insight into her struggle to comprehend and find her place in the Asian cultures she visits. It is the personal and self-reflective approach of her narrative, coupled with her microscopic journeying, which encourages a consideration of whether elements of her texts are particularly 'feminine' and what impact this has on the final travel narrative. A number of contemporary critics, such as Susan Bassnett and Sara Mills, have suggested the possibility of a differentiated female travelling gaze, and while remaining aware of the risks of stereotyping women's travel literature, it is nonetheless worthwhile searching to decipher questions of identity and also pondering how gender is performed in response to the circumstances of travel. My intention here is not to suggest any binary opposition in travel writing based on gender, nor to generalise about travelling femininities (however difficult it may be to avoid such generalisations), but rather to question how this one female traveller translates her personal encounter with Asian culture.

Travelling Relationships and Relationships with Travel

The two different types of travel presented in these texts have a significant impact upon the way the traveller experiences the other culture. In *Chambres d'ailleurs*, rather than choosing to focus exclusively on what happens around her in travel, Bernheim seeks also to present her journey as geographical, emotional and psychological, describing details of her own sensual needs and desires as readily as she portrays the landscape she travels through. Her focus is torn between her journey and her relationship. In *Saisons japonaises,* Bernheim presents herself as a vulnerable lone traveller and narrates both her journey towards integration into a community and her path towards gaining a better understanding of the travelling self. She narrates her personal interaction with one family, highlighting their individuality and her 'exceptional' interaction with them.

When travelling as part of a couple, Bernheim describes fleeting moments spent in a great number of different rooms, temporary sanctuaries and places for rest. It is perhaps surprising, then, that this account displays such an interest in the temporary ownership of, or belonging to, a place which can represent and replace home. In a sense, Bernheim shows each room as a dwelling place for her relationship, a more or less private space in which the focus can be sustained without too much disturbance from the busy other culture through which she and her partner travel. That is not to say that the intimacy afforded by the *'chambres d'ailleurs'* exists in isolation from the Asian culture but rather that these temporary homes allow the traveller to focus on the details of the travelling landscape without being overwhelmed by the constantly changing outside space. The anecdotal details of the rooms in which the traveller stays, coupled with the description of mundane activities, allow a glimpse of the domestic side of travel. The following passage reflects this interest in the banal and everyday:

> When you are elsewhere for a long time, it's impossible to live in constant curiosity. You end up forgetting that you are a foreigner in foreign lands. Sometimes we only go out to eat or we picnic face to face in the room, our room.
>
> Four walls, enclosed space. We could just as well be in Paris watching the telly. If you travel as a twosome, the day-to-day is stronger than the exotic. You have to be able to breathe without thinking of anything, to rest without admiring anything, to look after yourself, after the other, patch your clothes, wash them.[20]

Rather than focusing on the Asian landscape, Bernheim allows herself to come to a gradual understanding of the customs and quirks of the places she visits through the details of the diverse rooms she stays in. Her experience of the countries she visits is limited to these *chambres* and brief encounters with her hosts. Yet, to a certain extent, the constant evolution of her relationship with her partner overshadows the way in which Bernheim experiences the encounter with the other. Her deep involvement with her travelling companion is stressed from the very beginning of the text where she writes with satisfaction 'I'm in Tokyo, at the end of the world and I'm with you.'[21] However as the text progresses, Bernheim expresses her growing anxiety at the tension that has developed between herself as traveller and herself as lover. She describes this conflict of interests as follows:

> Writing instead of being with you. Writing is getting up without feeling your legs entangled in mine, it is taking the liberty of moving alone [. . .]. Writing is forgetting that you drive at my side [. . .]. Writing, really writing, for yourself and for others, is loving. The desire to love other than you is unbearable, a betrayal — so I repress it.[22]

Here, it seems that this tension almost endangers the creation of the travel text. The intimacies, tensions and fluctuations of her relationship appear to preoccupy the author to the point where the encounter with the Asian other is partially eclipsed by the interest in the other with whom she travels. *Le Monde*'s René de Ceccatty remarks that '*Chambres d'ailleurs,* could have been called '*Chambres de soi*, a self (soi) reduced by love, love for one man and love for mankind'.[23] De Ceccatty's assertion that the travelling self is diminished by the narrator's love for one man is accurate and yet Bernheim's love for humankind is less clear here than he suggests. Partly due to the nature of her travel, but mainly due to the focus on her travel companion, Bernheim's intercultural contact is largely reduced to brief, functional encounters with a succession of 'travellees', whose importance lies more in facilitating her journey, than in any true exchange of interests. This can be seen in the episode where Bernheim and her lover spend the night at the house of a customs officer in Pakistan. Once again the focus lies on the intimacy between traveller and co-traveller, on the moments they share alone, rather than on the reality of the lives of the people she meets. It can be suggested that, in the following quotation, Bernheim's fleeting comic-erotic interest in her hosts is perhaps the closest interaction with the cultural other that is narrated in this text:

> We lay down near to the red brick wall. Incense is burning somewhere, it smells good. The moon shines, the stars sparkle. The proximity of Farida and Hussein troubles me, are they going to make love? Are we, quietly . . . You caress me, I try not to laugh. Maybe the customs officer is doing the same.[24]

The preoccupation with a relationship can be seen as making *Chambres d'ailleurs* as much about a personal, intimate journey as about a travel encounter with Asia.[25] Bernheim is to some extent sheltered from the cultures she travels through by the presence of her companion and in this way is able to examine her otherness as distinct from the co-traveller rather than from the cultural other. Or perhaps it is more accurate to suggest that Bernheim actively seeks shelter in the relationship from the seemingly alien cultures surrounding her. The comfort offered by the familiar seems difficult to resist. In the two closing passages of the text, Bernheim reflects on her life with this co-traveller and examines the contradictory emotions his presence, in her life and her journey, inspired in her. In the conclusion of the second edition of this text, Bernheim describes the nostalgia she feels, almost thirteen years after *Chambres d'ailleurs* was first published, for the love that characterised her journey. It is telling that her final thoughts about this journey turn to her lover and travel companion, rather than to the countries she visited and the people she met. This raises important questions about the generic boundaries of travel writing. Perhaps this continued emphasis on the presence of relationships, be they real or imagined, present or absent, intercultural or intracultural, demonstrates how important their existence can be, and what a profound effect they can have upon the way the traveller experiences travel.

It is possible to see a real shift between this text and *Saisons japonaises*, which suggests an evolution in Bernheim's attitude to travel. From the interpersonal/intracultural approach in *Chambres d'ailleurs*, she progresses to a more interpersonal/intercultural approach which makes *Saisons japonaises* a very different text in content, approach and structure. In contrast to the earlier text, *Saisons japonaises* describes the encounter between two cultures, which have traditionally, and reductively, been seen as binary opposites: East and West. This solo experience of travelling-in-dwelling provokes a very different encounter with Asia. As we have already seen, the shelter afforded by her companion is absent in this text, and as such the author has to negotiate her own way into the Japanese community which she so fiercely desires to gain access to and understanding of, whether it be for her book, or for more personal reasons. Without any recourse to, or support from, her own culture, Bernheim has little choice but to be open to the intercultural encounter and experiences it all the more fully, perhaps, because of this *ouverture*. In a sense, this can be related to the *exercice de disparition*, or aesthetics of disappearance, that Jean-Xavier Ridon remarks upon in Nicolas Bouvier's work.[26] At some points in *Saisons japonaises*, the travelling self is partially eclipsed by the author's sustained interest in the host family and yet, in closing, the narrator's self-congratulatory tone in regard to how well she perceives herself as having integrated into the Japanese community suggests that her interest in the other was fundamentally inspired by self-interest:

> I am lucky to have been able to have created links (with a disappearing Japan) while so many *gaijin* say that such a thing is impossible, that Japan is always closed to strangers. As a good *baku*, I hope to have destroyed, swallowed these clichés.[27]

In *The Global Soul,* Pico Iyer, who spends much of his time in Japan where he has a Japanese partner and children, discusses the impossibility of a foreigner gaining acceptance into that community. Bernheim's claim, after a relatively short stay in Japan, that she has effectively gone where no [Western] traveller has gone before speaks of the level of self-performance present in this account. While the narrator lays claim to vulnerability, sensitivity and fascination with her host family, it would seem that the traveller's ultimate motivation is to claim access to the supposedly inaccessible.

Home in Travel

Bernheim's experience of microscopic travel in Japan, and of dwelling-in-travel in the succession of countries described in *Chambres d'ailleurs,* are of particular importance in terms of their renegotiation of the concept of home. Traditionally, within travel literature, women have often been limited to the representation of domestic space, while men have travelled into the foreign domain, using the (feminine) domestic sphere of home as a necessary point of reference and return. But of course 'home' is as much an imaginary space as a physical one. In her text *Moving Lives,* Sidonie Smith suggests that the link between woman and home is difficult to break:

> Whatever particular women might be doing in their everyday lives, the idea of woman as 'earth, shelter, enclosure', as 'home', persists, anchoring femininity, weighing it down, fixing it as a compass point. Moreover, the 'home' that is identified as feminine, feminized and equated with woman becomes that which must be left behind in the pursuit of agency.[28]

This necessarily leads us to question: What happens when a woman travels away from home? Can women leave the place and space which has been assigned to them? What happens to home when women travel away from it? The idea of home as a set, geographically situated location to which women are tied is now outdated, and we should see home as a shifting, mobile, imaginary place which can be taken with the traveller or adopted through rituals, objects or people. Through the study of a number of texts by travel writers, it becomes apparent that home is not always a fixed place, but can be recreated in travel by the traveller (male or female) wishing to feel at home. That is not to say that this only occurs in female-authored texts, but rather that this imaginary displacement of home can be seen as one of the many ways in which women travellers negotiate the physical separation from the domestic sphere traditionally assigned to them.

One of the first ways in which home is taken with the traveller is by attachment to place. This can be represented as home in many different ways in travel accounts, some more obvious than others. In *Chambres d'ailleurs,* the notion of being at home, of being comfortable, is a recurrent feature. Bernheim describes rooms in terms of the warmth and comfort that they provide: a temporary haven from the outside world. This is carried out through an interest in everyday objects which provide the traveller with a place to rest, a comforting home-replacement:

> The bed . . . two mattresses, the futons are folded away in the cupboard. You can spread them out wherever you feel like [. . .]. Tea and two cups wait on a tray [. . .]. I roll myself up in the warm and comfortable bed [. . .]. All is well.[29]

This concept of home being a provisional, temporary shelter, marked out as home by domestic customs and rituals, is extended, in *Saisons japonaises,* to the identification of a semi-permanent home. Bernheim stresses the importance of the comfort of this temporary home, describing her bed as '*un nid douillet*', a type of nest to which she can retreat and hide from the outside world. She marks this space out as her own by the Western furniture she installs in it and the home comforts she insists upon.[30]

It is clear in Bernheim's work that home is not necessarily limited to the idea of place, and that for many travellers home and feeling at home are as much about people as they are about place. In *Chambres d'ailleurs*, home is represented in terms of the physical presence and comfort her partner provides, whereas in *Saisons japonaises*, Bernheim's status as lone traveller forces her to recreate home through the adoption of surrogate family and friends. This supposedly reciprocal relationship is described in idealistic terms in *Saisons japonaises*:

> The way in which I tell them, the way that I see them, makes my relationships with the Japanese seem effortless. But it wasn't as easy as all that. [. . .] My relationship with the Imai family was built slowly, I had to prove my interest, my sincerity, from 'heart to heart' as they say. They know now that they can count on me, that I do what I say I will. I realise that from now on the doors that I have opened will remain open for life. [. . .] This family that has adopted me, I have also gradually adopted. Our friendship is based on reciprocal respect, on indispensable politeness without unwanted intrusions.[31]

From this passage, it becomes clear that Bernheim actively sought to found a friendship with the Imai family, and that this was a deliberate act to bring her closer to the Japanese community. From being an errant traveller who belongs nowhere, her friendship with, and acceptance by, her surrogate family allows her an intimate perspective on the Japanese culture, or at least the illusion of one for her European readers. At face value, the sentiments expressed here by Bernheim are worthy and represent the dream of many a traveller: to gain acceptance into a community and therefore to 'understand' it. Nonetheless, a more sceptical approach demands that this be read in terms of a professional journalist's attempt to claim authority and authenticity. The very fact that we are able to read about her 'adopted' family in this text suggests that this traveller was not solely motivated by a search for friendship but was also in search of material for her book.

Moreover, while Bernheim admits the financial motivations for this journey at the beginning of the text, and also the finances involved in her prolonged stay in Koyasan, she seeks to portray her presence there in more romantic terms: as part of a long-established love-affair with the place, with the traveller repeatedly drawn there by fate. She describes how she first visited Koyasan during the journey narrated in *Chambres d'ailleurs*, and subsequently revisited it when her hired car broke down in the vicinity, and then again when a newspaper asked her to write an article on the town. The fourth stroke of fate, when a magazine asked her to return once more to Koyasan, and the fortuitous grant she received from the Japanese foundation, prove to be the final motivations for her travel. This outwardly open admission of financial incentive, so often suppressed by travel writers, may perhaps be seen as an astute way of assuring the reader of her honesty, while she conveniently omits other details which would potentially undermine the image of the naïve and innocent traveller.[32] This impression is supported by the way that in the same paragraph where she writes of the intervention of fate in her decision to return to Japan, she also talks of her '*désir de Japon*',[33] revealing that her travels to Japan were not based on serendipity or finances alone, but also on her own wishes and desires.

Photography and the Gaze

Bernheim's attempts to indicate her immersion in the Japanese culture impact upon the way in which the gaze is presented in her narrative. The narrator's status as lone, female traveller is shown to make her particularly conscious that she is both observer and observed, so the gaze is reciprocal. As Clifford remarks in *Traveling Cultures,* in such circumstances, 'Who, exactly, is being observed?'.[34] The sense of mutual exoticism and of difference, in this case of being physically different, is emphasised in the following extract. Using her gender as a point of entry to an exclusively female domain, Bernheim hints at the stereotypical, male-written fantasy descriptions of sensual environments like the female section of the communal baths and the harems of old. However, while on some level hinting at this voyeuristic tradition, she also portrays the *onsen* as a family outing, and herself as amateur participant and alien body:

> Onsen with the Imai family. House bathrooms have rendered the traditional public baths virtually useless, but the thermal baths remain in fashion and are used by regulars. Men on one side, women on the other. Water at 50 degrees, steam. 'Maman Imai', Ikuyo and Sawako are naked with me in the deep women's pool. For now we are alone. They have quite dark skin, little breasts with tiny brown nipples. They are very slender. I feel like a giant next to them. The youngest, Ikuyo, decides to take me in hand, to show me how I must squat to wash myself, taking my time.[35]

In many respects this episode is not unlike that narrated in Lady Mary Wortley Montagu's description of the Turkish baths in *The Turkish Embassy Letters*.[36] Like Montagu, Bernheim is able to be observer and observed at the same time, to maintain the power and authority of the travel writer, while allowing herself the submissive role of participant. In this way she treads a fine line between hinting at more traditional ways of seeing the other, and particularly the female Asian other, as a sensual, exotic being, and excusing herself for this by demonstrating how she is equally strange and exotic in her own way. The possibility of a gendered solidarity, if not a solidarity based on language, class or ethnicity, is present in this episode. It would seem that the experience of sharing in the intimacy of the baths and allowing the reciprocal gaze to travel over the feminine body is designed to confirm and strengthen the impression of trust between female traveller and female travellees. In this way, this narrative seems to support Simone Fullager's claims about intercultural exchange between women when she suggests that 'a shared feminine embodiment may generate a sense of connection between women; a fleeting friendship and feeling of being at home, that is produced through an intersubjective cross-cultural relation.'[37]

And yet one must question just how reciprocal the gaze can ever be as long as it is the Western traveller who retains control of its narration and eventual publication. In some senses, the narrator sets these women up to serve as the perfect foils against whom she can project this particular version of her travelling persona. It is difficult to ascertain whether this episode is indicative of a possible shared intercultural experience in travel based upon gender (and possibly the female body) or, more cynically, whether it should

'Chambres d'Asie, chambres d'ailleurs' 191

be seen in terms of wish-fulfilment for the traveller desperate to prove her intimacy with the people she meets. Indeed, it is this very episode which brings back the warnings of Holland and Huggan about the inescapability of repetition when travelling to one of the zones they describe. In this extract, one of the most marked within this text, Bernheim seeks to accentuate how close she is to this Japanese family. But it is this very same episode which betrays her as the traveller-writer, who uses her gender to revise, and to add to, this familiar scene of intimacy.[38] While in many ways Bernheim's approach to the 'Oriental zone' has differed from previous accounts through its privileging of the traveller as experiencing subject, and her personal approach to travel, it seems that the temptation to improve upon the narratives that went before her, by gaining admission to, and participating in, the exoticised feminine Orient, was too great to resist. Her desire to illustrate reciprocity of experience with the people she meets, and to set herself up as an exception, is perhaps all too exaggerated in the text, and its authenticity, accordingly, must be questioned.

Nonetheless the fragility of this supposed bond and the vulnerability of the travel writer's accepted place within the culture are underlined by Bernheim later in the narrative. It is the use of photography that is shown to endanger the honorary position she claims for herself within this Japanese community. Bernheim demonstrates how this one act, perhaps due to photography's often negative links to tourism and invasive photo-journalism, and its power to highlight the presence of the gaze, has the effect of reminding her surrogate family of her difference: she is a journalist, observer and travel writer, and her presence in Japan is only temporary. The camera acts as a sign of intrusion for Etsuko, the mother of Bernheim's surrogate family, and she reacts accordingly:

> One day, Etsuko-san reproached me for taking photos of her family. I was given a never-ending speech, translated by Ikuyo. It went on and on. She explained that, to them, I am a friend. That she forgets that I am a journalist, a writer, that these photos bother her. What was I intending to do with them? With my tiny camera, I'm not a professional and I'm hardly a member of the paparazzi. [. . .] I promise to let her know. She calms down, invites me for a meal but she has undone the ties which bind us together. I wasn't expecting it and this prevents me from writing for several weeks.[39]

While it seems strange that a family from a culture which is generally held to adore photography should be concerned about the photos that Bernheim takes, perhaps this episode should be seen more as a reminder of the fragility of the position of the traveller-writer in other cultures. The presence of the camera reminds her adoptive family that she is the traveller-writer, and that neither they, nor she, can escape the inevitability of the gaze. This use of photography as a means of exploring intercultural instability is present in other travel narratives such as Robyn Davidson's *Tracks*,[40] and also François Maspero's *Les Passagers du Roissy-Express*, which explores this issue in an episode where a group of Malian men seek to explain why they took offence at the photograph that Anaik Frantz took of them without their permission.[41] Photography provides a useful reminder to the reader, the traveller and the travellee that the travelling gaze is present and that the intercultural encounter is not always as stable as the traveller might wish. The inclusion of this issue suggests an element of postcolonial anxiety and self-awareness in the traveller and situates Bernheim as having partially rejected certain imperialist modes of travel, while retaining a number of the familiar tropes.

Conclusion

Bernheim's travel narratives illustrate the recurrence of self-performance and construction of role in contemporary travel writing, creating an illusory rhetoric of intimacy which is thinly disguised by the traveller's claims to vulnerability and naivety. Moreover, they provide an often problematic example of the possibilities of a differentiated female gaze in travel where gender appears, albeit briefly, as a potential point of access from which cross-cultural relations can progress. However the space which this author creates to define the experience of the female traveller is an awkward one which reveals a further set of cultural and historical constraints. Most important perhaps, is the way in which these accounts remind us of the possibilities for a perception of the fluid notion of home in travel literature, and not only in the work of female travel writers. Authors and texts as diverse as Nicolas Bouvier's *Journal d'Aran et d'autres lieux*,[42] Ella Maillart's *Ti-Puss*,[43] Carole Pither's *Un Camion dans la tête*,[44] Jenny Diski's *Skating to Antarctica*,[45] and Carol Dunlop and Julio Cortázar's *Les Autonautes de la cosmoroute*,[46] all explore to varying degrees the ways in which a focus on the microscopic, the decelerated and the domestic in travel may prove as illuminating with regard to questions of identity and self-hood as the more traditional focus on geographical displacement. Fullagar's suggestion of moving towards finding new ways of being at home with ourselves and others, and Iyer's claims to a possible multiplicity of homes in contemporary life provide possible avenues for future enquiry.

13

World Journey of My Heart and *Homestay in the World:* Travel Programming and Contemporary Japanese Culture

Mark Meli

People all over the world who appreciate literature are familiar with the travel journals of the Japanese haiku poet Bashō, and maybe with the tradition of earlier wandering waka poets like the Buddhist priests Saigyō and Nōin. This older tradition of literary and religious travel in Japan has been well documented in academic as well as popular discussions of the country, by both Japanese and non-Japanese. Furthermore, as early as the seventeenth century, European visitors such as Engelbert Kaempher noticed the great Japanese fascination with travel. Kaempher, when making the trek from Nagasaki to Edo in order to pay homage at the Shogun's court in 1691 and again in 1692, estimated that roughly twice as many Japanese were moving about the country as in any contemporary European country.[1]

While many treatments of the place of travel in Japanese culture focus on the classical traditions of wandering poets or Buddhist monks, very few afford even a glance at travel writing in post-World War II Japan, or at its significance within contemporary Japanese cultural representation. Today, one cannot live in Japan without noticing the fascination with travel, especially overseas travel, that is displayed prominently throughout Japanese society in various media, and particularly in the cultural representations that the Japanese make of themselves. This is readily seen in the great volume of travel writing that is published both in magazine and book form, but to my eye, nowhere is it more evident than on television. In a country where multi-channel cable and satellite TV is far less prominent than in the United States or Europe, five or six major networks still command the great proportion of viewers, and the amount of time they allot to travel programming is quite remarkable. Table 13.1 shows a list of all the travel-related programming on network and national satellite television for the month of July, 2005. It has been prepared in order to give an idea of the amount and variety of travel programming that is regularly broadcast on the Japanese airwaves. In that month, four one-time specials on domestic travel, and two others, along with an eight-episode series focusing on overseas travel, were aired on network television. There were three weekly series dedicated to overseas travel and six to domestic travel, plus one that mixed both. Another two series introduced World Heritage sights, and one more focused on Japanese regional foods (and one should travel to the region in order to taste them in their proper environment). There was also a two-minute daily weekday spot on world train travel, and seven individual late-night reruns. On the national satellite network, another travel show was rerun three to four mornings a week. It is possible that there are others that have been overlooked. It should be recognised, moreover, that almost all of these shows are directly involved with the notion of actually travelling. With the exception of one of the World Heritage programmes, they are not simply programmes dealing with other cultures or places — they all centre on the concept of a member of the cast actually visiting another place. This is often emphasised by airline sponsorship.

There are two contrary cultural tendencies behind this interest in travel. Domestic travel tends to be focused on an urge to return to simpler times, to the image of a traditional Japan with its slower pace of life, traditional arts and religions, and healthy and simple fare. The relation between domestic travel and tourism and Japanese identity has been discussed by Marilyn Ivy in her *Discourses of the Vanishing* as one strategy in dealing with the social problems that have emerged as a result of Japan's rapid urbanisation and seeming 'Westernisation' after World War II, and particularly in the last forty years (Ivy, 29–65). The 'real Japan' is often shown to exist in the countryside, where, according to dominant nostalgic representations in the media, farming is still the main economic force; Western influences are less evident, and traditional ways of life still doggedly persist. This cultural tendency can also be seen, to give one example, in the persistent popularity of the travel writings of Shiba Ryōtarō (1923–96), the *Kaidō wo Yuku* (*Going Along Highways*) series. Although perhaps best known for his voluminous writings of historical fiction, Shiba's travel books, each of which is focused upon one historically important roadway or passage, stretch to some forty-three volumes.[2] For the great majority of these books, Shiba never leaves Japan; and when he does venture abroad, he usually deals with places that have a strong connection to Japanese history, such as areas in China where literary figures who are also

Table 13.1 List of all travel-related programming on network and national satellite television for July 2005

One-time specials (Overseas travel)
Sekai isan: itaria jūdan sanzen nen no tabi (Italy World Heritage: A Journey Crossing 3000 Years: 8 episodes, 9 hours)
Shiina Makoto no kandō niman mairu! (Writer) Shiina Makoto's Impressive 20,000 Miles)
My Dear Friend Nyū jiirando no kandō taiken (Impressive Experience in My Dear Friend New Zealand)

(Domestic travel)
Ichido tomatte mitai! Kurashikku hoteru no natsu (I Want to Stay There Once! Summer's Classic Hotels)
Gyōshi ga itonamu kakuyasu minshuku (Fisherman-run Dirt-cheap Pensions)
Seiryū no yado (Clean-type Hotels)
Umi, yama, daichi ga daisuki! Daishizen no gaido hito (I Love Sea, Mountains, and the Great Earth! Nature's Guide)

Weekly programmes (Overseas travel)
Sekai fushigi hakken! (Strange Discoveries of the World)
Sekai ururun taizaiki (Crying Homestay in the World)
Ainori (Riding (and Loving) Together)
Sekai no shasō kara (From the Train Windows of the World 5 per week)

(World Heritage, sometimes mixed with travel elements)
Sekai isan (The World Heritage)
Tanken roman sekai isan (Romantic Search for the World Heritage)

(Domestic travel)
Shin nihon kikō futatabi (New Japan Journey, Again)
Ganso debu ya (Our Fat Ancestor)
Haretara ii ne. Let's komimi tai (It's Great if it's Sunny. Let's Komimi Squid [eat])
Tōku e ikitai (I Want to Go Far Away)
Tabi no kaori, toki no asobi (Fragrance of Travel, Play of the Moment)
Ii tabi, yume kibun (A Great Journey, Feeling like a Dream)

(Mixture of domestic and overseas)
Asa da! Nama desu tabi sarada (Morning! The Raw Travel Salad)

(Food travel, mostly domestic)
Shokusai roman (Cuisine Romance)

Re-runs
Sekai: waga kokoro no tabi (My Heart's Journey in the World, 2–5 per week)
Minzoku ongaku kikō (Ethnic Music Journey)
Koi suru betonamu (Vietnam That/Where I Love. Weekly)
Eizō sekai tabi (World Video Journey, two times)

famous in Japan lived, or spots in Holland and Portugal that were significant in connection with the missionary activity or trade that these countries undertook with Japan. It is also worth noting that, throughout 2005, a magazine series of the same name was published wherein each week one of Shiba's travelogues was taken up and discussed by prominent literary figures and travel writers. These often included information that could be used should the reader want to re-trace Shiba's steps along some historically important highway.[3]

On the other hand, overseas travel tends to be represented more as the realm of the bourgeois urbanite, a mark of sophistication, cultural education and wealth, something enjoyed by college students, 'parasite singles' (young people, especially women, who work but live with and are basically supported by their parents, and who thus have money to burn on luxury items and leisure activities such as travel), and retired professionals with big pensions and lots of newfound time on their hands.[4] In Japan, as is certainly true in other consumer societies, overseas travel bears something of the prestige of wearing an expensive brand-name suit or dress. It might even be said to be something that people with money feel they must do to show their sophistication and wealth, whether or not they truly enjoy travelling overseas. We might point to certain group tours wherein Japanese food is consistently provided and no contact has to be made with anything native as evidence that such a tendency exists.

While there are, as we have seen, various kinds of overseas travel programming in Japan, little of it is concerned with the kind of practical travel tips that can be seen, for example, in the US on The Travel Channel's *Passport to Europe* or *Travel Café*. Almost all of these Japanese shows are more concerned with presenting interesting aspects of other cultures rather than in giving practical or promotional information. Many shows feature an individual traveller presenting rare and fascinating facts about a little-known place, and several include quizzes amongst panel contestants or the audience at home. Travel related to food, both foreign and domestic, is also immensely popular.

In two shows that have been persistently popular over the last decade, an individual's trip abroad is presented as a kind of visual journal, similar in many ways to the kind of representation seen in contemporary travel writing, particularly in that the traveller's impressions in response to the journey are brought to the fore. In the long-running *Sekai: Wa ga kokoro no tabi* (*World Journey of My Heart*) and *Sekai ururun taizaiki* (*Homestay in the World* is the official English title given on the website, although a direct translation would be *World Weeping Homestay Journal*), better- or lesser-known personalities travel abroad, with a camera following in order to create journals of their trips. These are the two programmes which I shall focus upon in the remainder of this chapter, for two main reasons. The first has to do with their longevity. *World Journey of My Heart* ran for just under ten years, from 1994 to 2003, and *Homestay in the World* celebrated its tenth anniversary in Spring 2005 and is still going strong. This is remarkable in a country where single-season dramas are the mainstay of network television. A second reason to focus upon these two shows is the contrasts that we can draw between them. *World Journey of My Heart* ran on one of the satellite channels of government-run NHK, which is known for commercial-free programming and seen as being more academic or educationally oriented.[5] The show featured well-known artists, musicians, intellectuals, writers and actors who related their journeys to their own lives and work. Most of the travellers were of middle age or older, a fact which allowed a primary place for memory during their trip, and dealing with personal memories often led to wider issues of Japanese cultural memory. *Homestay in the World*, on the other hand, is a prime-time show on commercial television that usually features young, up-and-coming actors, singers or other 'talents' who travel to other countries and do homestays with families there. Most of the issues presented here are less obviously rich in historical connotations; most themes are meant to appeal to younger viewers, and a moral is often presented. The show also features a regular cast of TV personalities in the studio, one which includes both veteran actors and trendy newcomers, evaluating the journey and taking part in quiz games related to obscure cultural facts. The criteria for selection of this cast seems to have no connection at all to the overseas experience or intercultural sophistication of these personalities.

Before proceeding with my analysis, one point needs to be made. Something that immediately stands out and grabs our attention is the repetitive use of the word *sekai*, 'world', in the programme titles, always at the very beginning. Just as in the case of *Sekai isan*, or 'World Heritage' (which is also the name of a TV show), we find *Sekai: Wa ga kokoro no tabi*, *Sekai fushigi hakken* (Strange Discoveries of the World) and *Sekai ururun taizaiki*. Why the need to constantly remind us that these trips are taking place in the world? It is, of course, a sure way to let us know that they are *not* taking place in Japan. The word *sekai*, however, does not usually mean 'overseas' (*kaigai*), or 'foreign country' (*gaikoku*); it literally means 'world,' and is usually used in much the same way as the English term to designate both the entire earth as well as any certain sphere within it — the academic world, for instance. This present usage shows a dialectic in Japanese thinking that cannot really be found in English. Whereas in English expression, both the domestic and the foreign are thought of as being parts of the greater whole that is the world, in Japanese it is often the case that the opposite of Japan is the world. There is a clear message here: that Japan and the Japanese are quite unlike anything that might be found on the outside. This usage also works to insinuate that, as opposed to Japan, which is so singular as to demand its own category, all the other cultures of the world can be grouped together in one bunch, thereby levelling off to some extent whatever cultural difference might appear between other parts of the world. This interpretation of the significance of the term *sekai* is supported, I think, by the analysis that follows.

World Journey of My Heart

Memory, both personal and cultural, plays a major role in *World Journey of My Heart*, as might be guessed immediately from its very nostalgic-sounding title. This is even clearer in Japanese as a result of the somewhat archaic *wa ga*, 'my', as opposed to the contemporary form which would be *watashi no*. A more literal translation might thus be 'World Journey of MINE Heart'.

World Journey of My Heart ran on the national satellite network NHK-BS2 from 7 October 1993 until 23 March 2003, for a total of 463 shows. For this research, I chronicled some 105 episodes, each featuring a different traveller going to some place that had been of great significance in his or her life. The travellers were all quite renowned in their respective fields, although some were less well known generally than others. The three most popular professions represented were artists (25), musicians (21) and writers of various types (18). The next most popular groups were actors, scholars (a pleasant surprise!), film directors or screenwriters and athletes. Other groups (including business personalities, photographers, explorers, chefs) each had less than five percent representation.

One very interesting aspect of this show, something that set it apart from all other travel shows I have seen in Japan, was the high representation of non-Japanese travellers. Whereas I have never seen a non-Japanese featured on any other travel show, in this survey eleven percent of the travellers were not of Japanese ethnicity, although all spoke excellent Japanese. These include five born outside Japan (four Europeans and one Taiwanese), as well as one Ainu and five Japanese-born and raised (*zainichi*) Koreans or Chinese. Also significant, at seven percent, was the number of Japanese travellers who were themselves born overseas or had nuclear family members who were. We might thus say that this show reflected the 'internationalisation' that was so much talked about in Japan during the time in which it aired. I also find it quite telling that it ended in 2003, a year when the media showed a clear increase in anti-foreign rhetoric (specifically anti-Chinese, because of a perceived increase in Chinese and other foreign crime in Japan).

While commendable for its very international and non-homogeneous approach, *World Journey of My Heart* is, at bottom, a show about memory, individual and cultural. In fifty of the 105 shows I surveyed, the traveller was re-visiting some place or places that had been important in his/her life and/or professional or artistic development. More than half of these took the typical format of people in their 60s or 70s making a visit, after several decades' absence, to overseas locations where their career was launched or greatly changed — where they studied, apprenticed, worked, performed or competed athletically. Almost all the other shows, those featuring a person's first visit to a place, went somewhere the traveller had long been interested in, either to better understand influences upon his/her own artistic or intellectual development (e.g. where Beethoven or Chopin lived, Henry Miller's Paris, Lee Wiley's New York, Lao Zi or Li Bai's home town), to understand things about a family member (e.g. where father died in China in World War II, where father played jazz in San Francisco), or, especially in the case of musicians, to seek out some new influence for their art (e.g. Persian lute, Korean or Cameroonian drumming, Inca flute playing).

Often overlapping this fascination with exploring individual memory is the category of cultural memory, which is most interesting to me. I found that forty of 105 episodes surveyed deal in some broader way with the cultural memory of the Japanese nation. Included in this category are the following recurrent themes:

- Tracing a historical Japanese personality's footsteps overseas (twelve episodes)
    (Catholic boys sent to Rome in the sixteenth century; nineteenth-century actress starring in Europe; twentieth-century steelmaker, playwright, athletes)
- Looking at Japanese immigrant communities overseas (seven episodes)
    (in Cuba, US internment camps, Macao, Lebanon)
- Dealing with the aftermath of World War II and Japan's preceding colonisation in Asia (four episodes)
- Looking for roots of Japanese culture (six episodes)
    (Lute, court music, Buddhism, Taoism)
- Drawing parallels between foreign places and people, and issues in Japan (eleven episodes)
    (Ethnic problems, class problems, historical relationships)

The conclusion can thus be drawn that in this programme, overseas travel for the Japanese and the foreigners who have been accepted into the fold, very often comes back to being a reflection upon Japan. In nearly forty percent of the episodes, the actual focus of the travel was Japanese history and culture, and not the destination. Moreover, many of these episodes reveal that, despite having achieved sufficient material affluence to travel regularly, there still exists a common sense of insecurity regarding the place of Japan in the greater world. Episodes directly related to Japanese imperialism and World War II are clearly thus, especially those undertaken by *zainichi* travellers who visit family members affected by Japanese imperialism,[6] but so are the first two categories listed above. The focus on tracing the journeys of an historical personality often leads to asking how the Japanese of an earlier generation were accepted by the people in the places they visited, just as the focus of the return journeys of many of the actresses and musicians on the show is the reliving of their memories of just how they as Japanese succeeded in wowing the foreign audience at some past point in time.[7] In the 18 February 2001 episode, manga artist Satonaka Machiko traced the travels of Hanako (given name Ota Hisa), a dancer and stage actress who garnered great popularity in Paris and London and posed as a model for Rodin at the end of the nineteenth century.

Journeys in search of immigrant communities reflect the same insecurity: how is it that these people, once Japanese just like us, have managed to make a new life abroad? How do the 'foreigners' there treat them? Don't they miss Japan? This was epitomised in the episode from 13 February 1994 when photographer Hashiguchi Kōji visited a Japanese-born woman, now in her nineties, who had emigrated to Cuba decades earlier. Astonishment was shown at the fact that she has somehow forgotten how to speak Japanese, and that she now considered Cuba her home, with no desire at all to visit Japan.

It must be said here that *World Journey of My Heart* is one of the more intelligent travel shows I have yet to see on television. It is certainly of a higher educational quality than any of the travel programmes that can presently be seen on Japanese TV. In that context, it appears original and daring in its use of intellectuals and other out-of-the-ordinary characters, few of whom were professional actors, and certainly in its use of non-ethnic-Japanese travellers in more than ten percent of the shows surveyed. It is unfortunate that it is no longer on the air. Those aspects which made it original and refreshing within the greater pool of Japanese media stand out clearly in comparison with *Homestay in the World*, which is still a current hit.

Homestay in the World

This show started with the premise that simple tourism and programming based on tourism fail to adequately grasp the culture of the tourist destination. *Homestay* aims to do better. This can be seen in the explanation of the show's concept as given on its official homepage:

> If, for example, a French television crew
> came to Japan and filmed Mount Fuji, geisha,
> and Akihabara on location,
> would they have captured Japan?
>
> We think that on television up to now
> there have been too many
> post-card like shots,
> too much miserable coverage.
>
> There are many different kinds
> of people in the world,
> living various kinds of lives.
>
> *Ururun* wants to film
> The everyday of the world.
>
> Shiroi Hiroshi
> Producer, *Homestay in the World*[8]

Simply going somewhere and talking about the landmarks for which the place is famous fails to give us an adequate picture of the culture of the place. This show tries to remedy this problem by having young Japanese do homestays over a period of several days with families around the world, so that they might get a personal glimpse of the lives of these people at close hand.

The premise is fine, but the show has one flaw that is often fatal. In order to feed the idol-making machinery of Japan, and possibly also to boost ratings among young viewers, *Homestay in the World* relies solely upon youthful actors and actresses to do the travelling, paying much more attention to their pretty faces than to their capacity for engaging a foreign culture. When watching, one often gets the feeling that the traveller might never have even been abroad before. Here the show certainly pales by comparison to *World Journey of My Heart*. Otherwise interesting scenarios are more often than not spoiled by the lack of intellectual capacity or the pretentious posing of the 'idols', and the only conclusion to be had is that this seems to be what the industry demands. It is well known that 'talent agencies' in Japan have nearly unrestricted control over who gets put on television and who otherwise gets publicised. The plan in this show seems to be that these relatively unknown actors will use their appearances here as a springboard to better things, and many of them have, as we also find out on the show's website, where the latter showbiz activities of all travellers are carefully compiled and presented in CV form. The website of the show strengthens the cult of the travelling idol by providing much biographical information, particularly lists of the TV shows or movies he or she has appeared in, CDs made and prizes received. When this programme is watched in conjunction with *World Journey of My Heart*, the lack of any relevant connection between most of these actors and their topic is unmistakable. First of all, these relatively inexperienced talents rarely have anything to inform us about the places they visit, unlike the older travellers who have either lived there in the past or have at least learned a lot about the place. Neither are their reactions to the new culture very interesting or convincing. While displays of emotion pour forth, many of the travellers reveal their lack of knowledge of and/or interest in their destinations with rude or superior comments upon the strangeness of smells, foods, or customs, boiling the main content of the show down to ubiquitous squeals of '*oishii*!!!' (it's so delicious!!!) or '*kawaii*!!!' (How cute!!!). This formula creates an atmosphere where the viewer is usually left wondering just how much of it was not scripted.

The travellers in *My Homestay in the World* are clearly symbols of Japan — both to the natives with whom they stay, and then again to the Japanese viewers at home, vis-à-vis the natives. They are signifiers of a beautiful, fashionable and wealthy homeland. This is clear at first glance, when travellers appear before their host families dressed in designer clothes, fully made-up, and wearing the same jewellery they might wear on the town in Tokyo. This is particularly interesting when seen against the backdrop of so many Japanese travel guides which warn Japanese travelling to developing countries not to wear anything too glittery or expensive-looking as it draws the attention of pick-pockets and other criminals. Singer Karazawa Miho was a good example, joining a rice-wine-making family in China and helping with the work, wearing a black sweater, white blouse underneath, fully made up, and with dangling silver earrings. The sight of her spreading manure in the barley field wearing brand new, white, high-top sneakers was amusing indeed. Might this seemingly deliberate incongruity, while obviously underlining difference in economic power and fashion sensibilities, also be read conversely as a comment on just how far contemporary Japan had separated itself from its earthy agricultural roots (23 January 2005)? Showing just how up on fashion a young Japanese idol can be, on the 6 March 2005 show, Sata Mayuko is seen driving Italian shoe designer Bruno Magli to the point of insanity with her particular and refined tastes as she tries to design the original shoes that he will make for her.

The authenticity of the travel experience is a key concept here. Travellers are shown coming to truly understand the life and emotions of the families they stay with. Travellers live with a family on location, and interact with its members, sometimes even going to work together with them. The travellers always use only Japanese, the voice of the interpreter kept carefully masked. Responses from the natives, however, are heard in their native tongue and rendered into subtitles, creating the illusion of unmediated communication between the guest and the host, as if each understood the other's language. The traveller sleeps in the bed provided by the family, eats with the family and works with the family. There are no overt signs of tourism — no hotels, no discussion of means of arrival at the site, no visible interpreter, no tour guides. As if this was not authentic enough, however, the traveller appears back in the studio to discuss his or her experiences with a cast of 'talents' who put the final stamp of approval upon the experience. It appears as if authenticity can finally be adjudicated only at home, in the eyes of one's Japanese colleagues. Further confirmation is provided by the re-creation of the major activities in the studio to gain the approval of the panel: all agree that 'real' Chinese wine tastes different from the stuff sold in Japan, or that Basque-style, pan-fried cod really is quite delicious (16 January 2005), no matter how strange the cooking style might seem.

On *Ururun*, it goes without saying that the traveller is always accepted into the host family and invited back. In fact, every year a couple of shows are made showing travellers from years past returning to find a grand welcome. There have even been specials where particularly interesting families who made a big hit on their first appearance, such as the 'Fat Family' gospel singing group from Brazil, have been invited to come and surprise their homestay student in Japan (26 December 2004). There is a strong sense in all of this that the travellers travel not simply as individuals, but as representatives of their country, and they are welcome wherever they go, if only they strive for authenticity. Although this authenticity is constructed and framed by the programme itself, it appears for the most part in the ability to display empathy towards the people one encounters, and to come to an understanding of the surface manifestations of their lives. Certainly any inquiry into the deeper political or socio-economic factors underlying their lives is not included in this concept.

A main tenet of the show is that the Japanese are loved and accepted throughout the world, or at least potentially so, and this is signified by the '*ururun*' in the show's title: the sound of weeping. If members of the host family do not shed tears at departure time, then the stay surely was not a success, and I have yet to witness an episode that did not end in weeping, although once in a while it does seem rather staged. It is not clear how far monetary rewards might go in inducing these tears. It is to be expected that families are compensated for appearing, and probably coached so that the show works better if they really seem to like their visitor and appear sorrowful at his or her departure.[9] Thought about practically, a homestay done in the face of the film crew that must accompany each traveller would certainly subtract from whatever feeling of family might ensue between host and guest. A vain young actor or actress spending hours every day in your bathroom making up and doing his or her hair might make some host families regret the whole affair. Often, however, the visitor is portrayed as a ray of beauty entering the aesthetically humdrum lives of the natives, as with Karazawa in China, where the oldest son seems to fall in love with her, his mother much approving of the match. The boy had given up on the family wine business, as he preferred drinking beer and wanted to find work outside of their small town, but he promises to become a fully-fledged wine-maker, so she can drink *his* wine the next time she visits.

As in the Karazawa episode, the Japanese traveller is very often portrayed as something of a saviour to the natives. She brings the family back together or convinces the love-struck young son to give up his job and return to the family business. He introduces fish prepared Japanese-style to seafood lovers abroad, adding a new aspect to their culinary experience that they might never have known. This theme coincides with something indicated earlier as a common theme in *World Journey of My Heart*, namely the strong interest in showing that Japanese celebrities and their arts are valued and appreciated overseas as well as at home. There is a very strong need to show what Japanese people can do for the rest of the world, whether seen in an ethical or an aesthetic light.[10]

In another vein, one that coincides with the manner of representation of domestic travel within Japan as witnessed in both television and writing, the traditional is often given a nod of approval, especially as opposed to the modern or the 'Western'. This fits in well with *Ururun*'s claim that it intends to find the 'real' culture of the places it visits. Real culture not only is not that which any tourist sees immediately, but is also portrayed as that pure form which lies there beneath layers of pan-global culture. Just as scholars in *nihonjinron* (theories of what it means to be Japanese) have long been and still remain in search of the essential characteristics of Japanese culture, many Japanese cultural media, including this programme, tend to assume that there is a certain essential fabric to the culture of every nation, one that can be exposed if we dig deeply enough through layers of Westernisation and McDonaldisation. That essential culture is always one of the things that this programme aims to find.[11]

In the episode that aired on 26 June 2005, tough young actress Kaneko Sayaka stayed with a boat family on the Amazon. The difficulty of their lives was clear, as was their poverty in comparison to the average Japanese viewer. What the programme stressed, however, was the harmony of the family: they *never* fought or argued, however implausible that might seem. What is this? The wealthy Japanese are very much aware not only of the breakdown of the traditional family system, as was expressed, starting over fifty years ago, in, to give just one well-known example, the films of Ozu Yasujirō, but also of the overarching dysfunctional nature of family life in general for many Japanese. These miserable folks living with ants and crocodiles on makeshift boats in the Amazon show Japanese viewers the true meaning of family. We may be more beautiful and much better off materially, but they might just be happier, and certainly they have a healthier social life. This sentiment again reflects back upon a Japan where many people, for reasons that are often contradictory, vocally mourn the loss of so-called traditional family- and village-centred values.

Conclusion

First of all, we should say that based upon the great variety and volume of travel-related media in contemporary Japan, and its role in the lives of so many Japanese, the value of critical cultural or sociological analysis of such media must be recognised. Travel, especially overseas travel, is a major element in contemporary Japanese culture, and yet the question of its cultural significance has been largely ignored by researchers. This is true in regard both to the more traditionally recognised genre of travel literature as well as to media like television. Aside from work on Basho and other classical travelling poets, even Japanese travel writing has been pretty much ignored by scholars inside as well as outside Japan.[12] It would also be very interesting to look at Japanese travel media in a comparative context, something which has not been my intention here, in order not only to highlight this aspect of Japanese culture, but also to show how paradigms of travel there might differ from, have been influenced by or have influenced paradigms from other cultural spheres.

We can draw several specific conclusions from the analyses undertaken above. As we have focused only on television programmes, and on only two programmes at that, it would be dangerous to generalise from these conclusions in order to say things about the consciousness of overseas travel in Japanese society. What we can do, though, is get a good look at the manner in which the notion of overseas travel has been represented in the media over the last ten to twelve years. Any specific connection between that and some wider consciousness regarding such travel would need to be based upon further empirical and statistical research, although we might expect that the views of people who have been educated through this media will tend to be particularly strong reflections of the ideas seen there.

In a manner reminiscent of the long-running debate in Anglophone travel writing and research, there is seen in these programmes from Japan a strong interest in the authenticity of travel, of being a 'traveller' rather than merely a 'tourist'. This may be interpreted partly as an attempt to escape or prove wrong the 'ugly Japanese' title associated with group tourism, duty-free shopping and sex tourism, although it may also function, like its counterpart in the West, as a way of solidifying pre-existing divisions in economic or educational level.

In viewing other cultures, we see here a persistent need to relate that culture back in an explicit way to Japanese culture, either by looking at historical connections, making comparisons, or simply looking to other Japanese peers to authenticate the experience. This manifests itself in seemingly contradictory ways. It can at times be taken as a form of cultural narcissism, but can also be seen as stemming from insecurities about the present state of Japanese society. Traditional aspects of other cultures, particularly those which are being lost in the face of globalisation, are often shown parallel to fading Japanese traditions.

Here we see a strong desire to be accepted by the other, and to have one's nation and culture accepted as well. In a Japan that has been kept off the UN Security Council even though it has the world's second biggest economy, has forsaken the use of force to solve conflict, and funds the UN more than any other nation; and at a time when Japanese who speak otherwise perfect English are still made fun of on account of difficulty in pronouncing *l*s and *r*s (remember *Lost in Translation*?) and when, though most Japanese travellers usually do have a genuine interest in learning about the people they meet overseas, they are more often than not singled out as rich, ignorant, duty-free-mad shoppers, we see through these shows that these people who have for so long made it a point to emphasise their differences to the rest of the world also want desperately to fit in and be recognised by the world.

World Journey of My Heart looks at other cultures through the lens of personal or cultural memory, or both, in an attempt to introduce foreign cultures through the manner in which they have influenced living people, either directly, that is through past personal journeys, or in any of a number of indirect ways. In a sense, we might say that this programme is primarily travelogue as biography. It often reaches a fine balance between biography and cultural description. *Homestay in the World*, while very self-consciously focused upon the traveller featured each week, really functions quite independently of the actor, as the match between traveller and destination usually seems almost arbitrary, with the young talent usually having little to add to our understanding of the other. It is the basic method of showing a young Japanese interacting with a family abroad, something that so many young Japanese are also actually doing as they study abroad, that is the show's strong point.

In their conscious quest for recognition by the other, and in their tendency to constantly point out how the foreign stands in relation to the Japanese — either that of today or that of memory — both these shows continue to push the implication that the world is something very different from Japan. This certainly follows the age-old *nihonjinron* way of thinking of Japan and the Japanese as irrevocably unique and categorically other. The focus of a visit to a foreign land is very often simply the Japanese who goes or has been there, or the culture back at home that is more or less similar or somehow connected to that seen abroad. The question that needs asking, in the end, is what impression this leaves upon the viewing audience. Certainly the outside world is represented as something interesting that is worth visiting, and as something that might well influence one's life, but it is still something that exists behind a cultural wall, something that 'we' as Japanese almost seem destined to confront together. One wonders what kind of world traveller these programmes help to create.

14

After the Bubble: Post-Imperial Tokyo

Steve Clark

I

Tokyo is too big to be contained, or even rendered intelligible, through conventional techniques of representation. A population of over 14 million, on a narrow definition, rises to 28 million on a fairly conservative estimate within a radius of thirty miles; and if the Kanto and Kansai conurbations down to Hiroshima are regarded as a continuous urban mass on Honshu, its overall size would approach 70 to 80 million.[1] It is tempting to invoke Paolo Soleri's thesis, in 'Arcology', that the city and nature, rather than being opposites, will increasingly be contained within a single integrated structure, or Constantin Doxiadis's vision of 'Ecumenopolis', an expanding world city extrapolated from existing patterns of coastline development, requiring a new discipline of ekistics, the science of human settlement.[2] Arguably, both have already happened and been called Tokyo.

Between 1600 and 1800, Edo (the pre-Meiji name for Tokyo, Eastern Capital) boasted a population of 1.3 million (compared to approximately 1 million for London at its largest); during two hundred years of self-imposed isolation (*sakoku*), it was the world's biggest city. There remained premodern aspects to its infrastructure: for example, disposal of raw sewage until the early twentieth century continued to be reliant on wagons carting night-soil away for fertilizers.[3] Nevertheless, even at this early period, Tokyo has no apparent boundaries: conversely there appears to be no inside to participant-observers, who instead undergo a peculiar kind of emptying out or self-evacuation. As Isabella Bird observed in 1880, 'The country presents itself to me as a complete blur, or a page covered with hieroglyphs to which I have no key', which makes it crucial 'to delay forming opinions as long as possible'.[4]

In contemporary Tokyo, the representation of place is rendered inherently problematic, not only because of the notorious lack of addresses, but also the difficulty of ascertaining direction when maps are not oriented towards standard north. It is almost as if the urban topography has been deliberately designed to resist cognitive mapping; there are seldom if ever immediately discernible paths or edges to delimit regions, only apparently randomly disconnected nodes.[5] Donald Richie, the most longstanding and authoritative of foreign residents, observes that Tokyo streets produce a collection of village-sized neighbourhoods: 'Otherwise there are no views at all. Everywhere you look is a chaos but what a fascinating chaos it is. It is mosaic city, a mélange city. It has no centre. It has no outside. It seems to lack even those structural supports we know from other cities'.[6]

This chapter will examine some recent attempts to produce an adequate equivalent (whether in travelogue, novel or film) to this 'mosaic'. What kind of narrative expresses such a lack of any sense of location? What are the ethics of inhabiting a city that one cannot begin to imagine, let alone comprehend? This will be balanced against a more historicist question: How have contemporary conventions of representation been altered by the collapse of the Bubble Economy in the early 1990s, and consequent shifts in the global balance of political and economic power? Tokyo is paradoxically presented as the centre of the world, newly-ascendant, with stupendous incomes and grotesquely conspicuous forms of consumption (gold dust on salads), but also in catastrophic decline, impoverished and claustrophobic. Before discussing the curious combination of supplication and schadenfreude that characterises recent travelogue, I wish to examine some specific examples of this urban phenomenology of deferred knowledge (or prolonged ignorance).

II

> My attempts to get around Tokyo proved as confusing as trying to understand the Japanese. Most of Tokyo was rebuilt during the years of poverty after the Second World War. It left the city with a makeshift air, of waterways hastily filled in and buildings knocked up from the cheapest materials. There are no vistas and few parks. Streets stretch in every direction, an interminable tangle of overhead cables, billboards, and cramped shabby dwellings fronted by bars and frosted glass . . .

Harriet Sergeant, in *The Old Sow in the Backroom* (1994), immediately equates sense of place with broader cultural understanding. Tokyo's 'makeshift air' is emphasised, its haphazard development attributed not only to the exigencies of post-war reconstruction but also to a kind of self-protective perversity. The Imperial Palace Gardens is cited as a primary exemplar of this tendency:

> The Japanese have surrounded their institutions, their culture and themselves with a series of earthworks. Life for the foreigner takes on the characteristics of siege warfare. As soon as you penetrate one barrier you are confronted by another. Sometimes you wonder if the whole point of Japan is the wall rather than the treasure inside.

This places the female travel-narrator in the unexpected position of a besieging army faced by obdurate resistance, outside looking in, seeking to 'penetrate' boundaries (in an oddly phallic usage) and grasp (if not loot) the 'treasure inside'.

> The foreigner learns to approach Tokyo not as a city but as a jungle or a desert. I never left home without two or three maps (invitations, whether from a business, a shop or a party always arrive with one), a Japanese language dictionary, the name of my destination written in Japanese (Japanese are nonplussed by even the most subtle mispronunciation) and the telephone number of where I was going. It was also vital to take note of my route for the journey back. Once I met a foreign woman crying in the street. She had moved in the day before and just popped out to buy milk. 'Now I can't find my way home', she wailed, 'I have been trying for half an hour'. Tokyoites navigate by landmarks, a striking skyscraper, a crossing or a peculiar pink coffee shop. Unfortunately Tokyo is in constant upheaval. Buildings are pulled down in a day. Just as I began to feel safe, a precious landmark would disappear behind white plastic curtains, several stories high. After a month the curtains opened to reveal a quite different building or sometimes the fresh tarmac of a new car park.
>
> Getting lost is the best way of getting to know a city. I started with my own neighbourhood.[7]

The comparison of the world's largest urban mass to 'a jungle or a desert' is disconcerting, as is the subsequent recourse to nautical imagery ('navigate'). The comic excess of precaution when venturing outdoors is balanced against the confidence with which the Japanese are said to be 'nonplussed' — what degree of linguistic expertise would be necessary to gauge what counts as 'the most subtle mispronunciation'? 'Getting lost' becomes itself a means of initiation; simply finding one's way around becomes a form of potentially redemptive knowledge. (In Barry Eisler's sequence of Tokyo-based thrillers, John Rain, Vietnam vet and Liberal Democratic Party hit-man, displays his charisma not by black-belt martial arts skills but by prowess at switching subway lines.)[8]

Sergeant's reiteration of 'journey back' suggests that even brief forays may be the occasion for personal metamorphosis, as a parallel to the 'constant upheaval' of Tokyo itself. Her previous emphasis on nondescript sprawl and squalid personal living conditions is difficult to reconcile with the almost animistic power of self-renewal implied by the continually frenzied activity of reconstruction.[9] The most frequent emblem of this economic dynamism and huge corporate wealth in recent representation of the city is the motif of the Smart Building. David Mitchell's *number9dream* opens with a description of the Panopticon 'fortress':

> It is a simple matter. I know your name, and you knew mine, once upon a time: Eiji Miyake. Yes, that Eiji Miyake. We are both busy people, Ms Kato, so why not cut the small talk? I am in Tokyo to find my father. You know his name and you know his address. And you are going to give me both. Right now. Or something like that. A galaxy of cream unribbons in my coffee cup, and the background chatter pulls into focus. My first morning in Tokyo, and I am already getting ahead of myself. The Jupiter Café sloshes with lunch-hour laughter, Friday plottings, clinking saucers. Drones bark into mobile phones. She-drones hitch up sagging voices to sound more feminine. Coffee, seafood sandwiches, detergent, steam. I have an across-the-street view of the Panopticon's main entrance. Quite a sight, the zirconium gothic skyscraper. Its upper floors are hidden in clouds. Under its tight-fitting lid Tokyo steams — 34 degrees C with 86% humidity. A big Panasonic display says so. Tokyo is so close up to you cannot see it. No distances. Everything is over your head — dentists, kindergartens, dance studios. Even the roads and walkways are on murky stilts. Venice with the water drained away. Reflected airplanes climb over mirrored buildings.[10]

The novel employs Dickensian motifs of orphan, lost father and searching for an inheritance, which partially distinguish its narrator from a more stylised traveller-persona. Just as Dickens uses the detective story as a means of bridging the class stratifications of Victorian London, and Chandler employs the hardboiled thriller as a means of bringing the urban sprawl of Los Angeles into spatial relation, Mitchell synthesises the influential genres of Tokyo noir and Cyperpunk in an attempt to map the city. There is a distinctive elision of past or future outside the text ('once upon a time' versus 'getting ahead of myself'); lack of financial specificity or indeed discernible professional skills (the epithet 'drone' would be perhaps better assigned to the idle observer than hyperactive salarymen); and a curious absence of psychological interiority or development. The ethic of *furusato*, of nostalgia for country and hometown, has also been adapted from Japanese cinema, where the city is customarily seen as site of alienation, test and ordeal.[11] Spatially, however, the conventions are extremely similar to recent travelogue: an address defines an identity more accurately than a name (the unusual kanji used by the narrator in his signature are repeatedly emphasised). 'Venice with the water drained away' refers to the erasure of the original water-city; the Yoshiwara pleasure quarter north of Akasuka would originally have been reached by boat.[12] 'Reflected airplanes climb over mirrored buildings' evokes the multiple refractions that make it difficult to distinguish what is image and what reflection in the city skyline. The skyscraper itself is 'hidden in clouds', a mixture of Swiftian Laputa and Foucauldian surveillance, a confinement reiterated in the image of 'tight-fitting lid' of both saucepan and coffin. Macrocosm and microcosm merge in the 'galaxy' within the 'coffee-cup'. The 'across-the-street view' results in being 'so close up you cannot see it. No distance'. Auditory stimulus is more immediate than visual: 'the background chatter pulls into focus'. The 'Friday plottings' prefigure what is later termed the impossibility of 'unplotted space': the city is always already narrated.

Sofia Coppola's *Lost in Translation* combines the motif of spatial derangement with emphasis on the high technology architecture of the future.[13] The film was made a decade after the Bubble economy but appears to inscribe the power relations of the previous decade, thus recalling the archaic sense of *translatio imperii* as a point of transition between empires (originally Roman and Christian, here transposed to the United States and Japan). Bob Harris, though paid 2 million dollars to make a whisky commercial in Tokyo, must also be regarded as a kind of chattel and licensed fool, scarcely entitled to his posture of sardonic world-weary detachment. The cooperation of the Suntory Corporation is acknowledged in the credits without apparent irony, so the satire at the very least can be read both ways.[14]

The Park Hyatt Hotel, in which Bob and Charlotte are staying, or perhaps more accurately are both incarcerated and put on exhibition, is one of a long line of Smart Buildings, that may be traced back as far as the mausoleum of the Tyrell Corporation in Ridley Scott's *Blade Runner*. The structure serves as a microcosm of the entire city, but is also replicated by high-tech devices within it, such as the exercise bike running amok, suggesting a *Terminator*-style rebellion of machines. The building contains numerous artificial plants and shrubs: there are paper sakura in the bedroom; the displays of ikebana in the foyer render distinctions between nature and artifice irrelevant. The guests inhabit the corridors of the hotel as parasitic organisms, easily equated with figments of a video game. Atriums within buildings are mirrored by nature as iconic decoration outside them, with numerous crossovers between animate and inanimate (speaking machines, caring robots, new generation toilets). Lamps within the bar merge with street-lights, buildings and signs outside in such a way that it becomes impossible to distinguish internal from external space. There is incessant mirroring on car-screens, TVs, adverts, windows, bars and video-games. The initial vista of neon signs is refracted via lift-mirrors and the car-window: visual stimuli that seem to have eluded any specific perceiver, in the same way that the image of himself which Bob perceives on the giant screen immediately after his arrival in Tokyo seems to have appropriated and possessed his own identity.

The discomfort in the big city felt by Bob and Charlotte, highly sophisticated and urbanised Americans, may appear somewhat incongruous, but the simultaneous urge to flee and awareness of the impossibility of that gesture remains powerful. The panorama of the city is depicted through successive panning shots and reflected gazes, with a striking chromatic flattening of urban vistas to a pointillism of red and blue dots. There is no perspective on the city despite the high skyline, and apparently dominant perspective. All attempts to escape culminate in the realisation of its infeasibility. 'Gotta get out of here as soon as I can': Bob's attempts to organise a prison break reveal that there is no outside to the room, foyer, bar, hotel, city or country. The guest, however pampered, remains abjectly dependent.[15]

Any distinction between city and country is dissolved. Premodern Japan is contained as a licenced space within the postmodern – as with the dinosaurs projected on the glass building at Shibuya – as a necessary condition of its survival. This is evident in the visit to the Nakano shrine in Tokyo and in the Kyoto scenes made possible by Shinkansen or bullet-train, but with no narration of how the temple was reached from the futuristic station. There is an absence of any consistent spatial logic. The announcement of arrival at Narita is followed by an immediate cut to moving through downtown Tokyo: the Park Hyatt hotel is itself located in Shinjuku to the west of the Imperial Palace, though Omote-sando outside Shibuya is given as the name of the subway station; the night-time cab ride heads outwards via Tokyo Tower and the Rainbow Bridge; the final journey to the airport is signposted to Haneda (which is restricted to domestic rather than international flights), then loops back into Ginza in the final sequence. The rapt attention directed at the subway map by Charlotte can offer no settled destination. The Japanese DVD of *Lost in Translation* provides a comprehensive street-map of locations (though no account of transition between them). The generic satisfactions offered by the film might be seen as at least as much cartographic as comic-romantic.[16]

I now wish to link this spatial mapping to some more general cultural analyses of contemporary Japan.

III

As early as 1959, in a footnote added to the second edition of his introduction to Hegel, Alexander Kojève was describing Japan as 'post-historical', in terms prefiguring Fukuyama's well-known thesis of the 'end of history'.[17] Its everything-all-at-onceness, accelerated processes of assimilation, are precursors of the Asia of global homogeneity documented and implicitly celebrated in Pico Iyer's *Video Night in Kathmandu*: nothing but universal simulation and hyper-consumerism.[18] All share the premise of Japan skipping from premodern archaism to postmodern hybridity with no modernity, instrumental reason, in between.

A dystopian version of this narrative is apparent even in Alex Kerr's valedictory *Lost Japan* (1993) which warns of a 'huge and terrifying machine, a Moloch tearing apart its own land with teeth of steel and there is nothing anyone can do about it'. In his later *Dogs and Demons* (2001), 'Japan's unlimited ambition to go forth and conquer like a giant blowtorch' is compared to the 'sorcerer's apprentice' (139): it is 'a demon escaped from the bottle in 1868 and it has yet to be tamed' (234). The culture is seen as addicted to 'construction scams, environmental catastrophe, information blockage, pork-barrel politics', and controlled by 'bureaucracies on autopilot' (11), committed to both protecting their vested interests and pursuing previously successful policies of breakneck industrialisation at all costs.[19]

Kerr's polemic jeremiad may be regarded as a somewhat histrionic variant on Karel van Wolferen's influential thesis in *The Enigma of Japanese Power*, of a nation without a state, with decision-making diffused among multiple non-accountable bureaucratic agencies: 'There is no political core to this geographical centre. To grasp the reality of the state is not easy in any country. In Japan it is like groping in the proverbial bucket of eels'.[20] The motif of power as absence combined with the accusation of predatory capitalism ('business as war') was popularised in Michael Crichton's *Rising Sun* (1992), which also draws on a wide array of traditional yellow peril motifs. The Nakamoto Corporation has colonised Los Angeles. Their new headquarters is constructed entirely out of imported material, with minimal involvement of American labour. It is the most conspicuous of a number of shadow worlds (of which the paradigm is the brothel for executive mistresses): Japanese power is presented as both contemptibly parasitic on and dangerously seductive to America. The ritual sacrifice of Cheryl, the gasper strangled on the boardroom table, is offered as a lurid analogy to the death-throes of the US economy in the asset purchases undertaken after the revaluation of the yen agreed in the Plaza accords in 1987.[21] As part of this massive capital transfer, Matsushita took over MCA and Universal Studios for $6 billion while the film was still in production; and it insisted the end of the novel be revised so the turncoat American lawyer, Richmond, takes the rap for his Japanese boss Ishihara rather than Ishihara sacrificing himself for his company. Sufficient ambiguity surrounds the ending, however, for conspiracy theories to run unabated: the quick-setting concrete dries and the routine graft of trans-Pacific business resumes unflustered.

The iconography of the lack of any apparent 'core' may be regarded both as displaying a consistent stratagem within a long history of Oriental duplicity, and as manifesting a pure absence of negation, the experience of the sublime of global capital at its most pure, intense and irresistible. Yet absence itself may be read in material terms. Roland Barthes's influential designation of Tokyo as 'Center City, Empty Center' may be empirically contested.[22] Historically, the Imperial Palace was not the traditional heart of the city. Its walls originally reached down to the harbour but were partly dismantled for landfill; the area on the east side to the seafront that gives the impression of a radial node is constructed upon relatively recently reclaimed land. There was also an overall economic and demographic shift from the Low City centred on the Sumida River, after the 1923 earthquake: the importance of waterways during the Edo period is concealed by the motorways built directly over them for the 1964 Olympics. As an infallible indicator of the westering of urban development, after 1984 Godzilla attacks the new government buildings at Shinjuku rather than the traditional site of Tokyo Tower. The major commuter terminuses — Shinjuku, Shibuya, Ikebukuro — have themselves provided a powerful stimulus to development. The stations were built by the same companies that owned department stores and so inevitably provided the axes for future growth primarily on the west side of the city.[23] What Barthes claims as *mu*, the 'emptiness of language' (somewhat speciously attributed to Zen) has an ideologically precise function; the 'empire' of the 'signs' is entirely omitted in, for example, the structural analysis of student radicals as devoid of intention rather than protesting quite precisely against the support of their government for the Vietnam war.[24]

The imagery of absence also pervades expositions of the collapse of the Bubble Economy, the greatest loss of wealth in human history. Following a peak in January 1990, the Tokyo financial markets were sixty percent down within two years, with land prices experiencing comparable falls; and the endemic problem of unrecoverable loans used as collateral for property speculation is still around more than fifteen years later.[25] The dissolution of a stock-market boom is as difficult to narrate as its emergence. Peregrine Hodson, in *A Circle around the Sun* (1993), opts for an increasingly paranoid diary parallel to the disintegration of the Japanese economy. An initially mystical apperception — 'the same everywhere. A sameness. Nothing, nothing, nothing. I have to believe there is a mystery: otherwise there is nothing' (6) — is juxtaposed with financial meltdown: 'If he says the bull market is over, it's over' (3). The narrative progresses from 'Tokyo's a money machine, the capital of a twenty-first-century empire' (49) to 'The market's a stuffed dodo' (102); 'The end of the party', said Roger, 'Tomorrow's the hangover' (109); 'The market's dead' (154); 'the market's like a frozen mammoth' (165).[26] Harriet Sergeant, in *The Old Sow in the Backroom* (1994), comes to Japan as the wife of a largely anonymous banker. The crash occurs offstage, with 'the latest banking scandals' merely a subject of trivial gossip (87), till in the final pages, 'our numbers [have been] somewhat diminished by the recent political and banking scandals' (181).[27] Alex Kerr, in *Lost Japan* (1994), claims to have been hired by the father of 'an old Yale classmate', Tramell S. Crowe, who, despite his lack of any prior business experience, insists 'At any rate let's make you an employee'. One might have thought this a recipe for disaster, but as with Sergeant, there is a complete disavowal of personal culpability and utter inability to recognise any complicity of foreign operatives as beneficiaries of that system. Kerr's repeated contrast of ten years of Japanese recession with US growth in the same period has become retrospectively incongruous after the collapse of Western stock prices with the demise of the dot.com boom and in the wake of the Enron scandal.[28]

The American Kerr heaps praise on the 'western-trained civil service regimes' of ex-colonies of European powers that have produced 'beautiful modern cities such as Hong Kong, Singapore and Kuala Lumpur' of formerly colonised Asian countries. In contrast, the emergence of Japan from the status of once emphatically subordinated satellite to genuine contender for power prompts distrust: the days of the occupation are nostalgically invoked, when 'foreigners lived well', automatically allocated the best houses, in contrast to a presumably near-starving indigenous population.[29] Donald Richie similarly laments: 'I am speaking of my regretting imperialism, I know. I ought to rejoice that Japan is no longer subject to it, but I do not want to. It was too much fun being treated as someone quite special. And one no longer is.'[30]

Other Anglophone residents remain more circumspect about such cultural triumphalism. Will Ferguson observes: 'It sure is great being a Canadian. You get to share all the material benefits of living next door to the United States, yet at the same time you get to act smug and haughty and morally superior.'[31] A particularly vivid example is offered by Peter Carey's *Wrong about Japan*, a text which offers an implicit meditation on Australian memory of past conflict with, and unease at present economic colonisation by, Japan.[32] The chart of samurai sword-cuts in executing prisoners (26) perhaps recalls atrocities against Australian captives; there is a passing reference to massacres in Penang when 'the swords of World War II' were 'enthusiastically wielded by their owners' (44); and Takashi's bow recalls the 'hint of sarcasm' in the 'house of a Japanese father's friend who had fought Australians and despised us all' (144). The traveller-narrator has no apparent qualm in projecting nuclear anxieties and depth memories of the firebombing of Tokyo onto comic-book apocalypse — 'the red-hot centre of the manga world' (145) — but receives the tart response from the actual illustrator himself: 'There is something in your own character that is interested in questions of national identity. As for Mr Tomimo, he has avoided it completely' (98). The 'avoidance' itself, of course, could be seen as a convenient form of cultural amnesia, but the possibility is also raised that Carey over-interprets, that the 'air of great inscrutability' and 'great secrets' which he claims to discern are themselves a projection, idealisation as a particularly pernicious form of stereotyping:

> I was weary of pulling out my lists of questions, of having insights that were apparently only figments of my foreign imagination, of forgetting to bring my business cards along to meetings conducted with all the formality of the Treaty of Versailles. (147)

Yet the recessive irony of questioning the 'list of questions', having 'insights' into lack of insight, encounters a recalcitrant historical allusion in the oblique reminiscence of Australian racism. If 'private guilt' is 'suffered . . . over my incomplete experience of the real Japan' (108), what about the public guilt of the Australian Prime Minister Billy Hughes vetoing the principle of equality of races proposed by the Japanese in the Covenant of the League of Nations drafted at the Versailles conference in 1919?[33]

Carey acknowledges that he is heavily reliant on Japanese connections to fix meetings but offers no extended discussion of his basic self-annulling premise: every foreign traveller not only is, but must also always remain, ignorant. I now wish to consider how this issue is negotiated in other travelogues, before returning to *Wrong about Japan*.

IV

Travel writing is collective and incremental rather than singular and aesthetic. Strictly literary modes of evaluation are secondary, if not wholly irrelevant: place takes precedence over psychology. Of recent travelogues on Japan, probably only Donald Richie's *The Inland Sea* (1971) would qualify as a 'great book', though it refers back to the introspective mode of inter-war autobiography rather than the vicissitudes of the postmodern tourist-traveller. It is also concerned with evoking rural rather than urban Japan, whereas, as Richie's more recent publications make clear, the latter is clearly where the action is and will continue to be for the foreseeable future.[34]

Richie's commendable openness about learning Japanese — specifically the difficulty of mastering honorifics — inevitably raises the issue of linguistic competence in other travellers.[35] As Will Ferguson notes in *Hokkaido Highway Blues* (1996), which is probably the best of the teaching memoirs despite its cumulatively tedious sub-Brysonian wisecrack-a-line idiom:

> Now one thing I have noticed about travel writers in Japan is that they tend to reproduce the conversations they have as if they spoke the language fluently. *'Why yes, my good man'*, I said to the chap in perfect Kanto dialect. *'I am able fully to converse in your language. Why what do you think we have been speaking all this time?'* At the same time any English spoken by Japanese is presented as being moronically inept. *'You no go Tokyo, Tokyo far. Go with car. Faar.'* After careful consideration I have decided to follow this time-honored self-aggrandizing method, even though I spoke Japanese in what would be best be presented as thick ungrammatical pidgin slang.[36]

Any depiction of travel in Japan invites enquiry as to basic problems of communication. Who are the interlocutors, how representative are they if prepared to discourse at length in English, and how dependent is the scenario on the intermediary of translators (a problem endemic from Isabella Bird and Lafcadio Hearn onwards)?[37] How plausible, for example, is the obligatory prefatory thank-you to Japanese teachers? How dependent are journalistic witnesses on the system of collective briefings through press-clubs?[38]

An implausible level of cultural competence is usually simply presumed, with no explanation of how it might have been attained. Expository guidebooks on Japan in particular give no account of 'Where was this learned'? 'Who told you that'? 'Can they be trusted'? In Joseph, there is a systematic excision of first-person pronouns and corroborative anecdote: the first usage of 'I' (rather than a continual present-tense address to an unspecified 'you') comes after nearly fifty pages ('I once bumped into a friend in Tokyo' [44]). Even in Kerr, whose

Lost Japan was originally written in Japanese, the personal context openly acknowledged when in other Asian cities tends to be almost completely elided for Japan.[39] Direct testimony would necessarily involve the possibility of error, making the endemic lack of dignity of the narrator an object of potential ridicule through continually misapplying of the categories of his or her home culture.

Japan is not usually regarded as a destination for casual tourism because of its reputed expense. Residence requires employment in a culture where, without extensive prior study, linguistic expertise will inevitably be painfully lacking. Considerable time and effort are required to achieve even low-level speaking competence. Ferguson concedes that 'if God had meant me to learn kanji he would have given me a bigger brain' (13); Sergeant fluffs her single line at the school Nativity play ('So much, I thought, for a year's Japanese lessons' [132]). Linguistic ability is demonstrated at the very beginning of a visit that at the very least is unlikely to be acquired till the end: in *Kill Bill*, the Okinawan sword-master advises the Bride 'You should learn Japanese — it is easy', impressed by the extent to which she has already mastered the language on the way from the airport.[40]

MacGregor's injunction — 'Don't try and understand them, mate, just report them' (1) — is heeded all too seldom: 'all-pervasive stereotyping' masquerades as ethnographic data. 'Journalist and scholars alike are turned into amateur anthropologists'(4) without, however, taking into account either the self-consciousness of participant-observer testimony or self-critique of the discipline over the last two decades.[41] The recycling of anecdote is generally overt and shameless. In Hodson, who has been on a previous year of cultural exchange, but whose level of linguistic expertise remains uncertain, there occur such hoary axioms as Japanese women being 'like Christmas cake ... After twenty-five no Japanese man wants us' (69) or 'the Imperial Palace was worth the same as the entire state of California' (81). Sergeant even claims, somewhat surreally and with no empirical basis whatsoever, that every weekend evening in Tokyo, 'across the sky helicopters ferried businessmen home from golf courses' (111).

Yet the almost obsessive reiteration of the group mentality ascribed to the Japanese only serves to reinforce the isolation and fallibility of the traveller. Tokyo defeats autopsy, the illusion of an experiential present.[42] It accentuates the counter-empiricist tendency of the genre of travel writing, which resists any narrative of gradual patient accumulation of knowledge: the travel-writer must already know, be aware of previous journeys and larger contexts.

I now wish to return to the issue of how *gaijin* ignorance alternates between means of cultural imposition and mode of continual humiliation in Carey's *Wrong about Japan*.[43]

V

'No Real Japan', said Charley. 'You've got to promise. No temples. No museums.'
'What would we do?'
'We could buy cool manga.'
'There'll be no English translations.'
'I don't care. I'd eat raw fish.'
'What else?'
'And slimy things, I'd eat everything.'
'What if we interviewed some anime directors', I asked, 'trying to figure out how to pay the airfares.' (12)

The final conundrum introduces an immediate split between buffoonish parental persona and established literati whose credentials are somewhat immodestly blazoned on the cover notes: 'The recipient of two Booker prizes [and so, one presumes, able to pay for his own flights] Peter Carey expands his extraordinary achievement with each new novel — and now gives us something entirely different'. The format may perhaps be regarded as innovative, with the text embedded in thirteen high-quality and carefully-selected anime illustrations.[44] The quick-dash impressionistic travelogue is, however, orthodox enough (Carey spends even less time in Tokyo than Barthes does), with the generic conventions of repartee between picaro and companion transposed onto a father-son relation.

The journey becomes the means of bonding and reconciliation, though no account is given of previous friction or estrangement except through fleeting references to Charley as a 'shy boy' (4). He is described as having a 'silent passion for Japan' (4) but it remains uncertain whether he can actually speak Japanese. The ambition — 'When I grow up I want to live in Tokyo' (4) — might be regarded as naïve and impossible to fulfil, or as an eminently practical career option for a young Australian eager to pay college fees, who has presumably taken the option of education in Japanese from primary school onwards in Australia. Internet contact has already been established with Takashi, and thumb-talk via cell-phone involves the son 'already adapting to a certain Japanese language' (51). It is claimed that manga is an area in which the 'the entire English language had been vaporized' (5), though Takashi converses extremely competently, and the Japanese involved in the production of anime seem shrewd, multilingual and cosmopolitan.

The Cretan liar's paradox of 'I'm a terrible reporter' (129) inevitably poses the question of who is exploiting whom? If taken at face value, the author is deceiving his publisher-financier, his Japanese hosts and his Anglophone readership. Similarly, Carey's rapacious pursuit of a free trip may perhaps be construed as the sign of the imminent demise of his reputation as a novelist (a clapped-out celebrity, like Bob in *Lost in Translation*). Before parting, there is an apparently confident self-designation — 'I'm a good enough traveller until I have to catch the plane' (156) – but the preceding text continually equivocates as to whether father and son should identify with or despise 'the first tourists of the day' (125). If 'the most interesting tourist experience of all' is 'exotic junk food in plastic bags' (129), what might constitute authentic travel? If 'it is the nature of tourism that one returns not only with trinkets and postcards but also with memories of misunderstandings, hurts ignorantly inflicted across the borderlines of language and custom' (92), what about the converse of novelty and delight? If 'misunderstandings' are recognised as such, do they become a kind of negative epiphany? Is a 'hurt' which is known to be 'ignorantly inflicted' thereby consciously redeemed?

In Carey, present ignorance is narrated from a position of future retrospect, with an implied reader located outside that framework of address. In enquiring 'How could I have known where this would lead?' (3), what status has the first-person pronoun? From the point of view of having written the book, the narrator-persona already knows but wishes to preserve the illusion of ignorance. 'Let me tell you Fremantle Jack, it is not that simple' (146): if an Australian interlocutor is implied, why is there not more on the specific history of relations between the two countries? 'Nor did I know we were staying at the heart of Japanese pop culture' (32): his guidebook would surely have informed him.

Similarly, there is an unanswered conundrum of studying the famously-uncensored genre of manga while attempting to shield Charley from what is 'sexually explicit and unpleasant' (107). The equation of nose and large penis is divulged to the reader but withheld from the son (at least until such point as he himself might choose to read the book [9]).[45] The smothering over-protectiveness towards Charley implies the unworldliness of the father-narrator, yet this comic persona who continually makes mistakes is framed by the traveller who already knows, who has diligently prepared, with access to a range of cultural reference denied mere natives. When the relation is pointed out between the 'origins of the tokonoma' (display case for one item) and sumptuary laws prohibiting ostentation by the merchant class, this is supposedly the 'only time I heard this intriguing suggestion' (23), despite the extended exposition given to the issue in 'Alex Kerr's sad and celebratory book, *Lost Japan*' (66). *Little Adventures in Tokyo* is cited as a 'handy guidebook', yet obvious and easily rectifiable errors remain in the text: 'anime' is a Japanese rather than French term (6); it is the long-term homeless rather than drunks who camp out in the parks (16); even the date of Parry arriving in Japan is given as 1854 rather than 1853 (8). Error is not located exclusively within present narration, but is transmitted as a form of contamination that also infects the extra-textual vantage of implied superiority:

> This is what it had seemed the trip had come to: everything falling apart. Takashi offended, studio Ghibli looking desolate, a looted museum in the last days of war.
>
> Now all of the above was what I thought had happened. Yet later when I checked my version of events with Mrs Miyagi I learned I had been horribly mistaken. (148)

Seeing 'through the lens of a foreigner's misunderstanding' necessarily raises the question of what understanding might consist of. The final vignette involves finding the residence of Takashi's grandmother using 'a piece of fine onionskin paper on which he drew the most exquisite map' (124), which also recalls the earlier references to global-tracking devices and finding locations as a kind of a quasi-military satellite-targeting. This is presented to a cabdriver: ' "We go" I said in perfect English . . . "OK" he said reading the map.' Charlie willingly hands over the manga encyclopaedia, previously presented as magic talisman for entering into the depth of the Japanese cultural psyche:

> 'I was surprised she kissed you. I didn't think they did that.'
> 'Must be the real Japan,' he said.
> 'Yes,' I said.
> 'Found it finally. Let's get out of here before we learn we are wrong.' (157–8)

Remembering how little one knows becomes a crucial mark of distinction, though this in turn can become a double-bluff of proclaiming the lack of need to comprehend the other, except in terms of momentarily diverting spectacle.

Thus it appears that travelogue on Japan can only be authenticated by failure; insofar as it claims authority, it must appear inevitably self-deluding. I now wish to relate this to some more general conventions of recent texts on Tokyo and Japan.

VI

Travel is unheroic in Japan: physical journeying is rarely possible in such an intensely urbanised environment: adventure and initiation must be at best highly metaphorical. Paul Fussell's often-cited dictum of the expiry of the genre of travel writing with the dissolution of travel into tourism has little relevance in this context.[46] Arrival will necessarily be by plane, with the only ordeal jetlag, seldom explicitly described, more a testimony to globalisation than entry into an exotic alternative realm. (Carey describes the route from Narita airport into Tokyo but not the experience of flying and actual moment of touchdown; only Ross gives a brief account of the flight and the anxiety of passing through Japanese customs [21–2, 28–9]). For an earlier generation, there would have been close restrictions on movement outside the treaty ports: the exceedingly well-connected Isabella Bird cites the tight restrictions on zones of access.[47] Ferguson intersperses his narrative with occasional quasi-choric laments: 'You are welcome as an outsider. The problem is not exclusion but partial exclusion. The door is open but the chain is on' (115).

The traveller undergoes as well as acts: journeying is not simple empowerment but oddly passive: often boring and so requiring tolerance of repetition as much as the overcoming of obstacles. Scenes that tend to be edited out but which are crucial in everyday life include shopping; paying bills to utility companies; registering at government offices; negotiating for visas with the fearsome embassy bureaucracy (which only Hodson describes the process of applying for (5–7)). It is never explained, for example, how to find property in Tokyo when landlords will not let to foreigners without additional deposits and guarantors.

Ferguson's route — copying Alan Booth's *Road to Sato* (401) — has to swerve away from expressways: he must repeatedly turn down lifts to Tokyo and the big bad city of Osaka' (187) which nevertheless exert a continuous gravitational pull.[48] He is repeatedly advised, 'There is no reason to hitchhike. That is why we built the bullet-train' (8). In contrast, travelogue on the United States appeals to the frontier, movement, velocity with multiple means of transport (boat, motorbike, car, truck), and re-enactment of the mythic journeys undertaken in cinema and popular music. It can assume instant recognition of icons such as the Manhattan skyline, or the pan-shot over Los Angeles: a landscape of desire which is always already known. For Japan, and in particular Tokyo, it is difficult to narrate movement, let alone depict it cinematically. In *Lost in Translation* there is a certain hasty snatched quality to the photography, due to the street-sequences being shot without formal permission: the simple complexity of Japanese licensing procedures is one obvious cause of the comparative rarity of depictions of Tokyo. Hence there is no immediately recognisable visual iconography for the city: perhaps the teenage crowds in Shibuya, the neon signs of department stores in Ginza, the sky-view from Shinjuku.[49]

Travel narrators may be distinguished from characters in realist fictions through absence of motivation, whether positive (curiosity/wonder) or negative (grief/flight). There is no direct answer to the question of why any of these narrator-personas have come to Japan, and a consistent elision of any explicit profit-motive. Yet why does the traveller travel if not to write travel books (Carey/Iyer), academic ethnography (Barthes) or journalism (Joseph, McGregor); or to earn an 'absurdly large salary' from JET/language teaching (Ferguson/Ross); or to engage in the chimerical and rapacious realm of stocks, real estate speculation and banking (Kerr/Hodson/Sergeant).[50]

No collective rationale is offered for the travellers (unlike the Japanese themselves): they remain poignantly vulnerable figures, however privileged. Their belatedness is evident in continued defensive allusions to a pre-ironic persona; Hodson boasts, 'I've read a hundred pages of *Morte D'Arthur*' (177) and Ferguson designates himself a 'direct descendent of Dr Livingstone' (44). Quest produces self-mockery and melancholy in a therapeutic rite. For all the quasi-heroic resonances, the trip is as much about the invention of difficulty as its circumvention. In Ferguson, the cherry-blossom front sweeping upward across Japan represents both omnipresent quest and mere arbitrary pretext; in Hodson, money is a similarly illusory object of pursuit; in Carey, any definitive interpretation of manga remains elusive; in Ross, the final tracking down of Mishima's sword, ostensibly the obsessive goal of the book, is both bathetic and inconclusive ('It had, in my failure to find it, remained intangible yet still vital', 240–1). There is a notable reluctance to dramatise any actual work-relations. Ferguson shows no disquiet at ridiculing the language teaching of which he is a part ('that's just the teachers. The students are even worse', 91); Hodson is never quite able to begin work (uncertain of what it would be); and Kerr is a translator/fixer, but gives no details of responsibilities, just assumes his own authority and competence; and Sergeant is a freelance journalist but offers no details of contracts, contacts or deadlines.

The older Japanese policy of closed borders (*sakoku*) is visible in still-current rituals such as the fingerprinting of visitors and biometrical inspection introduced in 2008. The stranger, however apparently weak, vulnerable and dependent, is imbued with threat, menace and doom: whether in the older guise of proselytising missionary or newer one of writer-commentator, the intruder must always be suspected as a potential informant and agitator. As Hodson muses, 'My arrival in the office is an invasion of company territory' (52): 'I was like a spy, like everyone who wants to understand a foreign country' (202).

This renders problematic any implied superiority of the traveller through mobility and the option of choosing to visit. Contracts are often extremely generous, but expertise is certainly bought and sold, fixed-term, both ultimately and immediately dispensable. The import of foreign workers as a form of technology transfer dates back to the Meiji Era: even then, however, as Bird notes, desirable skills should remain while their bearer remains transient.[51] The irresistible force of globalisation meets the immovable object of social cohesion, *nihonjinron*. Are the Japanese simply wasting their money on bringing these people over? There are financial experts who cannot foresee the collapse of the Bubble Economy; teachers who pride themselves on not teaching; journalists who claim omniscience; and writers who appear not qualified to write. This might be seen as the reverse of technology transfer, with *gaijin* simply hired to confirm their own irrelevance, fully deserving of Ferguson's comparison to tame dancing bears (92).

The principle of contingency is accentuated to the point where, in Ferguson, no closure can be offered, not even the termination of contract at the conclusion of his narrative when his employers implement their right to 'reconsider our options' (432). There appears no point of completion: the very concept of destination remains problematic. Action is placed in a past which, as Hodson puts it, 'isn't just another country, it's another universe' (2). The future implied by the temporal progression of the journey never coincides with maturation into an older self. The use of present-tense narration merges past and present selves, eliding any explicit markers of hindsight: there are strikingly few dates and a general compression of time. The persona is self-sufficient within its textual manifestation, separated from the biographical self: we simply do not know what will happen to the traveller.

The very fact of journeying implies motivation by deficiency and lack: the texts may be regarded as a plea for readmission, ultimate testimony to not having become Japanese. There is usually a lacuna concerning actual departure, and no dramatisation of any moment of eventual re-incorporation. Return must inevitably imply defeat and rejection as well as survival and resilience: Sergeant agonises, 'I had become a traitor to my own, a foreigner in my own land' (201). There appears no gain of knowledge and competence, but rather a gradual dispelling of what had previously been assumed. Travellers return and so cannot comprehend (in contrast to the settler or the fieldwork of the anthropologist). Extended residence would remove the original frisson of interrogation by and of the other. It is this quality of ignorance that is important for the foregrounding of cultural difference. It allows experiences of novelty, wonder and curiosity to remain unsated, though these are capable of instant reversal to a wounding sense of permanent exclusion.

While conducting an interminably prolonged interview in *Wrong about Japan*, Peter Carey confesses to feeling 'locked inside my skin, lost in space, emotionally disconnected from my fellow human beings' (101). This might be regarded as an explicit gloss on the title of Sofia Coppola's film: culture-shock, jet-lag and linguistic ineptitude as alienation. To be *Lost in Translation* might seem necessarily to imply misunderstanding or diminishment. Yet the term also involves movement heavenwards in a kind of stellification ('removal from earth to heaven, orig. without death as the translation of Enoch, but in later use said of the death of the righteous' [OED 1c]). In its verbal form, it may be glossed as 'to transport with the strength of some feeling; to enrapture, entrance (arch) (OED 6), which links to the positive sense of 'lost' one may be existentially thrown, but implies potential ecstasy as well as or as part of the experience of abandonment ('to become deeply absorbed or engrossed (in thought etc.); to be bewildered, overwhelmed in wonder; to be distracted, lose one's wits (from emotion or excitement)' [OED 10c].

After the talk-show interview, Bob flaccidly accedes to Charlotte, 'whatever you like I'm completely lost', and the post-coital soundtrack establishes a mood of sensual opulence in inverse proportion to depicted sexual activity. (The one-night stand with the singer occurs off-camera, behind closed doors.) There seems no obvious reason why the relation between Bob and Charlotte should remain unconsummated: the former unresponsive to the intrusive demands of his wife, the latter suspecting (though never finally confirming) infidelity by her husband. Arguably, a latent father-daughter incest taboo is operative: the singer is caustically dubbed by Charlotte as 'closer to your age', with the withering insult of 'growing up in the fifties', but it seems more an issue of spiritual rather than bodily integrity. If 'the more you know where you are the more you know what you want', is the converse also true? If you do not know where you are and never expect to find out, how does that redefine one's desires, particularly in a film suffused with a sense of karma, rebirth and release from sexual consummation? The lovers cease to be from anywhere and similarly have nowhere to return to; they are nostalgic perhaps not for authenticity but less flagrant modes of simulation. The evacuated quality of a postmodern consumerist lifestyle is simply intensified by an illusory shift of location.

Travel enlarges while exile demeans. Visitors to Japan seem to get narrower, contract through increasing awareness of their incompatibility with both their own and the alien culture; losing an old self without gaining any functioning newer identity. Hence the customary lack of any depiction of the journey back, even the gesture of booking the flight. The enormous tact of *Lost in Translation* lies in not permitting any overhearing of the final conversation between the lovers, locating its final scene of parting not at the airport, but on the public street. There is redemptive silence, crucial words withheld from the audience, who follow and empathise with Bob's final pursuit, only to be abruptly rebuffed. There is a refusal of disclosure — is this the ultimate parting or has a promise been made to meet again? — which becomes a more general disclaimer of knowledge of Tokyo, Japan, otherness. Thus the film, for all its occasional ethnocentrism, gains a kind of legitimate authority by showing the willingness of the lovers to depart from the hotel, meet and embrace on a street level, which refuses to accord them any particular priority.[52] As such, it might be seen as offering a more general model for negotiating the challenge of representing Tokyo itself.

Notes

Introduction

1 Most influentially in Edward Said's *Orientalism* (New York: Vintage, 1979), and Mary Louise Pratt, *Imperial Eyes: Travel Writing and Transculturation* (London: Routledge, 1992).
2 The term is a coinage from the Second World War as a field command, which became further established after the Vietnam War. The Chinese/Japanese term for the area is Nanyang, the South Seas. See Susan Morgan, *Place Matters: Gendered Geography in Victorian Women's Travel Books about Southeast Asia* (New Jersey: Rutgers University Press, 1997), 4.
3 See Colin Thubron, *The Shadow of the Silk Road* (London: Chatto & Windus, 2006).
4 See *An East Asia Renaissance: Ideas for Economic Growth* (World Bank, 2006).
5 Influential examples of this now extensive body of academic work include: Janet L. Abu-Lughod, *Before European Hegemony The World System AD 1250–1350* (Oxford: Oxford University Press, 1989); K. N. Chauduri, *Asia Before Europe: Economy and Civilisation of the Indian Ocean from the Rise of Islam to 1750* (Cambridge: Cambridge University Press, 1990); Andre G. Frank, *ReOrient: Global Economy in the Asian Age* (Berkeley: California University Press, 1998); Geoffrey C. Gunn, *First Globalisation: The Eurasian Exchange 1500–1800* (Lanham: Rowman & Littlefield, 2003); John M. Hobson, *The Eastern Origins of Western Civilisation* (Cambridge: Cambridge University Press, 2004); Dirk Hoerder, *Cultures in Contact: World Migrations in the Second Millennium* (Durham NC: Duke University Press, 2002); and Kenneth Pomeranz, *The Great Divergence: China, Europe and the Making of the Modern World Economy* (Princeton: Princeton University Press, 2000).
6 On luxury commodities, see Anne Bermingham and John Brewer (eds), *The Consumption of Culture* (London: Routledge, 1995) and Maxine Berg, *Consumers and Luxury* (Manchester: Manchester University Press, 1999).
7 See Susan Whitfield, *Marco Polo and the Encounter of East and West* (Toronto: Toronto University Press, 2003).
8 Said, *Culture and Imperialism* (London: Chatto & Windus, 1993), 22.
9 The title of Eliza Ruhamah Scidmore's *China: The Long-Lived Empire* (New York: The Century Co., 1900).
10 On early relations between Japan and China, and also their complex triangulations

with Korea, see W. G. Beasley, *Japan Encounters the Barbarian: Japanese Travellers in America and Europe* (New Haven and London: Yale University Press, 1995), 1–16.

11 For the impact of Chinese colonisation on Tibet, see Robert Barnett, *Lhasa: Streets with Memories* (New York: Columbia University Press, 2006). On the recent Chinese presence in Central Asia, see Thubron, *The Shadow of the Silk Road*, especially 'Kashgar', 138–50.

12 On naming in Cook, see Paul Carter, *The Road to Botany Bay: an Essay in Spatial History* (London: Faber, 1987).

13 See Madeleine Yue Dong, *Republican Beijing: The City and its Histories* (Berkeley: California University Press, 2006).

14 On early tribute missions, see Edwin O. Reischauer, *Ennin's Diary: The Record of a Pilgrimage to China in Search of the Law* (New York: Ronald Press, 1955). Beasley stresses the priority given to weaponry (particularly naval), industrial technology, and business expertise, and the variable reception which returnees received (178–99) but pays comparatively little attention to the generic form of the memoir or diplomatic report.

15 James Clifford, *Routes: Travel and Translation in the Late Twentieth Century* (Cambridge: Harvard University Press, 1997), 39.

16 See Stephen Greenblatt, *Marvelous Possessions: The Wonder of the New World* (Chicago: Chicago University Press, 1991).

17 See Akinori Kato, 'Package Tours, Pilgrimages and Pleasure Trips', in Atsushi Ueda (ed.), *The Electric Geisha: Exploring Japan's Popular Culture* (Tokyo: Kodansha 1994), 51–9; and John Clammer, 'Sites and Sights: The Consuming Eye and the Arts of the Imagination in Japanese Tourism' in *Contemporary Urban Japan: A Sociology of Consumption* (Oxford: Blackwell, 1997), 135–51.

18 Pratt, 'Scratches on the Face of the Landscape, or What Mr Barrow Saw in the Land of the Bushmen', *Critical Inquiry*, 12 (1985), 119–43.

19 Paul Fussell, *Abroad: British Literary Travelling between the Wars* (Oxford: Oxford University Press, 1980).

20 Clifford, 'Spatial Practices', in *Routes*, 52–91.

Chapter 1

1 Its popularity is evident in the number of reprints, its significance in the history of Japanese literature, the huge number of books connected to it (e.g. impressions and photography from people who travelled the same route), and last, by the many translations.

2 For other dimensions of the *Oku no hosomichi*, in particular as a masterpiece of *haikai* prose (*haibun*), see Haruo Shirane, *Traces of Dreams. Landscape, Cultural Memory, and the Poetry of Bashō* (Stanford: Stanford University Press, 1998), 212–53.

3   Thomas S. Kuhn, *The Structure of Scientific Revolutions* [1962] (Chicago: Chicago University Press, 1970).
4   What I am referring to with the concept of the Middle Ages is the Japanese term '*chūsei*', but in a much broader than the usual political sense, which is determined by questions of political power and movements of the capital (that would be from 1185 to about 1600). Some aspects of these Middle Ages will be shown in the text.
5   German: Luhmann speaks from 'funktionale Differenzierung des Gesellschaftssystems' (functional differentiation of the system of society) and 'Ausdifferenzierung einzelner Funktionssysteme' (differentiation of single functionsystems); see Niklas Luhmann, *Die Kunst der Gesellschaft* (Frankfurt AM: Suhrkamp, 1997), 115.
6   Gerhard Sauder, 'Formen gegenwärtiger Reiseliteratur', in Anne Fuchs and Thomas Harden (eds), *Reisen im Diskurs. Modelle der literarischen Fremderfahrung von den Pilgerberichten bis zur Postmoderne* (Heidelberg: Universitätsverlag C. Winter, 1995), 552–73 (553).
7   See, for example, Tōzō Suzuki, *Kinsei kikō bungaku nōto* (Tōkyō: Tōkyōtō shuppan, 1974); Yukihiko Nakamura, *Nakamura Yukihiko chojutsushū*, Vol. 6 (Tōkyō: Chūō kōronsha, 1982); Kenji Watanabe, 'Kinsei kikō bungaku no saihyōka', in *Kokubungaku, kaishaku to kanshō: Kinsei bungaku to tabi*, 55, 3 (1990), 147–53; Yōko Itasaka, *Edo no tabi to bungaku* (Tōkyō: Perikansha, 1993) or 'Kinsei no kikō', in 'Jidaibetsu Nihon bungakushi Jiten Henshu Iinkai' (ed.) *Nihon bungakushi jiten* (Tōkyō: Tōkyōtō shuppan, 1997); and other works by Itasaka. For useful observations and discussions of some travel diaries in English, see Donald Keene, *Travelers of a Hundred Ages* (New York: Henry Holt and Company, 1989), 323–94.
8   Watanabe, 'Kinsei kikō bungaku', 147.
9   See Yukihiko Nakamura, *Nakamura Yukihiko chojutsushū*, Vol. 13 [1984] (Tōkyō: Chūō kōronsha, 1991), 303, and Keene, *Travelers*, 325.
10 Itasaka, *Edo*, 85.
11 For the epistemology of the Middle Ages, see Robert F. Wittkamp, *Japans frühmoderne Reiseliteratur. Leben und Werk von Sugae Masumi (1754–1829)* (Hamburg: OAG, 2001), 31–7.
12 Translated by Nobuyuki Yuasa, *Bashō. The Narrow Road to the Deep North and Other Travel Sketches* [1966] (Middlesex, Baltimore, Ringwood: Penguin Books, 1968), 97.
13 Keene, *Travelers* , 324.
14 Yuasa, *Bashō*, 110.
15 Bashō worked over and polished this piece of *haikai* prose presumably until its publication in 1694.
16 Yuasa, *Bashō*, 105.
17 ———, 114. To be fair, one has to admit that there is no grammatical subject in the original text so it could also mean 'we'. But even if Bashō's intention was a

'we', this would only show how far the English translation is guided by the old paradigm (Yasuda is translating the whole travel sketch using 'I' where in theory 'we' could be meant just as well).

18 For further discussion of the history of *hyōhaku*-mentality ('strong desire to wander') in the context of religious studies, literary and folk studies (*minzokugaku*), see Robert F. Wittkamp, 'Hyōhaku — das stete Getriebenwerden. Beitrag zu einer Mentalitätsgeschichte des Mittelalters', in *Nachrichten der Gesellschaft für Natur- und Völkerkunde Ostasiens*, 173–4 (2003), 155–82 (159).

19 For Li Bo (Jap: Rihaku), see Nōichi Imoto, Hori Nobuo and Muramatsu Tomotsugu (eds), *Matsuo Bashō-shū* (*Nihon koten bungaku zenshū*) 41 (Tōkyō: Shōgakukan, 1972), 341.

20 A field of research developed in France at the beginning of the twentieth century; see Wittkamp, 'Hyōhaku', 157.

21 See Haruo Shirane, 'Matsuo Bashō's *Oku no hosomichi* and the Anxiety of Influence', in Amy Vladeck Heinrich (ed.), *Currents in Japanese Culture: Translations and Transformations* (New York: Columbia University Press, 1997), 171–83, and *Traces of Dreams*, 230–41. Shirane describes the *Oku no hosomichi* as *haikai* prose (*haibun*), which 'remapped the cultural landscape of the Interior' in *Traces of Dreams*, 212.

22 Yuasa, *Bashō*, 115–6.

23 Shirane, *Traces of Dreams*, 220–1.

24 See Wittkamp, *Japans frühmoderne Reiseliteratur*, 37–43.

25 See Keene, *Travelers*, 324, who is referring to the *Seihoku kikō* (Journey to the Northwest), the 'earliest Japanese diary I have read that contains not a single poem by the author'. The diary was written by Kaibara Ekiken in 1689, the same year in which Bashō made his journey along the *Narrow Road of Oku* (*Oku no hosomichi*).

26 See Wittkamp, *Japans frühmoderne Reiseliteratur*, 1–12.

27 This is the case in the works of Koshōken and Nankei too; see Harold Bolitho, 'Traveler's Tales: Three Eighteenth-Century Travel Journals', *Harvard Journal of Asiatic Studies*, 50, 2 (1990), 485–504 (489).

28 See Tsune'ichi Miyamoto, *Tabibitotachi no rekishi*, Vol. 2 (Tōkyō: Miraisha), 29–40.

29 Kōjin Karatani, *Origins of Modern Japanese Literature* [1993] (Durham and London: Duke University Press, 1994), 22; original: *Nihon kindai bungaku no kigen* (Tōkyō: Kōdansha, 1980).

30 See Karatani, *Origins*, 19. The original notion of 'landscape as landscape' (*fūkei toshite no fūkei*) is translated with 'landscapes as such'.

31 My translation; see Karatani, *Origins*, 20.

32 Karatani, *Origins*, 21 and 24.

33 For a sceptical view of Karatani's 'postmodern discourse on landscape', see Robert F. Wittkamp, 'Die Anti-Landschaft bei Bashō. Ergänzungen zur Kritik am postmodernen Landschaftsdiskurs', *Die Deutsche Literatur* (*Doitsu bungaku*), 48 (2004): 107–26, 107–9, and 'Konstruktivismus, Wahrnehmung und Gedächtnis:

Ein Plädoyer für einen konstruktivistischen Landschaftsdiskurs', in Andreas Moerke and Andrea Germer (eds), *Grenzgänge (De-Konstruktion kollektiver Identitäten in Japan)* (München: Iudicium, 2004 [Deutsches Institut für Japanstudien: Japanstudien, 16]) 239–56 (241 footnote 9).
34 My translation.
35 For Ekiken, see Keene, *Travelers*, 323–9.
36 For a development of a concept of landscape as an anthropological matter, a question of theory of perception, and as an epistemology based on (radical *and* cultural) constructivism, see Wittkamp, 'Konstruktivismus, Wahrnehmung und Gedächtnis'.
37 *Kikō bunshū* (1930), in *Shōwa-han teikoku bunko* (1928–30). For the *Kikō bunshū*, see also Karatani, *Origins*, 52.
38 For a short comparison of Koshōken, Nankei and Masumi, see Bolitho, 'Traveler's Tales'.
39 See Karatani, *Origins*, 52, quoting Yanagita: 'The first consists of a string of poems and lyrical essays; the second consists exclusively of description, narrated by a traveller who simply is a discreet presence hidden in the shadows of the actual scene'.
40 See Tōzō Suzuki, *Kinsei kikō bungei nōto* (Tōkyō: Tōkyōtō shuppan, 1974), 28.
41 Karatani, *Origins*, 32.
42 ———, *Origins*, 33; for Chapter 5, see 114–35.
43 Yuasa, *Bashō*, 120.
44 Bolitho, 'Traveler's Tales', 491.
45 Itasaka, *Edo no tabi*, 10.
46 See Masaki Taguchi, *Sugae Masumi dokuhon* (Akita: Mumeisha, 1994), 168–87, where he puts many of Masumi's descriptions together. For Niklas Luhmann's 'the observation [...] of children is now observed' ('das Beobachten des Kindes wird jetzt beobachtet'), see his 'Kontingenz als Eigenwert der modernen Gesellschaft', in, *Beobachtungen der Moderne* (Opladen: Verlag der Sozialwissenschaften, 1992), 93–128 (124).
47 Karatani, *Origins*, 40–1.
48 See Itasaka, *Edo no tabi*, 242–76; she identifies about six hundred titles connected to Hokkaidō and more than sixty works including the name '*kikō*' (travel literature) in their title.
49 The expression 'synchronical intertextuality' (quoting, complementing, correcting, criticising, etc.) is intended not to stress the relationships of these texts to the literature of the Middle Ages but to newer or contemporary literature.
50 Translated by Richard A. Jambor, 'Waga kokoro by Sugae Masumi (I)', in *Shōin joshi gakuin daigaku kenkyū kiyō* (Shoin Literary Review), 37 (1996), 1–22, and 'Waga kokoro by Sugae Masumi (II)', in *Shōin joshi gakuin daigaku kenkyū kiyō* (Shoin Literary Review), 38 (1997), 1–20; page numbers are taken from the offprints respectively.
51 The following *waka* poem is omitted; see Jambor, 'Waga kokoro (I)', 8.
52 Jambor, 'Waga kokoro (I)', 13.

53 ——, 'Waga kokoro (II)', 1–2.
54 ——, 'Waga kokoro (II)', 11.
55 See Yuasa, *Bashō*, 73 (*Oi no kobumi*: *The Records of a Travel-worn Satchel*). A more appropriate translation of the last two lines would be 'unless there are the freshness of [the Chinese poet] Su and the arresting elements of [the Chinese poet] Huang in them'.
56 For Japanese texts by Masumi, see Takeshi Uchida and Tsune'ichi Miyamoto (eds), *Sugae Masumi yūranki*, 5 vols (Tōkyō: Heibonsha [*Tōyō bunko*, translation into modern Japanese], 1965–68) and *Sugae Masumi zenshū*, 12 vols (Tōkyō: Miraisha, 1971–81). For translations of two travel diaries into German, see Wittkamp, *Japans frühmoderne Reiseliteratur*, 205–60.

Chapter 2

1 Samuel Holmes, *The Journal of Samuel Holmes*, 133.
2 Pratt's 'Scratches on the Face of the Country; or What Mr. Barrow Saw in the Land of the Bushmen' first appeared as a chapter in *Race, Writing, and Difference* (Chicago: University of Chicago Press, 1986a), and was later revised and included in *Imperial Eyes*. The full title of Barrow's Africa journal is *An Account of Travels into the Interior of Southern Africa in the Years 1797 and 1798* (London: T. Cadell and W. Davis, 1801–04).
3 *A Delicate Inquiry* is a thirty-one-page booklet published in 1818, two years after a second failed English embassy to China led by Lord Amherst.
4 Brief descriptions of each of the Macartney texts can be found in Cramner-Byng, 342–52.
5 On this day, the embassy was to travel through the Chinese capital to the famous Summer Palace where they would stay for several days before some members would proceed to the emperor's residence north of the capital. The Summer Palace and surrounding gardens were well known in England, and the anticipation of seeing the capital was no doubt matched by the excitement of staying at the 'Garden of Gardens'. The name 'Garden of Gardens' (Cranmer-Byng, *An Embassy to China*, 95) appears in Macartney's journal. Cranmer-Byng explains that the 'name literally means "round bright garden" and has the connotation garden of perfect brightness, or "the garden *par excellence*", 359.

The embassy travelled through the suburbs of Peking for about fifteen minutes before they reached the gates to the city, and then they only spent about two hours in the capital before heading to the Summer Palace. The Summer Palace was in such a state of disrepair that it was deemed 'unworthy the residence of the representative of a great monarch' (Anderson, *A Narrative*, 111). Therefore, the embassy (except for Barrow and several others who stayed to supervise the handling of the gifts that were stored at the palace) left the imperial residence after only three days and returned to Peking where they stayed at an estate (supposedly built by a merchant from Canton using bribes he received from English, or at least foreign, traders). On 2 September, eleven members of the embassy then proceeded to Rehe for the celebrated audience with the emperor.

6 Cranmer-Byng, *An Embassy to China*, 351.
7 ———, *An Embassy to China* 219.
8 Appleton, *A Cycle of Cathay*, 121.
9 Barrow tells the story of a near revolt that took place in Madrid when the monarchy ordered the construction of 'proper places of retirement' to be attached to houses in order to prevent the inhabitants from 'emptying their nocturnal machines out of the windows into the streets'. The inhabitants considered their rights violated before the doctors, who for financial reasons were opposed to the measure in the first place, managed to convince the citizens 'that if human excrement was no longer to be accumulated in the streets, to attract the putrescent particles floating in the air, they would find their way into the human body, and a pestilential sickness would be the inevitable consequence' (67).

Chapter 3

1 This work was supported in part by a grant from the City University of New York PSC-CUNY Research Award Program and Faculty Fellowship Publication Program (FFPP). As a new junior faculty member, I was also given time to research the article. A shorter version of the essay, 'Uneven Distribution of the China Craze: Travel Narratives, Periodicals, and Audiences in Nineteenth-Century Britain,' was read at the Mobilis in Mobile: International Conference on Studies in Travel Writing at the University of Hong Kong on 11 July 2005. I am thankful to the audience for their useful comments. I would also like to thank colleagues of the FFPP for their thoughtful feedback on a draft of the article.
2 *Ship Amherst. Return to an Order of the Honourable the House of Commons, Dated 17 June 1833* . . . (London: House of Commons 1833; reprinted in *Irish University Press Area Studies Series, British Parliamentary Papers: China*, Vol. 39, 127–233 [reprint page numbers]), 3 [original page number]. All future references are to page numbers of the original edition, not to reprint page numbers.
3 Hugh Hamilton Lindsay and Charles Gutzlaff, *Report of Proceedings on a Voyage to the Northern Ports of China in the Ship Lord Amherst* (London: B. Fellowes, 1833).
4 Charles Gutzlaff, *Journal of Three Voyages along the Coast of China in 1831, 1832, & 1833, with Notices of Siam, Corea, and the Loo-Choo Islands*, intro. William Ellis (London: F. Westley and A. H. Davis, 1834). Subsequent references abbreviated to *Journal*.
5 John Barrow, 'Free Trade to China', *Quarterly Review*, 50 (1833–34), 430–67 (449).
6 Nan Mu, 'Ya pian zhan zheng yi qian Ying chuan A Mei Shi De Hao zai Zhongguo yan hai de zhen cha huo dong' [The British *Ship Amherst*'s reconnaissances in

China's coastal waters before the Opium War], *Jin Bu Ri Bao* [The progressive daily], 13 September 1952, 2. All excerpts and quotations from Chinese sources such as this article are my translations.

7   See Kathleen Wilson, 'Introduction: Histories, Empires, and Modernities', in Wilson (ed.), *A New Imperial History: Culture, Identity and Modernity in Britain and the Empire, 1660–1840* (Cambridge: Cambridge University Press, 2004), 1–26.
8   Historians and literary critics who have treated travel books as primary sources include: P. J. Marshall and Glyndwr Williams, *The Great Map of Mankind: British Perceptions of the World in the Age of Enlightenment* (London: Dent, 1982); Colin Mackerras, *Western Images of China* (Oxford: Oxford University Press, 1989); Edward W. Said, *Orientalism* [1978] (New York: Random-Vintage Books, 1979); Mary Louise Pratt, *Imperial Eyes: Travel Writing and Transculturation* (London and New York: Routledge, 1992); and recently, Terence Bowers, 'Robert Curzon, Orientalism and the *Ars Peregrinationis*', *Political Matters,* special issue of *Victorians Institute Journal*, 33 (2005), 117–47.
9   Barrow, 'Free Trade', 431, original emphasis.
10 Marshall Broomhall, *Robert Morrison: A Master-Builder* (London: Livingstone Press, 1924), 194–5.
11 'Voyage of the *Amherst* to Northern China', *Eclectic Review*, 3rd series, 10 (1833): 326–43 (326); 'Gutzlaff's *Three Voyages, &c.*', *Eclectic Review* 3rd series, 11 (1834), 369–92 (369).
12 John Crawfurd, 'Voyage of *Ship Amherst*', *Westminster Review*, 20 (1834), 22–47 (47), emphasis added.
13 Richard D. Altick, *The English Common Reader: A Social History of the Mass Reading Public, 1800–1900* [1957], 2nd edn with a foreword by Jonathan Rose (Columbus, OH: Ohio State University Press, 1998), 276.
14 J. Don Vann and Rosemary T. VanArsdel, 'Introduction', in Vann and VanArsdel (eds), *Victorian Periodicals and Victorian Society* (Toronto: University of Toronto Press, 1994), 3–8 (3).
15 Barrow, 'Free Trade', 441.
16 Altick, *The English Common Reader*, 319.
17 Barrow, 'Free Trade', 431.
18 ———, 'Free Trade', 448, original emphasis.
19 Crawfurd, 'Voyage,' 40–1.
20 ———, 'Voyage', 41.
21 John Barrow, 'Gutzlaff's *Voyages along the Coast of China*', *Quarterly Review*, 51 (1834), 468–81 (468).
22 'China', *Missionary Register* (1834), 268–70 (269), original emphasis.
23 'Gutzlaff's *Journal*', *Quarterly Christian Spectator*, 5 (1833), 610–1.
24 George Borrow, 'To the Rev. J. Jowett', 13 October 1834, letter 17 of *Letters of George Borrow to the British and Foreign Bible Society*, World Wide School Library: http://www.worldwideschool.org/about.html (accessed 17 March, 2006).
25 'British Connexion with China', *Gentlemen's Magazine* [Wason Collection of

Cornell University Kroch Library, Containing Articles Relating to China and the Chinese Only], 5 [Wason's Vol. no.] (1834), 123–30 (127).
26 Patrick Brantlinger, *Rule of Darkness: British Literature and Imperialism, 1830–1914* (Ithaca, NY and London: Cornell University Press, 1988), 47–70.
27 John Crawfurd, 'Chinese Empire and Trade', *Westminster Review*, 21 (1834), 221–56 (221).
28 Quoted in Herman Schlyter, *Der China-Missionar Karl Gützlaff und Seine Heimatbasis* (Lund, Sweden: C. W. K. Gleerup, 1976), 28.
29 ———, *Der China*, 28.
30 Peter Ward Fay, *The Opium War, 1840–1842* [1975] (New York and London: W. W. Norton, 1976), 58.
31 Charlotte Elizabeth, 'Introduction', *Christian Lady's Magazine*, 1 (1834), 1–6 (6).
32 Charlotte Elizabeth, 'Politics', *Christian Lady's Magazine*, 1 (1834), 73–80 (74).
33 ———, 'Politics', 74.
34 Charlotte Elizabeth, 'China, India, and the East', *Christian Lady's Magazine*, 3 (1835), 540–2 (540).
35 ———, 'China', 540.
36 ———, 'China', 541.
37 ———, 'China', 541.
38 ———, 'China', 541.
39 ———, 'China', 542.
40 For a list of the Society's members and contributors, see Society for Promoting Female Education in China, India and the East, *Appeal* (London: E. Suter, Printer, 1835), front page and 9–16.
41 Elizabeth, 'China', 542.
42 Lydia, 'China, India, and the East,' *Christian Lady's Magazine*, 6 (1836), 498–502 (501).
43 J. S., 'China, India, and the East,' *Christian Lady's Magazine* 7 (1837), 540–3 (540–1).
44 ———, 'China', 540–1.
45 ———, 'China', 541.
46 Charles Knight, 'A Postscript to Our First Readers', *Penny Magazine*, 1 (1832), 8. The *Penny Magazine* cost six pence.
47 Altick, *The English Common Reader*, 338.
48 Quoted in Altick, *The English Common Reader*, 337, original emphasis.
49 Society for the Diffusion of Useful Knowledge, 'Committee', *Penny Cyclopaedia*, Vol. 11 (London: Charles Knight, 1838), no page.
50 'The East India Company', *Penny Magazine*, 3 (1834), 84–6.
51 'Chinese Inhabitants of Boats,' *Penny Magazine*, 3 (1834): 371; 'Chinese Women,' *Penny Magazine*, 3 (1834): 371; 'Opium,' *Penny Magazine*, 3 (1834), 397–99.
52 'Tea', *Mirror of Literature, Amusement, and Instruction* [Wason Collection of Cornell University Kroch Library, Containing Articles Relating to China and the Chinese Only], 2 [Wason's Vol. no.] (1832–40), 220–1.

53 'Siamese Barbarities', *Mirror of Literature, Amusement, and Instruction* [Wason Collection of Cornell University Kroch Library, Containing Articles Relating to China and the Chinese Only], 2 [Wason's Vol. no.] (1832–40), 365–6.
54 'Terrific Fire,' *Mirror of Literature, Amusement, and Instruction* [Wason Collection of Cornell University Kroch Library, Containing Articles Relating to China and the Chinese Only], 2 [Wason's Vol. no.] (1832–40), 366–7.
55 Homi K. Bhabha, 'Signs Taken for Wonders: Questions of Ambivalence and Authority under a Tree Outside Delhi, May 1817', *Critical Inquiry*, 12 (1985), 144–65; Gauri Viswanathan, *Masks of Conquest: Literary Study and British Rule in India* (New York: Columbia University Press, 1989).
56 See my article: Ting Man Tsao, 'Representing "Great England" to Qing China in the Age of Free Trade Imperialism: The Circulation of a Tract by Charles Marjoribanks on the China Coast', *Political Matters*, special issue of *Victorians Institute Journal*, 33 (2005), 179–95. See also Suzanne Wilson Barnett and John King Fairbank (eds), *Christianity in China: Early Protestant Missionary Writings* (Cambridge, MA and London: Harvard University Press, 1985).
57 For a brief introduction to the influence of Western knowledge on late Qing China, see Ssu-yü Teng and John K. Fairbank, *China's Response to the West: A Documentary Survey, 1839–1923, with a New Preface* [1954, 1979] (Cambridge, MA and London: Harvard University Press, 1982).
58 Carl T. Smith, 'Commissioner Lin's Translators', *Chung Chi Bulletin*, 38 (1965), 14–20; Teng and Fairbank, *China's Response*, 23–35; Jane Kate Leonard, *Wei Yuan and China's Rediscovery of the Maritime World* (Cambridge, MA and London: Harvard University Press, 1984), particularly Chapter 4.
59 For instance, Wei Yuan, *Hai guo tu zhi* [Illustrated gazetteer of the maritime kingdoms]. This influential geography book has several editions: 1844 (50 juan), 1847 (60 juan), 1852 (100 juan). It also has a Japanese edition.
60 Ying Baoshi, and Yu Yue, *Jiangsu sheng: Shanghai xian zhi (san)* [Jiangsu province: Gazetteer of Shanghai county (Vol. 3)] [1872], Zhongguo fang zhi cong shu, hua zhong di fang, di 169 hao [Collection of Chinese local gazetteers, Hua zhong region, no. 169] (Taibei Shi: Zheng wen chu ban she you xian gong si, [1975]) juan 11, 31; Zhou Kai, 'Daogong xia men zhi' [Daogong xiamen gazetteer], in Qi Sihe, Lin Shuhui, and Shou Jiyu (eds), *Ya pian zhan zheng* [The Opium War] [1955, second edn], Vol. 4 ([Shanghai]: Shi ji chu ban ji tuan, Shanghai ren min chu ban she, 2000), 349–56; Dong Pei, 'Guangxu yin xian zhi' [Guangxu yin xian gazetteer], Qi, *Ya pian*, Vol. 4, 403–13.
61 Zhang Dechang, 'Hu Xia Mi huo chuan lai Hua jing guo ji qi ying xiang' [The voyage of Hu Xai Mi's cargo ship to China and its impact], *Zhongguo jin dai jing ji shi yan jiu ji kan* [Studies in Modern Economic History of China], 1, 1 (1932), 60–79, reprinted in *Zhongguo she hui jing ji shi ji kan* [Studies in Social and Economic History of China] (Xianggang: Long men shu dian, 1968), juan 1, 2 (Vol. 1).
62 See advertisements in *Zhongguo jin dai jing ji shi yan jiu ji kan* 2, 1 (1933), reprinted in *Zhongguo she hui jing ji shi ji kan* [Studies in Social and Economic History of

China] (Xianggang: Long men shu dian, 1968), juan 1, 2 (Vol. 1).
63 See Evelyn Sakakida Rawski, *Education and Popular Literacy in Ch'ing China* (Ann Arbor, MI: University of Michigan Press, 1979), 162–7.
64 Pan Guangzhe, 'Zhongguo jin da shi de shu xie wen ti: guan yu zhongguo jin da shi zhi shi de sheng chan fang shi de yi xie si kao' [The problem of writing modern Chinese history: Thoughts on the production modes of modern Chinese historical knowledge], *Paradigm Shifts in the Study of Modern China Forum, Rethinking Modern Chinese History: An International Conference to Celebrate the 50th Anniversary of the Institute of Modern History*, Academia Sinica, Taibei, Taiwan, 29 June 2005, Academia Sinica, <http://www.mh.sinica.edu.tw/eng/download/abstract/abstract2-1-1.pdf>, 7 (accessed 19 March 2006).
65 See, for instance, Guo Tingyi (ed.), *Jin dai Zhongguo shi* [Modern Chinese history] (Changsha: Shang wu yin shu guan, Min guo, 29–30 [1940–41]), particularly the foreword. For the importance of Qing archives in the writing of modern Chinese history in Republican China, I rely on Pan, 'Zhongguo jin da shi', 5–13.
66 'Journals of Messrs. Lindsay and Gutzlaff', *Chinese Repository*, 2nd edn, 2 (1834), 529–53.
67 Charles Gutzlaff, *A Sketch of Chinese History, Ancient and Modern . . .* , 2 vols (London: Smith Elder, 1834), Vol. 2, Chapter 21.
68 Xu Dishan (ed.), *Da zhong ji: [Ya pian zhan zheng qian Zhong Ying jiao she shi liao]* [A collection of historical documents related to the intercourse between China and Britain before the Opium War] [1931] ([Taibei Xian Yonghe zhen]: Wen hai chu ban she, [1974]).
69 Zhang, 'Hu Xia Mi', 61.
70 ———, 'Hu Xia Mi', 66.
71 ———, 'Hu Xia Mi', 72.
72 ———, 'Hu Xia Mi', 72.
73 ———, 'Hu Xia Mi', 73.
74 These dynamic interactions were recoverable from the Qing archival sources tapped by Zhang: Xu, *Da zhong ji*.
75 For a critique of nationalist history writing, see Dipesh Chakrabarty, 'Postcoloniality and the Artifice of History: Who Speaks for "Indian" Pasts?' *Representations*, 37 (1992), 1–26. Cf. Prasenjit Duara, *Rescuing History from the Nation: Questioning Narratives of Modern China* (Chicago and London: University of Chicago Press, 1995).
76 Fang Hanqi (ed.), et al, *'Da Gong Bao' bai nian shi, 1902-06-17–2002-06-17* [A hundred year history of *Da Gong Bao*] (Beijing: Zhongguo ren min da xue chu ban she, 2004), 328.
77 Tianjin shi shi zi yun dong wei yuan hui [Tianjian City Literacy Movement Committee], 'Tianjin shi shi zi yun dong xun su kai zhan de yuan yin ji mu qian cun zai de wen ti' [The reasons for the rapid development of Tianjian City's literacy movement and currently existing problems], *Jin Bu Ri Bao* [The progressive daily], 13 September 1952, 2. Cf. Rawski, *Education*, 20 and 167–80.

78 Fang, '*Da Gong Bao' bai nian shi*, 328.
79 See, for instance, 'Xu yan' [Foreword], Qi, *Ya pian*, Vol. 1, 1–4.
80 Nan Mu, 'Ya pian zhan zheng', 2.
81 See Tsao, 'Representing "Great England" to Qing China'.
82 Nan's article was republished in Lie Dao (ed.), *Ya pian zhan zheng shi lun wen zhuan ji* [Collection of articles on the Opium War] (Beijing : Sheng huo, du shu, xin zhi san lian shu dian, 1958), 105–12.
83 Zhang's article, on the other hand, was referenced by a Chinese-American historian: Immanuel C. Y. Hsu, 'The Secret Mission of the Lord Amherst on the China Coast, 1832', *Harvard Journal of Asiatic Studies*, 17 (1954), 231–52.
84 For example, Gu Changsheng, *Chuan jiao shi yu jin dai Zhongguo* [Missionaries and modern China], di 2 ban [second edition] (Shanghai: Shanghai ren min chu ban she: Xin hua shu dian Shanghai fa xing suo jing xiao, 1991), 22–46. See also Gu's *Cong Malixun dao Situ Leideng: lai Hua xin jiao chuan jiao shi ping zhuan* [From Robert Morrison to John Leighton Start: a critical biography of protestant missionaries in China] (Shanghai: Shanghai shu dian, 2005), the chapter on Gutzlaff.
85 Fujian Shi fan da xue [Fujian teachers' university], *Ya pian zhan zheng zai Min, Tai shi liao xuan bian* [Selection of historical sources on the Opium War in Min and Tai] (Fuzhou: Fujian ren min chu ban she : Fujian sheng xin hua shu dian fa xing, 1982), 26–116.
86 For example, Nan's article is reprinted in the CCP's official website <http://military.china.com>. It is cited in 'Chuan jiao shi, ya pian fan, jian die — guo shi li' [Missionary, opium seller, spy — Gutzlaff], Zhongguo qing shao nian ji suan ji xin xi fu wu wang [China youth computer information service web], 19 March 2006 <http://cyc6.cycnet.com:8090/xuezhu/his_data/content.jsp?n_id=6340&pageno=1>.

Chapter 4

1 Nicolás Tanco Armero, *Viaje de Nueva Granada a China y de China a Francia*. The translations throughout this article are my own.
2 See 'Of Travel' by Francis Bacon.
3 Colonel Jackson's book, first published in Paris, in 1822, under the title *Guide du voyage*, appeared in English in several editions from 1841 under the title *What to Observe, or, The Traveller's Remembrancer*. I quote from the third (1861) edition, revised by Dr. Norton Shaw.
4 *Recuerdos de mis últimos viajes, Japón* (Madrid: Est. Tip. Sucesores de Rivadeneyra, 1888).
5 Reinaldo Arenas' sonnet in *Inferno* (1971), 'De modo que Cervantes era manco', plays with statements of the obvious: Cervantes lost a hand, Beethoven was deaf, Virginia Woolf drowned, etc. to go on and list homosexual authors in history, an issue for Arenas at a time when the Cuban regime was turning against its former

permissive policies. Aside from the sought rhyme (with 'manco'), the sonnet also reflects the circulation of studies on Tanco Armero's role in the island's racial history.

6 See Ángel Rama, *La ciudad letrada*, 23–30.
7 José María Cordovez Moure, a chronicler of nineteenth-century Bogotá, writes about a soireé hosted by the Tanco Armero family to welcome back the traveller in 1860. On such an occasion, pieces acquired while travelling were displayed for the guests, who 'could not decide what to admire most, since among those objects, just a single chess set had cost the intrepid traveller more than 2.000 pesos', *Reminiscencias*, Chapter III. Juan Pérez de la Riva in *El barracón*; an oft-cited study of slavery in Cuba, writes a reproachful portrayal of Tanco Armero as a 'capitalist', and points to the immense fortune he amassed, 98*ff*.
8 Frank Safford quotes a letter of Tanco Armero to a fellow Colombian exile in New York requesting an apprenticeship position for one of his nephews.
9 See Bourdieu's discussion in *Distinction: A Social Critique of the Judgement of Taste*, 267–82.
10 See *The Cuba Commission Report: The Hidden History of the Chinese in Cuba*. It must be pointed out, however, that the coolie trade in Cuba is not the origin of the sizable colony of Chinese, also from Southern China, that settled in the island throughout the last quarter of the nineteenth and early twentieth centuries.
11 Félix Tanco, Nicolás Tanco Armero's uncle, who established himself in Cuba and was active in an influential abolitionist group is the author of a novel with an anti-slavery theme, *Petrona y Rosalía* (1838).
12 Alexis de Gabriac, *Promenade à travers l'Amérique du sud: Nouvelle-Grenade, Équateur, Pérou, Bresil* (Paris: 1868). Gabriac, a painter and naturalist, is an example of the numerous European (mostly French) travel writers in post-independence South America.
13 Johann Gottfried von Herder, *Ideen zur Philosophie der Geschichte der Menschheit* (1784–91). As Anthony Pagden has noted, discussing the notion of incommensurability in cultural encounters, Herder's view posed the possibility that 'the very concept of a single human genus became, if not impossible to conceive, at least culturally meaningless', cited in Pagden, 180.
14 Bartolomé de las Casas (1484–1566) was a Spanish friar and historian who denounced the abuse against, and the plight of, the indigenous people of America under the 'encomienda' regime. Himself an 'encomendero', his defence of the native peoples led him to propose that Africans be brought to alleviate their burden. For a discussion on the epistemological meaning of las Casas's attitude, see for example the work of Tzvetan Todorov, *Conquest of America*, trans. Richard Howard (London: Harper & Row, 1984).
15 See Maurice Collins, *Foreign Mud: An Account of the Opium War*, 269–74.
16 That a century later this is the case with his native Colombia and cocaine seems a sad twist.

17 See John K. Fairbank, *Trade and Diplomacy in the China Coast: The Opening of the Treaty Ports, 1842–1854*.
18 See for example the discussion of the role of these concessions in the context of the rise of Chinese nationalism in Henrietta Harrison, *China*, 64.
19 See Fairbank, 19. Also quoted in Harrison, 58–9.

Chapter 5

1   I thank Maria Noelle Ng and Mark Meli for their constructive criticism. I also thank my colleague Michael Gardiner for extensively commenting on an earlier draft of this essay.
2   Ainu is the usual term — Bird herself refers to the 'Ainos'.
3   Isabella Bird, *Unbeaten Tracks in Japan: An Account of Travels in the Interior Including Visits to Aborigines of Yezo and the Shrine of Nikko* [1885] (London: John Murray, 1893), 242. All further references to this work, abbreviated 'popular edn', will be included in the text. The quote also appears in its first edition, *Unbeaten Tracks in Japan: An Account of Travels in the Interior, Including Visits to the Aborigines of Yezo and the Shrines of Nikko and Ise*, 2 vols (London: John Murray, 1880), 2, 59. For this edition, I will use the one reprinted in Volumes 4 and 5 of *Collected Travel Writings of Isabella Bird* (Bristol: Ganesha, 1997). All further references to this edition, abbreviated '1st edn.', will be included in the text. When quoted passages appear in both texts, their respective page references will be indicated.
4   For bibliographical information, see Shigetoshi Kusuya, 'Ba-do Nihon Kiko Kaisetsu', in Isabella Lucy Bird, *Ba-do Nihon Kiko* (Tokyo: Ushodo, 2002), 333–76. Bird also published a new, one-volume version of the first edition in 1900, which includes substantial geographical essays and reflections on victory over China in 1895.
5   This difference is reflected in the full titles of the travelogue. While the first edition is subtitled as 'An Account of Travels in the Interior, Including Visits to the Aborigines of Yezo and the Shrines of Nikko and Ise', the reference to Ise is omitted in the popular edition's full title.
6   Anna M. Stoddart, *The Life of Isabella Bird (Mrs. Bishop)* (London: John Murray, 1908), 168.
7   Shigetoshi Kusuya, 'Ba-do Nihon Kiko Kaisetsu', 374.
8   Evelyn Bach, 'A Traveller in Skirts: Quest and Conquest in the Travel Narratives of Isabella Bird', *Canadian Review of Comparative Literature*, 22, 3–4 (1995), 587–600 (592).
9   Mary Louise Pratt, *Imperial Eyes: Travel Writing and Transculturation* (London: Routledge, 1992), 78–9.
10 As is well known, Bird's early writings are based upon the letters she sent to Henrietta during her trip. As Kay Chubbuck points out in her edition, it was the

travel writer's routine to 'excise a mass of personal detail, while adding in its place intellectual gravitas' once she returned home. See *Letters to Henrietta* (By Isabella Bird) (Boston: Northeastern University Press, 2002), 12. Unfortunately, the original letters Bird sent from Japan do not appear to be extant (Chubbuck, *Letters*, 205).

11 Olive Checkland, *Isabella Bird and 'A Woman's Right to Do What She Can Do Well'* (Aberdeen: Scottish Cultural Press, 1996), 57.
12 For instance, the description of the 'Foreign Concession' in Tokyo (1st edn, 1, 32–3) is cut out in the popular edition.
13 Pratt, *Imperial Eyes*, 6.
14 The first edition's more frequent description of her visit to Western-style hospitals could be read in a similar light. Maria Noelle Ng concisely discusses how Bird's visit to hospitals during her trip reflects her social settings at home. See *Three Exotic Views of Southeast Asia: The Travel Narratives of Isabella Bird, Max Dauthendey, and Ai Wu, 1850–1930* (Norwark: Eastbridge, 2002), 53.
15 Kusuya, 'Ba-do Nihon Kiko Kaisetsu', 374.
16 For instance, at the beginning of her journey, the narrator-traveller notices the sweeping rice fields (1st edn, 1, 84; popular edn, 36). In the first edition, the narrative then explains in detail how to raise the crop. The explanation is excised in the popular edition.
17 Maria Ng discusses in detail how such views Bird held are culturally determined, and therefore resonate with those of her contemporaries. See Ng, *Three Exotic Views*, 41–7.
18 Checkland, *Isabella Bird*, xv.
19 ———, *Isabella Bird*, 168.

Chapter 6

1 John Gullick, 'Florence Caddy: A Biographical Note', in Florence Caddy, *To Siam and Malaya in the Duke of Sutherland's Yacht 'Sans Peur'* (Singapore: Oxford University Press, 1992), v–xiv (xi).
2 Susan Morgan, *Place Matters: Gendered Geography in Victorian Women's Books about Southeast Asia* (New Brunswick, NJ: Rutgers University Press, 1996), 168.
3 Emily Innes, *The Chersonese with the Gilding Off*, Vols. I and II [1885] (Kuala Lumpur: Oxford University Press, 1993), in II, 233. Further volume and page references will be given parenthetically in the text.
4 Sara Mills, *Discourses of Difference: An Analysis of Women's Travel Writing and Colonialism* (London: Routledge, 1991), 3.
5 Mills, *Discourses of Difference*, 1.
6 Barbara Watson Andaya and Leonard Y. Andaya, *A History of Malaysia* (Basingstoke: Palgrave, 2001) [1982], 164–5.

7 Isabella Bird, *The Golden Chersonese and the Way Thither* [1883] (Kuala Lumpur: Oxford University Press, 1967), 270. Further page references will be given parenthetically in the text.
8 Gayatri Chakravorty Spivak, 'The Rani of Sirmur', in Francis Barker et al. (eds), *Europe and Its Others, Volume One: Proceedings of the Essex Conference on the Sociology of Literature, July 1984* (Colchester: University of Essex Press, 1985), 128–51 (133).
9 Frank Swettenham, *British Malaya: An Account of the Origin and Progress of British Influence in Malaya* [1906] (London: George Allen and Unwin, 1948), 197.
10 Andaya, *A History of Malaysia*, 58.
11 ———, *A History of Malaysia*, 40.
12 Morgan, *Place Matters,* 159.
13 ———, *Place Matters*, 153.
14 ———, *Place Matters*, 150.
15 ———, *Place Matters*, 151.
16 ———, *Place Matters*, 147.
17 Isabella Bird, *Letters to Henrietta*, ed. Kay Chubbuck (London: John Murray, 2002), 305.
18 Bird, *Letters to Henrietta*, 267–8.
19 ———, *Letters to Henrietta*, 268.
20 Gullick, 'Florence Caddy', vii.
21 ———, 'Florence Caddy', viii.
22 Florence Caddy, *To Siam and Malaya in the Duke of Sutherland's Yacht 'Sans Peur',* [1889] (Singapore: Oxford University Press, 1992), 278. Further page references will be given parenthetically in the text.
23 Gullick, 'Florence Caddy', xi.
24 ———, 'Florence Caddy', xi.
25 Maria H. Frawley, *A Wider Range: Travel Writing by Women in Victorian England* (London: Associated University Press, 1994), 27.

Chapter 7

1 Eunice Tietjens, *Profiles from China: Sketches in Free Verse of People and Things Seen in the Interior* (New York: Alfred A. Knopf, 1919), 63.
2 'The collection is primarily composed of works first published in the nineteenth century, but, where appropriate, important works of the late eighteenth century and early twentieth century are also included. The principal guide for selection is Henri Cordier's Biblioteca Sinica, Paris, 1904–07 and Supplement, 1921. This is complemented by both rare and renowned material from the holdings of the British Library, primarily the Oriental and India Office Collections' < http://c19.chadwyck.co.uk/html/noframes/moreinfo/china.htm> (accessed 9 August 2006).

3   Robert Coltman, *The Chinese, Their Present and Future: Medical, Political, and Social* (Philadelphia: Davis, 1891); Archibald R. Colquhoun, *China in Transformation* (London: Harper, 1898); Robert L. Jefferson, *China and the Present Crisis* (London: G. W. Bacon, 1900); Arnold Henry Savage Landor, *China and the Allies* (London: Heinemann, 1901); Arthur Henderson Smith, *China in Convulsion* (Edinburgh: Oliphant, Anderson and Ferrier, 1901); William A. P. Martin, *The Awakening of China* (London: Hodder and Stoughton, 1907); Joseph King Goodrich, *The Coming China* (Chicago: A. C. McClurg & Co, 1911); John Stuart Thompson, *China Revolutionized* (London: T. W. Laurie, 1913).
4   This can also be seen in the above bibliography. See also the following: Colin Mackerras, *Western Images of China* [1987], rev. edn (Oxford: Oxford University Press, 1999), particularly Part I (i.e. Chapters 2–5).
5   Ellen Newbold LaMotte, *Peking Dust* (New York: The Century Co., 1919), 3.
6   See Isabella Bird Bishop, *The Yangtze Valley and Beyond: An Account of China, Chiefly in the Province of Sze Chuan and among the Man-Tze of the Somo Territory* [1899]. In ibid., *Collected Travel Writings*, 12 vols (Bristol: Ganesha Publishing, 1997), Vol. 11, and C. F. [Constance Frederica] Gordon Cumming, *Wanderings in China*, new edn, 2 vols (Edinburgh and London: William Blackwood, 1888).
7   Eliza Ruhamah Scidmore, *Westward to the Far East: A Guide to the Principal Cities of China and Japan* [1892], 2nd edn (Montreal): The Canadian Railway Company, 1892.
8   Throughout this chapter, I have adopted the Pinyin spelling for place names, which varies from the (erratic) Victorian conventions our women travellers use. I have included the non-Pinyin place name in brackets where necessary for clarification.
9   'The invalid at home, and the Samson abroad'. See A. Stodart Walker, *Edinburgh Medical Journal*, 16 (1904), 383. Cited by Olive Checkland, 'Collected Travel Writings of Isabella Bird' (1998) <www.ganesha-publishing.com/bird_intro.htm> (accessed 9 August 2006).
10 See Isabella Bird Bishop, *The Golden Chersonese and the Way Thither* [1883]. In ibid., *Collected Travel Writings*, 12 vols (Bristol: Ganesha Publishing, 1997), vol. 6.
11 See Marion Tinling's biographical outline of Bird in *Women into the Unknown: A Sourcebook on Women Explorers and Travelers* (New York: Greenwood Publishing, 1989), 47–55; Dorothy Middleton, *Victorian Lady Travellers* [1965], with a New Introduction (Chicago: Academy Chicago Publishers, 1982, rpt. 1993), 19–53; Alexandra Allen, *Travelling Ladies* (London: Jupiter, 1980), 225–66.
12 Middleton, 50, 53.
13 Isabella Bird, 'A Journey in Western Sze-Chuan', *The Geographical Society*, 10, 1 (July 1897), 19–50 (22–3).
14 Eliza Ruhamah Scidmore, 'Mrs Bishop's "The Yangtze Valley and Beyond" ', *National Geographic Magazine*, 11 (Jan/ Dec 1900), 366–9 (368, emphasis added).
15 Bird, *The Yangtze Valley*, 390.
16 ———, *The Yangtze Valley*, 390.

17 ———, *The Yangtze Valley*, 393.
18 I refer to the concise travel account 'Ningpo and the Buddhist Temples', reprinted in *The Century Illustrated Monthly Magazine*, 29 (May/Oct. 1882), 726–39 (726). A fuller, more detailed version of Cumming's stay in Ningbo is described in Chapters 22–28 of her *Wanderings in China* (276–350), which presents a wealth of material left out in the journal article, which, however, would have been the more popular version.
19 Cumming, 'Ningbo', 727, 729*ff*, 733*ff*.
20 ———, 'Ningbo', 737.
21 See Eliza Ruhamah Scidmore, *China: The Long-Lived Empire* (New York: The Century Co., 1900), and her many independently published articles, which include 'The River of Tea', *Century Magazine*, 58 (May/Oct. 1899), 547–9; 'Cruising up the Yangtsze', *Century Magazine*, 58 (May/Oct. 1899), 668–79; 'The Streets of Peking', *Century Magazine*, 58 (May/Oct. 1899), 859–73; 'The Greatest Wonder in the Chinese World: The Marvelous Bore of Hang-Chau', *Century Magazine*, 59 (Nov./ Apr. 1899–1900), 852–9. The articles were then republished, with only very slight revisions, in *China: The Long-Lived Empire*.
22 In *Westward*, Scidmore remains vague about the number of the stops on her own trip to Hong Kong. The map at the back of her guidebook gives two alternative routes from Shanghai to Hong Kong — one non-stop and one pausing on the way in Ningbo, Wenzhou, Fuzhou, Xiamen [Amoy] and Shantou. In her travel description, Scidmore briefly explains the main attractions in Fuzhou and Xiamen, which suggests that she actually went there. Fuzhou, she writes, is picturesquely hilly but largely devoid of shopping opportunities, and Amoy presents a colourful harbour site and is famous for its delicious pomeloes (37).
23 Cumming, II, 206.
24 ———, II, 209.
25 ———, II, 207 and 208.
26 ———, II, 211.
27 ———, II, 257.
28 ———, II, 162.
29 ———, II, 208.
30 ———, II, 265.
31 Scidmore, *Westward*, 41.
32 ———, *Westward*, 41.
33 ———, *Westward*, 42.
34 Scidmore, *China*, 83.
35 ———, *China*, 87.
36 Cumming, II, 263. The heading reads: 'shopping descriptions' (263–6).
37 Scidmore, *China*, 193–200.
38 ———, *China*, 200.
39 See Scidmore, *China*, 227–49 (The Great Wall) and 250–9 (Ming Tombs). See Mary Gaunt, *A Woman in China* (London: Werner Laurie, 1914), 113*ff* and

122–7. LaMotte acknowledges these places as familiar tourist destinations and writes: 'Day before yesterday four of us went up to see the Ming tombs and the Great Wall. Everything is so exciting in Peking that we could hardly bear to absent ourselves from it even for two days; having come all the way out to China, it seemed as if we really ought to see the Great Wall. I won't describe our trip. You can read descriptions of the wall in any book; all I can say is that it took two days to get there and back, and that we set off on the expedition most reluctantly', 86–7. See also Grace Thompson Seton, *Chinese Lanterns* (New York: Dodd, Mead and Co., 1924), 350. Seton remains vague about the dates of her visit to the Ming Tombs, but mentions seeing *another* Ming Tomb at Nanking, 340.
40 Gaunt, 117.
41 See Scidmore, *China*, Chapters XXIII–XXVI, 333–429.
42 See Mrs. Archibald [i.e. Alicia] Little, 'In the Wild West of China', *The Nineteenth Century*, 39 (Jan/June 1896), 58–64; 'A Summer Trip to Chinese Thibet', *Cornhill Magazine*, ser. 3, issue 6 (1899), 213–29 and 'A Journey of Surprises: Through Yunnan from the Yangtse', *The Cornhill Magazine*, 3, issue 20 (1906), 476–91.
43 For Mrs. Archibald Little's travel writing see, for example, *My Diary in a Chinese Farm* (Shanghai, Hongkong, Singapore and Yokohama: Kelly & Walsh, 1894); *Guide to Peking* (Tientsin: Tientsin Press, 1904); *Intimate China: The Chinese As I Have Seen Them* (London: Hutchinson, 1899); and *Round About My Peking Garden* (London: T. Fisher Unwin, 1905).
44 See Elizabeth Crump Enders, *Temple Bells and Silver Sails* (New York and London: D. Appleton and Co., 1925), from Chapter XIV. Elizabeth Kendall, *A Wayfarer in China: Impressions of a Trip Across West China and Mongolia* (London: Constable, 1913).
45 Tietjens, 33–4.
46 See Elizabeth Crump Enders, *Swinging Lanterns* (New York and London: D. Appleton and Co., 1923), 83, 153. LaMotte, 30*ff*, particularly 32.
47 In Shanghai, Enders and her husband Pierre employ — out of pity, it says — an amah for Elizabeth and a rickshaw boy, and they also pay for the room boys in their accommodation. In Beijing, where they settle down, the couple learn a little Chinese to communicate with their servants and their new friends (*Swinging Lanterns*, 10–11, 151). LaMotte and her travel companion also employ rickshaw boys for the month and they are 'much attached to them' (56). LaMotte even breaks up a fight in which her boy Kwong is involved, later using her Western identity to protect her servant when the police come (60).
48 Enders, *Swinging Lanterns*, 217*ff*.
49 LaMotte, 167.
50 Scidmore, *China*, 167–79.
51 ———, *China*, 179, and Hans-Georg Gadamer, *Truth and Method*, 2nd rev. edn, trans. rev. by Joel Weinsheimer and Donald G. Marshall (New York: Continuum, 1997), 388.
52 Seton, ix.

53 For Seton's biography, see Lucinda H. MacKethan, 'The Setons at Home: Organizing a Family Biography' at <http://www.nhc.rtp.nc.us:8080/biography/mackethan.htm> (accessed 9 August 2006).
54 Seton, 174.

Chapter 8

1 W. Somerset Maugham, *The Gentleman in the Parlour: A Record of a Journey from Rangoon to Haiphong* (London: Heinemann, 1930), 83.
2 Hugh Clifford, 'The Quest of the Golden Fleece', *Malayan Monochromes* (London: John Murray, 1913), 197.
3 Letter to Lytton Strachey, 2nd October 1908. *Letters of Leonard Woolf*, ed. Frederic Spotts (London: Weidenfeld & Nicholson, 1989), 137.
4 Julius Caesar, *The Gallic War*, with an English translation by H. J. Edwards, Loeb Classical Library (Cambridge, MA: Harvard University Press, 1917), Book VI.
5 Leonard Woolf, *Growing: An Autobiography of the Years 1904–1911* (London: Hogarth Press, 1961), 212.
6 Maugham, *Ah King and Other Stories* (Singapore: Oxford University Press, 1986 [1990]), 269–339.
7 Leonard Woolf, *The Village in the Jungle* [1913] (Oxford: Oxford University Press, 1981), 179.
8 Rudyard Kipling, 'Kaa's Hunting', *The Jungle Book* [1894], ed. W. W. Robson (Oxford: Oxford University Press, 1987), 22–47.
9 Kipling, 'The King's Ankus', *The Second Jungle Book* [1895], ed. W. W. Robson (Oxford: Oxford University Press, 1987), 104.
10 The phrase 'imperial Gothic' was coined by Patrick Brantlinger in his *Rule of Darkness: British Literature and Imperialism 1830–1914* (Ithaca: Cornell University Press, 1988), 227–54.
11 Hugh Clifford, 'A Dying Kingdom', *Macmillan's Magazine*, 86 (May/October 1902), 110.
12 Clifford, *Malayan Monochromes* (London: John Murray, 1913), 233.
13 Pierre Loti, *Un Pélerin d'Angkor* (Paris: Calmann-Lévi, 1912), 118.
14 Ibid. 'So there it is, this sanctuary which once haunted my childish imagination, and which I have attained only after so much wandering the earth, when the evening of my wayward life has already come!'
15 Maugham, *The Gentleman in the Parlour*, 209, 213–4. Such is the pervasive power of junglification, in Maugham's account, that not only the vegetation but also the ruins themselves have become tangled.
16 There is no agreement among historians on a single main cause for the decline and fall of Angkor, and no doubt a variety of factors — economic, political, cultural and environmental — were involved. See Ian Mabbett and David Chandler, *The*

Khmers (Oxford: Blackwell, 1995), 204–17. For other recent accounts, see, for example: Claude Jacques, *Angkor: Cities and Temples* (London: Thames and Hudson, 1997); Charles Higham, *The Civilization of Angkor* (Berkeley and Los Angeles: University of California Press, 2001); and David Snellgrove, *Khmer Civilization and Angkor* (Bangkok: Orchid Press, 2001).
17 Hugh Clifford, *Malayan Monochromes*, 245–6.
18 Clifford, *Further India: Being the Story of Exploration from the Earliest Times in Burma, Malaya, Siam, and Indo-China* (London: Alston Rivers, 1905), 161–2.
19 See J. A. MacGillivray, *Minotaur: Sir Arthur Evans and the Archaeology of the Minoan Myth* (London: Jonathan Cape, 2000).
20 Hugh Clifford, *The Downfall of the Gods* (London: John Murray, 1911), 335, 336.
21 Immanuel Kant, *Critique of Judgement* (1790), trans. with Analytical Indexes by James Creed Meredith (Oxford: Clarendon, 1952), 111.
22 Hugh Clifford, 'A Dying Kingdom', 108.
23 See Harry A. Gailey, *Clifford: Imperial Proconsul* (London: Rex Collings, 1982), and Kathryn Tidrick, 'Hugh Clifford, Administrator', *Empire and the English Character* (London: Taurus, 1992), 88–129.
24 Philip Holden, *Orienting Masculinity, Orienting Nation: W. Somerset Maugham's Exotic Fiction* (Westport, CT: Greenwood Press, 1996), 96.
25 Hugh Clifford, 'Mankind and the Jungle', *Living Age*, 278 (July/September 1913), 162.
26 *Rudyard Kipling's Verse; Definitive Edition* (London: Hodder and Stoughton, 1940), 487. 'Cities and Thrones and Powers' first appeared in *Puck of Pook's Hill* (1906).
27 The scientific and literary debate about civilisation, nature and progress is the topic of Brian Shaffer's study *The Blinding Torch: Modern British Fiction and the Discourse of Civilization* (Amherst: University of Massachusetts Press, 1993).
28 T. H. Huxley, 'Evolution and Ethics', *Evolution and Ethics and Other Essays* (New York: Appleton, 1911), 45. This bleak future is visited by the Time Traveller in *The Time Machine* by Huxley's pupil, H. G. Wells, published the following year (1895), and a reversion to the State of Nature also overtakes *The Island of Dr Moreau* (1896).

Chapter 9

1 Translated from the French 'Oases Interdites' by Thomas McGreevy.
2 Philip Krummich discusses the depth of their relationship in his unpublished article 'She/He Wrote: Two Accounts of a Crossing of Asia' (thanks to Dr Krummich of Moorehead University, USA).
3 See Izzard, *Freya Stark A Biography* (1993), 194, and Glendinning, *Rebecca West A Life* (1998), 161, for examples of the connection between these writers and government interests.

Chapter 10

1. Ayako Kano, *Acting Like a Woman: Theater, Gender and Nationalism* (New York: Palgrave, 2001), 99. Studies on Otojiro and Sadayakko in English include: Yoko Chiba, 'Sadayakko and Kawakami', *Modern Drama*, 35, 35–52; Shelley C. Berg, 'Sadayakko in London and Paris, 1900', *Dance Chronicle*, 18, 3 (1995), 343–404; and Leslie Downer, *Madame Sadayakko: A Geisha Who Bewitched the West* (New York: Gotham Books, 2003).
2. Otojiro also produced a variety of 'travel plays' including *Oshi ryoko* (Dumb Travel 1908) that Kano examines (104) and *Seiban tobatsu* (Conquering Indigenous Taiwanese 1911), both of which represent the 'twisted double vision'.
3. Even though Otojiro himself did not write about his travels, we can read interviews with him and his wife reproduced in several books, including Sotetsu Fujii (ed.), *Jiden Otojiro Sadayakko* [Autobiographies of Otojiro and Sadayakko] (Tokyo: San-ichi Syobo, 1984) and Tanejiro Kaneo (ed.), *Otojiro Sadayakko Manyu-ki* [Globe-trotting of Otojiro and Sadayakko] (Tokyo: Kaneo Bunshin-do, 1901). All translation from Japanese is mine.
4. Fujii (ed.), 58.
5. *Jiji Shimpo*, 21 December 1900.
6. *San Francisco Chronicle*, 26 March 1899.
7. ———, 22 May 1899.
8. ———, 10 June 1899.
9. Brian Miller, *The Life of Admiral George Dewey*< http://www.spanamwar.com/dewey.htm> (accessed 11 June 2006).
10. Goyo Narita, 'Japanese writings on Jose Rizal' <http://members.jcom.home.ne.jp/goyo/RIZAL/jasturiz.htm>.
11. *San Francisco Chronicle*, 25 June 1899.
12. 'Interview with Kawakami Otojiro', *Taiwan Nichi Nichi Shimpo*, 5 December 1900.
13. Onitaro, 'Haiyu Gassen (Wars of actors)', *Engei Sekai*, August 1903.
14. Nyozekan Hasegawa, 'News from Anglo-Japan Exposition,' *Tokyo Asahi Shimbun*, 8 July 1910.
15. 'If the Japanese Portrayed Us,' *St. Louis Globe Democrat* (4 December 1904). Quoted by Mari Yoshihara, *Embracing the East: White Women and American Orientalism* (Oxford: Oxford University Press, 2003), 87.
16. Fujii, 76.
17. Baron Suematsu, *The Risen Sun* [3rd impression] (London: Archibald Constable, 1895), 132–42.
18. 'On *Othello* at the Meiji-za Theatre in February,' *Yomiuri Shimbun*, 3 February 1903. This scene of the Taiwanese people singing in praise of Japanese colonial rule is not in Emi Sui'in's script (Emi Sui'in, *Othello*, The *Bungei Kurabu*, February 1903). 'The natives' in the above quotation refer to the indigenous Taiwanese, distinct from Taiwanese with Chinese ancestry.
19. *Miyako Shimbun*, 21 December 1902.

20 The *Taiwan Nichi-Nichi*, a newspaper published in Japanese in Taipei, reports famine in the Penghu Islands just before Otojiro's visit to Taiwan. See *Taiwan Nichi-Nichi*, 5 December 1902.
21 Emi Sui'in, *Othello*, Act 3.
22 Kaneo (ed.), 32*ff*.
23 *Eta*, or the *burakumin*, are the largest discriminated-against population in Japan. They are generally recognised as descendants of a caste ostracised since feudal times. When the social status system was established in the seventeenth century in the form of three classes (warrior, peasant, townsfolk), placed at the bottom of the society were *eta* (extreme filth) and *hinin* (non-human) classes. The *burakumin* are one of the main minority groups in Japan, along with the Ainu of Hokkaido and residents of Korean and Chinese descent. Their place in Japanese society is often compared to the Dalits, or *Untouchables*, in the culture of India. See Headquarters of Buraku Liberation League <http://www.bll.gr.jp/eng.html> (accessed 11 June 2006).
24 *Ryukyu Shimpo*, 21 May 1903.
25 *Ryukyu Shimpo*, 25 April 1903.
26 *Osaka Mainichi*, 9 February 1903.
27 For 'human showcases' and imperialism, see Paul Greenhalgh, *Ephemeral Vistas* (Manchester: Manchester University Press, 1991), 112–41.
28 Carol Ann Christ, ' "The Sole Guardians of the Art Inheritance of Asia": Japan and China at the 1904 St. Louis World's Fair', *Positions: East Asia Cultures Critique*, 8, 3 (2000), 676–7.
29 *Daily News*, 2 November 1910, cited in Hiroyuki Mutsu (ed.), *The British Press and the Japan-British Exhibition of 1910* (Melbourne: The University of Melbourne, 2001: originally printed in London 1910 and Tokyo 1911), 180–1.
30 *Taiyo Special Issue on the Anglo-Japan Exposition* (Tokyo: Hakubun-sha, 1908), 26.
31 Hasegawa, ibid.

Chapter 11

1 Unless otherwise stated, all references are to *The Writings of Lafcadio Hearn* [16 vols] (Boston: Houghton Mifflin, 1922). This edition's standardisation of Hearn's eccentric punctuation is followed throughout. Texts omitted from this edition will be separately cited.
2 Heimin: a term loosely denoting 'citizen' after Meiji, but in the Tokugawa period broadly designating the caste of merchants, artisans and peasantry below the samurai.
3 Paul Murray contests the tradition in Hearn studies which typifies the elderly widow, Sarah Brenane, as an intimidating Catholic zealot of 'fierce and prudish beliefs' (Dawson, 7), believing instead that she gave the young Hearn 'a life of cultured

leisure with, critically, untrammeled access to books of all sorts' (Murray, 16). Murray also attributes Brenane's misrepresentation in part to Hearn himself and 'the legend he was propagating' (Murray, 247).

4 See 'The New Orleans Exposition: The Japanese Exhibit', first published in *Harper's Weekly*, 31 January 1885.

5 Accompanying the frequent sense of déjà vu in reading Hearn's Japan texts are the surprise insertions of previous travel experience. *Exotics and Retrospectives* (1898) effortlessly switches its focus from Japan to the West Indies and back to Japan. Similarly, the penultimate story, 'Hi-Mawari' of the supernatural tales of *Kwaidan* (1904), witnesses Hearn substitute Japanese goblins for the more distantly remembered goblins of Wales, and where the singing voice of the ugly Welsh harper ('a quivering tenderness indescribable' [XI: 260]) is reworked in *Kokoro*'s 'A Street Singer' as that of the equally ugly blind samisen player ('A tenderness invisible seemed to gather and quiver about us' [VII, 295]).

6 Stevenson, 197, quoted from Edward L. Tinker's *Lafcadio Hearn's American Days* (New York: Dodds, Mead & Co, 1924), 328–9. Stevenson records Hearn's pleasure when he was mistakenly accepted as an 'Ainoku' — a half Japanese (265).

7 Hirakawa, 1997, 2–3.

8 Yuzo Ota's essay 'Lafcadio Hearn: Japan's Problematic Interpreter' states that Hearn's writing gained fresh appeal in the 1930s, as it was perceived to be 'in harmony with the conservative nationalisms which were becoming more and more dominant' (Hirakawa, 215–6). However, the 1920s saw the steady publication of Hearn's work in Tokyo, including the nine-volume complete translation into Japanese (1920–1923), and editions of Hearn's letters (Tanabe, 1921), (Ichikawa, 1925), literary criticism and literary history (Tanabe and Ochiai, 1927), and annotated selections in translation (Hagiwara, 1929).

9 Reading Hearn at length, stock words such as 'ghost', 'vapor' and 'glide' become [all too] familiar presences.

10 See George Hughes's authoritative overview, 'Lafcadio Hearn and the Fin de Siècle', which considers in detail the issue of indebtedness to Poe, Loti, Kipling, Gautier and Pater, whose rendition of the Mona Lisa is shown to be the origin of Hearn's Japanese farmer in 'The Stone Buddha' from *Out of the East* ('He himself is older, incomparably older, than his attire. The earth he tills has indeed swallowed him up a thousand times a thousand times' [VII, 126]). Hughes observes the 'equality' Hearn demonstrates between the high Western and Japanese traditions of visual art as achieved '[w]ithout forcing overt confrontation' (In Sukehiro Hirakawa [ed.], *Rediscovering Lafcadio Hearn* (Kent: Global, 1997), 93–94.

11 Hearn is able to stand back and undermine his conceit at this point ('Hackneyed to the degree of provocation this statement no doubt is' [V, 10]), while instituting a favourite shorthand for referring to the Japanese. Cf. 'The fairy mistress' hotelier in 'The Dream of a Summer Day' from *Out of the East* (VII, 12).

12 Cf. 'Hyogo, this morning ... Forms remain sharply outlined, but are almost idealized by faint colors not belonging to them; and the great hills behind the town aspire

into a cloudless splendor of tint that seems the ghost of azure rather than azure itself (VII, 330). The ideal light here seems to have its origins in symboliste 'azure' as much as in perceived phenomena. The frequent merging of the visual and the visionary evokes Hearn's biographically poor eyesight due to congenital myopia, and the hapless blinding of his left eye in school.

13 Matthew Arnold, *The Study of Celtic Literature*, original lecture given 26 May 1866, republished in *Lectures and Essays on Criticism*, ed. R. H. Super (Ann Arbor: Michigan University Press, 1970), 291–86.
14 Letter to Ellwood Hendrick of 7 October 1891, quoted in Stevenson, 239.
15 The issue of Hearn's linguistic ability remains controversial, with judgements ranging from Murray, '[a]ll sources agree Hearn's Japanese was poor' (Murray, 253) to Hirakawa, 'he had a very good understanding of spoken Japanese' (Hirakawa, 41). As Hearn's wife had no English, Hirakawa recounts the necessity of a competence able to transcribe and refashion in English the oral versions read to Hearn from the Japanese and Chinese written sources.
16 Setsuko Hearn, 'Reminiscences of Lafcadio Hearn', in *The Atlantic Monthly*, September 1918, 346–7. Translated from the Japanese by Paul Kiyoshi Hisada and Frederick Johnson.
17 Bisland, *Japanese Letters of Lafcadio Hearn*, 341.
18 *Some New Letters and Writings of Lafcadio Hearn*, Ichikawa, 203.
19 Letter to Basil Hall Chamberlain, 17 January 1893, in *The Japanese Letters of Lafcadio Hearn*, ed. Elizabeth Bisland (London: Constable, 1911) 35, 38.
20 After a visit to the local community of outcasts — the yama-no-mono — Hearn had a letter published in the 'Japan Mail' of 13 June 1891 in which he signalled an unequivocal (liberal journalist's) compassion for the 'victims of a prejudice so ancient that its origin is no longer known' (*Kokoro*, Appendix to the Tuttle edition, 334). Hearn later lectured on the subject at the Asiatic Society of Japan on 17 October 1894.
21 In stark contrast to his travelogue's popular manga images, Peter Carey illustrates his discovery of the Edo samurai Eiko Ikegami's diary account of blade testing on condemned prisoners with a period diagram of the cuts valued by sword appraisers ('Bunzaemon was excited about cutting into a human body, something he believed every true samurai should experience '). *Wrong About Japan* (Sydney: Random House, 2004), 26, 42–3.
22 For example, in 'The Role of the Samurai in the Development of Modern Banking in Japan', Kozo Yamamura demonstrates that both the heimin and former samurai classes were competitively involved in the formation of the Meiji [financial] system. *Journal of Economic History*, 27, 2 (1967), 198–220.
23 Louis Allen's detailed account of Hearn's time at Ushaw College notes the 'Tyne ... the home of the Armstrong shipyards, where were built many of the ships of the Japanese fleet which defeated the Russians at the Battle of Tsushima in 1905' (Zenimoto, 79).
24 Isabella Bird's preface to the 1900 edition of *Unbeaten Tracks in Japan*, after

empirical assessment of Japan's progressing war machine ('the Government is preparing for eventualities by doubling the army') acknowledges the arrival of a 'brilliant and successful Empire' now 'on equal terms in the family of civilised nations, the only Oriental power to which this intimate relationship has been conceded.' Isabella J. Bird aka Mrs. J. F. Bishop, *Unbeaten Tracks in Japan* (London: Newnes [1880] 1900, new edn), VI, vii.

25   The origins of the Zouaves can be traced to the *Zouaoua*, a Kabyli tribe living in Algeria and Morocco. In 1830 a number of Zouaoua joined the French colonial army, and were organised into two battalions of auxiliaries.

Chapter 12

1   This is not to suggest that travel is always inevitably fragmentary, but rather that this particular mode of travel is frequently interrupted, both in terms of geographical progression and in the way that the remembered journey is presented stylistically.

2   Marc Augé, *Non-Lieux. Introduction à une anthropologie de la surmodernité* (Paris: Seuil, 1992). In this text, Augé explores the possibilities of 'anonymous' spaces such as airports, trains, supermarkets and chain hotels. Bernheim's *chambres* are infused with meaning and personal associations and so can never be termed anonymous.

3   James Clifford, 'Traveling Cultures', in *Routes: Travel and Translation in the Late Twentieth Century* (Cambridge, MA: Harvard University Press, 1997), 17–46 (26). Clifford cites the example of a Hawaiian family's preservation of their 'Hawaiianess' during years of constant interaction with different cultures. He asks how 'in transient, hybrid environments, did they preserve and invent a sense of Hawaiian "home"?' Bernheim's approach to what we might call 'dwelling-in-travel' can be seen to go some way towards providing some possible answers to this question.

4   Simone Fullagar remarks upon the complexity of the notion of home in her 'Narratives of Travel: Desire and the Movement of Feminine Subjectivity', *Leisure Studies*, 21 (2002), 57–74 (69). She writes: 'Travel is, indeed, a paradoxical space, an elsewhere that is at once leaving home and encountering the multiple ways of being at home in the world that are as much temporal as spatial relations.'

5   For further critical exploration of this, see Michael Cronin, *Across the Lines: Travel, Language and Translation* (Cork: Cork University Press, 2000) and Charles Forsdick, *Travels in 20th Century French and Francophone Culture: The Persistence of Diversity* (Oxford: Oxford University Press, 2005). For further examples of microscopic travel, see Jacques Lacarrière, *Le pays sous l'écorce* (Paris: Seuil, 1980), Paul Fournel, *Poils de Cairote* (Paris: Seuil, 2004) and Nicolas Bouvier, *Le Poisson-Scorpion* (Paris: Gallimard, 1996).

6   Whether or not these modes of travel were a conscious choice on the part of the traveller is debatable. It is possible that instead these particular types of travel were a product of travelling in an unfamiliar culture which initially seems

impenetrable to the traveller. In *Chambres d'ailleurs*, Bernheim turns inwards, towards her companion, and so the *chambres* become a focus and a place of partial familiarity. In contrast, the narrator's solitude in *Saisons japonaises* necessitates the creation of a sense of stability through dwelling-in-travel and by imagining a home away from home, rather than constantly changing location.

7   This investment of time and money betrays her as a professional journalist with proto-anthropological pretensions.

8   Nicole-Lise Bernheim, *Saisons japonaises* (Paris: Payot, 1999), 13. Please note that all translations in this article are my own. 'Je suis solitaire, intriguée, disponible et heureuse de divaguer dans les ruelles bordées de temples et dans la nécropole. Ne parlant pas la langue, je deviens ici analphabète et sourde. C'est comme si je venais de naître — je ne sais plus ni parler, ni lire, ni écrire. Seulement absorber, comme une éponge.'

9   Cronin, *Across the Lines*. See Chapter 2, 'The Changeling', 39–67.

10 Cronin, *Across the Lines*, 41.

11 *Chambres d'ailleurs* narrates travel around Japan, Taiwan, Hong Kong, Singapore, India, Nepal, Pakistan and Sri Lanka whereas *Saisons japonaises* focuses exclusively on one town in one country.

12 Patrick Holland and Graham Huggan, *Tourists with Typewriters: Critical Reflections on Contemporary Travel Writing* (Ann Arbor: University of Michigan Press, 2000), 67. These, often hazily defined, geographical areas, that Holland and Huggan identify as 'the Tropics', 'the Orient', 'the South Seas' and 'the Arctic', are argued to be complex textual zones which repeatedly draw the attentions of contemporary Western travel writers. They stress the conservative nature of travel to these areas and write 'even when it strives to communicate change or fresh perception, the contemporary traveller's account will at best supplement earlier versions'.

13 Such a personalised approach to travel, where the emphasis is as much upon the traveller as upon the place, can be seen to challenge *fin de siècle* notions in France of an imminent *fin des voyages* (see Julia Przybos, 'Voyage du pessimisme et pessimisme du voyage', *Romantisme*, 61 [1988], 67–74). If the traveller is as important to travel literature as place, then the possibilities for difference in travel accounts are seemingly infinite.

14 For an introduction to the complexity of French-Asian transcultural exchange, see Charles Forsdick, 'Introduction', *Modern & Contemporary France*, 14.1 (2006), 1–4. Forsdick writes: 'the France/Asias encounter cannot be understood as taking place between two whole, fixed and finished entities. Throughout, the question must be asked: which "Asia" for which "France"?' As this extract suggests, there is no one form of French-Asian intercultural contact, just as the notion of a singular Asia is inherently problematic. Concepts of place, identity and interchange are constantly evolving.

15 Forsdick suggests that such a silence is indicative of contemporary French resistance to postcolonial thought, in '*Viator in Fabula*: Jean-Didier Urbain and the Cultures of Travel in Contemporary France', *Studies in Travel Writing*, 4 (2000), 126–40.

It is possible to argue that, here, Bernheim's avoidance of postcolonial issues is motivated by a solipstic desire to use elsewhere as a screen upon which to project the self.

16 Although it was, of course, occupied for a period of time after World War II.
17 As Akane Kawakami notes in her text *Traveller's Visions: French Literary Encounters with Japan, 1881–2004* (Liverpool: University of Liverpool Press, 2005), 1: 'Japan had been, over the years, a privileged object of the French gaze'. This particular interest in Japan, described by Kawakami in terms of literary interest, indicates how French travellers' approach to Japan is, to some extent, determined or coloured by their associations.
18 For further discussion of Iyer's experience of Nara as one of his several homes, see Chapter 7, 'The Alien Home', 269–98 in *The Global Soul: Jet-lag, Shopping Malls and the Search for Home* (London: Bloomsbury, 2001).
19 Holland and Huggan, *Tourists with Typewriters*, 81.
20 Nicole-Lise Bernheim, *Chambres d'ailleurs* (Paris: Payot, 1999) [1986], 191. 'Quand on est longtemps ailleurs, on ne peut vivre constamment en curiosité. On arrive à oublier qu'on est un étranger à l'étranger. Parfois nous ne sortons pas sauf pour aller manger ou encore nous pique-niquons face à face dans la chambre, notre chambre. Quatre murs, clos. On pourrait aussi bien être à Paris et regarder la télé. Si l'on voyage à deux, la quotidienneté est plus forte que l'exotisme. Il faut pouvoir respirer sans penser à rien, se reposer sans admirer, s'occuper de soi, de l'autre, recoudre son linge, le nettoyer.'
21 Bernheim, *Chambres d'ailleurs*, 11. 'Je suis à Tokyo, au bout du monde et je suis avec toi.'
22 Bernheim, *Chambres d'ailleurs*, 41–2. 'Écrire au lieu d'*être* avec toi. Écrire, c'est me lever sans entendre tes jambes dans les miennes, c'est prendre la liberté de les faire se mouvoir seules [. . .]. Écrire, c'est oublier que *tu* conduis à mon côté [. . .]. Écrire, écrire vraiment, pour soi et les autres, c'est aimer. Insupportable désir d'aimer ailleurs que toi, trahison — je le refoule donc.'
23 René De Ceccatty, 'Le Japon intérieur de Nicole-Lise Bernheim', *Le Monde*, 21 May 1999. (Available online at www.lemonde.fr). 'Chambres d'ailleurs, qui aurait pu s'entituler Chambres de soi, un soi démultiplié par l'amour, l'amour d'un homme et l'amour des hommes'.
24 Bernheim, *Chambres d'ailleurs*, 216. 'Nous nous allongeons près du mur en briques rouges. De l'encens se consume quelque part, ça sent bon. La lune brille, les étoiles scintillent. La présence de Farida et d'Hussein me trouble, vont-ils s'aimer ? Allons-nous, en douce . . . Tu me caresses, j'essaie de ne pas rire. Peut-être fait-il de même, le douanier.'
25 Even when there is a lack of interpersonal contact in travel, it can still be suggested that intercultural contact may occur through systems of signs, TV, etc. Although this is not particularly in evidence in *Chambres d'ailleurs*, it is noticeable in other travel narratives about Japan such as in Roland Barthes, *L'Empire des Signes* (Paris: Seuil, 1970).

26 Jean-Xavier Ridon, 'Pour une poétique du voyage comme disparition', in Christian Albert, Nadine Laporte and Jean-Yves Pouilloux (eds.), *Autour de Nicolas Bouvier: Résonances* (Geneva: Zoé, 2002), 120–35.
27 Bernheim, *Saisons japonaises*, 219. '[J]'ai la chance d'avoir pu le côtoyer, d'y avoir créé des liens alors que les *gaijin* (strangers) prétendent souvent que c'est impossible, que le Japon est toujours fermé aux étrangers. En bon *baku* (mythical creature capable of swallowing nightmares), j'espère avoir détruit, avalé ces clichés.'
28 Sidonie Smith, *Moving Lives: 20th Century Women's Travel Writing* (Minneapolis: University of Minnesota Press, 2001), x.
29 Bernheim, *Chambres d'ailleurs*, 16. 'Le lit . . . deux matelas, les futons, plies dans le placard, on les étale ou le coeur vous en dit [. . .]. Le thé et deux tasses attendent sur un plateau [. . .]. Je m'enroule dans le futon chaud et confortable. [. . .] Je suis bien.'
30 Yet, perhaps clinging to Western modes of home-making is precisely what prevents the traveller from experiencing the other culture to a greater degree.
31 Bernheim, *Saisons japonaises*, 96–7. 'Comme je les raconte, comme je les vis, mes relations avec les Japonais semblent aisées. Mais rien ne m'a été donné d'emblée. A Koyasan, j'ai d'abord logé dans plusieurs temples, erré de ci, de là. Les échanges avec les Imai se sont faits avec lenteur, il a fallu que je prouve mon intérêt, ma sincérité, « de cœur à cœur », comme ils disent. J'ai dû montrer ma vérité. Ils savent désormais qu'ils peuvent compter sur moi, que je fais ce que je promets de faire. A partir de là, je l'ignore pas, les portes que j'ai ouvertes le resteront pour la vie. [. . .] La famille qui m'a adoptée, je l'ai moi aussi peu à peu adoptée. Notre amitié s'est fondée sur le respect réciproque, l'indispensable politesse, sans intrusion non voulue.'
32 See Steve Clark, '"Bang at its Moral Centre": Ideologies of Genre in Butor, Fussell, and Raban', *Studies in Travel Writing*, 4 (2000), 106–25, for a discussion of the recurrent disguising of material circumstances behind the production of travel literature.
33 Bernheim, *Saisons japonaises*, 13.
34 Clifford, *Routes*, 20.
35 Bernheim, *Saisons japonaises*, 89. 'Onsen avec les Imai. Les salles de bains ont rendus presque inutiles les bains publics traditionnels mais n'ont pas démodé les stations balnéaires, souvent fréquentées par des habitués. Hommes d'un côté, femmes de l'autre. Eau à 50°, vapeur. Maman Imai, Ikuyo et Sawako sont nues avec moi dans la profonde piscine des femmes. Pour l'instant, personne d'autre. Elles ont la peau assez foncée, de petits seins à très petites aréoles brunes et sont très minces. Je me sens géante à cote d'elles. Ikuyo, la plus jeune, décide de me prendre en charge, me montre comment je dois m'accroupir pour me laver, en prenant vraiment mon temps.'
36 Lady Mary Wortley Montagu, *The Turkish Embassy Letters* (London: Virago, 1994) [1861].
37 Fullagar, *Narratives of Travel*, 71.

38 Holland and Huggan, *Tourists with Typewriters*, 68 write: 'Travel writers today, like most of their predecessors, tend to share with professional ethnographers the yearning to establish a reciprocity with the people and places they visit and about which they write. Yet in most cases, the traveller-writer mobilises fantasies, as much collective as personal, that are always entangled in the myths and experiential categories of the zone. [. . .] in Japan, the desire for a poetised eroticism seeks experience of the feminised Orient. [. . .] Thus, while travel writing sustains the allure of exchange and acquisition, it often ends up by collapsing back onto the reserves of previous journeys.'

39 Bernheim, *Saisons japonaises*, 103. 'Un jour, Etsuko-san m'a reproché de faire des photos de sa famille. J'ai eu droit moi aussi à un interminable discours, traduit par Ikuyo. Ca a duré, duré. Elle m'a expliqué que, pour eux, je suis une amie. Qu'elle oublie que je suis journaliste, écrivain, et que ces photos la dérangent. Qu'allais-je en faire? Avec mon tout petit appareil, je ne suis pas professionnelle et je n'ai rien d'un paparazzo. [. . .] Je lui promets de la tenir au courant. Elle se calme, m'invite à déjeuner. Mais elle a dénoué notre lien. Je ne m'y attendais pas et cela m'empêche d'écrire pendant plusieurs semaines.'

40 Robyn Davidson, *Tracks* (London: Jonathan Cape, 1980).

41 François Maspero, *Les Passagers du Roissy-Express* (Paris: Seuil, 1990), 127. In this episode the Malian men remark upon the issue of respect and authorisation, indicating that to take a photograph without permission shows a fundamental lack of courtesy.

42 Nicolas Bouvier, *Journal d'Aran et d'autres lieux* (Paris: Payot, 2001) [1990].

43 Ella Maillart, *Ti-Puss* (Paris: Payot, 2002) [1951].

44 Carole Pither, *Un Camion dans la tête* (Paris: Payot, 2003).

45 Jenny Diski, *Skating to Antarctica* (London: Granta Books, 1997).

46 Julio Cortázar and Carol Dunlop, *Les Autonautes de la cosmoroute ou un voyage intemporal Paris-Marseille* (Paris: Gallimard, 1983).

Chapter 13

1 The social, political and economic conditions surrounding travel conditions in Japan have been exhaustively treated by Constantine N. Vaporis in *Breaking Barriers: Travel and the State in Early Modern Japan* (Cambridge: Harvard University Press, 1995).

2 The true weight of this figure is felt when one tries to imagine a contemporary Anglophone equivalent. In comparison, Bill Bryson has written fewer than ten travel books, Paul Theroux fourteen, and Colin Thubron about twenty.

3 There were sixty volumes in this series, which was divided into two groups. The main portion of fifty volumes dealt with Japan and other places in Asia, and the second series of ten was subtitled 'The European-American Series'. This division seems to imply that countries in Asia share the same cultural sphere with Japan

and therefore deserve to be included in the main, un-subtitled group. Information about the serial (in Japanese) can be found at <http://www.kaidou.net/>.
4 Interestingly enough, there is a new genre of travel writing emerging, consistent with the greying of the population, that is written by retirees and focuses on cultural items usually ignored by the fashion-conscious, or language-studying, younger set. See, for example, Kanai Shige, *Nenkin fūbō Shige san no chikyū hoihoi kenbunroku* (Pension Vagabond Shige's Record of Things Seen and Heard) or Yamada Fusako, *65 sai bakkupakkaa sekai hitori aruki* (65-Year-old Backpacker Walking the World Alone). Dozens of books have also been published that give concrete advice to retirees who are hoping to travel or even live overseas. As far as I know, this theme has yet to be taken up specifically on television.
5 While known for the intellectual content of its programming, NHK is often also associated with a conservative slant, which should come as no surprise as it has been under the control of the Liberal Democratic Party during nearly all of its existence. NHK was much in the news in 2005 on account of a series of scandals, one of which involved well-supported allegations that news items that might have been seen as critical of the emperor were withheld from programming at the urging of ruling LDP party politicians.
6 It was only when the traveller was non-Japanese that the pain caused by Japanese imperialism to other peoples was actually dealt with (4 November, 1995). In the more numerous cases when a Japanese travelled through the former empire, the content was focused on the pain felt either by Japanese soldiers who fought there, or (more commonly) civilians who were left behind there after the end of the war (14 October 1995; 12 December 1998; 15 January, 2000; 5 May, 2002; 4 August, 2002).
7 To give just a few examples, singer Shirai Yoshiko (14 November 1993), blues musician Shirai Eiichi (21 December 1996), baseball pitcher Murakami Masanori (16 May 1998), and singer Sawada Kenji (30 September 2001).
8 From the 'What's Ururun?' page on <www.ururun.com>.
9 After taking students abroad where they also experienced homestays, I have heard several of them explain that when parting from their host families at the airport, they had mustered up tears they did not themselves 'feel', because this was the response they thought appropriate.
10 This notion was perhaps best emphasised by a chapter in one of the several *Sekai Ururun taizaiki* books that have been published. These generally report in more detail on the experiences of certain travellers on the show. Actor Harada Ryūji here reflects upon his experience teaching at an elementary school in rural Laos (*Sekai Ururun Taizaiki*, 15–32).
11 For a recent and very thorough discussion of *nihonjinron*, see Harumi Befu, *The Hegemony of Homogeneity*, (Melbourne: Trans Pacific Press, 2001).
12 In the past hundred years, much has been written about Bashō and Saigyō as travel writers, and much also has been done in relation to travel in the *Man'yōshū*, the first anthology of Japanese poetry, compiled in 759. There is also a reasonable

amount of research dealing with medieval travel diaries. More recently, a number of scholars, led by Itasaka Yōko, have been opening up the immense volume of travel writing of the Edo period (1600–1867) for closer inspection. Very little has been done with work after that. One outstanding exception is Joshua Fogel's work *The Literature of Travel in the Japanese Rediscovery of China* (Stanford: Stanford University Press, 1996).

Chapter 14

1. This and other details of urban topography are taken from the standard two-volume history of the city, Edward Seidensecker, *Low City, High City* and *Tokyo Rising* (both New York: Tuttle, 1983).
2. Paolo Soleri, 'Arcology: The City in the Image of Man' and 'The Characteristics of Arcology' (originally 1969); Constantin Doxiadis, 'Ecumenopolis, World City of Tomorrow' (also 1969): both in 'The Future of the City' section of Richard T. LeGates and Frederic Stout (eds) *The City Reader* (London: Routledge, 1996) 453–57, 458–67.
3. Seidensticker, *Tokyo Rising*, 313–4.
4. Isabella J. Bird aka Mrs. J. F. Bishop, *Unbeaten Tracks in Japan* (London: Newnes [1880], 1900), new edn, Letter II, 18.
5. See Kevin Lynch, 'The City Image and its Elements' (1960), also in *The City Reader* 98–103; the terminology was popularised by Fredric Jameson, *Postmodernism or the Cultural Logic of Late Capitalism* (Durham: Duke UP, 1991), 51–2, 415–7.
6. Richie, 'Walking in Tokyo', *A Lateral View: Essays on Contemporary Japan* (Japan Times: Tokyo, 1987; rev. 1991), 53–61 (58–9).
7. Harriet Sergeant, *The Old Sow in the Back Room: An Englishwoman in Japan* (London: John Murray, 1994), 22–3.
8. Eisler also prides himself on spatial verifiability: 'With two exceptions, I have depicted the Tokyo in this book as accurately as I could. Tokyoites familiar with Shibuya will know there is no Higashimura fruit store midway up Dogenzaka. The real fruit store is at the bottom of the street, closer to the station': *Rainfall* (New York: Signet, 2002), 366. There are now numerous sequels including *Hard Rain* (2003), *Rain Storm* (2004), *Killing Rain* (2005) and *The Last Assassin* (2006).
9. Donald Richie regards the phenomenon of urban impermanence as part of a more general aesthetic of transience, which may be contrasted with the Western city's function of preserving collective memory: *Tokyo: A View of the City* (London: Reaktion, 1999), 44–51.
10. David Mitchell, *no9dream* (London: Hodder and Stoughton, 1999), 8.
11. Donald Richie, 'Attitudes to Tokyo on Film', *A Lateral View*, 185–95 (196).
12. 'Venice of Japan', Seidensticker, *Low City*, 19.

13 *Lost in Translation*, starring Bill Murray and Scarlett Johannson, directed by Sofia Coppola: American Zoetrope / Elemental Films (2003): for further details see <www.lost-in-translation.com>.
14 Joe Joseph notes that 'Eddie Murphy was paid $3 million dollars for making his eyes pop out at the sight of a new Toyota saloon, although they may have been popping out at the sight of the cheque', *The Japanese: Strange But Not Strangers* (London: Penguin, 1993), 111.
15 Similarly in *number9dream*, Eiji can only escape from Tokyo by heading to the southernmost point of Japan, to be finally liberated only when an earthquake devastates the capital.
16 Where the English DVD includes an extended interview with Sofia Coppola, the Japanese version of *Lost in Translation* includes a pull-out map identifying a specific location for each of the twenty-four narrative segments of the film.
17 Alexander Kojève, *Introduction to the Reading of Hegel* ([1934]1959), footnote added to second edn, 161–2, cited in *Postmodernism and Japan*, eds Masao Miyoshi and H. D. Harootunian (Durham: Duke University Press, 1989), xii–xiii. Francis Fukuyama's 1989 essay, 'The End of History' was expanded into *The Last Man and the End of History* (1992; reprinted New York: Free Press, 2006).
18 Pico Iyer, *Video Night in Kathmandu; and Other Reports from the Not-so-far East* (New York: Vintage, 1989).
19 Alex Kerr, *Lost Japan* (Footscray: Lonely Planet, 1996: originally Utsukushi Nippon no Zanzo (Shincho-sha: Tokyo, 1993); *Dogs and Demons: Tales from the Dark Side of Japan* (New York: Hill and Wang, 2001).
20 Karel van Wolferen, *The Enigma of Japanese Power: People and Politics in a Stateless Nation* (New York: Vintage, 1987, 1993), 34–5.
21 For the Nakamoto building, see Michael Crichton, *Rising Sun* (Ballantine Books: New York, 1992), 22–3; strikingly conveyed in the film's opening sequences (1993: directed by Philip Kaufman, starring Sean Connery and Wesley Snipes).
22 'Center City, Empty Center', *Empire of Signs*, trans. Richard Howard (New York: Farrar, Strauss and Giroux 1970, 1982), 30–3.
23 Seidensticker, *Low City*, 154; *Tokyo Rising*, 3, 313–4.
24 Barthes, *Empire of Signs*, 4; 'The Writing of Violence', 103–6. Compare the Sword Polisher in Christopher Ross, *Mishima's Sword: Travels in Search of a Samurai Legend* (London: Harper 2006): 'There was a climate of violence and it seemed a watershed in retrospect — but at the time it seemed like revolution was possible, even likely. It was all about the US Security Treaty. And about Vietnam. Really I suppose it was about perceived American imperialism' (179).

Within a specifically Japanese genealogy, one might compare the political dimension of the Kyoto school's metaphysics of nothingness, with the celebration of the imperial household as ultimate place of absence by its leading theoretician, Nishida Kitaro.
25 See Kerr, 'The Bubble; Looking Back', *Dogs and Demons*, 51–76; Richard MacGregor, 'Beyond the Bubble', *Japan Swings: Politics, Culture and Sex in the*

New Japan (New South Wales: Allen & Unwin, 1996), 18–37; Joe Joseph, *The Japanese: Strange but not Strangers* (London: Penguin, 1994), 246–50.

26 Peregrine Hodson, *A Circle around the Sun: A Foreigner in Japan Inc* (New York: Knopf, 1993).

27 Sergeant claims independent cultural access by minimising her role in maternal care. Much is made of the amorality of Tokyo nightlife (36ff) though no hint of marital impropriety is given. Yet if 'in order to practice my Japanese, I decided to become a hostess', to what extent would this involve fraternising intimately with her clients (63)?

28 Kerr, *Lost Japan*, 151–3.

29 ———, *Dogs and Demons*, 177, 14.

30 Richie, *The Japan Journals 1947–2004* (Berkeley: Stone Bridge Press, 2004), 211.

31 Will Ferguson, *Hokkaido Highway Blues* (New York: Soho Press, 1998), 18.

32 Peter Carey, *Wrong about Japan* (New York: Borzoi/ Knopf, 2004). The economic relation may be seen as formally codified in the Friendship Treaty signed with then prime minister and formerly indicted class 1 war criminal Nobusuke Kishi in 1957: McGregor, 201.

33 McGregor, 198.

34 Donald Richie, *The Inland Sea* (Tokyo: Kodansha, 1970, 1993); for a selection of subsequent cultural commentary, see *The Donald Richie Reader: 50 years of Writing on Japan*, ed. Arturo Silva (Berkeley: Stone Bridge Press, 2001).

35 *The Inland Sea*, 34–40.

36 *Hokkaido Highway Blues* (1996), 16.

37 On Bird, see Ozawa elsewhere in this volume; on Hearn, see Taylor.

38 For preliminary thank-yous, see Joseph, xi–xii; MacGregor, vii.

39 The supposedly 'enormous amount of research and conceptualization' (*Dogs and Demons*, ix) comes from trawling websites, whose lack of detail is berated compared to those provided by the United States military engineering corps: 'This book is filled with statistics that I cannot verify' (*Lost Japan*, 128, 126).

40 *Kill Bill*, directed by Quentin Tarentino, starring Uma Thurman and Keith Carradine, part I (2003), where this scene occurs: part II (2004).

41 'Mostly Japan starts life as a monolithic entity with individuals only hazily visible through their thickly coated Japaneseness' (MacGregor, 2)

42 For detailed discussion of autopsy, see Francois Hartog, *The Mirror of Herodotus: The Representation of the Other in the Writing of History*, trans. J. Lloyd (Berkeley: California University Press, 1988).

43 On the paradoxical power of ignorance, see Eve K. Sedgwick *Epistemology of the Closet* (Berkeley: California University Press, 1990), 4.

44 Even this is governed by the basic fallacy that non-naturalistic forms must inevitably give deeper insight into Japanese culture. Compare Kerr, *Dogs and Demons*, 'only manga could do justice to the bizarre reality of modern Japan', 11.

45 In the entertainment district, of whose nature the teenager is all too well aware, irony is spared 'on a subject which he could not possibly comprehend', 35; in the

pleasure quarters, it is 'judged . . . best to withhold these fascinating details', 71; there are 'views of otakus [as perverts] that I had not shared with my son', 107, in which case why is Charley allowed to consort with the hitherto unknown Takashi?

46 Paul Fussell, *Abroad: British Literary Travelling between the Wars* (Oxford: Oxford University Press, 1980).

47 Nor can they pass beyond a radius of twenty-five miles from the treaty ports without a '"passport" of formal permission from the government' (Bird, 8).

48 As further examples of erasure of place, in *Lost Japan*, Alex Kerr gives details of locations in Iya and Kyoto, but none anywhere in Tokyo; Josie Dew's garrulous *A Ride in the Neon Sun: A Gaijin in Japan* (New York: Time Warner, 1999) abruptly ends after 431 pages on the outskirts of Tokyo; in *Wrong about Japan*, Peter Carey hugely exaggerates the distance of a short subway ride from Akasuka down to Akihabara; in *Kill Bill*, the shot of the plane flying over Ginza is impossible (international flights would go to Narita, or possibly if from Okinawa to Haneda on the bay).

49 Richie observes that 'unlike all other major cities, Tokyo is very rarely seen on film. Location-work in Tokyo is very rare. If one sees a crew in the street one may be fairly certain it is TV': 'Attitudes towards Tokyo on Film', *A Lateral View*, 185–95 (193–4).

50 Sergeant's husband's salary places her, as she does not hesitate frequently to point out, among 'Tokyo's wealthiest', 10.

51 'The retention of employees forms part of the programme of progress: "Japan for the Japanese" is the motto of Japanese patriotism; the "Barbarians" are to be used and dispensed with as soon as possible' (10); 'It is no part of the plan of the able men who lead the new Japanese movement to keep up a permanent foreign staff' (28).

52 As Barthes says, 'The city can only be known by activity of an ethnographic kind; you must orient yourself in it not by book, by address, but by walking by sight by habit experience' (*Empire of Signs*, 36).

References

Chapter 2

Anderson, Aeneas, *A Narrative of the British Embassy to China, in the Years 1792, 1793, and 1794; Containing the Various Circumstances of the Embassy, with Accounts of Customs and Manners of the Chinese; and a Description of the Country, Towns, Cities, etc., etc.* (London: J. Debrett, 1795).

Appleton, William, *A Cycle of Cathay: The Chinese Vogue in England during the Seventeenth and Eighteenth Centuries* (New York: Columbia University Press, 1951).

Batten, Charles L., *Pleasurable Instruction: Form and Convention in Eighteenth-Century Travel Literature* (Berkeley: University of California Press, 1978).

Barrow, John, *Travels in China, Containing Descriptions, Observations, and Comparisons, Made and Collected in the Course of a Short Residence at the Imperial Palace of Yuen-Min-Yuen, and on a Subsequent Journey through the Country from to Canton* (London: T. Cadell and W. Davis, 1805).

Cranmer-Byng, J. L., *An Embassy to China* [1972] (St. Clair Shores, MI: Longman, 1962).

Dupee, Jeffrey N., *British Travel Writers in China — Writing Home to a British Public, 1890–1914* (Lewistown, NY: E. Mellen Press, 2004).

Edwards, Philip, *The Story of the Voyage: Sea-narratives in Eighteenth-Century England* (Cambridge: Cambridge University Press, 1994).

Hobson, John M., *The Eastern Origin of Western Civilization* (Cambridge: Cambridge University Press, 2004).

Holmes, Samuel, *The Journal of Samuel Holmes, Sergeant-Major of the XIth Light Dragoons, during His Attendance, as One of the Guard of Lord Macartney's Embassy to China and Tartary, 1792–3* (London: W. Bulmer and Co., 1798).

Hsu, Immanuel C. Y., *The Rise of Modern China* (New York: Oxford University Press, 1990).

Innes, Sherri, '"Repulsive as the multitudes by whom I am surrounded": Constructing the Contact Zone in the Writings of Mount Holyoke Missionaries, 1830–1890', *Women's Studies*, 23 (1994), 365–84.

Porter, David, *Ideographia: The Chinese Cipher in Early Modern Europe* (Stanford: Stanford University Press, 2001).

Pratt, Mary Louise, 'Scratches on the Face of the Country; or, What Mr. Barrow Saw in the Land of the Bushmen', in Henry Louis Gates, Jr. (ed.), *Race, Writing, and Difference* (Chicago: University of Chicago Press, 1986a), 138–62.

———, 'Fieldwork in Common Places.' in James Clifford and George E. Marcus (eds), *Writing Culture: The Poetics and Politics of Ethnography*. (Berkeley: University of California Press, 1986b). 27–50.

———, *Imperial Eyes: Travel Writing and Transculturation* (London: Routledge, 1992).

Richardson, J. M., *A Delicate Inquiry into the Embassies to China, and a Legitimate Conclusion from the Premises* (London: Printed for George and Thomas Underwood, 1818).

Schaffer, Simon, 'Instruments as Cargo in the China Trade', *History of Science*, 44 (2006), 217–46.

Staunton, George, *An Authentic Account of an Embassy from the King of Great Britain to the Emperor of China* (London: G. Nicol, 1797).

Chapter 4

Bacon, Francis, 'Of Travel', in *Essays, Civil and Moral*, Vol. III, Part 1 (New York: P. F. Collier & Son, 1597, 1909–14).

Bourdieu, Pierre, *La distinction. Critique sociale du jugement* (Paris: Éditions de Minuit, 1979). [*Distinction: A Social Critique of the Judgement of Taste*, Richard Nice, trans. (Cambridge: Harvard University Press, 1987).

Collins, Maurice, *Foreign Mud: An Account of the Opium War* (London: Faber and Faber, 1946).

Fairbank, John K., *Trade and Diplomacy in the China Coast: The Opening of the Treaty Ports, 1842–1854* (Cambridge, MA: Harvard University Press, 1953).

Harrison, Henrietta, *China* (London: Oxford University Press, 2001).

Jackson, Julian, *What to Observe; or, The Traveller's Remembrancer* (London: Houlston and Wright, 1861).

Moure, José María Cordovez, *Reminiscencias* (Bogotá: Librería Americana, 1899).

Pagden, Anthony, *European Encounters with the New World: From Renaissance to Romanticism* (New Haven: Yale University Press, 1993).

de la Riva, Juan Pérez, *El barracón* [1975] (Barcelona: Editorial Crítica, 1978).

Rama, Angel, *La ciudad letrada* (Hannover: Ediciones del Norte, 1984). [Published in English as *The Lettered City*, John Charles Chasteen (ed. and trans.) (Durham and London: Duke University Press, 1996)].

Safford, Frank, 'In Search of the Practical: Colombian Students in Foreign Lands, 1845–1890', in *The Hispanic American Historical Review*, 52, 2 (May 1972), 230–49.

Tanco Armero, Nicolás, *Viaje de Nueva Granada a China y de China a Francia* (Paris: Imprenta de Simon Raçon y Comp., 1861).

———, *Recuerdos de mis últimos viajes, Japón* (Madrid: Est. Tip. Sucesores de Rivadeneyra, 1888).

Todorov, Tzvetan, *La Conquête de l'Amérique: la Question de l'autre* (Paris: Seuil, 1982). [*The Conquest of America: The Question of the Other*, Richard Howard (trans.) (London: Harper & Row, 1984)].

Various authors. *The Cuba Commission Report: The Hidden History of the Chinese in Cuba*. [1876] Introduction by Denise Helly (Baltimore and London: The John Hopkins University Press, 1993).

Chapter 9

Byron, Robert, *The Road to Oxiana* (London: Penguin, 1937/1992).
David-Neel, Alexandra, *My Journey to Lhasa* (London: Virago, 1927/1988).
Fleming, Peter, *News from Tartary* (London: Abacus, 1936/1995).
Fussell, Paul, *Abroad: British Literary Translation Between the Wars* (Oxford: Oxford University Press, 1980).
Glendinning, Victoria, *Rebecca West, A Life* (London: Phoenix, 1987).
Izzard, Molly, *Freya Stark: A Biography* (London: Sceptre, 1993).
Leighfermor, Patrick, *A Time of Gifts* (London: Penguin, 1979).
Maillart, Ella K., *Forbidden Journey from Peking to Kashmir* (London: Heinemann, 1937; translated from the French, *Oases Interdites*, by T. McGreevy).
———, *Cruises and Caravans* (London: Heinemann, 1942).
———, *The Cruel Way* (London: Virago Press, 1947/1986).

Chapter 11

The Writings of Lafcadio Hearn, 16 vols (Boston: Houghton Mifflin, 1922).
A Japanese Miscellany (1901) (Rutland, Vermont and Tokyo: Tuttle, 1967).
Exotics and Retrospectives (1898) (Rutland, Vermont and Tokyo: Tuttle, 1971).
Gleanings in Buddha Fields: Studies of Hand and Soul in the Far East (1897) (Rutland, Vermont and Tokyo: Tuttle, 1971).
Glimpses of Unfamiliar Japan (1894) (Rutland, Vermont and Tokyo: Tuttle, 1976).
In Ghostly Japan (1891) (Rutland, Vermont and Tokyo: Tuttle, 1971).
Japan: An Attempt at Interpretation (1904) (Rutland, Vermont and Tokyo: Tuttle, 1956).
Kokoro: Hints and Echoes of Japanese Inner Life (1896) (Rutland, Vermont and Tokyo: Tuttle, 1972).
Kotto: Being Japanese Curios, with Sundry Cobwebs (1902) (Rutland, Vermont and Tokyo: Tuttle, 1971).
Kwaidan: Stories and Studies of Strange Things (1904) (Rutland, Vermont and Tokyo: Tuttle, 1971).
Out of the East: Reveries and Studies in New Japan (1895) (Rutland, Vermont and Tokyo: Tuttle, 1972).
Shadowings (1900) (Rutland, Vermont and Tokyo: Tuttle, 1971).
The Romance of the Milky Way and Other Stories (1904) (Rutland, Vermont and Tokyo: Tuttle, 1974).

Arnold, Matthew, *The Study of Celtic Literature*, original lecture 26 May 1866, republished in *Lectures and Essays on Criticism*, R. H. Super (ed.) (Ann Arbor: Michigan University Press, 1970), 291–86.
Bird, Isabella J., aka Mrs. J. F. Bishop, *Unbeaten Tracks in Japan* (London: Newnes [1880] 1900, new edn).
Bisland, Elisabeth, (ed.), *The Japanese Letters of Lafcadio Hearn* (London: Constable, 1911).
Carey, Peter, *Wrong About Japan* (Sydney: Random House, 2004).
Dawson, Carl, *Lafcadio Hearn and the Vision of Japan* (Baltimore and London: The Johns Hopkins University Press, 1992).
Hearn, Setsuko, 'Reminiscences of Lafcadio Hearn', *The Atlantic Monthly*, 1918.
Hirakawa, Sukehiro, (ed.), *Rediscovering Lafcadio Hearn* (Kent: Global, 1997).
Ichikawa, Sanki, (ed.), *Some New Letters and Writings of Lafcadio Hearn* (Tokyo: Kenkyusha, 1925).
Murray, Paul, *A Fantastic Journey, The Life and Literature of Lafcadio Hearn* (London and New York: Routledge Curzon, 1993).
Reischauer, Edwin O., *Japan Past and Present* (Rutland, Vermont and Tokyo: Tuttle, 1946).
——, *The Japanese Today: Change and Continuity* (Rutland, Vermont and Tokyo: Tuttle, 1977).
Richie, Donald, (ed.), *Lafcadio Hearn's Japan: An Anthology of His Writings on the Country and Its People* (Rutland, Vermont and Tokyo: Tuttle, 1997).
Ronan, Sean G., (ed.), *Irish Writing on Lafcadio Hearn and Japan* (Kent: Global, 1997).
Stevenson, Elizabeth, *Lafcadio Hearn* (New York: Macmillan, 1961).
Tinker, Edward L., *Lafcadio Hearn's American Days* (New York: Dodds, Mead & Co, 1924).
Yeats, William Butler, *Uncollected Prose*, John P. Frayne (ed.) (London: Macmillan 1970, 175–82).
Yu, Beong-cheon, *An Ape of Gods: The Art and Thought of Lafcadio Hearn* (Detroit: Wayne State, 1964).
Zenimoto, Kenji, *Centennial Essays on Lafcadio Hearn* (Matsue: The Hearn Society, 1996).

Chapter 13

Ivy, Marilyn, *Discourses of the Vanishing: Modernity, Phantasm, Japan* (Chicago: University of Chicago Press, 1995).
Kaido wo yuku shūkan (Going Along Highways Weekly), 1–50, *Ōbei hen* (Euro-American Series), 1–10 (Tokyo: Asahi shinbun, 2005), official website: www.kaidou.net.
Kanai, Shige, *Nenkin fūbō Shige san no chikyū hoihoi kenbunroku* (Pension Vagabond Shige's Record of Things Seen and Heard) (Tokyo: Yama to Keikoku, 1991).

Shiba, Ryotaro, *Kaidō wo yuku* (Tokyo: Asahi bungei, 1–43).
Sekai ururun taizaiki (Tokyo: Seishun, 2002, 15–32).
Sekai ururun taizaiki, official website : www.ururun.com.
Yamada, Fusako, *65 sai bakkupakkaa sekai hitori aruki* (65-Year-Old Backpacker Walking the World Alone) (Tokyo: Bungeisha, 2000).

Index

NB: Bold type for page numbers indicates substantial reference to the subject. For references in footnotes, the page number is followed by 'n.pp', where 'pp' refers to the footnote number.

Ainu (indigenous people of Hokkaido), 8, 12, 20, 87–88, 91, 94, 160–1, 198
Amoy (Xianmen), 71, 81, 122, 246 n.22
Anderson, Aeneas, 5, 6, 33–4, **36–41**, 45, 234 n.5
Angkor, 3, 10, **135–9**, 248 n.16
Armero, Nicolás Tanco, 7, **71–86**, 241 n.7, 11: *Reciderdos de mis utimos viajes, Japon*, 72–4, 77; *Viaje de Nueva Granada a China*, 71, 73–4, 76–8
Arnold, Mathew, 170
authenticity of place, 8; cultural, 158, 165; in travel and travel writing,181, 189, 191, 203, 206–7, 227

Bach, Evelyn, 88
Bacon, Francis, 72, 84: 'Of Travel', 72, 84
Barrow, John, 5–6, **31–7**, 40–45, 48, 50, 52–4, 68, 235 n.9: 'Free Trade to China', 48, 50, 52–4; *Travels in China*, 5, **32–37**, **40–45**; *Travels into the Interior of Southern Africa*, 31
Barthes, Roland, 183, 216, 221, 225, 263 n.52; *mu* (emptiness of language), 216: *Empire of Signs,* 216, 263 n.52
Bashō, Matsuo, 5, **15–19**, 21, 24, 26–9, 193, 205, 259 n.12: *Oku no hosomichi* (*Narrow Road to the Interior*), **15–19**, 24, 26
Bassnet, Susan, 183

Bernheim, Nicole-Lise, 12–13, **179–92**, 255 n.6: *Chambres d'ailleurs*, 12, **179–92**, 255 n.6; *Saisons japonaises*, 12, **179–83**, 186, 188
Bhabha, Homi K., 61
Birch, J. W. W., 101
Bird, Isabella, 7–9, **87–97**, **99–106**, 108–9, 111–7, 120–2, 125–6, 129, 174, 210, 219, 224, 226: *The Englishwoman in America,* 99; *The Golden Chersonese and the Way Thither,* 8, 99, **104–9**, 116; *The Hawaiian Archipelago,* 99; *Letters to Henrietta,* 105; *Unbeaten Tracks in Japan,* 8, **87–97**, 99; *The Yangtze Valley and Beyond,* 9, 115, 117
bird's-eye view, 21, 56
Booth, Alan, *Road to Sato*, 224
Bourdieu, Pierre, 76
British Empire, 49, 60, 68, 105, 138, 161
British-Japan Exposition (1910), 156, 161
Brunei, 135, 137
Buck, Pearl, 9, 114
Buddhism, 4, 19, 166, 173, 199; Buddhist priests, 193; Buddhist sculptures, 164; Buddhist temples, 121
Butor, Michel, 183, 257 n.32

Caddy, Florence, 8–9: *To Siam and Malaya,* 8–9, 99, 100, **108–12**
Caesar, Julius, 5, 10, 132–3
cannibals, 159, 175

Canton (Guangzhou), 34, 35, 47, 49, 51, 59, 61, 67, 81–2, 99, 104–5, 111, 116, 126; *Canton Register, The*, 51, 53
Carey, Peter, *Wrong about Japan*, 218, **220–2, 224–6**, 253 n.21
caste (system), 159, 160, 176
Ceylon (Sri Lanka), 99, 132, 138, 179
Checkland, Olive, 90, 97
Chiang, Madame Kai-shek, 114
China, 1–3, 5–7, 9–10, 32–8, 40–69, 71–82, 84–5, 104, 111, 113–29, 141, 150–2, 158, 166, 177–8, 194, 199, 202, 204; *see also* People's Republic of China
Chinese Communist Party (CCP), 66–9
Chinese poetry, 18–19
chishiteki kikō (topographical travel literature), 17, 20
Christianity, 57, 79, 85, 95–7, 165–6; Christian periodicals, 53, **55–8**, 60; missionaries, 95–7
Christian Lady's Magazine, 55–7
Clifford, Hugh, 8, 10, 132, **135–9**: *The Downfall of the Gods*, 136–8; *Further India*, 136; 'The Skulls in the Forest', 135–6
Clifford, James, 4, 12, 179, 189
colonialism (British), 1, 100, 104–5, 108, 110, 112; colonial administrators, 4, 10, 99, 103–4, 132; colonial rule (Japanese), 149, 157; neo-colonialism, 3
comedy, 6, 8 11, 143, 147, 164; *see also* humour
coolie trade, 76, 69
Coppola, Sofia, *Lost in Translation*, 206, **213–5**, 222, 224, 227, 261 n.13
Crichton, Michael, 215: *Rising Sun*, 215
Cronin, Michael, 180–1: *Across the Lines: Travel, Language, Translation*, 180–1
Cumming, Constance Gordon, 9: *Wanderings in China*, 9, **113–7, 120–6**, 129

Dewey, George, 153
diaspora, Chinese, 3, 7; Japanese, 11
diplomatic travel, 31–46
domestic audience, 31, 105; ideology, 9, 104, 112, 148, 188, 192; sphere, of the, 12, 107, 109, 110, 114, 182, 184, 187; travel, 194, 204, 214; and women, 58, 104
Dutch East India Company, The, 103

East India Company (EIC), British, 6, 47, 48, 50, 52–5, 59–60
Edo (Tokyo), 27, 193, 209, 216; Edo (period), 176, 216, 260 n.12
Ekiken, Kaibara, 17, 19, 21, 24–5, 28–9, 232 n.25
Engeki kairyo undo (Westernisation of Japanese drama), 150
Exotic, Japan and Taiwan, 11, 157, 168
Exposition (British-Japan), 156, 161; Fifth Domestic Exposition (Osaka), 160; New Orleans World Exposition, 166; Paris Exposition, 150, 161

feminine (in travel and travel writing), 10, 57, 88, 104, 145, 183, 187, 190–1
Ferguson, Will, *Hokkaido Highway Blues*, 218–20, 224–5
Fleming, Peter, *News from Tartary*, 10, **141–8**; *One's Company*, 142
Free trade (to China), 6, 35, 48, 52–6, 58–60, 63–4; *see also* laissez-faire
Furukawa, Koshōken, 24
Fussell, Paul, *Abroad: British Literary Travelling between the Wars*, 10, 141, 180, 224

Gadamer, Hans-Georg, 128
gaijin (outsider), 171–2, 186, 220, 226
Gaunt, Mary, 115, 125
geisha, 11, 151–3, 155, 161, 201
Gentleman's Magazine, 52, 54

Gillray, James, *The Reception of the Diplomatique and His Suite, at the Court of Pekin*, 41
Gothic, 10, 12, 134, 172, 174, 212, 248 n.10
Gutzlaff, Charles, 6–7, **47–69**: *Ship Amherst* narratives, **47–69**; see also Lindsay, Hugh Hamilton

Haiku, 15, 18, 193
hara-kiri (ritual suicide), 155, 161
Harper's Magazine, 166
Hearn, Lafcadio, 12, **163–78**, 219, 252 n.5–12, 253 n.15: *Japan: an Attempt at Interpretation,* 171; *Glimpses of Unfamiliar Japan,* 167–171; 'My First Day in the Orient', 167, 170–1; *Out of the East*, 163–4
Heian period, 18, 20
Herder, Johann Gottfried, 7, 78–9, 241 n.13
history, 2, 16, 20, 34, 64, 68, 70, 123, 125, 132–8, 182; Chinese, 47, 63, 66–7, 70, 239 n.64; colonial, 2, 182; imperial, 14, 49, 236 n.7; Japanese, 16, 158, 176, 194, 200, natural, 4; writing (historiography), 19, 49, 61, 67–70
Hobbes, Thomas, 133–4
Hodson, Peregrine, 217, 220, 224–6: *A Circle around the Sun,* 217, 220, 224–6
Hokkaido, 20, 25–9, 87–8, 90, 94, 159, 160; see also Ainu
Holland, 13, 196
Holland, Patrick, and Huggan, Graham, *Tourists with Typewriters,* 182–3, 191
Hong Kong, 2, 3, 4, 79, 81–2, 99, 104–5, 111, 116–7, 122, 126, 128, 179, 182, 217
Huggan, Graham, *see* Holland, Patrick
humour, 85, 141, 144, 156; see also comedy
hyōhaku (strong desire to wander), 5, 15, 17, 19

India, 1,10, 53, 56–8, 61, 76, 79, 99, 105, 136, 141, 147, 179, 182; Indian 'Mutiny', the, 105; see also East India Company
Innes, Emily, 8–9: *The Chersonese with the Gilding Off,* 99–100, **105–9**, 112
Itasaka, Yōko, 17, 25–6, 260 n.12
Ito, Hirofumi, 150
Ivy, Marilyn, *Discourses of the Vanishing,* 194
Iyer, Pico, 14, 183, 187, 192, 215, 225–6: *The Global Soul,* 187; *Video Night in Kathmandu,* 215

Japan, 1–5, 7–9, 11–20, 27–9, 34, 74–6, 87–97, 99, 115–6, 122, 128, 141, **149–183**, **186–207**, **210–228**; Japanese food, 93, 194, 196, 204; theatre, 11, **149–183**; literature, 15–6, 21–6, 230 n.1; see also Japonaiserie; Sino-Japanese War; Taiwan as Japanese colony
japonaiserie, 12, 152, 161, 167
journalism, 148, 165–7, 191, 225
jungle, 10, **131–9**, 211

Kaempher, Engelbert, 13, 193
kanshi (poems in Chinese), 18
Karatani, Kōjin, *The Origins of Modern Japanese Literature,* 16, 21, 24–6
Kawakami, Akane, 183, 256 n.17
Kawakami, Otojiro, 11–12, **149–61**; see also Kawakami troupe
Kawakami troupe, the, **150–5**
Kendall, Elizabeth, 115, 126
Kerr, Alex, 215, 217, 219–20, 222, 225: *Dogs and Demons,* 215, 217; *Lost Japan,* 215, 217, 219–20, 222, 263 n.48
Kipling, Rudyard, 10, 134, 137–8: 'Judgement of Dungara, The', 137; *Jungle Book, The,* 134; 'Recessional', 10, 138; *Second Jungle Book, The,* 134
Kobe (Japan), 95–6
Kojève, Alexander, 215

Korea, 2, 28, 116, 150, 198–9
Koyasan (Japan), 180, 189
Kuhn, Thomas, 15–16
Kushibiki, Yumeto, 151–2, 155, 162
Kusuya, Shigetoshi, 88, 93
Kyoto, 214, 261 n.24

laissez-faire, 50, 52, 64; see also free trade
LaMotte, Ellen, 10, 115, 125, 127–8, 247 n.39, 47: *Peking Dust*, 10, 115, 125, 127–8
Li Bai, 5, 199
Li, Hung-chang, 128
Li Po, 5, 18–19
Li, Yuan-hung, 129
Lin, Yutang, 114
Lin, Zexu 61, 63, 65
Lindsay, Hugh Hamilton, 6, **47–69**: *Ship Amherst* Narratives, **47–69**; see also Gutzlaff, Charles
Loti, Pierre, 135, 183
lyricism, 4, 5, 13, 168

Macartney embassy, 2–3, 5, **31–46**; kowtow incident, the, 6, 34
Maillart, Ella, 10, 12, **141–8**: *The Cruel Way*, 146; *Cruises and Caravans*, 142; *Forbidden Journey*, 10–11, **141–8**; *Ti-Puss*, 192; *Turkestan Solo*, 142
Maistre, Xavier de, 180: *Voyage autour de ma chambre*, 180
Malaya (British), 8–9, 99–102, 104–12, 116, 138
Mandeville, Sir John, 4–5
masculinity (in travel and travel writing), 9–10, 55, 88–9, 100, 104
Masumi, Sugae, 5, 16, 19, 20–1, 25–9: *Waga kokoro* ('My heart'), **26–9**
Mathias, Thomas James, *Imperial Epistle from Kien Long, Emperor of China ...*, 41
Matsue (Japan), 172

Maugham, M. Somerset, 131, 133, 136, 137: *The Gentleman in the Parlour*, 131, 136; 'Neil MacAdam' (*Ah King and Other Stories*), 133
Meiji period, 2–3, 8, 11, 21, 25–6, 164, 170, 175–7, 226; Meiji government, 160, 177; Pre-Meiji era, 174–5, 209
Merchant of Venice, The, Japanese adaptation of, 156–7, 159
Michaux, Henri, 183
Mikado, The, 151, 155
Mills, Sara, *Discourses of Difference*, 100, 183
Mitchell, David, *number9dream*, 212–3
Modernity, 4, 7, 10, 75, 85, 75, 85, 108, 132, 138, 143, 154, 163, 168, 170, 176, 215; 'Chinese', 66
Montagu, Lady Mary Wortley, *The Turkish Embassy Letters*, 190
Moure, Pedro María, 76–9: *Viaje de Nueva Granada a China,* 76–7

Nagasaki, 193
Nan, Mu, 48, 61–2, 66–70, 235 n.6
nihonjinron (Japaneseness), 2, 13, 204, 207, 226
nostalgia, 12, 138, 164, 186, 213

Okinawa, 160–1, 220
opium trade, 7, 53, 59, 79–80, 82; Opium Wars, 2, 6–7, 47, 61, 64, 66, 69, 80–1
Orient (region), 76, 125, 131–2, 165, 167, 169, 170–1, 191; see also Lafadio Hearn, 'My First Day in the Orient'
Oriental, 155, 216; jungle, 135; sublime, 137; plays, 152; pastoral, 163; zone, 182, 191
Orientalism, 6, 41, 48, 73, 149, 154–5, 161
Othello, adaptation of, 11, 149, 151, 157–8, 160–1
otherness, 85, 113, 115, 126, 128, 137, 159, 169

Index 275

Pakistan, 182, 185
Pangkor Treaty, 100–1
Paris Exposition (1900), 150, 161
Pearl River Delta, 82
Peking (Beijing), 9–10, 32, **34–8**, 40, **42–5**, 91, 115, 120, 124–7, 129; Beijing, 3, 6, 51, 62, 65, 116, 120, **122–8**
Penghu Islands (the Pescadores), 149, 151, 158, 251 n.20
People's Republic of China (PRC), 48, 62, 66–69, 129; *see also* China
Penny Magazine, 58–60
Philippines, the, 7, 11, 76, 153–4
photography, 189, 191–2, 224
picaresque, 165
picturesque, 4–5; in Japan and Taiwan, 21, 87, 92, 153–6, 158–9
Pindar, Peter, *Ode to Kien Long, the Present Emperor of China*, 41
postcolonial studies and theories, 1, 4, 14, 49, 69–70, 192; 255–6 n.15
Polo, Marco, 2, 5
postmodern Japan, 214–5, 227; postmodernity, 12, 14
Pratt, Mary Louise, 3, 6, 31, 89: *Imperial Eyes: Travel Writing and Transculturation*, 31, 89

Qing government and officials, 7, 47–9, 51, 53–4, 56, 63–6, 68, 158; dynasty and culture, 48, 61–2, 64, 66, 68, 80, 114

Rama, Ángel, 75: *la ciudad letrada* (the lettered city), 75
Reischauer, Edwin, *Ennin's Diary: The Record of a Pilgrimage to China ...*, 176
Richie, Donald, 210, 217, 219: *The Inland Sea*, 219
Romanticism, 132, 165, 174
Royal Geographical Society, 8, 72, 174

Said, Edward, 1–2
Saigon, 99, 104–5, 111
Sadayakko, Madame (wife of Kawakami Otojiro), 150, 152, 155–7
sakoku (isolation), 4, 209, 225
samurai, 152–3, 155, 161, 164, **173–7,** 218
Satow, Ernest, 8, 89
Scidmore, Eliza 9, 115, 117, 122, **124–9**: *China: The Long-lived Empire*, 122, 125, 136; *Westward to the Far East*, 9, 115, 122, 125
Sekai (world), 13, 197–8
Sergeant, Harriet, 211–2, 217, 220, 225–6: *The Old Sow in the Backroom*, 211–2, 217
Seton, Grace, 115, 125, 128–9
Shiba, Ryōtarō, *Kaidō wo Yuku* (*Going Along Highway*), 194, 196
Shanghai, 48, 62, 64–5, 116–7, 120, 122, 126, 128–9
Siam, 3, 99, 109, 111
Sichuan, 116–7
Singapore, 3, 9, 49, 99–100, 102–5, 107, 109, 111, 179, 182, 217
Sino-Japanese War, 11, 116, 150, 154–5, 158, 177
slavery, 7, 74, 79–80, 101; in Cuba, 241 n.7
Soleri, Paolo, 209
Soong, Ching-ling (wife of Sun Yat-sen), 9, 129
Spivak, Gayatri, 101
Sri Lanka, 179
Stark, Freya, 10, 141, 147
Staunton, George, 5, 33–4, 36–7, 40, **43–6**: account of the Macartney Embassy, 5, 33–4, 36–7, 40, **43–6**
Stoddart, Anna M., 88
Suematsu, Baron Kencho, 150, 157, 161: *The Risen Sun,* 157

tabi no urei (suffering on a journey), 18, 27

Taiping rebellion, 80, 82
Taiwan, 11, 149, 151, 157–62, 179, 182; as Japanese colony, **157–62**
television travel programmes (Japan), **193–207**
Tibet, 10, 116, 124, 141, 146
Tientsin (Tianjin), 116, 120, 122, 126; Treaty of, 80
Tietjens, Eunice, 113, 115, 127–8: *Profiles from China*, 113, 127–8
Tokyo, 3–4, 14, 90, 149, 161, 164, 167, 184, 202, 209–24, 228; post-imperial, 209–24, 228; University of, 166, 174–5
tourism, 4, 5, 9, 11, 13; in China, 115, 117, 125, 129; Japanese, 191, 194, 201, 203, 206, 220, 222, 224
treaty-ports, 224; in China, 61; in Japan, 92

Van Wolferen, Karel, *The Enigma of Japanese Power*, 215
Viswanathan, Gauri, 61

waka poets and poetry, 18–20, 27, 193
Watanabe, Kenji, 17
Wei, Yuan, 61
West, Rebecca, 10, 141
Western civilisation, 87, 154, 177; Westernisation, 92, 150, 154, 175, 194, 205
Woolf, Leonard, 10, 132–3, 137–8: *Growing*, 133; Letter to Lytton Strachey, 132; *The Village in the Jungle*, 133, 137–8

Yamagata, 93
Yanagita, Kunio, 24, 27, 233 n.39
Yokohama, 91–2, 116, 153, 166–7; Bird, 91–2; 116; Hearn, 166–7

Zainichi (Japanese-born Chinese and Koreans), 198, 200
Zhang, Dechang, 'Hu Xia Mi ...' (article on significance of *Ship Amherst* voyage): **62–70**